HARVARD EAST ASIAN MONOGRAPHS

91

Studies in the Modernization of
The Republic of Korea: 1945–1975

Government, Business, and Entrepreneurship in Economic Development: The Korean Case

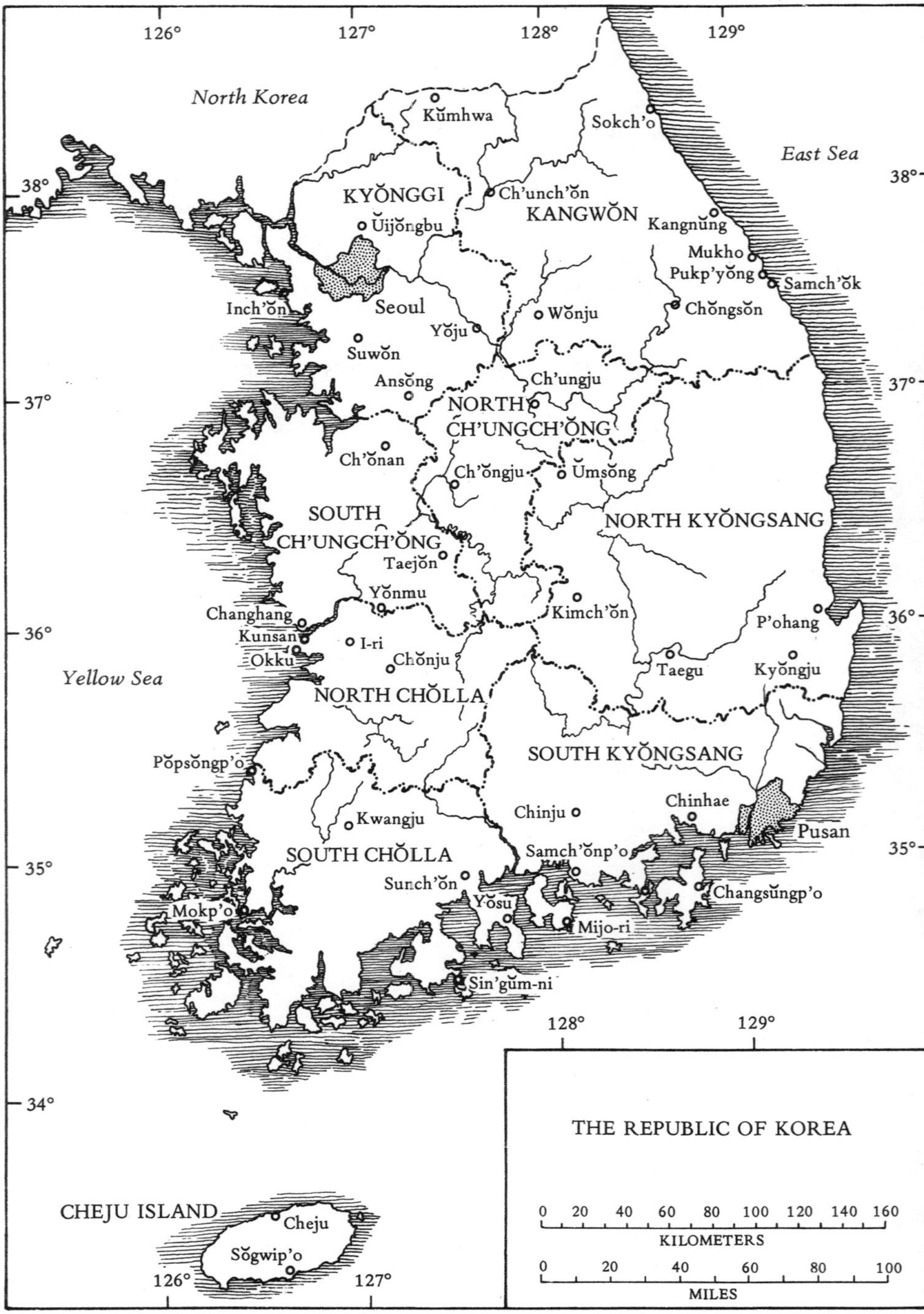

126°
127°
128°
129°
North Korea
East Sea
Yellow Sea
38°
37°
36°
35°
34°
KYŎNGGI
KANGWŎN
NORTH CH'UNGCH'ŎNG
SOUTH CH'UNGCH'ŎNG
NORTH KYŎNGSANG
NORTH CHŎLLA
SOUTH KYŎNGSANG
SOUTH CHŎLLA
Kŭmhwa
Sokch'o
Ch'unch'ŏn
Ŭijŏngbu
Kangnŭng
Mukho
Pukp'yŏng
Samch'ŏk
Seoul
Inch'ŏn
Wŏnju
Chŏngsŏn
Yŏju
Suwŏn
Ansŏng
Ch'ungju
Ch'ŏnan
Ch'ŏngju
Ŭmsŏng
Taejŏn
Yŏnmu
Changhang
Kunsan
Okku
I-ri
Chŏnju
Kimch'ŏn
P'ohang
Taegu
Kyŏngju
Pŏpsŏngp'o
Kwangju
Chinju
Chinhae
Pusan
Samch'ŏnp'o
Sunch'ŏn
Yŏsu
Mijo-ri
Changsŭngp'o
Mokp'o
Sin'gŭm-ni
CHEJU ISLAND
Cheju
Sŏgwip'o
THE REPUBLIC OF KOREA
0 20 40 60 80 100 120 140 160
KILOMETERS
0 20 40 60 80 100
MILES

Studies in the Modernization of The Republic of Korea: 1945–1975

Government, Business, and Entrepreneurship in Economic Development: The Korean Case

LEROY P. JONES
AND
IL SAKONG

PUBLISHED BY
COUNCIL ON EAST ASIAN STUDIES
HARVARD UNIVERSITY

Distributed by
Harvard University Press
Cambridge, Massachusetts and London, England
1980

The Council on East Asian Studies at Harvard University publishes a monograph series and, through the Fairbank Center for East Asian Research, administers research projects designed to further scholarly understanding of China, Japan, Korea, Vietnam, Inner Asia, and adjacent areas.

The Harvard Institute for International Development is Harvard University's center for interdisciplinary research, teaching, and technical assistance on the problems of modernization in less developed countries.

The Korea Development Institute is an economic research center, supported in part by the Korean government, that undertakes studies of the critical development issues and prospects of Korea.

Library of Congress Cataloging in Publication Data

Jones, Leroy P.
Government, business, and entrepreneurship in
economic development.

(Studies in the modernization of the Republic of
Korea, 1945-1975) (Harvard East Asian monographs ; v. 91)
Bibliography: p.
Includes index.
1. Korea—Economic policy. 2. Korea—Economic
conditions—1945- 3. Industry and state—Korea—
History. 4. Entrepreneur. I. SaKong, Il, joint
author. II. Title. III. Series. IV. Series:
Harvard East Asian Monographs ; v. 91.
HC467.J65 338.9519'5 79-28671
ISBN 0-674-35791-4

Foreword

This is one of the studies on the economic and social modernization of Korea undertaken jointly by the Harvard Institute for International Development and the Korea Development Institute. The undertaking has twin objectives; to examine the elements underlying the remarkable growth of the Korean economy and the distribution of the fruits of that growth, together with the associated changes in society and government; and to evaluate the importance of foreign economic assistance, particularly American assistance, in promoting these changes. The rapid rate of growth of the Korean economy, matched in the less developed world (apart from the oil exporters) only by similar rates of growth in the neighboring East Asian economies of Taiwan, Hong Kong, and Singapore, has not escaped the notice of economists and other observers. Indeed there has been fairly extensive analysis of the Korean case. This analysis, has been mainly limited to macroeconomic phenomena; to the behavior of monetary, fiscal, and foreign-exchange magnitudes and to the underlying policies affecting these magnitudes. But there are elements other than these that need to be taken into account to explain what has happened. The development of Korean entrepreneurship has been remarkable; Korea has an industrious and disciplined labor force; the contribution of agricultural development both to overall growth and to the distribution of income requires assessment; the level of literacy and the expansion of secondary and higher education have made their mark; and the combination and interdependence of government and private initiative and administration have been remarkably productive. These aspects together with the growth of urban areas, changes in the mortality and fertility of the population and in public health, are the primary objects of study. It is hoped that they will provide the building blocks from which an overall assessment of modernization in Korea can be constructed.

Economic assistance from the United States and, to a lesser extent, from other countries, has made a sizable but as yet unevaluated contribution to Korean development. A desire to have an assessment undertaken of this contribution, with whatever successes or failures have accompanied the U.S. involvement, was one of the motives for these studies, which have been financed in part by the U.S. Agency for International Development and, in part, by the Korea Development Institute. From 1945 to date, U.S. AID has contributed more than $6 billion to the Korean economy. There has also been a substantial fallout from the $7 billion of U.S. military assistance. Most of the economic assistance was contributed during the period before 1965, and most of it was in the form of grants. In later years the amount of economic assistance has declined rapidly and most of it, though concessional, has been in the form of loans. Currently, except for a minor trickle, U.S. economic assistance has ceased. The period of rapid economic growth in Korea has been since 1963, and in Korea, as well as in other countries receiving foreign assistance, it is a commonplace that it is the receiving country that is overwhelmingly responsible for what growth, or absence of growth, takes place. Nevertheless, economic assistance to Korea was exceptionally large, and whatever contribution was in fact made by outsiders needs to be assessed. One of the studies, *The Developmental Role of the Foreign Sector and Aid,* deals with foreign assistance in macroeconomic terms. The contribution of economic assistance to particular sectors is considered in the other studies.

All the studies in this series have involved American and Korean collaboration. For some studies the collaboration has been close; for others less so. All the American participants have spent some time in Korea in the course of their research, and a number of Korean participants have visited the United States. Only a few of the American participants have been able to read and speak Korean and, in consequence, the collaboration of their colleagues in making Korean materials available has been invaluable. This has truly been a joint enterprise.

The printed volumes in this series will include studies on the growth and structural transformation of the Korean economy, the foreign sector and aid, urbanization, rural development, the role of entrepreneurship, population policy and demographic transition, and education. Studies focusing on several other topics—the financial system, the fiscal system, labor economics and industrial relations, health and social development—will eventually be available either in printed or mimeographed form. The project will culminate in a final summary volume on the economic and social development of Korea.

Edward S. Mason

Edward S. Mason
Harvard Institute
for International Development

Mahn Je Kim

Mahn Je Kim
President,
Korea Development Institute

A Note on Romanization

In romanizing Korean, we have used the McCune-Reischauer system and have generally followed the stylistic guidelines set forth by the Library of Congress. In romanizing the names of Koreans in the McCune-Reischauer system, we have put a hyphen between the two personal names, the second of which has not been capitalized. For the names of historical or political figures, well-known place names, and the trade names of companies, we have tried to follow the most widely used romanization. For works written in Korean, the author's name appears in McCune-Reischauer romanization, sometimes followed by the author's preferred romanization if he or she has published in English. For works by Korean authors in English, the author's name is written as it appears in the original publication, sometimes followed by the author's name in McCune-Reischauer romanization, especially if the author has published in Korean also. In ordering the elements of persons' names, we have adopted a Western sequence—family name first in all alphabetized lists, but last elsewhere. This is a sequence used by some, but by no means all, Koreans who write in English. To avoid confusion, however, we have imposed an arbitrary consistency upon varying practices. Two notable exceptions occur in references to President Park Chung Hee, and Chang Myon, for whom the use of the family name first seems to be established by custom and preference. Commonly recurring Korean words such as si (city) have not been italicized. Korean words in the plural are not followed by the letter "s." Finally, complete information on authors' names or companies' trade names was not always available; in these cases we have simply tried to be as accurate as possible.

Contents

Tables

Appendix Tables

Figures

Abbreviations

AID	Agency for International Development
BOK	Bank of Korea
c.i.f.	cost, insurance, and freight
DPM	Deputy Prime Minister
EDC	Economic Development Council
EPB	Economic Planning Board
FKI	Federation of Korean Industries
FOA	Foreign Operations Administration
GDP	gross domestic product
GNP	gross national product
GTC	general trading company
ICA	International Cooperation Administration
IMF	International Monetary Fund
ISIC	International Standard Industrial Classification
KAL	Korean Air Lines
KATUSA	Korean Augmentation Troops to the United States Army
KDB	Korea Development Bank
KDI	Korea Development Institute
KFX	Korean Foreign Exchange
KIST	Korea Institute of Science and Technology
KOTRA	Korean Trade Promotion Corporation
KPC	Korea Productivity Center
KTA	Korean Traders Association
LDC	less-developed country
L/C	Letter of Credit
MCI	Ministry of Commerce and Industry
MPG	marginal product of government

NACF	National Agricultural Cooperative Federation
NCP	net commodity product
OEC	Office of the Economic Coordinator
ORB	Overall Resource Budget
ROK	Republic of Korea
SITC	Standard International Trade Classification
SOC	Social Overhead Capital
SNU	Seoul National University
UNKRA	United Nations Korea Reconstruction Agency

Acknowledgments

Our primary debt is to Edward S. Mason, who perceived the need for an unconventional study of this nature, convinced us to bear the risk of undertaking it, and provided guidance throughout its execution. Similarly indispensable was the advice and support of Mahn Je Kim, President of the Korea Development Institute.

In the design phase of our work, we benefited greatly from the assistance of Man-Gap Lee and Vincent Brandt. In preparing the questionnaire, they were invaluable in supplementing our narrow economic view with insights from their respective disciplines of sociology and anthropology. Man-Gap Lee also assisted in recruiting and training the interviewers, while Vincent Brandt contributed the case studies of small-scale entrepreneurship.

In administering our sample survey, we imposed upon many

Korean businessmen, and would like to thank those who cooperated with our interviewers. Special thanks are due to the following individuals who gave their time to discuss the issues with the authors: Pyŏng-ch'ŏl Yi (Chairman of Samsung), Chu-yŏng Chŏng (Chairman of Hyundai), Dŏk-chung Kim (Co-Chairman of Daewoo), Chŭng-hun Cho (Chairman of Hanjin), Tu-jin Paek (Chairman of the Yujŏnghoe), Ch'ung-hun Pak (Chairman of the Korean Traders Association and former DPM), Ki-yŏng Chang (Congressman and former DPM, deceased), Yong-wan Kim (former President of Federation of Korean Industries, FKI), and Ip-sam Kim (Vice-President of FKI). Employees of the above groups, plus Sam Yang, were most helpful in providing data for the large case studies. None of these individuals are to be held responsible for any of our conclusions.

Energetic research assistance and computer work at KDI were provided by: Hi Kang, Ki-hwan Pak, Chong-hyŏn Pak, Pyŏng-ch'an Kim, Chae-hun Yu, Chae-ok Yi, and Sŏng-suk An. Chin-sŭng Chŏng was especially helpful in coordinating the activities of various assistants and interviewers. Sŏk-je Yi was extremely useful in research assistance and computer work at Boston University. Yŏng-ch'ae Nam, Marianne Brinker, Mun-hyo Kim, and Susan Weise were exceptional in their ability to convert scrawl to manuscript. Interviewing was conducted by sociology students at Ewha and Yonsei Universities. We are heavily indebted to the following young women for their perseverance in a frustrating, non-traditional role: Hwa-jin Yi, In-sun Kang, Yŏng-ae Chŏn, Yŏng-nan Yu, Hyang-sun Yi, Kŭm-ju Kang, Pong-ji Yi, Sun-ji, Yi, Kwi-sik Sim, Ŭn-ju Kim, Yŏn-uk Pak, Kyŏng-ae No, Hŭi-ŭn Chŏng, Sŏng-sun Yi, Myŏng-sun Ch'a, and Yun-ja Kim. The diligence of Yŏng-nan Yu and Sun-ji Yi was especially notable.

Gustav Papanek and Gregory Henderson were kind enough to review the entire manuscript and provide valuable comments. Peter Kilby generously gave detailed advice on the entrepreneurship chapters. Kwang Suk Kim, Ian Little, Dwight Perkins, and

John Sheahan also gave useful advice. The volume has benefited greatly from all of these contributions, but we have refrained from complete responsiveness to the suggestion of any one individual, thus leaving all free to disassociate themselves from some of our more controversial observations.

Preface

It is a matter of common observation that governments in less developed countries play a larger role in economic processes than was true in Western countries at similar stages of development or, for that matter, than governments play in most Western countries today. This is evidenced not only by the importance of public enterprise in the industrial sector but also by the scope of government control over private economic activities. It follows that how the decisions of government relate to private decision-making in the allocation and use of resources has a good deal to do with the course of development. Yet these relationships are given short shrift in theories of development, and it is easy to see why this is so. They are closely bound up with the political and cultural characteristics of particular societies and do not lend themselves to the broad generalizations and cross-country comparisons that are the bread and meat of development literature. Yet government-business relationships are important in the development process.

To understand these relationships, it is necessary to examine the political forces that have shaped the structure of government and have determined its priorities; the way in which economic policies are formulated; the characteristics of the bureaucracy that implements these policies; the nature of business firms and the sources of business leadership. There are not many studies of the development process in the Third World that have undertaken this task, and this is one of the best.

The beginning of rapid economic growth in South Korea is usually dated in 1963, which followed by two years the assumption of power by military forces led by Park Chung Hee. Military leadership gave way to civilian government in 1962 under a constitution that concentrated power in the executive branch of a highly centralized regime. This regime, though increasingly authoritarian, brought political stability to the Republic of Korea, and political stability is a necessary, though not sufficient, condition of economic growth in any country. This is not to say that events preceding the military takeover had nothing to do with subsequent economic development. Two significant land-distribution programs had laid the basis for a relatively egalitarian and productive agricultural economy. The expansion of educational facilities had produced an unusually literate population with extensive training of upper ranks. And behind all this was the impact of the East Asian culture with its emphasis on education and individual and social discipline that has underlain recent rapid growth in all East Asian societies. Nevertheless, political stability in the hands of a government that gave the highest priority to economic development was the needed catalyst.

Although all sectors of the economy have grown at a respectable rate, it has been an export-oriented industrial expansion that has led Korean growth. Since 1963, industrial output (manufactures and mining) has expanded at the remarkable rate of 18 percent per annum, and exports (mainly of manufactures) at the even more remarkable rate of 40 percent. It is in this area that the relations between government and private activity have been closest and most significant. If there is a "Korea, Inc.," as there is alleged to be a "Japan, Inc.," it is the government that is the chairman of the board of the corporation. The absence of vigorous political life has not permitted business organizations, as in Japan, to compete for political power, and ownership by government of financial intermediaries and control of access to foreign capital have provided the principal instruments of government influence on business activities.

Although South Korea is thought of and, in the main, in fact is, a private-enterprise economy, government enterprise has played a remarkably large role, a role as large, in fact, as is common in developing countries following a "socialist pattern." Obviously this is not the product of ideology but of an essentially pragmatic policy that supports public enterprise where private-market failures or the inability of private enterprise to do the job are thought to exist. Over the last decade some 30 percent of total industrial investment has been directed to publicly owned enterprises, though these enterprises account for only 10 to 15 percent of total industrial employment. Although opinion in Korea considers public enterprise to be less efficient than private enterprise, the record indicates that it is highly efficient as compared with most public enterprises in other developing countries. The reason for this appears to be a government oversight that is not only well informed but intolerant of failure.

It is, however, in the relationship of government to private enterprise that the Korean experience is most worthy of study. The government has, in the main, eschewed those detailed and largely quantitative controls such as industrial licensing, price control, rationing, and allocation of foreign exchange that have characterized economic policy in India and many other developing countries. Nevertheless, the influence of public policy on private investment and output has been real. Beginning in the mid-1960s, a major orientation of this policy has been toward the promotion of exports. Domestic credit and foreign borrowing under government guarantee have been made available to firms showing a capacity to export. Imports have been made available at close to world market prices, and the government has actively participated in searching out export opportunities. Export targets have been set by product and region of destination, and the Minister of Commerce and Industry has kept close track of the performance of individual firms in meeting targets.

As might be expected in a society in which government leadership is evident, economic planning is taken seriously. The Economic Planning Board is under the direction of a Minister of Planning who is also Deputy Prime Minister. In addition to preparing five-year plans, the board is also charged with the preparation of annual Overall Resource Budgets and, since the expenditure side of the budget is in the hands of the Economic Planning Board rather than the Ministry of Finance, that board is the central focus of development strategy. Increasingly the Economic Planning Board, in conjunction with relevant ministries, is concerned with an examination of alternative courses of action. Planning in Korea is substantially more than indicative, since the public sector is large, and the private industrial sector is heavily influenced by government decision-making, but the resulting mix of public-private relationships falls far short of a command economy. Economic policy-making in Korea can be briefly characterized as being in the hands of relatively few people (though business and other interest groups are extensively consulted); conducive to rapid decisions (with equally rapid reversal of mistakes); and reaching rather far down in productive processes.

It is, however, in the area of policy implementation that the Korean economy differs most sharply from most developing economies. The manner in which individuals and firms are persuaded, cajoled, or compelled to follow government direction is a seriously neglected area of economic development research, and here the authors make an original and substantial contribution. They distinguish inducement from command procedures and discretionary from non-discretionary administration of these procedures. Liberal ideology favors non-discretionary inducement as the preferred method of policy implementation on the grounds that inducements offer possibilities of adaptation that command procedures deny, and that withholding discretion from administrative officials guards against corruption. The Korean government has made extensive use of non-discretionary inducements, but it has also used discretionary command procedures to good effect. This is possible only to governments possessing a well-trained bureaucracy that is either impervious to corruption or sufficiently supervised to make corruption unprofitable. No one would or could say that corruption is absent from the administration of Korean economic policies. Indeed, during the Rhee regime in the 1950s, it was endemic. But the absence of detailed government controls that characterize most Asian economies and the existence of a relatively well-trained bureaucracy in a government that is determined to produce results probably holds corruption down to modest proportions.

Despite the leading position of government in economic affairs, Korea is predominantly a private-enterprise economy. Over three-quarters of industrial output is produced in the private sector, and it is private enterprise, though acting within a policy environment designed by government, that is the operating mechanism responsible for rapid growth. Korean firms are universally individual—or family-owned—enterprises, and the general public is only beginning to participate in equity ownership. A great many of these firms, moreover, are still in the hands of the founding individuals or families. The rise of a large and active group of entrepreneurs is one of the striking aspects of Korean development. Jones and SaKong, using an extensive questionnaire and numerous personal interviews, have examined the regional, family, religious, and educational backgrounds and affiliations of this group. It is rather remarkable that, despite the fact that war and political convulsion had practically destroyed the basis of the old aristocracy and economic opportunities have been extensively broadened, the entrepreneurial class is, in the main, composed of descendants of former elite groups.

Public policy has tended to encourage the rise of large conglomerates, since domestic credit and access to foreign borrowing have been provided to those entrepreneurs who have shown a capacity to produce and to export. Preferred access to credit plus the fact that Korean corporations are highly leveraged, with a relatively small percent of capital represented by equity, have produced a high average rate of profits. Since Korean business leaders, at least in the first generation, have pursued a relatively austere lifestyle, most of these profits have been reinvested. A high percent of the expansion of industrial output has come from existing rather than new firms, with the result that economic concentration has grown rapidly. These large multi-firm enterprises in Korea are called chaebŏl and bear some resemblance to old style Japanese zaibatsu. The chief difference is that they do not control banks, which means that, since the distribution of credit is in the hands of the government, the Korean chaebŏl are unlikely to achieve that dominant position in the economy and in society attained by the old style zaibatsu. Nevertheless, the rapid increase in business concentration in Korea has become a public concern, and government is attempting to do something about it. How successful this will be is still to be determined.

The rapid industrialization of Korea and its emergence on the world scene as a formidable competitor are remarkable events in recent economic history. The role of government and the role of business have both been large, and the interrelationship of government and business has been at the heart of the development process. Jones and SaKong tell the story well and, in doing so, have made a significant contribution to the literature of development economics.

Edward S. Mason

Afterword

Park Chung Hee was killed on October 26, 1979, while page proofs for this volume were being corrected. We considered revising the manuscript to reflect this momentous event, but decided to let the original version stand unchanged.

This book will now appear at a time when there may be increased public awareness of the processes and consequences of economic decision-making under the Park regime. While this would undoubtedly be a healthy short-term corrective, we see no reason to alter the generally positive tone of our volume. Internationally (and in the longer run, in Korea itself), the dominant story is how the regime was able to achieve a sustained annual real increase in income of roughly 10 percent both for the country and for the poorest 40 percent of the population. The fact that in the process a relatively small number of individuals benefited disproportionately is important, but secondary when viewing the 1961 to 1979 period as a whole. Our primary concern has been to explain how the decision-making process achieved as much as it did, with somewhat less attention to how it might have done even better.

Nonetheless, when looking to the future, the weaknesses of the system deserve to be re-emphasized as they might be expected to be the focus of reform efforts. While a historical volume such as this is not the place for either prediction or prescription, it may be useful to underline those features of the existing system that are most likely to be altered in the future.

While change in the sphere of economic decision-making is likely to be much less dramatic than in the political arena, it is nonetheless liable to be significant. In the first place, exogenous political change will impact on the economic system; and in the second place, endogenous economic trends may produce reactions.

If the political changes emanating from the events of October 1979 constitute a move towards democracy and away from authoritarianism, then one consequence will be greater pluralism in economic decision-making. Additional actors will be appended to the rather narrow hierarchical structure we have described. The influence of legislators and politicians is likely to increase both in policy formation and in the critical day-to-day implementation decisions of civil servants. If democratic electoral success is in part dependent on availability of campaign funds, and if the dominant source of such funds is business, then the power of the chaebŏl may actually increase. Unions might well gain a significant role in the process. In short, there may be modifications in such characteristics of the system as executive dominance, speed of decision-making, and the use of discretionary command enforced by partial mutuality. In addition, system goals are likely to shift to give less emphasis to growth, with greater attention to equity and stability.

Turning to endogenous economic factors, it can be argued that, over time, there has been a marked increase in the cost/

benefit ratio associated with the existing system. First, the more than fivefold expansion of the economy from 1961 to 1979, plus equally dramatic alterations in structure, make control techniques appropriate to the simple environment of the 1960s inappropriate for the 1980s. Decentralization of decision-making, reduced reliance on command, increased use of field manipulation and the market, and reduced discretion of civil servants all become increasingly desirable in a more complicated environment where the information available to a small number of civil servants is a decreasing share of the total needed to run the economy. Second, demand for certain social goods may be highly income elastic: at $100 per capita the dominant concern may be simply to get jobs for people's hands and food for their bellies; with this accomplished at $1500 per capita, equity and social justice become far more important. Finally, while the level of business concentration was low in the 1960s, its rapid rate of growth creates increasing potential for abuse. Forty-odd chaebŏl producing, say, 10 percent of non-agricultural GDP is quite a different matter from the same number being responsible for 20 percent or more.

None of these changes occurred suddenly in 1979. Indeed, during the late 1970s, these sorts of concerns were being voiced with increasing frequency both within the government and outside it; and some policy changes were already taking place in the directions suggested above. What *has* changed discontinuously is the opportunity for actually implementing necessary changes in the decision-making process so as to fully reflect the realities of the 1980s as opposed to those of the 1960s. As always, the danger is that of overreaction, with the possibility that the very real strengths of the existing system will be undermined in the reform process. It is hoped that the present volume, in analyzing both the benefits and costs of the historical starting point, may contribute to a rational and balanced reform program.

Leroy P. Jones
Il SaKong

ONE

Introduction

ISSUES IN KOREAN GROWTH

A striking feature of post-war Korean history is the coincidence of economic and political turning points. On May 16, 1961, a military coup brought Park Chung Hee to power. Under previous regimes the economy had grown at a real annual rate of slightly more than 4 percent; thereafter it averaged nearly 10 percent.[1] The question naturally arises as to whether this relationship is accidental or causal.

Korea in 1961 represented a stage of suppressed growth potential in that the level of social development was conducive to a standard of economic achievement far higher than that actually attained. This is crudely reflected in Adelman and Morris's finding that, of seventy-four developing countries, Korea was sixtieth in 1961 per capita income but fourteenth in a composite indicator of socio-cultural development.[2] The question is why this gap developed and what happened in the early 1960s to allow tapping of the potential.

The marked discontinuity in the growth rate may be explained in terms of: 1) some sort of "stage theory" of economic development in which "preconditions" established in the 1950s allowed "take-off" in the 1960s; or, 2) differences in government actions. The truth is undoubtedly a mixture whose proportions we will not attempt to estimate here. Ours is the more modest goal of contributing to an answer by comparing selected aspects of the government's economic role under two political regimes.

When an economist evaluates the government's role, he is prone to think in terms of policies. From this perspective, the difference between the Rhee and Park periods can be explained by the shift to a set of rational economic policies such as export promotion, and equilibrium exchange and interest rates. A generation of Western economists has been going around the world urging less-developed countries (LDCs) to adopt this strategy of "getting the prices right." The aim is to achieve growth by substituting the invisible hand of market forces for the visible hand of government intervention. There has been a notable absence of success in convincing countries to follow this advice for any extended period of time, but the Korean experience is often cited as vindicating the process. Gilbert Brown provides a particularly ebullient exposition of this view:

> The almost irresistible conclusion from Korean development experience is that with proper economic policies and a continuation of reasonable international aid levels most developing countries can achieve at least a 6 per cent annual growth rate, and many countries could sustain growth rates as high as 10 per cent.[3]

Without denigrating the importance of "proper economic policies," we will argue that they are only a part of the causal mechanism and that similarly endowed nations could espouse equally appropriate policies with far less dramatic results. There is, after all, much to be done between a proclamation of export priority and the appearance of Korean shirts on Sears shelves or "Pony" automobiles on Riadh streets. Fixing an import substitution target for fertilizer does not automatically result in an adequate supply of domestic urea in three years rather than seven. Reasonable exchange and interest rate policies may be necessary for such results but they are far from sufficient in the context of a developing economy.

The missing element is implementation—the translation of an administrative abstraction into concrete action by a production unit. In Korea, this link has emphatically not been provided by sitting back and letting market forces reign. On the contrary, the Korean government under Park Chung Hee has been actively and pervasively interventionist. The "Korean miracle" is not a triumph of laissez faire, but of a pragmatic non-ideological mixture of market and non-market forces. Where the market works, fine; where it doesn't, the government shows no hesitation in intervening by means that range from a friendly phone call to public ownership. Implementation via intervention will be a major theme throughout this book.

A second major concern is the obverse of the first. To start again from the view that policies "explain" growth, how are these policies themselves to be explained? The basic elements of a rational growth-oriented strategy may not be particularly obscure to economists, but political leaders in LDCs have not proven enamored of the prescriptions of mere "academic scribblers." It is thus of interest to push the explanation of growth one step deeper and ask how basic strategic decisions came to be adopted. Even more important, how are the more difficult and more numerous tactical decisions arrived at and continually modified in light of changing conditions in an open economy? Korea's long-term planning process, reflected in a succession of five-year plans, is well known. We shall argue, however, that its rapid and flexible short-run adjustments to changing economic conditions are even more important in explaining rapid growth.

The concern of this volume, then, is not government policy itself, but the way in which it is formulated and implemented. This is a rather broad mandate, and it is necessary to narrow the focus somewhat. We therefore leave to companion papers the government's macroeconomic role in aggregate demand management via monetary and fiscal policy and its microeconomic role in providing and financing public and merit goods. The reader will be excused for momentarily wondering if anything remains, since we have explicity excluded virtually the entire content of traditional Western courses on "Public Economics." The answer is an area of particular importance in developing mixed economies, namely the state's contribution to increasing production in the organized enterprise sector.[4] This may be accomplished either through direct government participation in public enterprise or through guiding, stimulating, and controlling private entrepreneurial activity.

In light of Korea's capitalistic ideological reputation, its reliance on public enterprise has been surprisingly heavy, and we shall devote a chapter to explaining this paradox. The bulk of industrial growth, however, has come in the private sector, so that the extraordinary growth of the 1960s is manifest in a concomitant blossoming of entrepreneurial activity. Our concern with implementation, broadly conceived, thus necessitates substantial attention to the roles of private entrepreneurs and managers. Most of our earlier questions on the role of government thus can, indeed must, be reformulated in terms of the complementary role of the private sector. To what extent is this higher rate of business success attributable to identifiable government action, as opposed to independent evolution of entrepreneurial talents or a situation in which some critical mass of success leads to mutually reinforcing self-perpetuation? No definitive answer is possible, but perspective will be provided by surveying the history of Korean industrial entrepreneurship, the social backgrounds of a large sample of entrepreneurs, and a limited number of case studies of individual businessmen. The results will suggest that Korean culture and history have combined to produce a substantial stock of entrepreneurial intent, but that only after 1961 were these energies channeled into socially constructive outlets through government intervention.

In sum, this volume considers the interaction of government and business in formulating and implementing policies aimed at expanding industry. The primary goal is to broaden our understanding of the dynamics of Korean development by looking behind the changes in empirical economic magnitudes. A secondary goal of this Korean case study is to contribute to an understanding of more general issues concerning the interaction of government and business in developing a mixed economy. We now briefly sketch the outlines of these broader theoretical questions. Readers interested only in the Korean case may proceed directly to the Overview below.

THEORETICAL PERSPECTIVES

VISIBLE VERSUS INVISIBLE HANDS

The debate over the appropriate role of government is hardly new. Indeed, modern economic theory is rooted in Adam Smith's exposition on the merits of the invisible hand of the market over the visible hand of government. Although the topic is currently out of favor on the frontiers of the profession, there is nonetheless a very substantial body of literature on what John Maynard Keynes termed "the chief task of economists at this hour, [namely] to distinguish afresh the *Agenda* of Government from the *Non-Agenda*."[5] In the space available we must necessarily be highly selective.[6] The purpose here is twofold. First, we wish to outline the theoretical framework within which the study is conducted and thus expose our biases at the outset. Second, we hope to demonstrate that the Korean interventionist path to growth, far from being an aberration, is actually to be expected on purely theoretical grounds.

MEANS VERSUS ENDS

To put the issue in perspective, it is useful to recall the terms of Smith's original response to mercantilist economic philosophy. According to Eli Hecksher, the foremost authority on mercantilism, the dispute was not primarily over basic values: "On principle, mercantilist authors and statesmen not only believed in, but actually harped upon 'freedom' especially 'freedom of trade' . . . [Instead, there was] . . . one fundamental difference, namely, in the mercantilists' disbelief and the liberals' belief in the existence of a pre-established harmony." In the eyes of mercantilists the desired results were to be effected "by the dextrous management of a skilful politician; they were not expected to follow from the untrammelled forces of economic life."[7]

The visible and invisible hands may thus be seen as alternative means to desired ends. The choice then depends upon the results expected under the two methods and this will vary, first, with the particular decision and, second, with historical circumstance. The task is to choose a judicious combination appropriate to a particular time and place. This pragmatic approach is in sharp distinction to the ideological one in which a particular public-private combination is codified into some sort of "ism" which then attains the stature of an end in itself. Even if such a combination represents a judicious choice in its original historical context, it is not directly transferable to another time or place.

CLASSICAL MINIMALISM

Classical laissez faire can be viewed as leading to a minimal role for the state as reflected in the often quoted passage from Keynes:

> The most important Agenda of the State relate not to those activities which private individuals are already fulfilling but to those functions which fall outside the sphere of the individual, to those decisions which are made by no one if the State does not make them. The important thing for Government is not to do things which individuals are already doing, and to do it a little better or a little worse, but to do those things which at present are not being done at all.[8]

The minimalist scope originally included the "night watchman" functions of Lasalle and Smith's "certain public works and public institutions which can never be for the interest of any individual to erect or maintain."[9] In a more complex twentieth-century economy, Keynesian aggregate demand management has been added.

An ideological minimalist (or a maximalist seeking a strawman) would confine the state to these functions in perpetuity. A pragmatist would observe that the Keynsian supplement to the minimal list was in itself a response to changing conditions and that Keynes is subject to a much broader interpretation if the emphasis is changed to "those things which *at present* are not being done at all." As the "present" changes, so do the problems left to government to solve: for example, pollution and control of multi-national corporations in the contemporary West. While the relevant external conditions are infinitely variable, it is possible to suggest some general determinants of the public-private mix.

EXOGENOUS DETERMINANTS

The determinants of an economic system may be broadly classified into two groups—economic and socio-historic. The pragmatic approach emphasizes the role of economic factors and views government intervention as a response to private market failures. This is represented by William J. Baumol, who "attempt(s) to determine which, if any, are the circumstances in which people composing an economy will find that a particular extension of the authority of their government is requisite for the most efficient pursuit of their own economic interests."[10] General equilibrium theory establishes certain very stringent conditions under which a competitive equilibrium exists and is Pareto efficient; any deviation from these conditions then establishes a presumptive case for government intervention.[11] Such market failures being ubiquitous in the real world, a rigorous presentation of the beauties of the invisible hand ultimately proves a brief for the visible. The pragmatic market failure approach thus does not reflect a pro-laissez-faire bias, but only provides an analytic frame of reference.

If the normative market failure approach is coupled with an assumption of social rationality then it leads to descriptive propositions such as Kenneth J. Arrow's that "when the market fails to achieve an optimal state, society will, to some extent at least, recognize the gap, and non-market social institutions will arise attempting to bridge it."[12] A natural corollary is that societies facing similar problems in a similar environment will evolve similar solutions. This is reflected in various convergence theories which see the United States and the Soviet Union, or socialist and capitalist LDCs moving toward similar patterns of government-business interaction.

In fact there are real limits to convergence due to sociohistoric factors. The first of these is ideological. In theory, one could start with a "government failure" model and, with a given set of constraints, arrive at the same public-private mix as by starting at the opposite market failure extreme. In practice, ideological taboos will constrain the search pattern to marginal changes, and commonality will be approached from one side or the other rather than by iterative bracketing. Given an inevitable range of real world indeterminancy, convergence will then stop at opposite sides of this often broad band. Further, as Albert O. Hirschman argues, "New problems continually arise and they will presumably again result in initially quite different probing and search patterns (so that) convergence in one area will be paralleled by renewed divergence in another."[13] From the point of view of the present study, the important point about ideology is that it can reduce the speed of adjustment and the scope of search. In an LDC where both government and market failures are pervasive, the rate of growth may be a function, not of ideological orientation, but of ideological flexibility.

The second non-economic system determinant might be termed sociological. Talcott Parsons identified four interrelated functional needs of societies: maintenance of prevailing social and cultural patterns, integration of persons and groups within society, attainment of systemic (group) goals, and adaptation to environmental conditions.[14] The relative importance of these functions varies with the evolutionary stage of society, and Bert Hoselitz has suggested that the scope of government activity varies with the nature of the dominant problem.[15] Thus a "new" state facing problems of integration and systemic goal attainment may be more likely to rely on collective action than a "mature" state facing primarily problems of individual needs and environmental adaptation.

A third non-economic system determinant is cultural. Regardless of the economic and social problems faced by a nation, a particular cultural heritage may make government activity more or less efficacious as a tool. For example, it may be that the Confucian hierarchical heritage is conducive to a stronger government in East Asia than in the individualistic West, even with identical environment and goals.

ENDOGENOUS SYSTEM DETERMINANTS

While external factors affect the need for collective action, endogenous elements may limit its efficacy. Two of these are of primary importance—information and motivation.

Rational economic decisions require extensive information on such things as consumer preferences, technology, domestic and foreign resource availability, and conditions in related output markets. Moreover, future as well as present conditions must be considered. Since acquiring such information is a difficult and expensive task at best, the well-known advantages of the invisible hand offer substantial rewards both in improving the speed and accuracy of results and in conserving resources devoted to it. The von Mises-Lange-Hayek controversy centered on the drawbacks of the visible hand in this respect and led to the theory of Market Socialism.

With private decision-making, many of the consequences of action fall directly upon the decision-maker and, compared with a disinterested bureaucrat, this may spur greater energy and accuracy in seeking information and implementing decisions. Keynes provides a uniquely balanced presentation of the argument:

> Profit accrues, under *laissez-faire*, to the individual who, whether by skill or good fortune, is found with his productive resources in the right place at the right time. A system which allows the skillful or fortunate individual to reap the whole fruits of this conjuncture evidently offers an immense incentive to the practice of the art of being in the right place at the right time. Thus one of the most powerful of human motives, namely, the love of money, is harnessed to the task of distributing economic resources in the way best calculated to increase wealth.[16]

Use of the phrase "skillful *or* fortunate individual" is judicious for it points to the endogenous distributional drawback of laissez faire. Keynes again provides an articulate summary:

> Many of the greatest economic evils of our time are the fruits of risk, uncertainty, and ignorance. It is because particular individuals, fortunate in situation or in abilities, are able to take advantage of uncertainty and ignorance, and also because for the same reason big business is often a lottery, that great inequalities of wealth come about.[17]

Once the choice is made, explicit attention needs to be given to offsetting undesirable side effects. Reliance on government requires bolstering information flows and motivation, while dependence on private decisions suggests attention to limitation of unproductive windfall gains. In sum, regrettably but inevitably, the alternative to market imperfection is government imperfection and vice versa.

SYSTEM DETERMINANTS IN LDCS

Heterogenous though the set of LDCs may be, there is sufficient uniformity of circumstance to lead various authors to generalizations concerning the appropriate role of the state.[18] Since most of these arguments are based on the various exogenous and endogenous determinants already enumerated, they may be dealt with rather briefly as four classes of illustrative propositions:

1) The need for government intervention will tend to be greater the lower the absolute level of development, since market failures will be more widespread. In particular, fragmented capital markets and information scarcity will retard productive private entrepreneurship. Further, the ubiquity of disequilibrium markets will reward rent-seeking zero-sum entrepreneurial activity.
2) The demand for government action will increase with the relative degree of backwardness, because of the tensions created by expectation gaps. Rapidity of escape from the various vicious circles of poverty may be seen to require concerted collective action.
3) The capacity for government action will increase with relative backwardness, since follower nations relying on borrowed technology require a less innovative form of entrepreneurship. Also, information requirements are lower in a simpler economy, and centralized decision-making can economize on the use of scarce trained manpower.
4) The capacity for government action will be lower in poorer countries, since administrative and bureaucratic efficiency is lower.[19]

While the need for intervention thus seems clearly greater in LDCs, the judgment on its efficacy is mixed (that is, factors #3 and #4 work in opposite directions). The scarcity of competent decision-makers affects public and private sectors alike. It might be said that the problem is to allocate scarce administrative and managerial resources so as to equate the marginal products in each sector. It might also be said that the problem is to harness the "animal spirits" of private capitalists to the service of broader social goals. Neither formulation is particularly illuminating in an operational sense, and the problem remains of determining a reasonable distribution in a particular time and place.

SYSTEM DIMENSIONS

Thus far we have proceeded rather simplistically as though the choice between visible and invisible hands were one-dimensional. In order to broaden the discussion, it is first necessary to restrict it by eliminating collective consumption. The government must necessarily organize and finance consumption of public and merit goods. The expansion of this dimension of intervention is largely explained by income levels and is, in any event, quite independent of decisions as to intervention in production—witness Sweden's combination of high public consumption and low government intervention in production.

Even confining ourselves to the production side, a single-dimensional continuum—say between capitalism and socialism—is quite meaningless. The two-dimensional comparison of market socialism, market capitalism, command socialism, and command capitalism makes a step in the right direction by distinguishing between the independent dimensions of ownership of capital and the locus of resource-allocating decisions. While the ownership dimension is fairly well defined, the command-market continuum is not. For one thing, there is the obvious problem of specifying and weighing interventions in various markets. Much more important, within a given market there is seldom a clear choice between a visible public hand and an invisible private one. On the one side, the prevalence of scale economies relative to the size of the market means that private decisions will often be taken by one (or a few) individual(s) whose hands are just as visible (and arbitrary) as that of government. On the other side, government decisions commonly evolve through a process that may be just as "invisible" as the workings of the market. Many critical decisions are reached through a complex and subtle interaction between private and public actors, so that a decision formally announced in one sector is not necessarily functionally attributable to that sector.

Other elements of multi-dimensionality abound. The intervention of the government is not confined to "commands," but also includes marginal incentives, provision of information, and subtle persuasion. Decisions in one market may be affected, intentionally or unintentionally, by actions in another. Intervention may operate on price or quantity and may apply to the entire economy, an industry, or a particular company. The choice between these various methods of intervention is not a mere matter of detail but one of substance. Even where the same primary result can be achieved by various tools, the secondary effects—desirable and undesirable—will be quite different. This is so, not just because of the exogenous interdependence of markets, but also because the endogenous strengths and weaknesses of intervention vary in importance from tool to tool.

These elements of interdependent multi-dimensionality will be elaborated on at length in later chapters. Here we wish only to flag their importance, since they affect the methodology of the entire paper.

METHODOLOGY AND OVERVIEW

The foregoing surveys of Korean and theoretical issues should suffice to demonstrate that this study addresses subtle questions whose answers are inherently slippery. As Patrick and Rosovsky observe about the comparison of the Japanese with Western European systems, "We really do not know, both because we do not know a great deal about the actual state of government-business relations in any country, and because we do not have good techniques of comparison."[20]

The theoretically ideal way of dealing with the problem is represented by Koopmans and Montias, who suggest a detailed morphology to deal with complexity, followed by econometric analysis to sort out correlation and causation.[21] Outcomes (consumption, growth, power, efficiency, equity, stability, and so on) are viewed as a function of environment (resources, technology, international markets, and so on), of the economic system (participants, organizations, interactions, orders, information flows, motivations, nature of organization, authority structure, and so on) and of policies. Economic and organization theory suggest the functional forms of the interrelationships, and norms can be expressed as a function of outcomes. Armed with time series and cross-section observations on the variables, one could ascertain the role of policy and systems in particular environments by estimating first and second derivatives of outcomes with respect to the various independent variables.

We hasten to reassure (dismay?) the reader by announcing that we have no intention of attempting anything nearly so rigorous. The Koopmans-Montias analysis represents the ultimate extension of the pragmatic approach, while we shall be operating near the opposite pole of sophistication, close to what Ward has termed "intuitive groping."[22] Nonetheless, the same logical framework underlies our analysis. One need not be immediately striving for Nirvana to be called a Buddhist. While the relationships we shall be examining are similar to those which concern Koopmans and Montias, we rely on verbal description rather than parameterization and support our generalizations with anecdotes rather than correlation coefficients. The results are undeniably "soft."

To some extent our approach is dictated by the virtual absence of prior work in this field in Korea. In dramatic contrast to the situation in neighboring Japan, Korean scholars have virtually ignored the areas of government-business interaction and entrepreneurship. To bolster our intuition and build up our stock of anecdotes, it has therefore been necessary to undertake a fair amount of primary research. This primary material has been relegated to appendixes, since it interrupts the analytic flow of the main text. It, nonetheless, constitutes an integral part of the whole effort. It has two components—a broad-based survey, and detailed case studies—as described below.

To provide breadth, an entrepreneurship survey was conducted among a one-sixth random sample of all Korean manufacturing firms employing more than fifty workers. Using trained college students, interviews were solicited with the chief executive and top manager of each firm, and a questionnaire was administered covering enterprise history, personal background, government-business relations, values and attitudes. Appendix C gives a detailed description of the survey design, and comments on problems and limitations of the questionnaire method. An English version of the questionnaire is given as Appendix D.

To provide depth, we conducted detailed case studies of small and medium enterprises (Appendix A) and of large chaebŏl (family-based industrial conglomerates),[23] (Appendix B). In each case study, the goal was to reflect the relative roles of government and business in industrial entrepreneurship; the extent, vehicle, and impact of government intervention; and the sources of private entrepreneurs. Our conclusions were checked through a number of interviews with prominent government and business leaders (see "Acknowledgments" for a list).

Our interpretation of the results, organized according to the theoretical issues given above, is presented in the main text. We begin with a historical survey of developments in the colonial period (Chapter 2), and then deal with the process of policy formulation (Chapter 3), the importance and means of implementation (Chapter 4), the role of public enterprise (Chapter 5), the sources of expansion of private entrepreneurship

(Chapter 6), the social environment producing the supply of private entrepreneurs (Chapter 7), and government efforts at controlling private economic power (Chapter 8). Conclusions are summarized in Chapter 9.

In sum, "methodology" is perhaps an overly grandiose term for the approach followed here. It would be more accurate to say that we simply intend to tell a story about how things work in Korea. The test of the story is that it be consistent with facts available to knowledgeable Koreans and that causal interactions be explained logically in light of economic theory and international experience. Alternative explanations are possible, and our preliminary generalizations will undoubtedly be modified following further work in this underdeveloped area of inquiry.

TWO

The Colonial Heritage

Past is not always prologue, but the possibility must be considered. We, therefore, begin with a survey of the industrial base upon which post-war growth was built. The rapid rise of a Korean entrepreneurial class is impressive in any case, but it would become positively epical if it could be shown to have emerged spontaneously with little or no prior history. Such a tale can be built on three not implausible premises: first, under the Yi dynasty there was no industrial entrepreneurship and only a very weak mercantile class; second, under the colonialists, modern economic activity was overwhelmingly dominated by the Japanese; and third, such limited indigenous entrepreneurs as emerged under the Japanese lost their physical capital, if not their lives, during the chaos of the Korean War.

While these premises will be shown to be broadly accurate, we shall, nonetheless, reject the pure hypothesis of immaculate conception. Rather, we shall point out that the colonial era did leave behind a substantial growth potential consisting of impressive stocks of both physical and human capital. The putative bureaucrats, entrepreneurs, and managers had largely "learned by watching" rather than by "doing," but had, nonetheless, learned a great deal. This experience could have been translated into fairly rapid growth when combined with the inherited stock of Japanese factories. Instead, this heritage was dissipated through years of political and military conflict, the former being no less destructive of the industrial potential than the latter.

Throughout this chapter, we shall be concerned solely with the industrial sphere. Parallel developments in social structure, education, and the like, while critical to explaining overall post-war growth, will be largely ignored given our focus on manufacturing entrepreneurship and government. We now proceed chronologically, beginning with the traditional economy of the Yi dynasty.

YI DYNASTY ENTREPRENEURSHIP

The study of Yi dynasty economic history is far less developed than its political and cultural counterparts, so this section will necessarily be perfunctory and tentative.[1] We shall describe the Yi economy as "traditional dualistic." It was "traditional" in relying on small-scale, labor-intensive "handicraft" production techniques. It was "dualistic" in being segmented into royal-aristocratic and commoner segments. The more sophisticated needs of the former were supplied by government handicrafts factories and Chinese imports, while the cruder needs came from levies on the population. The commoner economy was characterized by household production and limited exchange. The link between the two economies was an extractive system based on land taxes and commodity tribute.

Private sector activities were strictly controlled in theory.

Manufacturing outside the government monopolies was originally prohibited except in strictly limited areas. Trade was confined to tribute contractors and government-licensed merchants. The degree to which these prohibitions were effective is subject to interpretation, but there can be no question that the Confucian heritage restricted the Yi economy to a particularly limited form of traditional dualism.

Following the Hideyoshi invasions (1590s), the general decline of the dynasty was reflected in a deterioration of the aristocratic sector of the economy. As a result, the government factory system was weakened and private artisanship grew. Whether the commoner economy benefited more from the reduced constraints and increased trade, or suffered more under increased extractions and general societal malaise, is not altogether clear. What is apparent is that the degenerate traditional dualistic economy of the late Yi dynasty was extremely weak and undifferentiated and is not to be compared to its late Tokugawa counterpart.

THE TRANSITION PERIOD, 1876–1910

The opening of the ports beginning in 1876 introduced a transition period lasting until formal Japanese annexation in 1910. The competition of foreign powers for influence, and the increasing role of the Japanese, combined to introduce dynamic elements into the static traditional economy. By the end of the period, Russians had established a match factory and were involved in lumbering and mining; Americans owned a gold mine and a power station and were active in rail and tramway construction; French, German, and British interests operated in mining and rail construction.[2] Primary impetus, however, came from an influx of Japanese. According to official statistics, in 1908 there were 79 incorporated Japanese manufacturing firms employing an *average* of 41 workers, compared with 6 owned by Koreans employing a *total* of 92 people.[3]

TABLE 1 Industrial Occupation of Household Heads, 1910

Industry	*Japanese*	*Korean*	*Total*
Agriculture	2,210	2,433,450	2,435,660
Fishing	1,423	33,646	35,069
Mining	–	1,429	1,429
Manufacturing	5,619	22,943	28,562
Commerce	14,568	178,780	193,348
Civil Service	8,724	15,758	24,582
Other	16,730	177,647	194,500
Unemployed	1,718	31,123	32,841
TOTAL	50,992	2,894,776	2,945,991[a]

Source: Chōsen Sōtokufu, *Chōsen Sōtokufu tōkei nenpō, 1909, 1910,* pp. 63–79, 81–87. Reported in: Sang-Chul Suh, *Growth and Structural Changes in the Korean Economy,* 1910–1940 (Cambridge, Mass., 1978), pp. 34, 36.

Note: [a]These figures reflect a slight discrepancy arising from the original source.

To supplement these selective observations, it is useful to consider the single set of comprehensive data available. This is the 1910 household survey reported in Table 1. It shows that at the end of the transition period, there were 5,619 Japanese families active in manufacturing (11 percent of the immigrant group) compared with 22,943 Korean households. Regrettably, the survey does not distinguish occupations, so that owners, technicians, and laborers are lumped together. Nonetheless, the data are consistent with a pattern of Japanese dominance of "factory" manufacturing, with Koreans confined to household industry and the role of unskilled labor in Japanese-run firms.

The role of Korean aristocrats in the early period is particularly interesting. Banking apparently had a great appeal to this group, and six Korean banks were founded during the transition, three of which quickly failed.[4] Of the surviving banks, one was founded by the royal family with a crown prince as president, a second by Korean aristrocrats, and a third by "businessmen." The three failed banks all were founded by aristocrats, and members of the upper class were found in managerial positions throughout the sector. In addition, several rail lines were formed by former government officials.[5]

Ki-Zun Zo argues that these early aristocratic efforts must be seen as part of the nationalistic effort to thwart foreign domination.[6] His argument is in many ways similar to the once-popular characterization of early Meiji entrepreneurs as patriotic and community-centered and is subject to many of the same criticisms.[7] When profit and social goals coincide, there is always room for skepticism as to the prime mover, but the intensity of anti-Japanese feeling in some Korean circles may give Ki-Zun Zo somewhat stronger grounds for stressing business as one weapon in the nationalists' arsenal. In any event, the longer-run impact of these early efforts was minimal, but it is clear that the aristocrats were by no means aloof from economic activity.

At the other end of the social hierarchy, the role of merchants must be mentioned, since their accumulated mercantile capital and experience with calculations of profit and loss make them, a priori, a potential source of industrial entrepreneurship. The opening of the ports led to an expansion of foreign trade from a near zero base to 20 percent of domestic commodity-product plus import in 1911–1915.[8] To what extent did domestic merchants profit from this expansion? Daniel S. Juhn argues that while domestic merchants, particularly innkeepers, were active in the early years, they were ultimately unable to compete with the foreigners, particularly after the abolition of monopoly trading rights in 1895.[9] He concludes that "Japanese merchants completely dominated foreign trade by the early part of the twentieth century."[10] A similar story is told by Ki-Zun Zo, who asserts:

> The Japanese merchants came to Korea together with their goods and had Japanese retailers to sell their goods in towns and even in rural villages. The Japanese also purchased farm products directly from farmers for export to their country. At the beginning, the

> Japanese merchants hired Korean brokers for collection of farm products, but gradually removed such brokers and dealt directly by themselves as Japanese came in large numbers. The indigenous merchants of Korea were therefore excluded from trade with Japan.[11]

The positions taken by these two leading experts on early Korean entrepreneurship history are not inconsistent with the limited household survey data given in Table 1. There were nearly 15,000 Japanese families active in "commerce" (some 30 percent of the immigrant group) versus about 180,000 Korean households. It is thus possible that the Japanese—who represented 7.5 percent of "commerce" households— dominated foreign trade and its feeder chain, while the 92.5 percent Korean component was confined to small domestic trading activities and unskilled employees of Japanese. The evidence of foreign dominance, however, is weaker for commerce than manufacturing.

In sum, at the end of the transition period, we have less than 1 percent of Korean households active in manufacturing and 6 percent in commerce. In both sectors, available evidence suggests foreign dominance of the larger and more important enterprises. Limited though they were in numbers, these early Korean businessmen, nonetheless, made a significant contribution to modern growth by spawning modern entrepreneurs.

COLONIAL PERIOD, 1910–1945

The Japanese occupation brought rapid industrialization and a high rate of economic growth, as shown by the net commodity-product (NCP) series in Table 2. Over three decades, real manufacturing NCP grew at an annual compound rate of 10 percent and increased seventeenfold, while total NCP tripled. The share of manufactures in NCP grew from less than 4 percent to over 20 percent. Impressive though this record is, Korean observers stress that its contribution to post-war growth

TABLE 2 Net Value of Commodity-Product, 1910–1940
(in million K¥)

Period	*Value of Net Commodity-Product*[a] *Total*	*Manufacturing*	*Share of Manufacturing in NCP*
1910	645	21	3.3
1914	864	25	2.9
1919	814	69	8.5
1924	970	80	8.3
1929	1,141	137	12.0
1936	1,478	290	19.6
1940	1,661	364	21.9

Source: Sang-Chul Suh, pp. 170–171.

Note: [a]In 1936 constant prices.

was limited by three factors: the "colonial enclave" industrial structure; the dominant role of Japanese owners, managers, and technicians; and the North-South split. These will be discussed in turn.

The structural pattern of the Korean economy followed from the role assigned to Korea within the Japanese Empire. During the first two decades, the emphasis was on Korea as a supplier of foodstuffs, and the result was an "agriculture first" policy. From 1910 to 1920 manufacturing activity was actively discouraged by the Company Regulations that made formation of new corporations subject to government approval, and this was granted selectively.[12] After repeal of the regulations in 1920, large numbers of small factories were established, but it was not until the late 1920s that the rate of growth of factory output outstripped that of household industry.[13] The period may then be summarized as a rather typical colonial dualism with the periphery providing raw materials to the center. The expansion of manufacturing during the period was substantial, but dominated by small-scale agricultural processing and household industries supplying consumer goods.

As shown in Table 3, the rate of expansion of Korean entrepreneurship was high, with the number of wholly Korean-owned companies increasing from 27 in 1911 to 362 in 1929. The Japanese were also expanding rapidly, but a comparison is made difficult by the existence of jointly owned companies about which little is known. If the latter were Japanese-dominated, then the Korean share of paid-in-capital declined steadily from 17 percent in 1911 to 6 percent in 1929. Even so, the Korean partners in jointly owned firms undoubtedly played a major role in the critical learning process of the period.

Today's Sam Yang and Whashin, the two most important and prosperous business groups throughout the colonial period, originated in this period. The Sam Yang Group began when a Japanese-educated son of an aristocratic landlord took over a small financially troubled textile company and built it into the well-known Kyungbang Limited Spinning Company. He also established today's *Dong-A Ilbo* (Dong-A daily newspaper) around this time and later took over a private school that eventually became today's Korea University.[14]

The 1930s brought a new element as a consequence of Japanese war preparations, and the encouragement of Japanese zaibatsu investment in the colonies. The result was a substantial expansion of heavy industries from 23 percent of factory product in 1930 to 50 percent in 1940.[15] Most of this relative growth was in the chemical industry, taking advantage of abundant cheap hydroelectric power in the north. The output of these producer goods went to supply Japanese industry, and the share of exports in total manufacturing increased from roughly a third in 1930 to two-thirds in 1940.[16] With the output of modern industries largely exported, forward linkages were few. Backward linkages were necessarily low in chemicals and mineral processing. Even in textiles, the Japanese built integrated modern weaving and spinning plants instead of relying on small-scale weavers supplied by large-scale spinning.[17]

The common agricultural dualism of the earlier period was thus complemented by a rather unique manufacturing dualism

TABLE 3 Enterprise Expansion, 1911–1929

	Number of Companies				
	Korean	*Japanese*	*Joint*	*Foreign*	*Total*
1911	27	109	16	0	152
	(17.8)	(71.7)	(10.5)	(0.0)	(100.0)
1919	63	280	22	1	366
	(17.2)	(76.5)	(6.0)	(0.3)	(100.0)
1929	362	1,237	165	4	1,768
	(20.5)	(70.0)	(9.3)	(0.2)	(100.0)
	Paid-in Capital (wŏn)				
1911	2,742,355	5,063,020	8,104,450	0	15,909,825
	(17.2)	(31.8)	(50.9)	(0.0)	(100.0)
1919	11,403,615	83,375,962	10,982,000	2,000,000	107,761,577
	(10.6)	(77.4)	(10.2)	(1.9)	(100.0)
1929	19,877,512	193,736,669	95,785,106	1,221,500	310,620,787
	(6.4)	(62.4)	(30.8)	(0.4)	(100.0)

Source: Chōsen Sōtokufu, *Chōsen Sōtokufu tōkei nenpō, 1931,* pp. 190–193. Includes all partnerships, limited partnerships, and joint-stock companies whose main offices are in Korea. Later editions do not distinguish ownership in a manner consistent with that presented here.

in the 1930s. In both sectors, the "colonial enclave" structure minimized the spread effects of the rapid economic growth.

The impact was further reduced by the dominant role of foreign owners, managers, and technicians. Japanese owned virtually all large-scale establishments and more or less split with Koreans in small-scale factories. The result was that, by 1941, Japanese owned 59 percent of the manufacturing firms representing 91 percent of paid-in capital.[18] For all industry in the same year, Juhn reports that the Korean share drops to 2 percent, as shown in Table 4. Even with allowance for substantial under-reporting of the smaller-scale Korean establishments, it is apparent that foreign ownership of the modern sector was virtually complete.

Further exacerbating the enclave structure, Japanese were

TABLE 4 Sources of Industrial Capital, 1941
(%)

Japan-based corporations	74
Japanese residents in Korea	12
Government corporations	12
Koreans	2
TOTAL	100

Source: Daniel Sungil Juhn, "Enterpreneurship in an Underdeveloped Economy: The Case of Korea, 1890–1940," Ph.D. dissertation (George Washington University, 1965), pp. 176–177.

TABLE 5 Occupations of Active Male Population, 1944
(1,000s)

	Japanese	*Koreans*
Managerial	3.4	7.2
Professional and technical	14.5	27.9
Clerks and other white collar	53.4	172.4
Civil servants and small businessmen	38.2	122.1
Laborers	74.6	6,292.3
TOTAL	184.1	6,622.3

Source: George M. McCune, *Korea Today* (Cambridge, Mass., 1950), pp. 330–331.

recruited to fill many of the managerial, technical, and even laboring positions. Throughout the colonial period, Japanese constituted roughly one-fifth of total manufacturing employment.[19] In skilled categories, the dominance was even greater: in 1943, Japanese held 81 percent of the "technician and engineer" positions in manufacturing.[20] For the economy as a whole, in 1944, Koreans outnumbered Japanese in white-collar positions by only two or three to one (see Table 5). This is again consistent with foreign dominance of the large-scale sector and substantial participation in smaller-scale activities.

TABLE 6 Regional Shares of Net Commodity-Product, 1939–1940

(%)

	South	North
A. By Industry		
Agriculture	60	40
Forestry	53	47
Fishery	63	37
Mining	24	76
Manufacturing	46	54
TOTAL	54	46
B. Manufacturing Breakdown		
Chemicals	17	83
Metals	11	89
Ceramics	27	73
Textiles	83	17
Machines and Tools	72	28
Wood Products	56	44
Printing	86	14
Foodstuffs	64	36
Others	72	28

Source: Sang-Chul Suh, pp. 137, 141.

The colonial contribution to post-war growth is further limited by the north-south industrial distribution. Northern Korea produced 90 percent of the nation's electricity and led in manufacturing and mining while the south held the larger shares of agriculture, forestry, and fishing. (See Table 6, Part A).

THE LEGACY EVALUATED

We have seen that the impressive industrialization of the colonial period had several "enclave" features which circumscribed its potential contribution to the growth of an independent South Korean entrepreneurial class. Nonetheless, a substantial legacy was left in several areas. Foremost among these was the inheritance of the entire Japanese productive machinery, including an impressive infrastructure of communications and transportation. The results and implications of this physical heritage will be elaborated in the next section. Here we only identify the components of the legacy and note that the opportunity presented thereby is most significant.

In terms of manpower, Japanese dominance should not be allowed to obscure the fact that many Koreans did gain substantial exposure to the world of industry. Korean employment in manufacturing increased from 23,000 household heads in 1910 to 440,000 males in 1940.[21] By 1944, there were nearly 1,900 Korean engineers and technicians employed in manufacturing, another 1,300 in mining, and 2,600 in service industries outside government.[22] Overall, there were more than 7,000 Korean managers and 28,000 professional and technical workers.[23] As early as 1937, there were 2,400 Korean-owned manufacturing factories, and 160 of these employed more than 50 workers.[24] Chapter 7 shows that few of these early industrialists participated directly in the modern growth of the 1960s, but their offspring played a major role.

In terms of the North-South split, the northern dominance of manufacturing was confined to chemicals, metals, and ceramics, with the south having a substantial advantage in all other sectors, most notably in textiles and machinery (see Table 6, Part B). If a few giant chemical plants in the north are excluded, then the south actually produced manufacturing product 50 percent *greater* than the north.[25] It thus seems highly probable that the south had a substantial advantage over the north in the number of indigenous entrepreneurs. Overall statistics are not available, but this hypothesis is to some extent substantiated by the fact that by 1939, Seoul produced nearly one-fifth of total manufacturing output, and two-fifths of this was in Korean-owned establishments.[26] The northern manufacturing advantage is thus overrated in terms of its implications for post-war growth.

Less quantifiable, but no less important than the foregoing, was the "demonstration effect" of exposure to modern technology and organization. The traditional economic structure was exposed to modernity not in the form of fancy goods mysteriously arriving on ships, but from factories down the street. Further, these establishments were run not by strange looking foreigners, but by people not unlike the indigenous colonials. Thus it is at least possible that the demonstration effect of the colonial period may have had a more effective and personal impact in Korea than in the typical European enclave. There might also have been "reaction" effect. Gregory Henderson argues:

> These things—perhaps especially those which were most unforgiveable—created in Koreans a fierce desire to modernize and to equal, if not overtake, those who had enslaved them. . . Contemplating the results of the ruthless Japanese hand one wonders whether alien colonial regimes, if developmental, are successful modernizers in proportion to their intensity, especially when what is intense is cruelly disciplinarian, creative of the maximum in outrage.[27]

One further modern reflection of the colonial heritage deserves special mention—export orientation. The open economy strategy of the 1960s did not achieve the relative "foreign" trade share of the colonial period until 1973.[28] There are, of course, substantial differences in that the early period was foreign-dominated and based on resource extraction and exploitative taxation, while the latter was indigenous and manufacturing-oriented. Further, the trade was not strictly "foreign" in terms of the geographic boundaries of the day. Nonetheless, Koreans in general became aware of the existence of external demand for their produce, and some actively participated in these markets: for example, Kyungbang Limited had a branch in Osaka and was extremely active in Manchuria (see Appendix

B); Whashin, one of the most successful Korean ventures, also turned outward, opening offices in Bangkok and Saigon, (with plans for a department store in Manila) and hired an American advisor to assist in plans for expansion in the United States and elsewhere.[29] In addition, after the war, some 2.5 million Koreans returned to the south after working abroad. While most of these had served in menial occupations, the stock of experience thus accumulated must have helped reduce the difficulty of entering unknown foreign markets. To be sure, neither the government's role nor the export orientation was passed directly to the Park regime, but the reintroduction of these critical patterns in the 1960s must have been substantially eased by familiarity with similar patterns two decades earlier.

None of this should be taken in any way as a defense of the colonial period. One can conceive of indigenous processes of development which could have produced equal or superior results at lower costs. The point made here is simply that Korea gained independence with a very significant base on which domestic industry could have been built. The colonial industrial heritage was far from negligible. We now consider the immediate use to which that patrimony was put.

HERITAGE DENIED, 1945–1951

The Japanese left behind physical facilities constituting one of the largest "turnkey" projects in history. The Republic of Korea inherited over 2,500 operating industrial and business enterprises, as well as infrastructure, inventories, real estate, and 15 percent of the nation's land; the official count was 166,301 items of such so-called "vested property."[30] The legacy of land was distributed constructively and contributed greatly to both the substance and process of land reform and rural development.[31] The industrial heritage, in marked contrast, was dissipated and contributed remarkably little to independent industrial growth. The process of deterioration will now be described.

During the U.S. Military Government (September 1945 to

August 1948), industrial output plummeted. Consistent data are not available, but Kim and Roemer estimate that, even in 1948 after recovery was underway, industrial output was still only 14 percent of the 1938 level.[32] The explanation must be sought largely in the vested-property sector which, in late 1947, accounted for about 30 percent of operating plants and 55 percent of employment.[33]

A few of the largest enterprises taken over from the Japanese were turned over for management to the nascent government departments (for example, electricity, railroads, communications, tobacco, coal mining).[34] Some were also leased to Korean businessmen, but the bulk were entrusted to the American Office of the Property Custodian who delegated operating responsibility to selected Korean managers. The failure of the process is reflected in the following official report issued in January 1948:

> Clarification of the status of Vested Property, its maintenance and preparation for eventual disposition moved ahead in a uniform and relatively uneventful way during January as procedures and programs previously set up were continued and their functions expanded to include measures for the revival of a consistently increasing segment of the national economy. The end of January saw more than 20 percent of vested or formerly vested industrial properties in partial or full operation.[35]

How was it that two and a third years after Liberation, only 20 percent of vested industry was in operation? There are two sets of explanations—economic and political. The economic argument follows from three features of the enclave structure previously discussed—the absence of trained manpower, the closing of markets in Japan and Manchuria, and the separation from output and input markets in the north (most notably, the electricity supply).

Important though these economic factors were, the political and administrative elements may have been even more critical. On the American side, there was little or no preparation for occupation, and continual and conflicting policy changes.[36] On the Korean side, the sudden opening of a political vacuum generated intense conflict between myriad groups and subgroups of diverse political persuasion, morality, and ability.[37] This combination of well-intentioned ignorance and political anarchy created a chaotic situation on all fronts. In the industrial sphere, the absence of policy and the shortage and rotation of occupation manpower were such that the Office of the Property Custodian was unable even to make a comprehensive survey of its assets for more than two years.[38]

The flavor of what went on is illustrated by E. Grant Meade's detailed description of the process in South Chŏlla province.[39] The civil affairs officers did not arrive there until more than two months after the Japanese surrender. They found 42 of the province's 50 factories in operation. Most of these had been Japanese owned, and the foreign managers and executives had already departed. The enterprises were being operated either by the Korean workers on a profit-sharing basis or by the local People's Committee.[40] The Americans then took control, designated Korean trustees, and actually got additional factories running. It was not until late 1946 that industrial activity slowed to a standstill as a result of politically induced labor strife and nationwide shortages of demand and inputs.

In South Chŏlla province, at least, the departure of Japanese technicians does not seem to have been a critical factor. Years of "learning by watching" seem to have allowed many Koreans to step up to supervisory and technical jobs when the situation demanded. It is, of course, impossible to generalize from a single description of one province's experience, but we must at least suggest the possibility that the Japanese departure was less significant than the political chaos and market disruption.

The presence of large stocks of "liberated" property created a further problem in that anyone could perceive himself as legitimate heir to at least a portion. As a result, "The property custodians were subject to all sorts of pressures from high-ranking military officers, representatives of national agencies, their civil affairs colleagues, and Korean friends."[41] Efforts at reliberating from American control what had already been liberated from the Japanese took every form from outright theft, to padded payrolls, to Byzantine legal efforts to prove prior title. Given American naiveté, the task was not a difficult one. Success in such efforts provided a stake for not a few budding entrepreneurs.

At Independence in August 1948, title to virtually all of the vested properties (except land, which had largely been sold) was passed to the new government (See Table 7). The immediate benefits of the inheritance were marginal, since a good deal of stripping had already occurred, many of the plants were not operating, and the remainder were highly inefficient. In George M. McCune's words:

> Instances of misappropriation, one may suppose, were much more common than the official record indicated. There was also an important problem as to the efficiency of enterprises ostensibly not operated for the direct profit of their managers but at the same time held only very loosely responsible to the Property Custodian. Cases where numbers of employees greatly exceeding reasonable need were noted in a number of enterprises under government operation . . . . The fact that the management of a "vested" enterprise may not have felt any particular incentive to maximize profits, may have made management indifferent to achieving the most efficient level of employment.[42]

In short, all the infamous characteristics of public enterprises were exacerbated by chaos and ignorance on the part of the foreign controllers.

The new government was in no position to improve the situation for, in Joungwon Kim's words:

> South Korea at the end of the American occupation was in chaos and on the brink of civil war . . . Inflation had gotten completely out of hand. People were pouring into cities where mobs of unemployed were attracted into "youth corps" of opposing political tendencies. These groups, together with the hated police force, survived in part by extorting "voluntary" contributions from an intimidated populace. Enthusiasm in South Korea had been replaced by fear, bitter-

TABLE 7 Vested Enterprises, 31 December 1948

	Seoul	*Kyŏnggi province*	*Kangwŏn province*	*Ch'ungch'ŏng province*	*Kyŏngsang province*	*Chŏlla province*	*North Korea*	*Japan*	*Total*
Banks	22	1	0	7	9	2	0	2	43
Chemicals	24	11	0	0	15	5	1	4	60
Commerce	56	5	1	16	32	17	0	9	136
Electricity	24	2	3	3	9	1	2	7	51
Entertainment	16	0	0	1	4	2	0	0	23
Farm	23	4	6	10	18	24	0	4	89
Fibre	64	16	18	20	90	19	0	21	248
Fish	6	0	5	0	13	6	1	0	31
Food & brewing	56	29	16	56	222	85	0	8	472
Fuel	11	3	2	2	12	12	0	0	42
Furniture	2	2	2	0	13	3	0	0	22
Insurance	2	0	0	3	1	1	0	20	27
Leather	14	2	0	1	4	0	0	0	21
Machinery	129	25	2	17	109	29	1	10	322
Metal	25	15	1	8	32	2	0	1	84
Mill	11	11	3	23	21	25	0	2	96
Mining	38	8	3	8	10	2	0	5	74
Nitrogen	7	14	0	7	28	5	0	0	61
Oil	17	3	1	2	8	3	0	1	35
Painting	17	3	0	0	5	0	0	1	26
Paper	13	3	1	4	5	3	1	2	32
Pharmacy	35	4	0	3	11	3	0	4	60
Printing	43	5	2	8	27	16	0	1	102
Contracting	65	7	2	1	12	9	0	15	111
Rubber	19	5	1	0	12	1	0	0	38
Ship operation	0	0	0	0	3	2	0	0	5
Transportation	19	9	5	12	19	10	1	0	75
Carpentry	21	11	14	12	31	11	1	1	102
Other	37	14	3	10	12	9	0	3	88
TOTAL	816	212	91	234	787	307	8	121	2,576

Source: United States Armed Forces in Korea—National Economic Board, *South Korean Interim Government Activities*, November–December 1948, p. 7.

> ness, and antagonisms which would be perpetuated for decades to come.[43]

Under these circumstances, it is not surprising that the new government was unable to utilize effectively the vested properties. They were as poorly run under the government as under the Americans. Naiveté may have been replaced by sophisticated profit sharing, and random distribution of benefits consolidated in a political and bureaucratic patronage system, but operational inefficiency and deterioration continued.

A further shock to the already debilitated industrial system was given by the Korean War. Physical damage in the first year of the war has been officially estimated at 1.8–2.0 billion dollars or more than the entire gross national product in the year prior to the war.[44] Some 45 percent of industrial units nationwide suffered "substantial" damage.[45] In Seoul "over eighty percent of industry, public utilities and transport, three-quarters of the offices, and more than half of the dwellings were in ruins."[46] The dissipation of the physical Japanese inheritance was thus nigh complete.

The unsatisfactory operation of the government-run factories did not go unnoticed, and even before the war a major attempt at divestiture was made in conjunction with the land reform of 1949. Landowners were paid with land bonds which could be used in purchasing vested properties. Little progress was made before the war, however, and even in 1953, only two-thirds of the enterprises (in value) had been sold.[47]

The effort at converting landlords into capitalists is generally held to have been a failure. A typical description runs as follows:

> [The land bonds were] sold to the public at rates between 30 and 70 percent of the actual value . . . . Korea's land reform forced landowners to make a sacrifice and contribute only to the formation of capital by newly-rising capitalists.[48]

In addition, it is widely believed that favoritism in sales led to illicit gains for the fortunate few, with a low sales price financed by long-term low interest loans and a variety of government privileges. This accusation is somewhat anomalous: on the one hand the lack of industrial initiative is deplored; on the other, those who took advantage of the opportunity are deprecated. Given the deterioration, destruction, and uncertainty, it is not surprising the plants brought a low price. Given the political context, it is also probable that the plants were actually sold at a still lower price.[49] Still, it must be recognized that those who did take over the properties performed a positive social service by returning debilitated establishments to productive use. Several modern industrial groups originated in this way: the OB (Oriental Brewery) beer company was taken over by a Korean minority shareholder in the parent Japanese Kirin company; a technician in a Japanese textile firm became acting manager under the Americans, later bought the plant, and built it into the Sunkyung Group; a similar sequence was followed by the only Korean employee of a Japanese explosives firm, and it grew into today's Korea Explosives. At least a small portion of the Japanese physical inheritance was thus rescued for the post-war period.

We have told this story of "heritage denied" emphasizing the causality of political maladministration and deemphasizing the role of manpower shortages.[50] We take this position because there is some evidence that the enterprises ran quite well for more than a year after the departure of the Japanese, and because of the degree to which we have been impressed with the abilities of Korean entrepreneurs. These qualities were demonstrated both under the constraints of the Japanese period and in the supportive environment of the Park regime. It is, of course, impossible to accurately assign responsibility between political and economic factors until far more research has been done. Causality may be in doubt, but the fact remains that the period 1945–1951 witnessed the destruction of the impressive industrial structure built by the Japanese.

The implications of this period for post-war growth are not merely physical. In Chapter 8, we shall argue that a major characteristic of Korean entrepreneurship in the 1950s was that it was far easier to make money from government-derived favors than from productive competitive activity, and entrepreneurs naturally followed their pocket books. In Chapters 3 and 4 we shall argue that in the 1950s there was neither an effective leadership commitment to growth nor a "hard" administrative structure and that as a result the government failed to channel private entrepreneurial energies into constructive outlets. All of these elements of government-business relations that characterized the low-growth years of the 1950s are but a continuation of the pattern of the 1945–51 period. Those negative interactions did not wither away, but were cut back with the imposition of a "hard," growth-oriented regime in 1961.

In sum, the colonial period left a heritage which was both physical and human. The physical structure was largely dissipated by a combination of maladministration and war. The human capital was not destroyed, but was diverted into largely non-productive activities by chaotic government economic management.

THREE

Government Economic Decision-Making Process

PLANNING AND IMPLEMENTATION

Any goal-directed activity involves an explicit or implicit hierarchy of means and ends. This hierarchy begins with a primary end that is valued in and of itself, then branches to various means for attaining the primary end, branches again to incorporate means for attaining the various secondary ends, and so on. For example, one branch emanating from the primary end of economic growth[1] might run through export promotion, and ultimately down to the stitching of shirts, loading them on ships, selling them abroad, and repatriation of earnings. No path in the hierarchy is unique: for example, exports can be promoted through equilibruim exchange rates, bonus vouchers, or simple commands. Neither are the chains independent; for instance, while both export bonus vouchers and equilibrium exchange rates may have identical primary effects on exports, the associated secondary impact on import substitution and capital transactions will be quite different.

"Planning," in the broadest sense, is the working out of reasonably consistent means-ends hierarchies, taking into account the various possible chains and the interdependence of those actually chosen. Planning is "complete" to the extent that it carries the chain down to the lowest level of requisite human actions, such as the order in which buttons are sewn on. Planning is "vertically consistent" to the extent that the "ends" at one level are achieved by the "means" of the next lower level. Planning is "horizontally consistent" to the extent that the various chains do not provoke behavior offsetting that required in another chain.

"Implementation," in the broadest sense, is the conversion of an idea into action, or the means by which ends are attained. That is, one tier of the means-ends hierarchy is "implemented" by all the tiers below it. If planning is complete and consistent, then implementation is taken care of by definition. In practice, however, no government planning is ever complete, and some part of the planning is left to production units, even if it is only the order in which to sew buttons on shirts. In a mixed economy, of course, the gap is at a much higher level, at, say, the point where a decision is made to build and operate a plant to produce the shirts. There is thus a crucial discontinuity in the means-ends hierarchy at the point where government's direct control stops and private planning begins. The implementation issue becomes critical at this point. It is essential that this gap be crossed, and that mechanisms be provided whereby private compliance is assured. "Implementation," in the narrow sense used in the remainder of this volume, then refers to the manner in which decision-makers in production units are induced to act in accord with the preferences of government planners. The lowest tier of government action then becomes a set of compliance mechanisms whereby the interface between government and private decision-makers is breached.

In sum, economic planning begins at the highest level of the means-ends hierarchy with the formulation of national priorities and determination of the relative importance to be attached to economic growth. Moving down the hierarchy, we reach a critical discontinuity where decisions on means-ends relationships pass from government to private hands. We call the crossing of this critical interface "implementation" (in the narrow sense). Everything above this point is government decision-making, and is the subject of this chapter; the crucial implementation phase is discussed in Chapter 4; and private decision-making at the lower end of the hierarchy is considered under the heading of entrepreneurship in Chapters 6 and 7.

This chapter begins with the highest level of government decision-making, namely, the priority attached to economic growth. We then discuss the formal planning process and its contribution and short-term policy formulation. In both cases, the emphasis is not on the policies pursued, but the processes by which decisions are reached and the relative influence of various participants. The influence of the business community is a particularly important question and this is given separate treatment. We conclude by considering business's evaluation of the government's role.

LEADERSHIP COMMITMENT TO GROWTH

The highest tier of the means-ends hierarchy is the establishment of national priorities. The importance assigned to growth, relative to other goals, determines the allocation of scarce government decision-making talent. If government attention has a positive marginal product (MPG), then the tautological result is that leadership commitment produces a higher rate of growth. Adelman and Morris's factor analysis of seventy-four developing countries suggests that the MPG is near zero at the lowest levels of socio-economic development, but strongly positive at the upper level (including Korea), once certain minimum social standards are achieved. At this level: "The extent to which economic change can take place is significantly conditioned . . . by a single political characteristic, the extent of leadership commitment to economic development. . . . It is . . . the absence of national mobilization for development which in general constitutes the prime political obstacle to development."[2] If social and political variables are considered alone, leadership commitment itself accounts for 60 percent of cross-country differences in growth rates.[3] It also correlates highly with various economic variables,[4] which suggests that if the top leadership really cares about growth, finding talent to formulate and execute the necessary policies is not an insuperable obstacle.

This sort of analysis provides a plausible partial explanation for the discontinuity in the Korean growth rate in the early 1960s. Syngman Rhee was preoccupied with political and integrative tasks, while Park Chung Hee has enshrined growth near the top of the regime's value hierarchy. These differences will be apparent throughout our discussion of planning and implementation, but we here present an overview.

The orientation of Syngman Rhee can be put in perspective by viewing him as one of the generation of Third World political leaders who were active in independence movements and led their newly sovereign nations into the post-colonial era. Rhee was prominent in the anti-Japanese movement in the first decade of the century, served time in jail, spent thirty-three years in actively oppositionist exile, returned to the political chaos of the interwar period, and led the country through the devastation of the Korean War and its aftermath. Success in this environment required charisma and expertise at political intrigue rather than administrative and managerial talent. Like others with similar careers, such as Sukarno, he was far better suited to the creation and integration of a new nation than to the development of an existing one. This is not to belittle his actual contributions to his country, but only to argue that he remained in power too long. Cole and Lyman describe the situation in the late 1950s as follows:

> At least on the part of the regime in power, politics moved more to resist than to accommodate to the social changes taking place. Neither Rhee nor his lieutenants were oblivious of the changes wrought by the war. Indeed, perhaps earlier than many Rhee saw the new attitudes of economic and military power that South Korea would need to survive in the post Korean War period. But in common with many of his goals, he saw these attributes in grand terms, in broad strokes. He never faced the technical and administrative complexity that they demanded for the society. Part of the problem was Rhee's age and his preoccupation with the past and with reunification. His goal was a very different Korea from the one he had inherited. In addition, his jealousy of his associates as potential rivals and his reliance on personal charismatic authority made it impossible for him to build the political, bureaucratic and private institutions that could absorb and channel the new energies and resources in the country for purposes of modernization . . . Thus the tasks of reconstruction and development in the South, in Rhee's time, on which a new national identity might have been built never gained the priority and attention they demanded.[5]

Rhee thus devoted energy to political action rather than administrative development and subsumed economic goals to integrative ones. For example, his anti-Japanese measures retarded trade with a natural and traditional partner, and his faith in reunification was carried to an extreme:

> There was an unwillingness to build up the South as an independent and integrated economy. The possibility that unification would again give access to the electric power and heavier industries of the North was given as a reason for holding down the growth of such facilities in the South.[6]

Even within the economic sphere, Rhee's concerns were not with growth, but with short-term objectives of reconstruction and maintenance of minimum consumption standards, both of which were to be achieved by aid maximization rather than investment and production.[7]

Park's value hierarchy could not have been more different. In the first place, economics took priority over politics. In his own words from 1962:

> In human life, economics precedes politics or culture.[8]

> In order to ensure efforts to improve the living conditions of the people in Asia, even undemocratic emergency measures may be necessary. . . . It is also an undeniable fact that the people in Asia today fear starvation and poverty more than the oppressive duties thrust upon them by totalitarianism. . . . In other words, the Asian peoples want to obtain economic equality first and build a more equitable political machinery afterward. . . . The gem without luster called democracy was meaningless to people suffering from starvation and despair.[9]

Second, higher ends such as reunification and national defense (as well as deferred objectives such as democracy) were seen as being furthered by, rather than in conflict with, economic growth. In 1964 he asserted:

> A sound development of democracy and national power accumulation for the unification of the nation by winning over Communists are ultimately dependent on the success or failure of economic construction.[10]

Third, he is scathing in his denunciation of the consumption-oriented aid strategy of the Rhee period:

> American aid during this period (1955–1959) was extremely tight fisted towards the productive facilities which we desired and generous with regard to consumer goods which we did not require.[11]

Words are of course cheap, but in this case the professed leadership commitment to growth has been translated into action. There are two aspects to this commitment. The first is the share of the chief executive's time devoted to economic matters. The second is the degree of support given to growth-oriented bureaucrats, technocrats, and entrepreneurs. Both elements will, it is hoped, be amply illustrated in the remainder of this volume.

FORMAL PLANNING

PLANNING IN THE RHEE REGIME, 1948–1960

At the beginning of the Republic in 1948, the Office of Planning was established under the Prime Minister with responsibility for budgeting, economic planning, resource mobilization, pricing policy, and research activities. The head of the office, however, ranked below ministers and lacked power. The Office of Planning did prepare a five-year plan during the Korean War and issued it in revised form in 1953. It was essentially a "collection of individual projects recommended by the various Ministers rather than an integrated comprehensive program."[12] Of course, the plan was never implemented, and the office dealt primarily with short-term stabilization policies until it was merged into the Ministry of Reconstruction in 1955.

Another five-year plan was prepared, not by the office, but by foreigners. In 1952, the United Nations Korea Reconstruction Agency (UNKRA) hired Robert R. Nathan and Associates to prepare a post-war reconstruction program. The resulting five-year "Nathan Plan," delivered in 1954, never really affected Korean decision-making. This was partly due to the Nathan group's poor relationships with the Rhee regime. These in turn stemmed in part from Nathan's appointment by UNKRA without prior consultation with the Korean government, and perhaps partly from Rhee's reading of American domestic politics.[13]

Political conflict alone, however, is hardly the whole explanation for the failure of the Nathan Plan. There is a real question as to whether or not Rhee's value hierarchy was compatible with the Nathan type of planning. Cole and Nam argue that the 1950s leaders:

> rejected the idea of overall planning and were not interested in trying to define the longer-run economic objectives or an integrated set of policies. This probably reflected a belief on their part that they could retain more flexibility and achieve better results in

> negotiations with aid donors by proceeding on an *ad hoc* basis and avoiding the overall commitments and constraints of a plan. Clearly the Nathan Plan called for very forceful policy action by the Korean government and set ambitious targets of self-support which the Koreans were not prepared to accept. To have agreed to the plan would have exposed the government to serious political risks.[14]

In 1955, the Rhee regime did show some interest in improving the national planning apparatus when it established the Ministry of Reconstruction with responsibility for "overseeing and coordinating overall planning regarding the rehabilitation of industrial economy."[15] This institutional change was made with full realization that "if he [the Minister who is responsible for planning] is just one among many, he is not likely to have the necessary authority."[16] Accordingly, the Minister of Reconstruction was made chairman of the Reconstruction Committee of Economic Ministers. This gave him a theoretical position of seniority which was not replicated in fact.[17]

Another step forward in economic organization came in April 1958 when the Economic Development Council was established within the Ministry of Reconstruction. The council was able to attract a capable staff including a number of young, foreign-educated Koreans. In Hahn-Been Lee's words:

> In order to season the work of these academically oriented experts with the benefits of practical experience, senior civil servants and industrial experts were invited to frequent and active discussions with the members and staff of the Council. Thus, many conditions auspiciously converged to make the EDC a valuable forum for the formulation of a plan that would reflect the consensus of the diffused thinking for the future which had been fermenting in many "innovational enclaves" of the period.[18]

Within a year of its founding the council prepared a Three-Year Economic Development Plan for the period 1960–1962.[19] The Three-Year Plan was submitted to a cabinet meeting in the spring of 1959 but was shelved for a year "by the Liberal cabinet, whose prior concern at the time of its submission was the expediency of retaining political power."[20] Ironically, the

Three-Year Plan did finally get approval a few days before the Rhee regime fell to the Student Revolution of 1960.

In sum, the Rhee period saw an evolution of economic decision-making machinery, and the Three-Year Plan can be seen as "a systematic crystalization of the future-oriented thinking in the Korean society."[21] Nonetheless, the planners were inexperienced and isolated from the operational levels of government so their impact was minimal.[22] More important, the political leadership commitment to development was missing, so that "a potentially useful instrument for development was thus relegated to the status of merely a document for later reference."[23]

PLANNING IN THE CHANG MYON REGIME, 1960–1961

From its inception, the short-lived Chang Myon regime expressed its foremost interest in the nation's economic development. As soon as it took power, the regime directed the Economic Development Council to prepare a five-year economic plan and invited a Rand Corporation expert to advise in its formulation. In addition, in November 1960, the regime organized public hearings in the areas of administrative reform, public finance and banking, industrial structure, public enterprises, international balance of payments, employment and standard of living, and regional development.

The government also established a Committee on Government Organizational Reform, one of whose tasks was to devise a new administrative structure to efficiently execute economic development plans. In its 1961 report, the committee recommended the establishment of an independent ministry of economic planning and an economic development research institute, both along the lines actually implemented under Park (see below). The Economic Development Council also prepared a Five-Year Economic Development Plan, which was approved by the Park cabinet in May 1961.

The later economic orientation of the Park regime was thus in no sense a sudden innovation. The actions of the interim Chang Myon regime suggest that there was widespread recognition of a need for a change from the Rhee period. It is an open question how successful the Chang Myon government might have been in translating these aspirations into reality.

ORGANIZATION FOR PLANNING IN THE PARK REGIME, 1961–1979

Immediately after the Military Revolution (May 16, 1961), Park Chung Hee unofficially directed one of his ten revolutionary associates to draft a five-year economic plan.[24] At the same time, the Military regime wasted no time in officially announcing its intention to launch a five-year plan beginning in 1962. The Park Military Government also introduced various institutional changes necessary for effective economic decision-making.

These administrative changes form a second major distinction between the Rhee and Park periods. Effective planning requires not only that growth be emphasized at the top of the means-ends hierarchy but also that consistent chains emanate downward to insure implementation. Limits on top leadership time and technical specialization require that there be an effective apparatus for intermediate-level economic decision-making. Improvements in this respect took two forms: first, obvious structural changes; and second, a fundamental shift in administrative philosophy.

Several Korean writers stress the importance of the change in organizational approach. Hahn-Been Lee asserts:

> The most general contribution of the military to the development of administration in Korea was its introduction and vigorous application of a "managerial approach." This approach took many concrete forms, including the adoption of a long-range development plan, institution of a comprehensive planning and control system, and revamping of many sluggish government corporations.[25]

In a similar vein, Sŏk-chun Cho characterizes the Military Government's administrative philosophy as consisting of three elements: first, a strong goal orientation and a high regard for institutions as a means for carrying out those goals; second, a willingness to replace inappropriate means with alternative means; and third, a willingness to expand institutions as necessary to achieve its goals.[26] The change in attitude is rather natural, in view of the backgrounds of Rhee and Park. Rhee was a politician and often a loner; Park was a military man who knew how to use a staff. Rhee consequently used political parties, youth groups, and cronies to a much greater extent than Park who increasingly relied on the government bureaucracy as his chosen instrument of control.

This reliance was not misplaced. The Confucian cultural heritage inculcates a value system based on "correct" superior-subordinate relationships of the sort conducive to a smoothly operating hierarchy. Further, the prestige attached to government work, the stress on education, and the competitive merit-based selection procedure insure civil service quality. Collectively, these features give the Korean bureaucracy the potential for highly effective decision-making, once they are given clear leadership guidance and support. If one gives credence to Max Weber's theories on the superiority of bureaucracy as an organizational form, then it is possible to argue that a part of the economic success of Korea (and East Asia in general) is attributable to a cultural compatibility with effective hierarchical organization.[27] In any event, in moving from Rhee to Park, the bureaucracy was not simply reoriented and somewhat reorganized but shifted to the forefront of the economic decision-making effort.

Structurally, a major institutional innovation was introduced in June 1961 when the government organized a powerful planning agency, the Economic Planning Board (EPB).[28] It took over planning responsibility from the recently established Ministry of Construction[29] and absorbed the Bureau of Budget from the Ministry of Finance and the Bureau of Statistics from the Ministry of Home Affairs. The head of the board was given the title of Deputy Prime Minister (DPM). This elevated position for the chief of the national planning agency signified the seriousness of the regime's planning effort and was necessary to coordinate and control conflicts among the various economic ministries.

The Military Government also established the Central Economic Committee, consisting of the Prime Minister as chairman, the DPM as vice chairman, all ministers concerned with economic affairs, and a few outside experts. Other structural changes will be described below in the context of plan and policy formulation.

FIRST FIVE-YEAR ECONOMIC DEVELOPMENT PLAN, 1962–1966

The First Five-Year Plan was officially adopted in December 1961. The formulation of this Plan was strongly influenced by a group of four civilian advisers to the Supreme Council, who prepared directives for plan formulation.[30] Directives were quite specific, and so the EPB planning staff's primary responsibility was to fill in details in cooperation with a 20-member working committee including government officials, businessmen, and scholars, in addition to the above-mentioned advisers. This First Five-Year Plan was, however, rather hurriedly prepared in a short period of time without good statistical data or a sophisticated planning apparatus.[31] When the Plan was publicly announced, the general feeling was that the real growth target of 7.1 percent was over-ambitious, given historic Korean growth performance. At the same time, academics and professionals were skeptical because of the crudeness of the plan and doubted its consistency.

This Plan had a bad start due to a poor harvest and the fiasco of the monetary reform in 1962. It was revised in 1964, but even the new version was more or less ignored for several reasons: the government's preoccupation with stabilization, the lack of confidence engendered by "expert" criticism, and the continued pressure to scale down a plan which eventually proved to be too pessimistic rather than too optimistic.[32]

The First Five-Year Plan was, however, significant in various ways. It showed the people that the government was seriously committed to the nation's development. At the same time, rather inexperienced political leaders and government officials began to appreciate the complexity of the planning process and gained useful experience for the future. The overachievement of growth targets during the later period also started building self-confidence on the part of both the people and the economic policy-makers.

SECOND FIVE-YEAR ECONOMIC DEVELOPMENT PLAN, 1967–1971

The First Five-Year Plan was prepared under constraints of time, data availability, and inadequate planning techniques and experience. In contrast, Second Five-Year Plan preparation started long before the actual plan period.[33] The Second Five-Year Plan utilized a reasonably accurate input-output matrix and a rather sophisticated dynamic projection model for testing the consistency of the overall plan as well as estimating sectoral investment and import requirements.

The Plan put much emphasis on "strengthening planning machinery," "strengthening implementation machinery," and "translating the plan into an Action Program."[34] With regard to the first point, the Plan proposed the establishment of an economic research institute to provide basic research.[35] Because the First-Plan formulation had suffered from the lack of reliable statistics, the Plan stressed data collection and processing. At the same time, the Plan foresaw the necessity of wider participation and support by various government bodies and civilians.

Unlike the First Five-Year Plan, the preparation of the Second Five-Year Plan began with some general guidelines. Within these broad terms of reference, EPB and various working committees[36] formulated plan proposals which were in turn cross-checked and coordinated by The Second Plan Deliberation Joint Meeting and The Second Plan Consultative Council Meeting. The Joint Meeting included ministers of concerned ministries, members of the Economic and Scientific Council,[37] and representatives from foreign-aid missions. The Consultative Council Meeting consisted of vice ministers of concerned ministries, vice presidents of national banking institutions, representatives of economic research institutes, scholars, journalists, other professionals, and representatives of various business associations. Although the meetings were not open to the public, primary content was often made available to the news media.

As a result of the improved formulation process, the final Second-Plan document had wide credibility both abroad and in Korea.[38] Further, as the official planning document of the Third Five-Year Plan states: "The successful completion of the first two plans has instilled new hope in the minds of the people whose attitude has been plagued by negativism and pessimism . . . It has given them self-confidence and courage to say, 'We, too, can be rich and strong.'"[39] In addition, "The planning function and the planners became an integral part of the government's decision-making process."[40] Despite these positive achievements, the Second Five-Year Plan was, nonetheless, rapidly outstripped by events with the result that "the Plan was put on the proverbial shelf, to be brought down only infrequently to point proudly at the fantastic overachievement of most targets."[41]

THIRD FIVE-YEAR ECONOMIC DEVELOPMENT PLAN, 1972–1976

Preparation of the Third Five-Year Plan started in February 1969. The initial work was primarily macro analysis to provide overall structure. Guidelines were prepared in about ten months, and, based on them, a tentative macro plan was drafted in April 1970. At this stage of planning, various foreign as well as domestic scholars were invited to participate. These guidelines were examined by the Working Committee on Economic Planning[42] and the Review Committee of the Third Five-Year Plan.[43] Ministries and concerned institutions were to make concrete plans and develop necessary policy measures in close cooperation with the planning authorities. These detailed plans were then discussed, integrated, and adjusted by the Coordinating Committee.[44] As pointed out by Westphal and Adelman, however, "Planning closer to the ministerial level of the organization chart tended to be more window dressing than anything else."[45]

Most details of planning were carried out by the young, energetic, and competent lower-echelon bureaucrats. This rather decentralized aspect of Third-Plan formulation contrasts with that of the Second Five-Year Plan, when "the EPB did not rely in a systematic way upon any other institutions within the economy for assistance in formulating the plan."[46]

A second change involved a shift from modeling and macro consistency emphasis to "policy planning." The focus was now on how "to formulate policies which will lead to the 'desired' allocation of resources within the framework of private decision-making in response to price incentives. Analytical work focuses on the system of incentives and the government's role as an economic catalyst."[47]

A major reason for these changes in planning technique was that the economy had become far more complex. In addition, ministries other than EPB had gained confidence in their capabilities in planning and were vying for the prestige and influence of participation.

FOURTH FIVE-YEAR ECONOMIC DEVELOPMENT PLAN, 1977–1981

This Plan is very similar to the Third Five-Year Plan in terms of its methodology and formulation processes. It also adopted decentralized "policy planning" procedures. There were twenty-two working groups, each headed by a high government official from a concerned ministry. Each group consisted of government officials of concerned ministries, and experts from research institutes (such as the Korea Development Institute–KDI), banks, industries, business associations, and universities. EPB officials acted as secretaries to each team.

These working groups were to develop detailed plans following guidelines prepared by EPB. Plans prepared by these groups were to be coordinated by the Economic Plan Coordination Committee chaired by the vice minister of EPB with members from concerned ministries and various public and private organizations. Finally, these plans were to be examined by the

Economic Plan Deliberation Committee chaired by the Prime Minister. As in the case of earlier plans, these committees were, in fact, a sort of formality, but did ensure that plan technicians were exposed to a wide variety of opinion.

Actual plans were prepared by young bureaucrats in close cooperation with KDI staff. The Fourth Five-Year Plan again utilized foreign consultants in twelve specific areas. They were hired independently using United Nations Development Program money under the auspices of the World Bank. Their opinions were evaluated by the Korean technicians and incorporated as appropriate. The aforementioned committees then debated and approved the drafts with relatively minor adjustments. In addition, KDI sponsored ten Economic Policy Conferences in important policy areas. At these conferences, related working committees' plans were presented and commented on by participants from all walks of life. Nearly 250 people, in addition to concerned government officials, were invited to participate in these conferences.

THE CONTRIBUTION OF FORMAL PLANNING

Korean planning has been only partially successful in charting a detailed path for the economy to follow. More important, it has functioned as a sort of economic topographic survey which educated officials and allowed them to make the intelligent short-run policy decisions that really drive the economy. It has also had a major "announcement effect" in articulating leadership commitment and giving the general guidelines and implicit promises of support that facilitate private planning.

Table 8 compares plan targets with actual achievements. Two features are noteworthy. First, actual growth always exceeded planned growth, particularly in mining and manufacturing. Second, during the first two plans, the actual ex post sectoral resource allocation shares diverge substantially from those planned ex ante (social overhead taking more than expected and mining

TABLE 8 Plan Targets and Actual Performance (%)

	First Five-Year Plan (1962–1966)		*Second Five-Year Plan (1967–1971)*		*Third Five-Year Plan (1972–1976)*	
	Planned	*Actual*	*Planned*	*Actual*	*Planned*	*Actual*
GNP Growth Rate (annual average)	7.1	8.3	7.0	11.4	8.6	11.2
Agriculture, forestry and fisheries	5.7	5.5	5.0	2.0	4.5	5.8
Mining and manufacturing	15.1	14.8	10.7	20.9	13.0	20.1
Social overhead capital and other services	5.4	8.9	6.6	13.2	8.5	8.5
Industrial structure (terminal year)						
Agriculture, forestry and fisheries	34.8	37.9	34.0	24.2	22.4	20.3
Mining and manufacturing	20.6	19.8	26.8	29.9	27.9	36.0
Social overhead capital and other services	44.5	42.3	39.2	45.9	49.7	33.7
Investment as share of GNP (annual average)	22.6	16.9	19.0	30.6	24.9	27.0
Domestic savings as share of GNP	9.3	6.7	11.6	15.5	19.5	17.0
Foreign savings as share of GNP	13.3	10.2	7.4	15.1	5.4	11.8
Allocation of resources by industrial sector [a]						
Agriculture, forestry and fisheries	17.4	15.4	16.3	9.5	11.8	11.5
Mining and manufacturing	33.2	26.2	30.7	23.8	25.8	25.8
Social overhead capital and other services	49.4	58.4	53.0	66.7	62.4	62.7

TABLE 8 (continued)

Sources: Kyŏngje Kihoegwŏn (Economic Planning Board), *Kyŏngje paeksŏ* (Economic white paper), 1972, 1976, 1977.
Kyŏngje Kihoegwŏn (Economic Planning Board), *Che samch'a yondŏ ch'ongjawŏn yesan, 1977* (Overall resources budget for 1977).
Bank of Korea, *Monthly Economic Statistics*, January 1977.

Note: [a]Inventory changes are included in the plan estimates, but the "actual" national income accounts data do not provide this on a sectoral basis. These data were therefore estimated from IO tables to provide consistent sectoral allocations inclusive of inventory adjustments.

and manufacturing less). These facts may be interpreted as follows. The government put primary emphasis on rapid growth of the mining and manufacturing sector and devoted its implementation efforts towards achieving that goal. The extraordinary response of private businessmen to these measures resulted in more rapid than planned growth in manufacturing. This then created bottlenecks in the social-overhead-capital sector (which the government controls directly), and required larger-than-planned formal allocations.

Another noteworthy feature of Table 8 is that investment was not underestimated as heavily as growth, implying that actual incremental capital-output ratios were lower than anticipated. This is particularly noticeable in the First Five-Year Plan period when actual investment was substantially lower than the planned level, but annual growth rates were substantially higher. Similarly, during the Third Five-Year Plan the achieved investment share was quite close to that planned, but actual growth was 11.2 percent rather than the planned 8.6 percent. The First Five-Year Plan result is, in part, due to increased capacity utilization, but overall we would suggest there was an increase in "X-efficiency." In Chapter 6 we shall argue that this is due to the rapidity of the learning being done by entrepreneurs and other economic actors.

For present purposes, however, the major point is that the actual behavior was substantially different from plans. This is hardly unusual by international standards; what is unique is that the deviations were generally positive. We take this as evidence of superior short-term policy-making and implementation. This conclusion is not inconsistent with the expectations of Korean planners themselves. As early as the Second Five-Year Plan, there was official recognition that

> The value of a development plan lies not in the plan itself but in how much the plan contributes to the development of the economy by implementing the plan properly. It is preferable to have a poorly-designed plan implemented appropriately rather than a good plan

> implemented inappropriately if the poor plan so implemented contributes to the rapid economic development of the nation.[48]

This view was manifest in the change in emphasis of the Third and Fourth Five-Year Plans away from modeling and consistency and towards "policy-planning." It was institutionalized from 1967 onwards in the form of annual Overall Resource Budgets (ORBs). The ORBs provided a framework for consistent short-run policy-making. They reviewed past performance, set short-term targets and allocations, and formulated appropriate implementation policies.

More important than the actual results of the plans may have been the economic education provided to officials. Under Rhee, planning was isolated and educated no one save a very small band of domestic and foreign technocrats. Thereafter, there was a steady expansion of participation and education. There was both a vertical extension of planning concerns from the top to the bottom of the hierarchy, and a horizontal extension to other agencies within the government. There was also formal involvement of a broader spectrum of lay society. This was somewhat illusory, but did facilitate information flow. Planning thus played a major role in educating officials as to the complexities and interactions of the economy.

The learning by Koreans is reflected in the diminishing role of foreigners. The preparation of the Second Five-Year Plan was heavily influenced, not to say dominated, by foreign advisors, but by the Fourth Five-Year Plan, foreign consultants were invited in only on a case-by-case basis to comment on particular topics. The process was controlled by Koreans, and the vast bulk of the analysis done by them.

In sum, formal planning has not been as important in charting a particular course for the economy as it has in mapping the economic terrain, providing a focus for dialogue, training bureaucrats, and announcing government commitment to businessmen. We now consider the resulting short-term policies. Growth is the objective, and the Koreans do not generally confuse means and ends. The formal Five-Year Plans were merely the first iteration in the process leading to the short-run procedures that actually drive the economy.

POLICY FORMULATION

Policy formulation is a much more diffuse effort than planning and cannot be summarized in the same fashion. In this section, we therefore attempt only to specify the most important participants and identify the major distinguishing features of the process. Our discussion will regrettably be largely confined to the Park period.

EXECUTIVE DOMINANCE

A major characteristic of Korean policy formulation is that the executive branch is the overwhelmingly dominant government partner. This will come as no surprise to most readers, as the story of the emasculation of the legislature is well known to the most casual observer of the Korean scene. The point, however, is much more fundamental and goes well beyond the short-term decline in democratic formalities. In Japan, the executive branch dominates the legislature despite formal legal provisions to the contrary.[49] One quantitative comparison involves the share of legislation initiated by the government as opposed to members of the legislature: in Japan, the figure is more than 90 percent;[50] in Korea, it has averaged 84 percent in the 1970s.[51] The similarity is in part due to the common cultural background and a similar historical tradition. On the economic side, it may also have something to do with the increasing technicality required to compete internationally and the necessity of speedy decisions to respond to a rapidly changing international environment.[52] Whatever the reason, it is clear that the executive branch overwhelmingly dominates not only execution but policy formulation as well.

Within the executive branch, the ultimate power is of course the President, and major decisions and disputes are ultimately decided by him. Given Park's personal preoccupation with growth, this is no rubber-stamp formality. Within the Blue House (the executive mansion), there is a small but extremely powerful economic secretariat. Prior to August 1973, the First Economic Secretary held the rank of minister; from then until 1974 he was a vice minister; and since then he has been at the assistant-minister level. This reduced status may reflect a long-term policy of power decentralization, but it is just as likely to be an adjustment to the President's confidence in incumbent ministers (as of the mid-1970s, the DPM had a United States PhD in economics and was formerly Minister of Finance; the Minister of Finance was previously First Economic Secretary of the Blue House).

The formal mechanism for conflict resolution is the Economic Ministers' Meeting, begun in 1964. The meeting is chaired by the DPM and consists of all economic ministers and the Minister of Foreign Affairs. The meeting is currently held twice a week. More informal interaction takes place every Saturday morning at the Economic Ministers' Round-Table. Economic policy proposals agreed to at this formal meeting are sent to the cabinet meeting which is largely a rubber stamp.

Despite these mechanisms, disagreement arises. Chitoshi Yanaga's description of interministerial conflict in Japan also serves for Korea:

> To a bureaucrat, possession of power is the goal. To maintain power and, if possible, increase it is his primary concern. Efforts to increase power inevitably result in sectionalism and jurisdictional conflicts, which have been exploited on occasion by both business and political parties. Power struggles are common not only within the ministries and agencies themselves but also between ministries over jurisdictional and budgetary matters . . . Jurisdictional conflicts arise because of the complexity of the problems handled by administrative agencies whose jurisdictions overlap.[53]

Even though the expression "power struggle" seems to be a bit strong for the Korean situation, there exists a keen competitiveness among economic ministries. For example, setting an annual export target can be a subject of heated discussion between the EPB on the one hand and the Ministry of Commerce and Industry (MCI) on the other. Grain price policy is another example of difficult coordination. EPB, concerned with price stability, would like to keep the price paid to farmers at a relatively lower level, while the Ministry of Agriculture and Fisheries (concerned with output incentives) may want to see the price increased as much as possible. Such disagreements are ultimately resolved either through interministerial bargaining or through the arbitration of the Blue House.

Interministerial conflict is hardly unique to Korea. What is somewhat rarer is that the disputes are predominately settled on the basis of who is most convincing on *economic* grounds. Given the dominant leadership commitment to growth, ministers prove themselves by the novelty and success of their economic ideas. Similarly, subordinates prove their worth within their ministries by conducting the staff work necessary to generate and support their ministers' programs. The incentive system flowing from leadership commitment to growth thus permeates the hierarchy and insures long bureaucratic hours devoted to making executive supremacy work in the economic sphere.

SPEED AND FLEXIBILITY

When the checks and balances of a multi-polar political system are rejected in favor of the tightly focused hierarchical structure already described, there are potential benefits in the speed and coherence of policy-making in a rapidly changing environment. There are also potential costs in that inadequate scrutiny may lead to errors that might otherwise have been avoided.

In Korea, journalists regularly deplore the hastiness of such measures as the 1971 Law on Restraining Real Estate Investment, which is claimed to have resulted from a twenty-four hour "study," and the 1973 Law on Price Stability, which is said to have taken a comparatively leisurely three days of preparation.[54] While there is undoubtedly exaggeration in these examples, there can be no doubt that speed and flexibility are fundamental characteristics of the government economic decision-making process. Businessmen often complain about the sudden shifts in policy direction, and (at a decidedly lower level of importance) academics are regularly frustrated when their critiques of policy become outdated before reaching print.

We can illustrate the process by giving one version of the response to the 1973 oil crisis.[55] While the oil price increase was initiated in October, the permanent dimensions of the problem were not apparent for more than a month. In late December, the Blue House economic secretariat began an intensive effort to produce a policy response. Their work was closely guarded, involving only a few technocrats from KDI and selected government bureaucrats. At the ministerial level, it is said that only the Minister of Finance was aware of the project. Though the Offices of National Tax Administration and Customs Duties were to be heavily affected by the outcome, these offices were not deeply involved (though senior officials were called upon to provide data). In situations such as this, the custom is to operate out of a suite of hotel rooms in order to avoid interruptions, preserve secrecy, and allow around-the-clock efforts. In this case, a Presidential Emergency Decree was issued on January 14, 1974, some three weeks after the study had begun. It was a quite sophisticated document, combining a respect for allocative efficiency (increase in price of petroleum products to more or less world levels) with a concern for equity (taxes were widely realigned to reduce the net burden on the middle class and increase it on the rich). There was also a recognition of the dangers of adjustment windfalls (petroleum product price increases and allowable pass-throughs by users were to be allowed only after scrutiny of profit and loss accounts).

This example is quite typical in reflecting executive dominance, speed of action, and relative sophistication in outcome. The secrecy of the process is less typical and may, in part, be explained by a desire to minimize the excess profits which could have accrued to anyone with foreknowledge. Perhaps more important, it was desired to avoid popular debate on an issue that boiled down to one of just how to redistribute income from Koreans to Arabs. In such a negative-sum game, debate is likely to produce deadlock (as in the United States) rather than illumination. The sudden fiat approach allows a quick absorption of the necessary deadweight loss and permits the country to get on with operating under the new reality. In any event, action was quick and decisive.

The costs of swift decision are also real. Better policy alternatives, or ill effects, or both are often found after a new policy has been quickly announced.

As one example, consider the government's approach to adopting the Japanese structure of general trading companies (GTCs). The justification for GTCs is that there are economies of scale in exploiting overseas markets and that these impose excessive transaction costs on many small volume products. The GTC reaps these economies by being horizontally integrated across products. It facilitates export expansion by playing an active entrepreneurial role in seeking out foreign markets for virtually any commodity and then finding someone to produce it. It thus contributes to the process of functional differentiation of entrepreneurship. While this pattern of corporate activity had been evolving informally for some years, the government decided to formalize it in 1975. While no explicit financial advantages are given to GTCs, the implicit administrative support makes such status highly desirable. Initially, firms qualified for GTC status by meeting such objective criteria as export volume, product diversity, number of countries exported to, corporate size, and so on. This led to an overabundance of GTCs negating the scale economies and, in August 1977, it was decided to limit the number of GTCs to ten to be effective January 1978.[56] This in turn led to artificial efforts (such as dumping some products in some markets) in attempts to qualify for one of the ten coveted spots. Accordingly, policy was again reversed in December 1977, before the old policy even became effective. As a result, firms who at some cost had altered their behavior to comply with the earlier regulations, were unable to reap any benefits. Their dissatisfaction was articulately summed up by one journalist:

> The Korean bureaucrats of economic affairs are undoubtedly geniuses of extemporization. They come up with new measures, institutions and regulations in a dizzying speed only to change them almost daily afterwards. Korean bureaucrats deserve to be called actors of thinking while running. To be recognized as a capable bureaucrat, they have to continuously come up with new ideas and new proposals for revisions. It is not unusual for them to formulate policies without thorough evaluation and preparation. Consequently, trial-and-error processes are repeated under the name of measures of modification of original ideas and sometimes basic directions are repeatedly changed only to confuse concerned parties. This is the reason why the economic bureaucrats can dominate the business world.[57]

The general indictment is, of course, applicable to the whole process of short-term policy formulation.

While the costs of "thinking while running" are certainly real, it is necessary to recall the benefits. There is great uncertainty in answering such questions as: "Should we have GTCs, and if so, what is the optimum number to exploit economies of scale?" Rather than studying the problem to death, the government moves quickly to achieve the perceived benefits immediately and then modifies its position quickly as deleterious side effects become apparent. Flexibility thus substantially reduces the costs of speedy decision-making.

In short, there are two polar approaches to short-term policy formulation. One is to study problems in depth, making certain that all factors are taken into consideration before taking action. The second is to react quickly, monitor the results, and continuously adjust policy as necessary to achieve the desired outcome. The Korean method is far nearer the second pole than the first. The costs of inaction are deemed greater than those of adjustment. This may be inevitable in an open economy growing at such a high rate. Rapid structural change and unpredictable exogenous shocks continually produce new imbalances which outdate earlier policies and require quick adjustments if growth is to be sustained. Speed and flexibility of government decision-making may thus (in part) be both cause and consequence of the sustained 10 percent growth rate.

PRAGMATISM, PARTICULARISM, CENTRALIZATION, AND OPENNESS

Other characteristics of the policy-formulation process include pragmatism, particularism, centralization, and openness. These are best illustrated by examples given elsewhere in this volume, and we here provide only a summary.

By "pragmatism" we mean the willingness to experiment with any available tool for achieving a desired end. This is to be contrasted with an ideological approach that attempts to apply some received formula focusing on means rather than ends: for example, centralization and public ownership on the one hand, or laissez faire and private capitalism on the other. Preconceived notions as to the appropriateness of particular tools are present in Korea, as elsewhere, but provide only a starting point for the search. The outcome is a balance between market forces (for example, in the foreign exchange market) and direct government intervention; and coupling extensive government ownership with heavy reliance on private entrepreneurship. Where the market works, fine; where it does not, the government is quick to intervene. This pragmatic absence of ideological predilection substantially expands the opportunity set of government tools and helps explain the sustained high growth rate.

"Particularism" refers to the practice of making policy decisions with a low level of generality: for example, with application to only a single firm at a particular time (see Chapter 4, especially the section on Discretion and Command: A Case

Study. The decisions may be codified in a "measure," "directive," "order," or other legal form, but are so often highly specific that the outcome may be characterized as more of a "rule of men" than a "rule of law." The advantage of the system is that it allows fine tuning of decisions in a rapidly changing environment where once-and-for-all general regulations inevitably conflict with a changing environment. The disadvantage is that it is often extremely difficult for medium to large businesses to know what is permitted without personal consultation at the concerned ministry. The accumulation of particularistic law emanating from various ministries is often impenetrable as to precedent. This difficulty being particularly acute with regard to foreign business, a unified foreign-investment code was promulgated in 1966. A similar effort by EPB to promote a uniform domestic Investment Promotion Law has thus far met with strong resistance from concerned ministries protecting their turf. The resulting particularism gives great scope for individual discretion (and attendant corruption) among bureaucrats. This aspect of the topic is considered in greater detail in Chapter 4.

Virtually all economic decisions of any importance are made in Seoul. This "centralization" is in no sense confined to the economic sphere and is hardly of recent origin. The historical causes and contemporary consequences of the broader phenomenon are detailed in Henderson's *Korea: The Politics of the Vortex*.[58] For present purposes, we need only note that centralism reinforces executive dominance and facilitates speed and flexibility.

The final noteworthy characteristic of Korean economic policy formulation is "openness." We mean this in the somewhat restricted sense of being open to a wide range of opinion inputs, even though the final decision process itself is usually closed. This openness is a somewhat surprising characteristic in an authoritarian regime and, even in Korea, can hardly be said to extend to the political arena. Nonetheless, within the strictly limited realm of economic affairs, there is virtually unlimited freedom of expression and dissent. Critics may have to be careful to attribute existing shortcomings to concerned ministers rather than the President or the regime as a whole. These, however, are minor restrictions and a variety of economic opinion is not only tolerated but often heeded. One manifestation of this process is the Fourth Five-Year Plan's shift in emphasis towards "social" development in the form of increased attention on health, education, and regional and urban problems. If implemented, this would soothe many earlier academic critics.

It is important to note the absence of organized labor as a significant participant in the economic decision-making process. While labor unions exist, they are so weak that not only do they not provide much opinion input, but their potential reaction is seldom considered as a constraint. While it is arguable that workers' interests are to some extent protected by the government's implicit value system and by the explicit criticisms of the journalistic and academic communities, it is clear that labor's direct contribution is minimal. Given the minor contribution of labor and the major role of the business community, it is worth examining the latter in greater detail.

THE INFLUENCE OF BUSINESS

IS THERE A "KOREA, INC."?

The nature and extent of business influence on government is a profound issue with ramifications well beyond the economic realm. Here we attempt only to present an overview. One relevant paradigm of government-business interaction is represented by the notion of "Japan, Inc.", that is, "the proposition that economic growth policies have been jointly decided and jointly executed by politicians and appointed officials together with representatives of private business."[59] There is some difference of opinion as to where dominance lies: some would have government dominating business, others the reverse, and a third group would say it makes no difference, because they are one and the same.[60] The journalistic popularity of this description notwithstanding, the concept's academic repute is not particularly high.[61] However, since the parallel notion of "Korea, Inc." has begun to appear in print,[62] a brief comparison of the Japanese and Korean "corporate" structures provides a convenient heuristic device for focusing our discussion.

Given the Korean government's dedication to growth and its substantial (though by no means exclusive) reliance on private-sector activity, the success of government requires the success of business. Indeed, the very survival of Park Chung Hee rests on economic performance and thus on the achievement of private business. This mutuality of interest implies a partnership and, to this extent, there is indeed a "Korea, Inc." parallel to "Japan, Inc."

This partnership is reflected in extensive interaction between government and business in the process of policy formulation. These relationships are facilitated by a network of personal ties between businessmen and bureaucrats, and by interchange of personnel between the two sectors (though the latter is decidedly less extensive in Korea). In these respects, there is again a similarity between Japan and Korea, in large part due to the common cultural heritage.

There is, however, one decisive difference between the two countries. In Korea, the dominant partner is unequivocally the government, whereas, in Japan, the reverse may be closer to the truth. A major study of the Japanese scene concludes that "big business (is) predominant and unrivaled as an influence in Japanese politics. Its wishes are tantamount to commands, and the government does not dare take them lightly."[63] A similarly bald description of the situation in Korea would be provided by rotating the subjects in the last sentence: the *government's* wishes are tantamount to commands, and *business* does not dare take them lightly.

This reversal of dominance follows from differences in political structure. In Japan, ascension to the top of both executive and legislative branches requires success in electoral politics, and this in turn depends heavily upon the financing and support of business. In Korea, Park's original power base was the military, and his current base is a broader mix of the military and other executive agencies, supported by broad-based (though by no means total) popularity derived heavily from economic success. Real private consumption expenditure roughly tripled in fifteen years under Park, and that buys a lot of votes. When elections have been held, they have, of course, been financed by levies on the business community. This has taken, however, the form of an unavoidable political tax levied by a powerful incumbent, rather than a discretionary contribution that imposes obligations on the recipient.

Another way of describing this difference would be to say that in Japan the business community can dismiss most politicians by withholding support in an election. In Korea, the business community could dismiss Park only by shutting down operations and ruining themselves in the process. Conversely, the Korean government can ensure the failure of any businessman, should it care to do so.

Eugene Kaplan argues that "business as well as government sits on the board of directors of 'Japan, Incorporated,' "[64] and it "should not be thought of as an organization with the bureauracy in command."[65] If the same corporate analogy were applied to Korea, it would be far closer to the truth to say that the President chairs a policy board composed of ministers, with businessmen as operationally independent managers or production units. The success of the conglomerate depends on the performance of the managers whose counsel is valued (and the more important are quite influential), but they are emphatically not members of the board.

In sum, in Korea the government is dependent upon the success of business, but not upon its political support. It therefore must listen to the business community and frame policies that are in the long-run best interests of entrepreneurs in general. At the same time, however, it is in a position to take actions that are inimical to certain short-run interests. In Chapter 8 we will describe these latter elements as: first, constraining the license-seeking entrepreneurship of the Rhee period and forcing businessmen into generally socially productive activities; and second, constraining private wealth *utilization* while allowing virtually unlimited wealth *accumulation.*

For present purposes, however, the critical point is that in Korea there is indeed a harmony of interest between government and business, and this is reflected in close working relationships between the two in a manner which could be crudely described as "Korea, Inc." The term is, however, misleading in implying an equal partnership as in Japan. Rather, government is clearly the senior partner in Korea. These propositions should not be terribly surprising. Intimate government-business interaction may be contrary to the American ideal of countervailing power but represents the actuality in many Western nations such as France. In Korea, government dominance follows from the authoritarian government and the relatively weak business power base in 1961. Granted that the actual interaction is far more complicated than that implied by the corporate analogy, the idea of "Korea, Inc." does not provide a bad starting point for understanding the relationship.

THE PATTERN OF BUSINESS INFLUENCE

The pattern of government-business interaction under Park was set in the first months of the regime. One of the first acts of the new government was the passage of a Law for Dealing with Illicit Wealth Accumulation. The law itself is described in greater detail in Chapter 8. Here we only note that, under its provisions, most of the country's leading businessmen were arrested and threatened with confiscation of their assets. Soon thereafter, ten of the leaders were summoned to a meeting with Park, then Vice Chairman of the Revolutionary Council.[66] A deal was struck whereby:

1) The government would exempt most businessmen from criminal prosecution.

2) With the notable exception of commercial bank shares, existing assets would not be confiscated.
3) Businessmen would instead pay off their assessed obligations by establishing new basic industrial firms and donating the shares to the government.

In other words, from the beginning Park tried to channel entrepreneurial energies into growth-producing activity. In the end, only a few plants were established under the program (on the argument that foreign loans were unattainable), and even those were not turned over to the government. Instead the fines were paid in cash. Nonetheless, the basic pattern was set, with buinessmen in a decidedly subordinate role.

THE MEANS OF BUSINESS INFLUENCE

A second outcome of the foregoing episode was the initiation of business input into government economic policy-making. The thirteen businessmen with the largest fines to pay received governmental permission to go abroad and solicit foreign capital. Upon their return, they made a variety of policy recommendations, including the establishment of an industrial port at Ulsan, a proposal that was immediately implemented. In addition, they formed an association that evolved into the Federation of Korean Industries (FKI). In addition to FKI, the most important Korean business associations are the older Chamber of Commerce and the newer Korean Traders Association (KTA) which is financed by a government mandated levy of 0.55 percent on all imports. In addition, there is the Cooperative Association of Small and Medium Firms and a plethora of "industrial associations" representing particular industries.

The role of business associations has been shown to be central to government-business interaction in Japan. Indeed, one observer asserts that "*zaikai* [loosely, big business] literally presided over Japanese society."[67] In Korea, their power is far less, for reasons already explained, but they do provide a major vehicle for the transmittal of business ideas on economic policy. For example, in 1974 KTA made 167 formal recommendations to the government and 76 percent were adopted, at least in part.[68]

In addition to such formal submissions, important Korean businessmen have regular opportunities to discuss economic policy with top government officials. Most notable is the Monthly Export Promotion Meeting and the more select luncheon that follows, both attended religiously by President Park.

Personal contacts with government officials are a traditional means of influence in East Asia, and Korea is no exception.[69] Many such contacts evolve from the close ties generated by school, region, or family, and by the recruitment of ex-civil servants for government positions. Since officials exercise great discretion in policy-making, there are obvious dangers in these relationships, as will be discussed in Chapter 4. Here we note only that, in addition to providing opportunities for transmittal of individual needs, they also serve to inform officials of business concerns in general.

It is, of course, impossible to quantify the importance of these various means of influence, but we did ask our sample survey respondents how important they thought various conduits were. Their responses, reported in Table 9, must be liberally discounted for response bias, but the following points seem worthy of note. First, direct appeals to the government[70] are used most often, with indirect appeals through politicians or political parties virtually never used by anyone. Second, indirect appeals through business associations are "sometimes used" by many of the respondents, with small industry-specific associations (for example, for cement or fertilizer) being far more influential than the larger broad-based groups. Third, there is extremely high variance in the responses (for example, for direct formal appeals, 30 percent respond with #1 or #2, 30 percent with #3 and 40 percent with #4 or #5, for a 3.38 mean). Surprisingly, decomposition into "exporters" versus "nonexporters" and "large" versus "small" firms does little to explain the variance. T-tests show only four cases of significant differences in means (at 5 percent): two of these are tautological, (exporters are more likely to use the Korean Traders Association,

TABLE 9 Methods of Business Influence on Government

Question: "If you have some influence on government economic policy, how frequently are the following methods used?"

Response Categories:

Used very often		Sometimes used		Never used
1	2	3	4	5

Mean Responses:	*All*	*Small*[a]		*Large*[b]
Direct formal impersonal appeal to government	3.38	3.51	c	2.82
Direct informal personal appeal to government officials	4.05	4.20	c	3.55
Indirect appeal through business association				
Industrial Trade Association	3.19	3.17		3.29
Chamber of Commerce	4.28	4.27		4.32
Small and Medium Industrial Association	4.41	4.28	c	4.91
Federation of Korean Industries	4.60	4.65		4.43
Korean Traders Association	4.19	4.11		4.47
Indirect personal appeal through politician	4.73	4.76		4.60
Indirect impersonal appeal though political party	4.90	4.90		4.91
Indirect impersonal appeal though newspaper	4.78	4.78		4.79
n =	109	86		23

Source: Entrepreneurship Survey, see Appendix C.

Notes: [a]Large firms are those in top quintile of respondents by value added.
[b]"Exporters" and "non-exporters" are not presented since the differences are significant at the 5% level only for use of the Korean Traders Association.
[c]Indicates difference significant at 5% level.

and small firms are more likely to use the Small and Medium Industrial Association); and two are reasonable—large firms make greater use of both direct personal and direct impersonal appeals. Still, the relatively small difference between "large" and "small" and between "exporters" and "non-exporters" is puzzling. Part of this is undoubtedly due to the inherent weakness of the question and to response bias, and part is probably due to the fact that, though small firms exert less influence, they use similar methods when they do so. In addition, however, we must consider the possibility that in some respects the government's treatment of different groups is somewhat more evenhanded than commonly thought. This will be elaborated on in the next section.

THE DEGREE OF BUSINESS INFLUENCE

Respondents were asked, "To what extent can you (or your company) influence government policies affecting your business?" Answers (detailed in Table 10) included: "frequently," 27 percent; "sometimes," 43 percent; and "seldom," 23 percent. These results are not surprising, given the foregoing argument that, while government is quite responsive to business needs, it is also clearly in the driver's seat.

What is surprising is that, while large firms feel themselves to be more influential than smaller firms by a small but statistically significant amount, exporters and non-exporters respond in a virtually identical fashion. This may seem to conflict both with the popular perception of export bias and with evidence we present elsewhere that shows that exporters see themselves as receiving significantly greater benefits from tax and tariff privileges (Table 36), and also view the government as being more "helpful" in establishing, operating, and expanding their businesses (Table 11). This is at least consistent with the following hypothesis: the government initiates policies favoring particular sectors, but is then roughly neutral in responding to complaints across sectors (for example, an exporter appealing for additional privileges may get short shrift given the general privileges already accorded).

TABLE 10 Degrees of Business Influence on Government

Question: "To what extent can you (or your company) influence government policies affecting your business?"

Response Scaling:

Can Get Anything	Can Frequently Affect	Can Sometimes Affect	Seldom Affect	Affect Not at All
1	2	3	4	5

Responses:

	% Distribution of Responses[c]							
	1	*2*	*3*	*4*	*5*	*n*	$\overline{x}$	*t*
All	1.6	26.7	43.0	22.8	5.9	182	3.05	–
Large[a]	2.8	33.3	45.9	18.0	0.0	37	2.79	1.96
Small[a]	1.3	25.0	42.3	24.0	7.4	145	3.11	
Export[b]	2.5	25.7	43.9	20.4	7.5	79	3.05	-0.00
Non-export[b]	0.9	27.5	42.3	24.6	4.7	103	3.05	

Source: Entrepreneurship Survey, see Appendix C.

Notes: [a]"Large" companies are those in the top quintile of respondents when ranked by value added.

[b]"Exporters" are those who derive more than 50% of revenue from exports.

[c]n ≡ number of observations
$\overline{x}$ ≡ mean response
t ≡ t values

BUSINESS'S EVALUATION OF GOVERNMENT

This chapter has been concerned with government economic decision-making, and we conclude by presenting businessmen's evaluation of the outcomes of that process. Our respondents were asked to evaluate the role of government as positive, neutral, or negative in a number of different areas. Results are summarized in Table 11, with the following points worthy of note:

1) The Park Government is ranked as superior to the Rhee Government in every respect (all differences are significant at the 5 percent level). The differences are greatest for "foreign finance," "foreign marketing," and "long-range

TABLE 11 Businessmen's Perceptions of Government Helpfulness

Question: "The government affects your operations in many ways. In each of the following areas, would you rate their involvement as having a positive, negative, or neutral effect upon your business. If you were in business under the Rhee Government, please rate them on the same items.

Response Scaling:

Very Positive		Neutral		Very Negative
1	2	3	4	5

Mean Responses:

	Now		*Rhee*	*Small*		*Large*[a]	*Non-Exporter*		*Exporter*[b]
Establishing business	2.28	*[c]	2.82	2.36	*	1.95	2.40	*	2.12
Operating business	2.19	*	2.80	2.23		2.02	2.34	*	2.00
Expanding business	2.25	*	2.90	2.31		2.00	2.36	*	2.10
Foreign marketing	2.26	*	3.26	2.29		2.16	2.38		2.12
Domestic marketing	2.66	*	3.08	2.63		2.78	2.52	*	2.85
Foreign financing	2.33	*	3.23	2.45	*	1.87	2.36		2.31
Domestic financing	2.22	*	2.90	2.24		2.16	2.44	*	1.94
Stimulating general level of economy	2.22	*	2.91	2.22		2.25	2.27		2.15
Controlling prices	2.68	*	3.00	2.59	*	3.04	2.70		2.65
Long-range planning	2.20	*	3.14	2.24		2.05	2.20		2.20
Controlling unfair competition	2.63	*	3.04	2.56	*	2.92	2.62		2.66
Controlling labor unrest	2.40	*	3.11	2.46		2.21	2.45		2.34
SOC provision	2.18	*	2.98	2.29	*	1.79	2.14		2.23
number	172		73	138		34	95		77

Source: Entrepreneurship Survey, see Appendix C. Some response categories are abbreviated here.

Notes: [a]"Large" companies are in the top quintile of respondents when ranked by value added.

[b]"Exporters" are those who derive more than 50 percent of revenues from exports.

[c]* indicates significant difference at 5% level.

planning"; and least for "controlling prices" and "controlling unfair competition."

2) Overall, the evaluation of the current government is mildly positive, but hardly wildly enthusiastic (mean responses are on the neutral side of positive). The only items on which the government was ranked closer to "neutral" than to "positive" were "controlling prices," "controlling competition," and "domestic marketing."
3) Large firms generally give the present government a higher rating than do smaller firms,[71] though the differences are often not significant. Even where statistically significant, the differences are not strikingly large (that is, mean responses of both groups are generally closer to "positive" than to either "very positive" or "neutral").
4) Exporters generally rate the government more favorably than do domestic producers.[72] The absolute differences remain small, however, though they are more often significant than with the "small" versus "large" distinction.

The relatively low explanatory power of the "small" versus "large" and "export" versus "non-export" distinctions requires attention. One hypothesis runs as follows: because of information imperfections and uncertainty, exporting is much more difficult than import substitution, and the government therefore must intervene in favor of exports to reduce the gap between expected private and social gains. The question then is not the qualitative one of whether or not the government should favor exports, but the quantitative one of how much is necessary to roughly equate returns from export and domestic sales. Has the government gone overboard and induced entrepreneurs to ignore domestic opportunities in favor of exports which, at the margin, are socially less advantageous? Or, have exporters received proportionally greater policy attention only to the extent necessary to offset the market imperfection? The relatively small differences in our empirical results provide some weak support for the view that in practice the government has largely intervened to redress an existing imbalance and has generally not gone so far as to create a new one. This is, of course, a testable hypothesis (in terms of average rates of return on domestic sales and exports), but we are unable to find any relevant data and so leave the exercise to others. In any event, the possibility must at least be considered that the government is reasonably even-handed in dealing with different sectors, with exporters having greater problems and thus meriting, and receiving, greater attention.

The judgments of businessmen presented above are, of course, only partly due to the government economic decision-making process—the top tier of the planning heirarchy. They are even more closely related to the cutting edge of planning where government decisions are transmitted so as to actually alter the behavior of production units. It is to this "implementation" level of planning that we now direct our attention.

FOUR

Implementation of Government Policy

IMPLEMENTATION AND COMPLIANCE MECHANISMS

Government planning, if it is to alter the path of a mixed economy, must ultimately be reflected in the actions of individuals and enterprises. This link is by no means automatic. In the words of Eli Hecksher: "Even in large countries ruled by strong governments, economic statutes and laws have ever so often remained pious wishes exerting little or no effect on the course of economic development."[1] This has been particularly true in post-World War II LDCs. "Development planning" has run the gamut from simple lists of "goods" to the most sophisticated programming models without conspicuously influencing grassroots behavior. Nehru's judgement on India, "The real question is not planning but implementing the Plan—I fear we are not quite so expert at implementation as at planning,"[2] is reflected in a growing emphasis in the planning literature on the cruciality of implementation and its inadequacy in most LDCs.[3] We believe that Korea is a notable exception, and that, in contrast to the Indian situation, Koreans are even better at implementation than at planning. Our argument will be structured according to four organizing principles.

We have broadly defined planning as the working out of an ends-means hierarchy in which "implementation" refers to the means whereby a given end is achieved; that is, any one tier in the hierarchy is implemented by all the tiers below it. In this scheme, there is a crucial discontinuity between government and private planning, and crossing of this interface is the critical bottleneck in implementation. The lowest tier of government planning is a set of mechanisms whereby individual and enterprise compliance is stimulated, forced, or cajoled. A discussion of implementation can usefully concentrate on these means whereby the crucial interface is crossed. Our first organizing principle is thus to focus on intervention mechanisms.

Intervention mechanisms may be classified in two ways: first, in terms of the instruments of intervention (taxes, exchange rates, rationing, subsidies, and so on); and second, in terms of the kinds of pressures brought to bear on individual behavior in order to insure compliance. Our second organizing principle is that we are primarily concerned with behavioral compliance mechanisms.

Behavior may be modified by field manipulation or by command. The former expands an individual's opportunity set, leaving him free to alter his behavior or not, while the latter constricts it. Since government's efforts at field manipulation are well known, a major concern of this chapter will be to describe and explain the command elements. The command versus field manipulation distinction is thus a third major organizing principle.

Both field manipulations and commands may be discretionary or non-discretionary, depending on the degree to which administrators are free to alter their applicability. A related distinction is the degree of particularism with which mechanisms are applied to individual or larger groupings of enterprises. The choice between discretionary and non-discretionary intervention is a fourth organizing principle.

These principles are elaborated on in theoretical terms in the next section (which may be skipped by those interested only in the Korean case). Pages 85–127 then detail Korean usages of non-discretionary and discretionary variants of field manipulation and command. The section, Discretion and Command: A Case Study, demonstrates how the various mechanisms interact to alter the behavior of a particular enterprise. We conclude by characterizing the Korean implementation system as a Myrdalian "hard" state and evaluate the costs and benefits of this status (pages 132–140).

THEORETICAL DIMENSIONS OF INTERVENTION

Our discussion of compliance mechanisms is hobbled by a lack of previous work on the subject, both in Korea and elsewhere. One notable exception is Gunnar Myrdal's discussion of what he terms "operational controls," but as he observes:

> In no other major field of South Asian economic policy is there such a lack not only of scientific analysis but of systematic and specific knowledge of the empirical facts. The operational controls are not planned, they are clearly not coordinated, and the manner of their application is usually not disclosed in any detail.[4]

This neglect is not confined to South Asia, and a natural consequence is the absence of an accepted paradigm, model, or framework for dealing with this complicated set of interrelationships. Our purpose here is not to present a detailed morphology, but to suggest its more important dimensions and thus provide a structure for our discussion of implementation as practiced in Korea.

INSTRUMENTALISM VERSUS BEHAVIORALISM

Two broad structuring principles of compliance mechanisms are possible—instrumental and behavioral. The instrumental approach is most completely developed in the work of E.S. Kirschen et al. They define instruments as "something which the Government itself can change in order to produce an economic effect," and classify them into five groups—public finance, money and credit, exchange rate, direct control, and changes in the institutional framework.[5] The behavioral approach is reflected in the work of Dahl and Lindbloom, Koopmans and Montias.[6] Here the focus is on the nature of the interaction which alters behavior, and this cuts across instrumental categories. For example, Kirschen's tax, credit, and exchange rate instruments are basically similar in altering resource allocation by acting on enterprise profits and self-interest. From the behavioral point of view, the crucial microeconomic question is not so much *which* particular element of the profit function is being manipulated, but *how* it is manipulated. That is, how much administrative discretion is there in application? How are underpriced resources allocated to competitors? How easy is it to avoid compliance, and so forth? Such questions are of interest for a wide range of instruments, and their answers have much to do with whether or not the policies remain mere "pious wishes." The process of control dominates the tool of control as a determinant of efficacy.

The behavioral and instrumental approaches are, of course, not mutually contradictory but two dimensions of the same issue. Nonetheless, we choose to organize our presentation along behavioral lines because it seems more suited to understanding the microeconomic problems LDCs face in making policies work. In addition, the instrumental approach is reflected in companion papers. We now elaborate somewhat on the behavioral categories.

Dahl and Lindbloom distinguish four broad socio-political techniques through which one social organism can produce a response in another.[7] Briefly, these are:

1) Spontaneous field control: pursuit of one's own interests affects another's behavior without conscious intent.
2) Manipulated field control: intentional alteration of another's opportunity set so as to stimulate a desired response.
3) Command: hierarchical direction enforced by expectations of penalties for non-compliance.
4) Reciprocity: bilateral or multilateral interaction employing combinations of the other three techniques.

In the present context, spontaneous field control is represented by the invisible hand of the market, government intervention is accomplished via manipulated field control or command, and reciprocity is the linkage between compliance mechanisms and business influence on government. Spontaneous field control is not itself an intervention mechanism so that it appears in this chapter only in specifying the opportunity costs of command and field manipulation. Interactive reciprocity is discussed in explaining how command is enforced by field manipulation.

COMMAND VERSUS FIELD MANIPULATION

The distinction between command and field manipulation can be clarified by considering the motivation behind compliance.[8] Both ultimately act on the controllee's self-interest by altering his perceived opportunity set. In field manipulation, compliance or non-compliance is up to the controllee's decision and is its own reward. With command, on the other hand, compliance is not perceived by the controllee as being advantageous in and of itself, so that it must be accompanied by an explicit or implicit threat for non-compliance.

Command thus implies compulsion, which may either be a penalty for non-compliance, or the removal of an existing (or potential) privilege. The latter method we shall refer to as "partial mutuality." In the words of Koopmans and Montias, this occurs

> when an individual undertaking an effective action incurs some, possibly temporary, disutility in order (a) to forestall an action by one or more participants which would inflict on him an even greater loss in utility or (b) to accumulate credits for future benefits.[9]

No better description of the Korean method of enforcing command could be found, as we shall see.

As an example of our behavioral morphology, consider the fiscal instrument of taxation. An income tax is imposed by command, conferring no advantage in and of itself, and it must therefore be enforced by threat of penalty.[10] Tax variances, exemptions, holidays, and other loopholes, on the other hand, consist of offers of advantage in return for particular actions. They are, therefore, field manipulations. Finally, the threat to withdraw exemptions (or to enforce inoperable tax commands) in the absence of a specified action represents partial mutuality in operation.

Field manipulation may, in turn, take two forms, which we shall call parameter manipulation and field augmentation. The former signals desired reallocations by marginal adjustments of prices, taxes, interest rates, exchange rates, and the like. Field augmentation, on the other hand, operates through expanding information about existing opportunities. The controllee considers his *perceived* opportunity set that includes only a finite number of feasible alternatives due to limited information. The controller can expand the decision-maker's perceived opportunity set by filling this information gap and thus lead him to reevaluate alternative courses of action and the expected outcomes associated with those alternatives.

In sum, field manipulation either expands the perceived opportunity set (field augmentation), or alters expected payoffs from particular courses of action (parameter manipulation). Command, on the other hand, reduces the feasible opportunity set, assuming there is sufficient compulsion to make it operable.

The main point is that a given instrument can be used to alter behavior in a variety of ways, and the process chosen is often as important as the instrument in determining the outcome. Where intervention is deemed necessary, field manipulation would seem preferable to command on several theoretical grounds: it increases liberty; it takes maximum advantage of the market forces of self-motivation and private knowledge and flexibility; and it conserves on administrative costs of enforcement and information acquisition. As we shall show, however, the Korean government has relied heavily on command, often with good effect. A major task of our discussion of implementation will be to explain this paradox.

DISCRETIONARY VERSUS NON-DISCRETIONARY INTERVENTION

The second dimension must now be added to our behavioral typology. Myrdal's discussion of operational controls utilizes such a two-dimensional classification scheme. One of these distinguishes "positive" from "negative" controls in a manner compatible with, but far from identical to, our command versus field manipulation categorization.[11] His second dimension defines a "non-discretionary" control as one in which "application follows automatically from the laying down of a definite rule, or from induced changes in prices, the imposition of tariff duties or excise duties, or the giving of subsidies to a particular branch of industry without the possibility of discrimination in favor of particular firms."[12] On the other hand, the application of discretionary controls "involves an individual decision by an administrative authority with power to act at its own discretion."[13]

Myrdal describes the heavy reliance of LDCs on discretionary controls and classes them as "illiberal states" on this count, in distinction to the use of non-discretionary controls in the "liberal" West.[14] He argues forcibly for liberalization on the ground that "the scarcity in South Asia of administrative personnel with both competence and integrity should make discretionary policies all the more difficult to execute with reasonable effectiveness and reliance on them more hazardous, even morally. With this consideration in mind, . . . it would be desirable if non-discretionary controls were used to the maximum extent possible."[15]

This argument is similar to Hirschman's hypothesis that "an untrained labor force will perform better in machine-paced operations" than in "operator-paced operations."[16] In both cases one conserves on scarce decision-making powers by relying on automaticity.

The formulation of well-designed generalized controls is, however, not a sufficient condition for non-discretionary application. Myrdal admits this by saying:

> In regard to all controls except those non-discretionary ones that work through induced changes in prices, there are wide differences in the degree of administrative discretion, depending on how firm and specific the governing directives and how literally they are observed.[17]

For example, under the law, tax holidays might be allowed to a wide class of investors, but in practice there may be substantial room for administrative discretion.

Again, examination of the Korean case will yield a paradox. Myrdal argues for non-discretionary controls, but the Koreans have successfully relied heavily on discretionary methods. We now describe the application of control mechanisms in Korea and return to an explanation of the double paradox at the end of the chapter.

NON-DISCRETIONARY FIELD MANIPULATION IN PRACTICE

In theory, non-discretionary field manipulation is the preferred form of intervention, since it achieves a desired deviation from pure market behavior while taking maximum advantage of the motivational and informational advantages of the invisible hand. In Korean practice, it is not so pervasive as one would gather from the writings of some economists, but, nonetheless, it plays an important role. The single most important realm of application of non-discretionary field manipulation is the market for foreign exchange. Other forms of intervention are also used in this market, and to maintain continuity we shall also consider them here. After the detailed examination of the foreign exchange market, we shall make more limited references to other uses of non-discretionary field manipulation.

The foreign exchange market is particularly important because of Korea's "export-led" growth. In 1962, exports were roughly fifty million dollars but, under the Park Government, they rose at a nominal average annual rate of 42 percent to a level of eight billion dollars in 1976.[18] This represented an increase from 6 percent of GNP to 38 percent.[19] More important, this was not cheap and easy natural resource-based growth: in 1976, 90 percent of the exports were manufactured products.[20] It is, therefore, of interest to ask what role government intervention played in the process. The traditional answer is that the change was wrought by a move to an equilibrium exchange rate and the addition of export incentives: namely, by parameter manipulation. We find little evidence to sustain this view and instead argue for the importance of field augmentation. We shall first examine the setting of the foreign exchange rate and demand side interventions in the form of tariffs and quantitative restrictions. We then consider supply side interventions through export promotion schemes.

THE FOREIGN EXCHANGE RATE AND ALLOCATION MECHANISMS

The basic change in the exchange rate regimes between the Rhee and Park periods is generally characterized as a move from a disequilibrium to an equilibrium system. This is suggested by Table 12 that calculates the demand for foreign exchange as the sum of the official rate, tariffs, and estimated distortion premia accruing to importers.[21] Under Rhee, foreign exchange was heavily undervalued with the demand price for dollars roughly three times the official rate. Under Chang Myon, devaluation resulted in the demand price falling to twice the official price. Following the 1964 exchange rate reform, the demand price was only 15 percent above the official rate and this declined steadily to some 7 percent in 1975.

Some of the gap between demand and official prices is taken up by tariffs, but in the 1950s the remaining distortion premia were still such that an importer who obtained foreign exchange at the official rate could earn a profit ranging from 100 to 175 percent if he brought in a tariff exempt commodity (compare columns A and B of Table 12) and in the 90 percent range if he paid an average tariff (compare columns A+C with B).

The resulting excess demand for foreign exchange at the official rate was allocated by a complicated system including a variety of privileged access categories for some products from some sources, and a series of competitive auction and bidding procedures for other uses and sources, notably including export earnings.[22] Estimates of activity in privileged and (relatively) competitive markets are given separately in Table 13. It appears that in 1958 something like 80 percent of imports came in via privileged access and this dropped to about 50 percent in 1959 and 1960.

The rates within the non-privileged sector varied substantially (Table 13). Exporters sold freely to importers at a competitive rate while International Cooperation Administration (ICA) and Korean Foreign Exchange (KFX) auctions yielded prices between the export and official rates. There were two reasons for this. First, ICA and KFX dollars were more restricted in use than were export dollars. Second, the auctions suffered from imperfections of information, collusion among bidders, and accusations that allocations were not always made to the highest bidders. Regrettably, we are unable to quantify these two factors, although their respective magnitudes are critical in assessing the restrictiveness of the system. In any event, the weighted average import rate ranged from 10 percent above the official rate in 1958 to 40 percent above in 1959 and 1960.

Three important conclusions emerge from this discussion.

TABLE 12 Foreign Exchange Market Distortions, 1955–1975

(current wŏn per dollar)

Year	*A* *Official Rate*[a]	*B* *Distortion Premium*[b]	*C* *Tariffs and Taxes*[c]	*D* *Demand Price*	*E* *Distortion Factor*[e]
1955	31.3	48.1	5.9	85.3	2.72
1956	50.0	52.9	7.0	109.9	2.20
1957	50.0	58.9	9.4	118.3	2.37
1958	50.0	64.0	20.3	134.3	2.69
1959	50.0	84.7	47.8	182.5	3.65
1960	63.8	83.9	52.0	199.7	3.13
1961	127.5	N.T.	30.8	222.5[d]	1.74
1962	130.0	N.T.	28.8	245.2[d]	1.89
1963	130.0	39.8	21.0	268.0[d]	2.06
1964	214.3	39.7	36.8	290.8	1.36
1965	266.5	0.0	41.0	307.5	1.15
1966	272.2	0.0	37.2	309.4	1.14
1967	272.5	0.0	39.0	311.5	1.14
1968	276.8	0.0	46.9	323.7	1.17
1969	286.8	0.0	38.7	325.5	1.13
1970	310.1	0.0	40.6	350.7	1.13
1971	346.1	0.0	34.4	380.5	1.10
1972	391.8	0.0	37.0	428.8	1.09
1973	398.4	0.0	29.1	427.5	1.07
1974	406.0	0.0	27.7	433.7	1.07
1975	484.0	0.0	34.8	518.8	1.07

Notes: [a]Twelve month average from Wontack Hong, *Factor Supply and Factor Intensity of Trade in Korea* (Seoul, 1976), p. 140.

[b]Estimate of windfall profit accruing to importer with privileged access to foreign exchange at official rate.

1) From 1955 through mid-1961, and again in 1963 and 1964 there was a competitive market for foreign exchange earned by exporters. The resulting exchange premia are taken from: C. R. Frank, K. S. Kim, and L. E. Westphal, *Foreign Trade Regimes and Economic Development: South Korea* (New York, 1975), pp. 70–71.
2) From mid-1964 on, a series of devaluations maintained a reasonable approximation to an equilibrium rate. Parity rates calculated by Frank, Kim, and Westphal (p. 235) and Wontack Hong (p. 141) show, if anything, undervaluation rather than overvaluation. A thin black market has existed with a very stable

TABLE 12 (continued)

premium of about 30 wŏn per dollar from 1965 through 1975 with the exception of the post-Vietnam psychological scare. The stability of this premium at an absolute rather than a relative rate, as well as its small size, suggests that it is largely a risk premium in an illegal market. We conclude that disequilibria premia after 1964 are virtually zero.

[c]Estimates of tariffs (including foreign exchange tax prior to 1962) per dollar of final consumption imports. Average rates per dollar were first calculated from the BOK *Economic Statistics Yearbook* and multiplied by an estimate of the ratio of actual consumer goods rates to the average. For the 1964 to 1967 and 1967 to 1972 tariff regimes the estimates are derived from Frank, Kim, and Westphal (p. 61). For early years the estimates are based on highly subjective examinations of legal rates and for later years on collections by SITC codes which do not distinguish endusers. The resulting estimates are indicative only of broad orders-of-magnitude.

[d]Confusion accompanying a plethora of reforms in the early years of the Park Military Government made the data for these years unreliable. Accordingly, we substituted a linear extrapolation.

[e]Demand price over official rate.

First, the degree of effective undervaluation of foreign exchange was substantially less than appears from looking at the official rate alone. Second, exporters in particular received close to a competitive rate. Third, there remained substantial room for excess profits from privileged access (in the KFX and ICA auctions as well as at the official rate). Together with the benefits from discretionary credit allocations, these economic rents constituted the prime movers of entrepreneurial activity in the 1950s and lead us to describe the Rhee period loosely as one of "zero-sum entrepreneurship" (see Chapter 8). These excess profits were allocated by a system of quantitative restrictions which will be considered in the section on discretionary command. Here we only note the shift in the behavioral foreign exchange allocation mechanism from one which relied in part on discretionary command (quotas and licenses) under Rhee to one which is virtually wholly non-discretionary field manipulation (official rate plus tariff) under Park.

The second intervention on the demand side is via tariffs. These are also field manipulations in altering allocation by affecting the access price. We now compare the use of tariffs under Rhee and Park. Under both regimes, they were administered in a largely non-discretionary fashion, though there was an important shift towards greater particularism under Park. In addi-

TABLE 13 Import Markets, 1958–1960

	1958	*1959*	*1960*
Imports (US $ million)	378.2	291.7	325.2
Source of import dollars (US $ million)			
Exports	16.5	19.2	31.8
ICA auction	50.9	124.9	128.2
KFX auction	13.0	24.4	11.3
Other[a]	297.8	123.2	153.9
Sources of import dollars (%)			
Competitive[b]	21.3	57.8	52.7
Official rate	78.7	42.2	47.3
Acquisition rate (wŏn per dollar)			
Exports[c]	114.0	134.7	146.4
ICA auction	74.2	79.1	99.8
KFX auction	79.8	104.2	105.9
Other	50.0	50.0	62.5
Weighted average	56.9	72.6	86.9

Source, except as noted: EPB, *Korea Statistical Yearbook, 1961* (Seoul, 1962).

Notes: [a]Calculated as a residual, but basically consisting of foreign aid allocations.
[b]At least somewhat so.
[c]Frank, Kim, and Westphal, p. 70.

tion, the level of effective manipulation declined between the two periods. The following summary draws heavily on Frank, Kim, and Westphal.[23]

In 1946, a uniform tariff rate of 10 percent was imposed on all imports except those financed by foreign assistance. In 1950, there was a move toward greater particularism and increased nominal levels. According to the new customs law, more than a thousand distinct import items were specified with an average nominal tariff of 40 percent. The many exemptions reduced average collections to less than 20 percent. In 1952, exemptions were extended for some capital goods and intermediate input users. In 1957, there was a minor restructuring which added 4 percent to the average rate and in 1958 a uniform foreign exchange tax was added. The first major reform came under the Park Military Government in July 1961 when a Temporary Special Customs Law was enacted "to capture the windfall profits that would otherwise accrue to importers receiving import licenses for restricted items."[24] A similar system of special tariffs was superimposed following the May 1964 devaluation. Adjustments in the regular tariff classification were made periodically. In 1967, there was a major shift from positive to negative list systems. The tariff law became even more flexible administratively in 1968 when it was provided that "under certain conditions, emergency duties, countervailing duties, and so-called beneficial duties could be levied. The government had the authority to change statutory rates by as much as 50 percent by administrative decree."[25] A further increase in flexibility accompanied the tariff reform of 1973 that allowed the government to adjust the tariff rates within 100 percent of the legal rate. The government subsequently used this authority to reduce the cost-push pressure from increases in world prices of major industrial raw materials.

Two trends should be emphasized in the foregoing summary. First, there was a steady decline in the level of tariffs as a percent of the demand price (compare columns C and A of Table 12). Second, and much more important, there was a dramatic increase in particularism and flexibility between the Rhee and Park periods. Under Rhee, the tariff system was relatively stable, and intervention in the structure of the national import bundle was achieved through discretionary application of quantitative restrictions. Under Park, allocation was increasingly accomplished by shifting relative tariffs on particular commodities in a non-discretionary fashion, and these changes came with great frequency.

In sum, the instrument for intervention in the allocation of foreign exchange under Rhee was a mixture of discretionary command and non-discretionary parameter manipulation. Under Park, the system became wholly non-discretionary, though highly particularistic, parameter manipulation.[26]

THE GENERATION OF FOREIGN EXCHANGE

Under Rhee, the dominant source of foreign exchange was foreign aid, and this was maximized by maintaining an overvalued domestic currency on the assumption of price inelasticity of donor supply. The wisdom of this policy may be questioned, but it emphatically did *not* have the effect of discouraging exports as is widely asserted. Recall that export earnings were converted by a variety of special means at well above the official rate, beginning with the export-import link system in 1951. By the late 1950s these premia were substantially greater than the official yield and produced an effective direct return to exporters that was as high (or higher) in the 1950s as in the 1960s and 1970s (see Table 14, columns A, D, and F).[27]

What then produced the export boom? The usual, though incorrect, answer is a variety of export subsidy schemes which increased the net profit from a given wŏn yield per dollar. Wontack Hong has prepared an extensive survey of export-promotion schemes and these are summarized in Table 15. Readers interested in the details of the schemes may refer to Wontack Hong's paper.[28] Here we only identify the trends. The first thing to note from Table 15 is that under Rhee export promotion subsidies were by no means absent. In addition to the premia already described, there were a variety of tax, tariff, and credit exemptions. Under Park such subsidies multiplied and diversified, but the crucial question is what the total effect was on net export earnings.

Calculating effective subsidies is a difficult task that has been attempted by Frank, Kim, and Westphal. Their estimates were given in Table 14, and the results are surprising. In constant 1965 wŏn per dollar the effective exchange rate on exports, inclusive of subsidies, has remained remarkably stable (in the vicinity of 300 from 1958 through 1970). If anything, there was a net decline between the late 1950s and the early 1960s.

Now these figures are subject to argument, particularly the credit subsidy estimation, and do not incorporate all of the

TABLE 14 Foreign Exchange Market, 1958–1970

	Effective Exchange Rate on Exports[a] (1965 won/dollar) (A)	Effective Exchange Rate on Imports[b] (1965 won/dollar) (B)	Ratio (A/B) (C)	Percentage Components of Effective Exchange Rate on Exports			Percentage Components of Effective Exchange Rate on Imports	
				Premia (D)	Subsidies (E)	Official Exchange Rate (F)	Tariff and Tariff Equivalents (G)	Official Exchange Rate (H)
1958	288.7	160.4	1.80	55.5	1.0	43.5	22.5	77.5
1959	333.3	202.9	1.64	62.2	1.0	36.8	39.6	60.4
1960	326.5	221.6	1.47	56.7	0.8	42.5	37.6	62.4
1961	294.1	287.1	1.02	9.7	5.6	84.7	13.2	86.8
1962	270.5	261.4	1.03	0.0	14.1	85.9	11.2	88.8
1963	280.6	219.4	1.28	21.3	10.3	68.7	12.2	87.8
1964	309.6	271.7	1.14	14.1	9.7	76.2	13.2	86.8
1965	304.6	293.1	1.04	0.0	12.8	87.2	9.4	90.6
1966	296.8	272.4	1.09	0.0	15.9	84.1	8.4	91.6
1967	287.6	255.8	1.12	0.0	18.2	81.8	8.6	91.4
1968	283.0	241.6	1.17	0.0	21.9	78.1	8.5	91.5
1969	271.7	233.4	1.16	0.0	20.6	79.4	7.8	92.2
1970	272.3	230.6	1.18	0.0	21.8	78.2	7.6	92.4

Source: Frank, Kim, and Westphal, pp. 70–75.

Notes: [a]Return to exporter deflated by wholesale price index. Includes official exchange rate, export premia, direct subsidies, tax and tariff exemptions, and interest rate subsidies.

[b]Price to importer deflated by wholesale price index. Includes official exchange rate, tariff and FX tax collections and export premia.

TABLE 15 Major Export-Promotion Schemes

Types of Incentives	*Duration*
Tax Incentives	
Commodity tax exemption	April 1950–
Business tax exemption	January 1962–
Reduction of corporation and income tax by 50% on earnings from exports	January 1961–December 1972
Accelerated depreciation on allowance for fixed capital directly used for export production in mining, fishing and manufacturing	January 1961–
Tax credit for foreign market development expenditures	August 1969–
Tax credit for losses due to operations in foreign markets	March 1973–
Tariff Incentives	
Tariff exemptions on capital equipment for export production	March 1964–December 1973
Tariff payments on an installment basis for capital equipment used in export production	January 1974–
Tariff exemptions on raw material imports for export production	April 1961–June 1975
Tariff drawback on imported raw material used for export production	July 1975–
Wastage allowance	July 1965–
Financial Incentives	
Financing for export sales	February 1948–July 1955
Export shipment financing	June 1950–July 1955
Export promotion fund financed by counterpart fund	November 1959–January 1964
Financing imports of materials to be used in export production	October 1961–February 1972

TABLE 15 (continued)

Export credits (trade credit before 1961)	June 1950–
Financing suppliers of U.S. off-shore military procurement	September 1962–
Fund to promote the export industry	July 1964–September 1969
Fund to convert small and medium size firms into export industries	February 1964–
Fund to prepare exports of agricultural and fishery products	September 1969–
Foreign currency loans	May 1967–
Financing exports on credit	October 1969–
Other Promotion Schemes	
Foreign exchange deposit system	June 1949–January 1961
Trading license based on export performance	January 1953–
An export bonus with preferential foreign exchange	? 1951–May 1961
Payment of export subsidy	? 1954– ? 1955 and ? 1960– ? 1965
Discount on railroad freight rates	? 1958–
Monopoly rights on exports of specific items to specific areas	April 1960–
Creation of exporters associations on various export products	September 1961–
Financing KOTRA	? 1962–
Export-import link system	November 1962–
Discount on electricity rates	? 1965– ? 1976
Waiver issuance for shipping	? 1965– ?
Local L/C system	March 1965–
Differential treatment of traders based on export performance	February 1967–
Export insurance	January 1969–
General trading company	May 1975–
Export-import bank	June 1976–

Source: Wontack Hong, "Trade, Distortions and Employment Growth in Korea," pp. 82–83.

subsidies listed in Table 15.[29] Nonetheless, the results are striking and suggest that export growth was not primarily a result of direct financial incentives, since the sum of exchange premia, exchange rate, and export subsidies were at least similar in periods of stagnation and rapid growth. What then made the difference? We suggest five contributing factors: reduction in opportunity costs, simpler input acquisition, lower variance in export return, field augmentation, and non-pecuniary parameter manipulation.

The most important cause of the change was probably the reduction of alternative higher-yielding sources of entrepreneurial income. If you can make 100 percent in a few months with little risk, through privileged access to foreign exchange, there is little point in devoting effort to the difficult and complicated task of exploring export markets and putting together internationally competitive productive combinations. The exchange rate reforms closed out the zero-sum sources of rent, reduced opportunity costs, and drove rent-seekers into productive positive-sum activity.[30]

A second factor also stemmed from the import side. The shift from discretionary field manipulation in allocating foreign exchange made it easier and cheaper for exporters to obtain imported raw materials, spares, and capital equipment. This, however, would be equally applicable to domestic production and does not serve to explain the increased share of exports.

While the mean value of the price received by exporters did not change appreciably from the 1950s to the 1960s, the variance was substantially reduced, thus removing an element of uncertainty in the expected yield. Prior to reform, premia constituted over 50 percent of the total return (see Table 14), but this value depended on an auction system in a thin market and fluctuated widely. Further, access to the market (and its variants) did involve some transaction costs, and there may have been further uncertainty as to whether the special rates would be maintained in the future. For these reasons, the reforms may have induced greater exports by increasing the expected return even though the mean yield was unchanged.[31]

Field augmentation was particularly important. At the highest level, this followed from the introduction of political stability by a regime which gave top priority to growth and ensured a "favorable business climate." This lengthened time horizons and made manufacturing a much more feasible alternative to commerce as a field of entrepreneurial activity. In the export field itself, the Monthly Export Promotion Meeting chaired by the President was a forum of multi-faceted information exchange. In 1962, the Ministry of Commerce and Industry began setting annual export targets classified by commodity, region, and country of destination. This had an announcement effect in suggesting profitable markets and in implicitly promising non-quantifiable government support in pursuit of those targets. In addition to such indirect field augmentation, the government established, or expanded, a variety of special purpose entrepreneurial support institutions. Best known of these is the Korean Trade Promotion Corporation (KOTRA) which is financed through a government-mandated contribution of 0.55 percent of the c.i.f. value of imports and channeled through the Korean Traders Association. Other support institutions include a variety of special purpose banks and financial intermediaries.

Also in the realm of field augmentation are diplomatic efforts. Indirect augmentation is provided by the mere fact of representation and interaction. Rhee's periodic embargoes of trade with Japan sorely hurt exports to the major traditional market[32] and were in marked contrast to Park's normalization of relations with Japan in 1964. More recent efforts include drives to establish relations in the LDCs and Eastern Europe and expand them in Western Europe. Direct action on the diplomatic front includes commercial attachés who actually performed marketing functions in the early years and who, more recently, have made a significant contribution to the construction industry's expansion in the Middle East. Removal of restrictions on foreign travel by businessmen has also improved information flows.

Non-pecuniary parameter manipulation also played a role. As Chapter 7 will show, entrepreneurs are not motivated by profit alone, and it is arguable that a rise in non-pecuniary incentives may increase their total return and thus the level of activity. In contrast to Rhee, Park has placed primary emphasis on industrialization, and this has led to government recognition and approval of successful entrepreneurs. November 30 is "Export Day" and the highest ranking exporters are, with great fanfare, awarded "industrial merit-medals" of gold, silver, and bronze pagoda rank.[33] In addition, special awards are given to those exporting over U.S. $100 million worth of goods.[34] These medals are presented personally by the President, and the competition is taken seriously. The competitors sometimes get carried away as Export Day nears. In 1976, Samsŏng Mulsan arranged prepayments amounting to U.S. $68 million and Daewoo managed $51 million. The referees managed to keep on top of the game, however, and since 1977 prepayments no longer count.

With due attention to income distribution, non-pecuniary incentives are not confined to the first decile. At an international Youth-Skills contest in the mid-1970s, a Korean delegation won top honors. They were met at the airport by the Deputy Prime Minister and several ministers, given a ticker tape parade through a carefully marshaled crowd estimated at 300,000, and were personally received by President Park. Jaded skeptics may chortle, but to the hairdressers, pipe-fitters, and welders it may well provide a non-pecuniary incentive to excell.

FOREIGN EXCHANGE MARKET: SUMMARY

Korea's export spurt is generally attributed to devaluation and export incentives; that is, to getting the price right. We find surprisingly little evidence for this position. Available calculations suggest that the total wŏn return to exporters was similar in periods of stagnation and of rapid growth. Both regimes intervened via non-discretionary parameter manipulation to a similar degree. Exchange rate reform was, nonetheless, important, though not in the fashion usually described. The move from discretionary command to non-discretionary parameter manipulation on the import side drove entrepreneurs out of zero-sum arbitrage activity, and into positive-sum production. Field augmentation and non-pecuniary parameter manipulation provided further support. We conclude that, even in the foreign exchange market where non-discretionary parameter manipulation is dominant, it is essential to look at non-price interventions to comprehend the dynamics of Korean development.

TAX COMPLIANCE INCENTIVES

Non-discretionary field manipulation is not used only to promote growth; it is also used in efforts to control business behavior. These attempts have not been notably successful, but are considered here to suggest the limitations of the mechanism.

The Corporate Tax Law defines "green-return corporations,"[35] as: publicly held corporations, corporations listed on the Korean Stock Exchange, public (that is, government) corporations established by special laws, and joint-stock companies in which the government's equity share is over 50 percent. In addition, any company may become a "green-return corporation" if it convinces the government that its reported taxable income is substantially correct over a period of years. Once a corporation attains this status, it enjoys various privileges including:

1) Assessment of tax based on tax reports alone.
2) Generous treatment in calculating expenses.
3) Tax installment payment privileges.
4) Special depreciation allowances.

As of 1975, there were only 282 "green-return corporations" out of 12,532 corporations.[36] This included 142 corporations in the automatic status, so enterprises with an acceptable tax return record are very few indeed.

A related incentive is the Office of National Tax Administration's "sincere-return corporations." These corporations are exempted from various tax investigations, and tax calculations are based on their reports alone. In July 1976, there were 59 "sincere-return corporations" and 857 "semi-sincere-return corporations."[37]

The effort at inducing firms to go public included similar incentive mechanisms, but largely failed, and discretionary command was resorted to as will be described below. In all of these cases the magnitude of the parameter manipulation was too small to be effective.

OTHER NON-DISCRETIONARY FIELD MANIPULATIONS

Price controls represent field manipulations from the point of view of the buyer, but commands from the viewpoint of the seller. They are generally highly discretionary in Korea. Exceptions involve the provision of subsidized goods and services by public enterprises. Worldwide, there is a temptation for government to generate political favor by such policies, and they can generally be justified (rationalized) in the name of consumption or production externalities. Korea under Rhee was no exception; a combination of inefficiency and populist pricing resulted in large deficits which were repudiated by the Park Military Government. In contrast, Brown's study of the pricing policies of six of the largest enterprises leads him to conclude that under the Park Military Government "pricing changes were consistently in the direction of moving toward and approximating opportunity cost prices."[38] While this is a fair assessment, it should be emphasized that the trend is more reflective of a concern for cost efficiency than of a basic aversion to subsidies. The government's willingness to use parameter manipulation in setting prices for publicly produced (or traded) goods and services is reflected in the continuing massive deficits arising from sales of fertilizer, grain, and electricity.[39] The overall level of this form of parameter manipulation may have been reduced between the Rhee and Park periods, and its incidence more easily justified, but intervention remains.

Together with the foreign exchange and wage rates, the interest rate is one of the fundamental factor prices. In Korea, with the exception of at most a few brief years, interest rates have not been determined by market forces. Instead, there has been government intervention on both the supply and demand sides. On the supply side, deposit rates have been set by the government, but administered in a largely non-discretionary fashion. There has been some particularism in that certain classes of small savers have been allowed higher rates than others, but parameter manipulation has by no means been eschewed. On the allocation side, intervention has been both particularistic and discretionary.

DISCRETIONARY FIELD MANIPULATION IN PRACTICE

CREDIT VULNERABILITY OF KOREAN FIRMS

Under the Park regime, allocation of under-priced credit has been by far the most important single instrument of government microeconomic control. Under Rhee, it was also important but shared top billing with foreign exchange allocation. In behavioral terms, it is a form of parameter manipulation which has been non-discretionary in theory, but generally highly discretionary in practice.

Credit is the life-blood of business enterprises everywhere, but it is particularly critical in Korea where debt-equity ratios in manufacturing have been in the three to four range in the first half of the 1970s.[40] This high level of credit dependence has been largely a product of the Park period since the ratio rose steadily from 1.2 in 1966 to a peak of 3.9 in 1971.[41] The sources of the change are shown in Table 16 which gives real flow-of-funds sources for private corporations from 1963–1974. Over the entire period, only 14 percent of the cash flow came from new equity. Another 20 percent was generated internally, but two-thirds came from borrowing. Of the borrowing, 53 percent came from domestic banks and financial institutions, 29 percent from foreign sources, and 19 percent from miscellaneous sources including the curb market.[42]

There are many consequences of leveraging of this magnitude, but two are germane here. First, businessmen have been able to prosper with relatively small infusions of their own funds, thus pyramiding the growth power of the limited stock of effective entrepreneurs (see Chapter 7). Second, businessmen have paid a price in the form of increased government control

TABLE 16 Real Private Corporate Sources of Funds, 1963–1974

(%)

Source		1963–1969		1970–1974		1963–1974
Internal savings[a]		18.6		20.8		19.9
New equity		7.2		18.2		13.7
Debt		74.2		61.0		66.4
Commercial banks	13.1		23.4		19.2	
Special banks and financial institutions	13.3		17.4		15.7	
Foreign loans	26.4		18.0		19.0	
Other[b]	27.4		2.2		12.6	
TOTAL		100.0		100.0		100.0

Source: Current flows from: BOK, *Flow of Funds Accounts in Korea: 1963–1975* (Seoul, 1976). Converted to constant 1970 prices by implicit GDP deflation from: BOK, *Economic Statistics Yearbook: 1976* (Seoul, 1977).

Notes: [a]Depreciation allowance plus retained earnings.
[b]Trade credit, "miscellaneous" and adjustments.

over their activities. With massive debt shares, firms are totally dependent upon credit, not only for expansion, but for survival. In Korea's institutional framework, this translates into dependence on government. As shown in Table 16, over half of the total fund flows come from domestic financial institutions and foreign sources, and both of these sources have been subject to effective discretionary government intervention.

Government intervention in the credit market is not confined to the power to set interest rates and provide allocation guidelines. Much more important is the power for direct discretionary intervention in the allocation process. This follows from two institutional factors. First, both special-purpose and commercial banks have been public enterprises in the sense that government controlled internal decision-making through the power to appoint top management. Second, all foreign loans (save short-term suppliers' credits) must be subjected to government approval and guarantee.

SOURCES OF CONTROL

In 1945, all commercial banks were Japanese-owned and were transferred to the government at Liberation. Initial government direct and indirect shareholding amounted to some 70 percent, and this was reduced by a series of six public offerings between 1954 and 1957. Dilution of control was minimal, however, since single-bidder sales and resales were forbidden in an effort to prevent decisive accumulation by any single private group. In 1957, this policy was reversed, and controlling interests were sold to various chaebŏl groups. Their control was short-lived, however, and in 1961 the Park Military Government confiscated the banks as part of the "illicit wealth accumulation" purge (see Chapter Eight). Since then, shares have again been sold publicly until the government's direct and indirect share in 1973 ranged from 30 to 65 percent.[43] This, however, was sufficient to ensure government control since the Temporary Law on Financial Institutions of June 1961 precluded anyone (save the government) from voting more than 10 percent of the outstanding shares. Government control over the banks was further strengthened by the 1962 revision of the Bank of Korea Law that shifted final responsibility for monetary policy to the executive branch. In sum, the government is able to affect domestic credit allocations at all levels from monetary policy to final bank decisions on individual end-users.

Three mechanisms of foreign credit allocation may be distinguished. Public loans (namely, those to the government or from international agencies or foreign governments) have since 1974 been covered by the Public Loan Inducement and Management Law which specifies the process for government guarantee. The previous procedures are unknown to us but, under both Park and Rhee, all public loans were subject to government approval and guarantee. The second category is private long-term loans (over three years' maturity). These are now covered by the Foreign Capital Inducement Law which allows guarantee by the government, the Korea Exchange Bank (formerly part of the Bank of Korea), or the commercial banks. In practice, the first procedure dominated up through about 1968, and the second has been preeminent since that time. Commercial bank guarantees have been increasing, but are still relatively small. The third category is private short-term credit which comes under the Foreign Exchange Management Law. In contrast to the first two forms, transactions under this law are relatively automatic and non-discretionary so long as the terms correspond to international banking practice. In sum, in both the Rhee and Park periods, the government has had the power to exercise discretionary control over foreign loans for capital goods (largely long-term), through the guarantee requirement. Financing of short-term intermediate inputs and exports, in contrast, has been largely non-discretionary, at least under Park.

EXERCISE OF CONTROL: DISEQUILIBRIUM INTEREST RATES

Governments everywhere regulate loan rates, and Korea is no exception. Throughout the post-war period, interest rates on domestic loans have been regulated, generally at levels well below their equilibrium values. Precise estimates are impossible since there have been a variety of loan rates, and the risk-free opportunity cost of capital is ephemeral. The general picture, however, is apparent from Table 17 which shows that: first, the general bank rate has typically been half of the curb-market rate; and second, the real bank rate has often been negative and generally below even the most conservative estimates of the opportunity cost of capital. The result has been excess demand followed by the necessity of non-price rationing devices.

DISCRETIONARY ALLOCATION IN THE RHEE REGIME

Under Rhee, rationing was accomplished by a variety of selective control schemes including BOK determined loan ceilings for various end-uses and financial institutions and priority end-use specification. In principle, these mechanisms could be used

TABLE 17 Real and Nominal Interest Rates and Opportunity Cost of Capital, 1954–1976

Year	*Nominal Loan Rate*[a]	*Curb Market Loan Rate*[b]	*Inflation Rate*[c]	*Real Loan Rate*	*Real Rate of Return on Capital in Manufacturing*[d]
1954	18.3	—	31.6	-13.3	9–18
1955	18.3	—	65.3	-47.0	"
1956	18.3	—	30.7	-12.4	"
1957	18.3	—	20.4	- 2.1	"
1958	18.3	—	- 0.5	18.8	"
1959	17.9	—	2.6	15.3	"
1960	17.5	—	9.6	7.9	"
1961	17.5	—	15.1	2.4	"
1962	15.7	—	13.9	1.8	9–26
1963	15.7	52.6	28.7	-13.0	"
1964	16.0	61.8	32.1	-16.1	"
1965	26.0	58.9	8.2	17.8	"
1966	26.0	58.7	14.3	11.7	"
1967	26.0	56.5	14.0	12.0	16–38
1968	25.8	56.0	11.8	14.0	"
1969	24.5	51.4	10.1	14.4	"
1970	24.0	49.8	13.2	10.8	"
1971	23.0	46.4	11.5	11.5	"
1972	17.7	39.0	14.5	3.2	17–40
1973	15.5	33.4	9.4	6.1	"
1974	15.5	40.6	26.7	-11.2	"
1975	15.5	41.3	24.1	- 8.6	"
1976	17.5	n.a.	15.7	1.8	"

Notes: [a]Interest rate on general bills up to one year. BOK, *Economic Statistics Yearbook*, various issues.

[b]BOK, *Survey of Business Financing and Unorganized Money Markets*, various quarterly issues.

[c]Annual rate of change in the GNP deflator. BOK, *Economic Statistics Yearbook*, various issues and *National Income in Korea, 1975*.

[d]Range of estimates reported in: Wontack Hong, *Trade, Distortions and Employment* (Seoul, 1977).

to allocate subsidized credit to socially profitable end-users. In practice, there can be no question that the actual allocations were highly discretionary in pursuit of non-economic ends. As one observer typically laments: "How one could expect a desirable development of financing under such a socio-political environment where loans were arranged not according to the importance of projects or ability to repay, but based on political decisions, private favoritism, or under-the-table dealings."[44] Such assertions are fairly easily documented since a good deal of data was made available after the Student Revolution of 1960 and the subsequent Special Law for Dealing With Illicit Wealth Accumulation.[45] The act actually defined "illicit wealth accumulators" as those with more than U.S. $200 thousand in foreign loans or more than 100 million hwan (10 million wŏn) in domestic bank loans,[46] thus reflecting popular belief in the corruption involved in credit allocation.

Of particular interest was the dominant role of politics in distributing foreign-aid credits in the early period. According to Joungwon Kim, the Liberal Party "was believed to have had a substantial interest in at least 50 percent of all the private projects receiving American aid."[47] The government was also able to put pressure on the banks, and this seems to have been heavily used especially at election time. For example, according to a report based on statistics provided by the BOK and the prosecutor's office, prior to the March 1960 election, loans amounting to more than 10.7 billion hwan (equivalent to U.S. $21 million in 1960) were kicked back to Rhee's Liberal Party as campaign contributions.[48] On a company by company basis, the kickbacks varied from 10 percent to 100 percent.

DISCRETIONARY ALLOCATION IN THE PARK REGIME

In the Park period, the domestic loan ceiling system was abandoned.[49] Specification of desirable end-uses, however, was retained and intensified. Differential rates and target industry allocations are set with great particularity and flexibility.

Though the pressure points changed somewhat, the potential for discretion remained. The system could have been non-discretionary had the priority system been highly specific so that anyone fitting a particular description automatically received an allocation. In practice, someone must ultimately decide whether or not even highly specific criteria are met, and this decision remained in government hands.

A fairly recent illustration is provided by the "industrial rationalization" component of the August 3rd Emergency Measures of 1972. The stated objective was to make Korean industries more productive so that they would contribute toward stabilizing the domestic price level and become more competitive in the world market. Criteria were established under which chosen firms would get long-term loans with relatively lower interest charges, preferential tax treatment, and various administrative privileges. Applications were to be examined by the Industrial Rationalization Council (established under the Prime Minister's office), with the President having final approval.[50]

There were two sets of screening criteria. The first step was to select companies in:

"1) Industries which produce goods or services indispensable for stabilization of the nation's livelihood and, further, whose rationalization and development will reduce significantly the burden of the people.
2) Key industries which will widely promote related industries and substantially benefit the overall national economy.
3) Machine and raw material manufacturing industries whose productivity will rise significantly through their rationalization and development.
4) Export industries, tourist business and other foreign exchange earning industries whose rationalization and development will improve the balance of payments.
5) Farmer's subsidiary business or agricultural-fishery processing industries, which can increase farmers' and fishermen's income significantly."[51]

Enterprises in such industries may then be given special status if they aim at:

"1) Specialization and vertical affiliation of production.
2) Optimum scale and method of production and other goals through consolidation of enterprises.
3) Liquidation or transformation of business.
4) Optimization of equipment investments (including replacement or expansion of equipment).
5) Increase of capital and other improvements in financial structure.
6) Development of technology and innovation.
7) Other necessary matters not specified above."[52]

In addition, "When small and medium industries or enterprises are designated, the criteria for rationalization may be determined separately taking into consideration the special characteristics of those industries."[53]

It is apparent that this specification leaves virtually complete discretion to the Industrial Rationalization Council. It would be difficult to imagine an enterprise which could not construct an argument for privileges under some provision of the law. Discretion is thus inevitable, and the question becomes whether it is exercised in the spirit of the allocation criteria or in pursuit of individual interests.

It is rather difficult to document the manner in which discretion is actually exercised under the current regime so we shall simply tell the story as we see it. Discretion undeniably remains and, given excess demand at an artifically low rate, there is substantial room for the recipient to share his benefits with the grantee. In this, there is no difference from the Rhee period, though the profit to be shared may be somewhat smaller. Under the current government, however, allocations are generally made in the spirit of the priority system. A genuine effort is made to ascertain whether the applicant fits the economic eligibility criteria. Gratitude, if shown by the borrower, is in the nature of a uniform transaction tax. This is distinct from the Rhee period when the payment was not only necessary, but often sufficient to obtain a loan. Under the Rhee regime, discretion was exercised in a manner which resulted in resource misallocation, whereas under Park, a portion of the profit may be reallocated, but resources generally get to qualified users. This is a direct result of the bureaucratic hierarchy's response to leadership commitment to growth. Personal bias may be, and is, exercised at the margin, but egregious deviations from sensible allocations are precluded by the self-interest of the hierarchy.

CREDIT: THE FULCRUM OF PARTIAL MUTUALITY

If the foregoing is correct, then can we conclude that discretionary allocation of industrial credit under Park is unimportant beyond diverting resources from low to high priority uses? The answer is emphatically no. There is a second function of the credit mechanism which is subtle, but critical. This is its role as the major means whereby command is enforced, and this follows from its discretionary potential.

We have already pointed out that, in Korea, command is generally backed up by partial mutuality rather than police action. Partial mutuality is effective in proportion to the importance of the advantage which might be withheld. Since credit is the lifeblood of any enterprise, it provides the most powerful basis for partial mutuality. If credit were unavoidably allocated in a non-discretionary fashion, then either command would have to be abandoned or police action would have to be stepped up. The knowledge that the government can cut off the credit tap at any time is sufficient for the operation of partial mutuality. The threat need only be carried out occasionally.

Recognizing the importance of this mechanism is central to understanding how business-government relations work in Korea. In Chapter 8 we shall argue that private concentrations of economic power are in a decidedly weaker position vis-à-vis government than in many other Asian nations at similar stages of development. A major reason for this is government control of credit. In pre-war Japan, banks were the central pillar of each zaibatsu group. Banks played a similar role in maintaining the power of India's industrial houses and Pakistan's twenty-two families.[54] With their own internal sources of finance, these groups were dramatically less dependent on government favor and proportionally less responsive to government control. In Korea, the chaebŏl groups are young, rapidly growing, and heavily leveraged so credit is not only for expansion but for survival. Government discretionary manipulation of the credit instrument is therefore the fulcrum on which partial mutuality pivots.

NON-DISCRETIONARY COMMAND IN PRACTICE

All nations utilize command to impose obligations which would not be met voluntarily. For example, taxes must be levied by command, as no one has yet developed a field augmentation technique that will convince citizens to voluntarily contribute substantial amounts to collective consumption. The first operational question with command, then, is not whether or not it is to be used, but whether or not it can be enforced. A major characteristic of intervention in Korea is that commands are not only used widely, but used effectively.

The second operational issue with command is whether it is applied in a discretionary or a non-discretionary fashion. This distinction requires some clarification since enforcement of command (almost) necessarily involves discretion, whether or not the command itself is discretionary. For example, the personal income tax in the United States is non-discretionary, even though it is enforced by selective examination with some individual tax bills being set at the discretion of the tax examiner. This is to be sharply distinguished from the discretionary procedure in some LDC's where the original tax bill is set by negotiation between two tax assessors and the individual. Not uncommonly, the "bad-guy" assessor sets the full legal rate;

the "good-guy" partner then comes along and sets a lower rate, and the difference is split among the actors. This is discretionary administration.

In Korea, taxes are administered in a largely (though not wholly) non-discretionary fashion even though enforcement is selective. This is discussed below. A second example of non-discretionary command is the prohibition of certain forms of consumption.

TAXES

Consider the first operational question of enforcement. Table 18 gives the historic shares of central government tax collections as a percent of GNP. The trend is upwards, roughly doubling from a 7.5 percent average in the 1953–1960 period to 15.5 percent in 1972–1976. This increase is of course partly due to rising income which in turn facilitates tax extraction. To correct for this, we rely on Lotz and Morss who have estimated the rate at which tax collections vary with income for a sample of fifty-two LDCs in the mid-1960s (we have added an observation for Korea in the mid-1970s).[55] Results are summarized in Table 19 which shows a dramatic increase in the relative ranking of the Republic of Korea from 1962–1964 to 1974–1976; for example, from forty-eighth to eighteenth in the equation relating tax burden to per capita GNP. Even granting the many ambiguities in international comparisons of this sort,[56] we take this as clear evidence that tax collections in Korea have increased far more rapidly than can be explained by the rise in per capita income alone. The tax burden in Korea started at a low level by international standards (due largely to the substitution of AID revenues in the 1950s), but has risen rapidly under Park, particularly in the 1970s.

Enforcement is reflected not only in the level of tax collections, but (perhaps more important) in the composition of the tax burden. A widely held tenet of public finance is that direct taxes are superior to indirect taxes since they are less regressive and do not distort marginal incentives for the production of

TABLE 18 Tax Burden Trend, 1953–1976

(%)

Year	Tax/GNP		Year	Tax/GNP
1953	4.8		1965	8.6
1954	6.8		1966	10.8
1955	6.1		1967	12.0
1956	5.9		1968	14.4
1957	7.5		1969	15.1
1958	8.5		1970	15.4
1959	10.1		1971	15.6
1960	10.2		1972	13.5
1961	9.5		1973	13.2
1962	10.8		1974	15.1
1963	8.9		1975	17.1
1964	7.3		1976	18.3
		1953–1961 Average	7.71	
		1962–1966 Average	9.28	
		1967–1971 Average	14.50	
		1972–1976 Average	15.44	

Source: Central Government Taxes as percent of GNP from BOK, *National Income in Korea, 1976* (Seoul, 1976).

various goods and services. Nonetheless, LDCs around the world rely heavily on indirect taxes, most notably in the particularly pernicious form of import duties. This has less to do with LDC disagreement with economic precepts than with simple administrative expediency—it is a relatively simple matter to assess and tax goods at the dock; it is extremely difficult to assess and tax income and wealth. Reliance on import duties is thus a matter of necessity, not choice.

Korea is something of an exception to this rule. This is suggested by Table 20 which gives direct taxes as a share of total taxes for Korea as compared with that projected at Korea's level of income (based on Raja J. Chelliah's regression coefficients for fifty LDCs in 1966–1968).[57] Korea is seen to have had a substantially higher than average reliance on

TABLE 19 Korea's Tax Effort Ranking (among 52 LDCs)

	Indicator[b]	Korea[c] 1962–1964	Korea[d] 1973–1976
A.	T/Y	50	19
B.[a]	$T/Y = a_1 + b_1\, Y/P$	48	18
C.[a]	$T/Y = a_2 + b_2\, Y/P + c_2 \frac{X+M}{Y}$	46	26

Notes: [a]Ranking based on percentage deviation from trend lines estimated in source as:

B. $T/Y = 12.98 + 0.0080\ Y/P$
C. $T/Y = 10.21 + 0.0085\ Y/P + 0.0712 \frac{X+M}{Y}$

Jorgen Lotz and Elliot Morss, "Measuring 'Tax Effort' in Developing Countries." In *I.M.F. Staff Papers,* November 1967, pp. 478–499.

[b]$T \equiv$ total central and local tax receipts
$Y \equiv$ GNP
$P \equiv$ Population
$X \equiv$ Exports
$M \equiv$ Imports

[c]Ibid., pp. 488–489.

[d]Korean data from BOK, *Economic Statistics Yearbook, 1976* (Seoul, 1977), Constant dollar conversions from constant wŏn series made at rate used originally by Lotz and Morss.

direct taxes even in the Rhee period, but the gap widened markedly under Park.

Both of the foregoing tests (on relative size and composition of taxation) are low-order and hardly definitive. At minimum, however, they do not conflict with our hypothesis that tax collection is more rigorously enforced in Korea (particularly under Park) than in other LDCs at similar levels of income. A major reason for this is the Park Government's ability to collect corporate and personal income taxes, inheritance taxes, and the like. Again, this is a highly relativistic statement. In a dynamic society where the information gap is large and personal connections are traditionally strong, tax "irregularities" remain widespread. Nonetheless, the trend of collections is upwards and the level of compliance, while low by United States standards, is perhaps not dissimilar from that in France and decidely above that in most LDCs.

The second issue in the use of command is whether it is

TABLE 20 Direct Taxes as Percent of Total Taxes

Period	*Projected*[a]	*Actual*	*Actual/Projected*
1953–1955	25	34	1.36
1966–1968	28	42	1.50
1973–1976	33	50	1.50

Note: [a]Based on share expected at Korea's income level from: Raja J. Chelliah. "Trends in Taxation in Developing Countries," *I.M.F. Staff Papers,* July 1971, pp. 278, 283.

discretionary or non-discretionary. Worldwide, indirect taxes are predominantly administered in a non-discretionary fashion. This is because, with few exceptions, (for example, antiques exported by tourists), quantity or value or both are readily ascertainable and a per-unit or percent-of-value tax is easily and objectively calculated. This clarity of assessment is reflected both in the well-known preference of LDCs for indirect taxes and in the non-discretionary application of the command to pay. Korea is no exception to the latter rule, with indirect taxes administered in a largely non-discretionary fashion.

For administration of direct taxes, the story is more complicated. The Office of National Tax Administration was established in 1966 to increase tax revenue and to make the tax administration as non-discretionary as possible by elimination of corruption, tax evasion, and arbitrary tax assessment procedures. Enforcement is generally via the selective application of police action. This is reflected in the recent announcement of a tax investigation of 27 corporations based on The Law for Punishment of Tax Criminals.[58] If tax evasion is discovered through the investigation, the corporation will not only have to pay the additional taxes due plus a penalty of twice the additional tax, but the management will also be subject to criminal prosecution. The latter is not a laughing matter in Korea, and corporations consequently dread a tax investigation. The selection of the 27 corporations was based on the "degree of sincerity" in filing tax documents. Out of a total of 14,864 corporations filing tax returns, 916 corporations are classified as either "sincere-return corporations" or "semi-sincere-return corporations." The remaining 13,948 firms were eligible for audit, but only 27 were chosen in the first round. Substantial selectivity is apparent. A somewhat broader approach to the problem is represented by a recent announcement of the National Taxation Office that all cases of delinquency exceeding one million wŏn will be publicly announced.[59]

Despite such broad-based efforts, the essence of the enforcement mechanism remains highly selective police action. Selection is not based solely on the perceived possibility of non-compliance with tax laws. A firm is just as likely to be audited for non-compliance with various discretionary commands. Suppose the government has made a company aware of its patriotic duty to contribute a little extra to national defense in a time of national crisis. Suppose further that the company ignores its duty. It is then imaginable that the company may appear on the select list of those to be investigated. Good and sufficient grounds will undoubtedly be found for penalizing the firm for non-compliance with non-discretionary tax laws, but the managers will be excused for believing that they are really being penalized for ignoring a command. More important, other owners may have their patriotic conscience raised by the example.

In sum, selective enforcement of non-discretionary tax laws has two effects. First, it serves as a means of backing up partial mutuality, though it is decidely secondary to credit in this role. Second, it encourages firms to reduce their liability by filing increasingly accurate tax returns. Much remains to be done in this respect, but as the tax figures cited above show, Korea already does a highly creditable job of enforcing non-discretionary command.

CONSUMPTION BANS

One readily observable use of command is the prohibition of certain forms of consumption seen as immoral or contrary to specific economic interests. As examples, we consider non-tariff barriers to trade and the ban on foreign cigarettes.

Under both Rhee and Park, the government has endeavored to control imports, in part through non-tariff barriers. In both periods these controls have been administered with a mixture of discretion and non-discretion. However, two trends have been apparent. First, the mixture has shifted increasingly away from discretion. Second, enforcement of prohibitions has been stiffened.

Conceptually, one may think of three classes of imports:

1) Unrestricted items which may be imported in any quantity;
2) Restricted items which may be imported in limited quantity; and
3) Prohibited items which may not be imported at all.

Unrestricted items do not require intervention (except in the allocation of foreign exchange, considered above). Restricted items necessarily require discretion in allocation (assuming the quota is binding in that there is excess demand). Absolute prohibition is, by definition, non-discretionary command.

From 1946 to 1949, there was a permit system which simply distinguished between prohibited and permitted items.[60] There were no quantitative restrictions within the permitted list, so the only constraint was access to foreign exchange. The system was thus non-discretionary since there were no restricted items.

In 1949 a quota system was introduced, placing quantitative restrictions on catagories of permitted items, end-use, and source. The restricted category was thus added and discretion introduced. This led to much of the corruption and excess profits from imports already noted.

Following the 1955 devaluation, a more flexible system was introduced with the addition of a "positive" list of items whose import was unrestricted. Some items were thus removed from the discretionary realm.

Thereafter, there was a general movement of items out of the restricted category and into the unrestricted group, where tariffs were used to control quantity. A major change came in 1961 with the introduction of a "negative list" system under which items not otherwise specified were automatically placed in the unrestricted category. Nonetheless, the restricted category remained substantial. In 1970, out of 1,312 "basic" items, 73 were prohibited, 524 were restricted, and 715 were unrestricted.[61] In addition, special approval was required for imports from countries with whom Korea showed a trade deficit.

While ample room for discretion thus remains in the system, it does not seem to be particularly problematic. Unlike the Rhee period, there are few, if any, complaints of favoritism and bribery in allocation of quotas. This is due to some combination of three factors. First, the equilibrium exchange rate reduces the excess profit to be gained from privileged access. Second, some of the restrictions may be non-binding. Third, the bureaucracy seems to use reasonable economic criteria in allocating permission to qualified end-users (that is, to producers needing particular intermediates). While the discretionary realm was thus reduced between the Rhee and Park periods, a more important difference was the manner in which discretion was exercised.

A second issue involves the degree to which prohibited items (and over-quota restricted items) are effectively banned. No hard information is available, but the incentives for under-invoicing and smuggling were greater under Rhee and enforcement almost certainly more lax. Under Park, enforcement has been serious, if not foolproof. The best known case involved the excessive import of saccharine (legitimately needed in small quantities as a catalyst) for the Korean Fertilizer Co., Ltd.'s plant in 1966, and resulted in the bulk of the plant's equity being forfeited to the government.[62]

The effectiveness with which non-discretionary command is enforced under Park may be illustrated with regard to foreign cigarette manufacture. The government enjoys a monopoly of domestic cigarette production, so that it not unsurprisingly bans imports. This was true under Rhee as well as Park, the difference being the level of enforcement. Under Rhee, the situation was similar to many countries (such as the pre-martial-law Philippines) with the ban ignored by all concerned. Today, foreign cigarettes are still sometimes smoked in private, but seldom, if ever, in public. This is not primarily due to reduced PX supply, since this would result in a much higher mark-up (not observed) unless demand also shifted. Part of the reduction in demand is due to a change in the popular attitude towards foreign cigarette smoking, which is now considered to be "un-Korean." There has also been a marked step-up in enforcement.

The Cigarette Monopoly Law of December 1972 provides explicit and severe penalities for buying, selling, or using foreign cigarettes. In the case of selling and buying for resale, the fine ranges from 50,000 up to 1,000,000 wŏn depending on the quantity of cigarettes involved. In the case of giving, receiving, or possession of cigarettes worth more than 1,600 wŏn, the fine ranges from 30,000 wŏn up to 500,000 wŏn depending on the quantity involved. In both cases, both buyer and seller are subject to punishment and may also be sent to jail (for up to ten years in the case of buying for resale). Further, rewards are provided to those who inform on illegal smokers and to those who arrest them. These rewards are large enough that small boys are sometimes found where passenger cars wait for traffic signal changes and report observed smoking violations to inspectors with whom they share the bounty. The Park Government is obviously serious about the ban.

Other luxury imports are also banned under the 1961 Law Prohibiting Sales of Special Foreign Products. Again, offenders are severely punished, being subjected to up to ten years' imprisonment and/or a fine of five to twenty times the price of the commodity. The government rewards informers with an amount equivalent to 30 percent of the price of the commodity at the time of the confiscation. This is not mere formalism. In 1974, a diamond smuggling scandal among wives led to the resignation of two ministers and other high government officials and public enterprise executives.[63]

In sum, non-discretionary command is widely used in Korea.

The unique thing is not its level, but the fact that it is generally enforced.

DISCRETIONARY COMMAND IN PRACTICE

Discretionary command is, in principle, the least desirable form of intervention because it combines compulsion with the potential for administrative abuse. It has, nonetheless, been extensively used in Korea, often to good effect. We consider three variants: informal guidance, formal directives, and price controls.

INFORMAL GUIDANCE

The first type of discretionary command occurs when someone in the government decides that a particular action should be taken by a particular firm and communicates this desire with more or less subtlety. This may have the objective of collecting contributions for some quasi-public purpose, but it may also take the form of a quick and expedient solution of a problem which is not generalizable. Use of this mechanism is difficult to document, but a few stories serve to illustrate the phenomenon.

One widely told tale along this line concerns a Seoul skyscraper which remained unfinished for an extended period due to a variety of administrative and financial difficulties. It is said that President Park was driving by one day, noted the lack of progress and the blight on the skyline, and instructed an aide to make the problem go away. The building quickly changed ownership and was completed in record time. Another example is President Park's alleged response to the news that no international finance could be found for the Hyundai shipyard, and the project would have to be abandoned. His initial angry response was a thinly veiled threat of the form— "If you only want to do what's easy, then you'll get no more help from us." This was followed, after an interval, by an impassioned patriotic plea for the national interest. The result was a renewed effort by Hyundai and the successful completion of a project which would not have gone forward without the personal "urging" of the President.[64]

A third example occurred in late 1975 when large trade deficits raised international doubts about the nation's ability to service further foreign debt. This was particularly troublesome, since at the time a major effort was being made to increase foreign borrowing. To convince foreigners that long-term export prospects were as good as the government felt they were, it was obviously desirable that 1975 export figures be as high as possible. Accordingly, it is said that exporters were given a strong suggestion to speed deliveries and to make whatever paper adjustments they could to enhance December performance figures.

Stories such as these may be apocryphal in any given instance, but occur so frequently, and are given such currency, that they clearly represent a common phenomenon. Informal guidance is ubiquitous, but its quantitative importance is impossible to assess.

FORMAL COMMAND: FORCING FIRMS TO GO PUBLIC

Discretionary command is more readily documented when the instructions are formalized. One major variant occurs when field manipulations fail to achieve a given end with sufficient rapidity, and certain firms are chosen to volunteer for the privileges being conferred. A revealing example of the use of command to supplement inadequate field manipulation involves the series of measures designed to "encourage" closely held private companies to make public offerings of their shares. We outline a series of four measures aimed at this end between 1968 and 1975. These show a clear trend towards increasing use of discretionary command to replace (or supplement) non-discretionary field manipulation.

The 1968 Law for the Promotion of the Capital Market had

as its objective "The development of the capital market by inducing privately-held firms to go public and creating a favorable investment environment in which people's participation in business affairs and domestic resource mobilization are to be facilitated."[65] As incentives, the law provided for various tax privileges for firms that "went public," but these proved ineffective. A new and stronger law was legislated in December 1972—the Law for Inducing Business Corporations to go Public. Field manipulation incentives were expanded but, more important, command provisions were added. Punitive measures could now be taken against certain corporations that failed to "go public." Provision was made for unfavorable tax treatment including a 20 percent penalty on the company's corporate income tax and a similar levy on the personal income tax of majority shareholders. Perhaps more important, the Minister of Finance was allowed to direct financial institutions to restrict credit to these firms. Further, targets were to be selected in a discretionary fashion. According to the law, the Minister of Finance shall select "appropriate corporations" based on the total paid-in capital, financial situation, ability to pay dividends, stock trading prospects, the general securities market trend, and so on, from among "eligible corporations."

The impact of the law was positive. In 1973, firms listed on the Korean Stock Exchange increased by 41, roughly equivalent to the 42 firms added during the entire 1968–1972 period. This was largely due to field manipulation as the command powers of 1972 law were not used.

Nonetheless, few of the chaebŏl group firms participated in the program, rejecting the benefits in favor of traditional closely held management pattern. Concern over the chaebŏl problem led to the May 29 Presidential Special Directives of 1974. These placed rather extraordinary restraints on chaebŏl behavior (for example, certain groups were prohibited from receiving further foreign loan guarantees, establishing or acquiring new companies, investing in stock, or acquiring non-operating real estate). These measures are described in detail in

Chapter 8 in the specific context of the problem of business concentration. Here we only note that the command elements of the 1972 law were now brought into play and applied to particular groups and firms selected in a discretionary fashion.

In the year following the special directives, 48 additional firms went public, but again with less than desired response from major chaebŏl. Accordingly, the August 8 Measure of 1975 extended coverage to the main holding companies (only subsidiaries had previously been included), and established a specific time schedule for compliance.

This example has illustrated the way in which formal discretionary command is used to supplement supposedly non-discretionary field manipulation. It also suggests the perseverance of the bureaucracy in pursuing an objective established at the top, and the flexibility of the search for a tool to achieve that end. To date, the effort can hardly be termed a success, though the number of firms listed in the stock exchange has increased from 66 at the end of 1972 to 251 as of October 1976. Nonetheless, a learning process has been taking place and the trend is clear.

PRICE CONTROLS

Price controls are the final variant of discretionary command that we consider. These are field manipulations from the point of view of the buyer, but commands from the perspective of the seller. The former element dominates when the primary goal is to subsidize consumers through low public enterprise prices, as discussed above. The command element dominates when there is a broad-based effort to control private prices as part of an anti-inflationary effort. It is this latter use which is considered here.

Price stabilization policies include:

1) Aggregate demand management via fiscal and monetary policy,
2) Aggregate supply management through foreign-aid financed imports,
3) Indirect price controls via wage-good price policies (for

example, through Public Law 480 imports and domestic grain price manipulation), and

4) Direct administrative price controls.

Briefly, in Korea the second and third (AID related) methods predominated in the post-Korean War Rhee period and were gradually supplanted by more conventional aggregate demand management policies. Administrative price controls were heavily used during the inter-war and Korean War years, withered under Rhee, and were reimposed under Park, though with varying degrees of intensity.[66] It is these efforts to stabilize prices administratively (microeconomic intervention) which will concern us in the remainder of this section.

Before detailing the rise and fall of administrative price control efforts, it is useful to distinguish three distinct sets of circumstances in which they might be used:

1) Sustained across-the-board efforts as a substitute for aggregate demand management,
2) Short-term, across-the-board efforts aimed at controlling excess profits in the disequilibrium wake of a shock such as devaluation, revolution, tax reform, or the oil price explosion, and
3) Selective efforts designed to achieve competitive price levels in monopolistic or oligopolistic markets.

The first method is typically, though not necessarily, administered in a non-discretionary fashion. The latter two, if rational, are necessarily non-discretionary. The first takes the form: "Thou shalt not raise prices more than X percent" and is thus non-discretionary. The others take the form: "Thou shalt raise prices only to the extent justified by real increases in costs." Ascertaining "real increases in costs," of course, requires case-by-case discretionary examination, whether in United States regulatory practice or in determining legitimate pass-throughs of oil-price increases.

Sustained across-the-board price control (#1 above), although beloved of politicians, is probably doomed to failure for the traditional "squeezing a balloon" set of reasons. Selective short-term controls (in circumstances #2 and #3 above) are certainly justifiable government interventions, though their efficacy varies with the wisdom of their administrators.

Under Park, with one notable exception, price controls have generally been either selective or short-term, and in pursuit of defensible economic goals. They have therefore been largely and necessarily discretionary. The exception is the 1972 to 1973 period when controls were used in a sustained broad-based effort to control prices, with predictable deleterious results.

The first instance of short-term price controls under Park occurred in May 1961 when the new Military Government announced a temporary freeze on prices at their pre-revolutionary levels. The goal was to prevent profiteering in an unsettled environment when uncertainty gives sellers a temporary disequilibrium advantage over buyers. Two months later, the freeze was replaced by the Temporary Law on Price Control which placed price ceilings on "critical" commodities such as rice, barley, coal, and fertilizer. These were largely under the control of public enterprises in any event. More items were added later, but the system withered away following the re-emphasis on aggregated demand management with the financial stabilization program of 1963.

The balance of the 1960s saw what Soon Chough calls an "informal price supervision" system.[67] That is, there were no formal control procedures, but the government exercised "persuasion" on various producers' associations to forestall "undesirable" price increases. Enforcement of these discretionary commands was through partial mutuality–implicit threats of credit restraint, tax investigation, stricter applications of sanitary standards, and so on. As Chough puts it: "There is no legal basis for the working of this system, but the government influence goes beyond what laws or regulations stipulate."[68] Application of these methods was discontinuous, with efforts intensified during the big spending sprees preceding Ch'usŏk (Autumn Moon Festival) and Sŏl (Lunar New Year).

A major change in the price control system followed the August 3, 1972 Emergency Measure Regarding Economic

Stability and Growth. One announced goal of the measure was to keep annual price increases below 3 percent. This ambitious target was to be achieved, in part, by a series of administrative controls which were broad-based and across-the-board rather than selective.

The policy was similar to, and clearly influenced by, the Nixon freeze of one year earlier, but was pursued with a uniquely Korean vengeance. A freeze on prices of all commodities was announced. If unbearable cost-push pressures developed in any one industry, they were to be offset not by a cost-pass-through price increase but by offsetting indirect subsidies. The Office of National Tax Administration set up 460 "mobile price control patrols" and 80 "price assurance forces" to check for price increases. Where "gouging" was found, violators were subjected to an immediate tax investigation, a special excess profits tax, and curtailment of credit. Moral suasion was also attempted through a major meeting between government and business leaders.

Results of these efforts were predictable. Producers resorted to under-the-table payments, product-mix realignments and other devices to avoid the controls. The government responded with quantitative restrictions (production quotas) and daily checks on shipments of major producers. In March 1973, a Law on Price Stability was passed prohibiting sales at greater-than-ceiling prices and prohibiting restricted shipments. In December 1973, the freeze was lifted, but prior approval was required for price increases. Sixty-three major commodities were controlled by EPB, and the remainder by concerned ministries. For EPB-controlled commodities, there was provision for special tariff reductions, import financing, and capital equipment and operating loans as an alternative to price increases. The usual partial mutuality penalties for non-compliance were also listed.

The pressures that built up under the system were exacerbated by the 1973 oil shock and led to a return to the old philosophy of selective controls on February 5, 1974. The DPM described the change by announcing that, "unlike the past price stability measure relying primarily on the administrative direct control power the new measure will be operated according to the natural price mechanism supplemented by some administrative control."[69] Prior restraint was abolished on all but 32 items, and for these products, price increases of 9.1 percent over February 5 prices were allowed (21.5 percent over November 15, 1973 base prices).

A new chapter in the price control story was added with the Law on Price Stability and Fair Trade of December 1975. This shifted the focus of selective control from temporary disequilibria (motive #2) to controlling oligopolistic and monopolistic markets (motive #3). Reflecting the government's increased concern with the problem of industrial concentration, this law was applicable to firms which:

1) Captured more than 30 percent of sales in any industry.
2) Captured more than 20 percent of sales in a concentrated industry (defined as having a three-firm concentration ratio of 60 percent).
3) "Practically dominate those industries which supply critically important goods and services for the national economy."[70]

Temporary disequilibria controls were of course not abandoned. In July 1977, the government introduced a value-added tax and accompanied it with intensive checks on 850 commodities to preclude pass-throughs in excess of those justified by the tax increases.[71]

In sum, the Park Government has throughout its tenure used administrative price controls in short-term across-the-board efforts aimed at controlling excess profits in disequilibrium situations such as revolution, devaluation, oil shock, tax reform, or holidays. More recently, it has used them in an effort to achieve competitive price levels in monopolistic or oligopolistic markets. Both motivations are completely rational from the standpoint of market-failure analysis—the unregulated market fails so the government can usefully intervene. In both cases, the behavioral intervention mechanism is necessarily discretionary command.

The major exception to the foregoing generalization is the brief one-and-one-half year period from August 1972 to February 1974. Here the government attempted sustained across-the-board controls. The predictable failure, and consequent reversal, of this effort should not be interpreted as illustrating the ultimate triumph of any underlying laissez-faire government philosophy. If anything, the reverse may be true. The government's readiness to intervene was overcome only by blatantly unsatisfactory economic consequences. Certain forms of intervention simply do not work, and sustained across-the-board price controls is one of them. This having been demonstrated, the government's dominant concern for efficiency and growth asserted itself at the expense of an interventionist proclivity in February 1974. The one-and-a-half year attempt at broad-based price controls was thus a brief aberration. Nonetheless, it illustrates several features of intervention in Korea: first, a willingness to intervene directly and pervasively via command; second, the capacity to enforce the command (insofar as price controls are ever enforceable); third, the willingness to try out a new control system (stimulated here by United States price control efforts); and fourth, flexibility in reversing direction once a conflict with growth and efficiency became apparent.

DISCRETION AND COMMAND: A CASE STUDY

We have argued that the Korean government actively uses its discretionary powers to intervene in the operation of individual business enterprises. We now illustrate the process in detail through a case study of the Korean Machinery Manufacturing Corporation (henceforth, "Han'gi"—a contraction of its Korean name).

The origin of the company dates back to June 1937 when it started under Japanese ownership as the Chosun Machinery

Manufacturing Company. After Liberation, the company became a departmental enterprise operated directly by the Ministry of Commerce and Industry. Control was transferred to the Ministry of National Defense in 1950 and then back to the Ministry of Commerce and Industry in 1961. In May 1963, however, it became an autonomous public corporation, established according to a special law. These earlier status alternations represented typcial bureaucratic conflicts over control of a major public enterprise, while the 1963 shift was an attempt at moving towards more autonomy and rational management.

The paid-in capital was officially 214 million wŏn in 1964, but this was a paper transaction in the sense that the government converted a KDB (Korea Development Bank) loan into equity. No cash was paid in. In 1964, the government again increased its capital base to 627 million wŏn simply by the revaluation of existing assets. The first actual government cash input came in 1965 when 73 million wŏn was provided to finance the plant and equipment and increase the company's capital base to 700 million wŏn. Given this equity base, the company had no choice but to rely on external debt for financing both operations and investment. In addition, the company had never experienced an operating surplus. The result was a continuing financial burden on the government, and a state in which Han'gi's very existence was in danger.

In 1968, the government initiated a policy of divestiture under which a number of public enterprises were to be sold to the private sector. As part of this process, Han'gi was sold to Shinjin Automobile Manufacturing Company. Some of the shares were to be sold publicly, but as with other divestitures at the same time, these were heavily undersubscribed. As a result, the government assigned roughly one-third of the equity shares to various of its commercial banks in lieu of paid-in capital. In addition, because of the large loans made or guaranteed by KDB, and the shaky financial position, the company was placed under the supervision of KDB's Special Administration Division. This meant that KDB appointed one director and followed the company's affairs closely.

Nonetheless, the company was under private operational control, the stated objective of the divestiture having been to improve the company's efficiency and financial performance by rationalizing management. Deficits, nonetheless, continued and the company eventually filed a petition to the government for its rescue in August 1971. The petition argued that the company was the "backbone" of the machinery industry which in turn was strategic for the nation's development.

Upon getting the petition, the concerned economic ministers adopted Measures for the Korean Machinery Manufacturing Corporation Account Improvement in December 1971 in view of "the company's position in the machinery industry." These measures were reported to the President in a meeting on the promotion of machinery, heavy, and chemical industries in January 1972. Then, actual measures were taken in April 1972 according to the Prime Minister's directive on Measures for Korean Machinery Manufacturing Corporation.

The major thrust of these measures was to relieve the company from its immediate debt service burden by replacing high-interest loans with low-interest loans, extending loan repayment schedules, making provisions for installment payments, and converting some KDB loans into equity. Cheaper KDB funds, tagged for promoting the machine industry, were used to replace a large portion of more expensive commercial bank and curb-market loans. Repayment of some outstanding KDB loans was postponed with an installment provision. At the same time, some interest charges in arrears on KDB loans were written off. In addition, the government promised tariff protection on diesel engines Han'gi planned to produce.

In return for all these favors, Shinjin was asked to increase substantially its equity base in Han'gi. Even more important, a substantial portion of the newly-planned diesel engine plant was to be financed by Shinjin itself.

These measures were effective in the short run, but continuing operating deficits and requirements for expansion forced the firm back to debt funding, including high-interest curb-market loans. By 1974 the company was in even worse condition than at the time of the 1972 rescue operation.

While the company's financial picture got grimmer and grimmer, the government issued its so-called May 29 Presidential Special Directives and the follow-up Measures on Bank Credit and Business Concentration issued by the Ministry of Finance. These required chaebŏl groups with high debt/equity ratios to correct their financial structure by selling off some firms and divesting themselves of non-operating assets. Han'gi, as a member of the Shinjin Group, was subject to these regulations.

In July 1974, the Council on Correcting the Financial Structure of Business Corporations, presided over by the Prime Minister, adopted specific measures for the Shinjin Group in general and Han'gi in particular. The council was worried that Han'gi's diesel engine and railway passenger car projects were underfinanced, might not be completed rapidly, and might face operational problems if completed. This was unacceptable because: both diesel engines and railway passenger cars were deemed critical products; and the government had arranged and guaranteed a West German loan for the diesel engine plant.

The council, therefore, ordered the Shinjin Group to sell off all its firms except Han'gi itself and Shinjin's joint ventures (for example, General Motors Korea Co., Ltd. and Shinjin Jeep), and to further divest itself of all non-operating real estate owned either by the companies or by the majority shareholders. The proceeds were then to be ploughed back into Han'gi. With the equity base thus improved, the government would then order domestic financial institutions to support Han'gi by: replacing high interest short-term loans with low interest long-term loans; postponing repayment of short-term loans; and designating Han'gi as "an industrial rationalization firm."

The Shinjin Group was directed to file with the Board of Bank Supervision a detailed plan for implementation of these directives, and this it did. However, in January 1975, the group filed a revised plan proposing that proceeds from real estate sales and divestiture be used to build up Shinjin Autombile Manufacturing Company (the group's holding company) and not for Han'gi. The group argued that the parent company was in trouble since it produced nothing itself, was earning minimal dividends from its troubled companies, and yet was burdened with paying foreign debts inflated by the recent devaluation. Shinjin therefore proposed that group resources not be used to bail out Han'gi, but that Han'gi should expand its own equity base. A public offering of Han'gi stock being deemed impossible because of low market valuation, it was suggested that most bank debt be converted into equity. This would have made KDB the majority shareholder and the company would have returned to the status of a full-fledged public enterprise.

Segments of the government are known to have considered this proposal seriously, but within a few months the issue was resolved by sale of Han'gi to Daewoo Group.[72] It is not known whether the government or Daewoo took the initiative in effecting this sale, but it is certain that the deal would not have been consummated without approval from the highest levels of the hierarchy. From the government's perspective, the sale was desirable as a means of bringing improved management to what was perceived as a growth sector. Shinjin had proven incompetent, and the KDB option was not particularly appealing given the government's general policy direction to sell off some of her existing subsidiaries. Daewoo held promise as the fastest growing new group, the only question being whether expertise gained primarily in light industry could be adapted to machinery.

Whatever the future of Han'gi, its past illustrates several features of government-business interaction in Korea. First, the government is pragmatic in choosing between public and private operation on rational rather than ideological grounds. Second, the government is prepared to intervene at any level deemed necessary to promote economic growth. Third, there is no reluctance to use direct command as opposed to indirect parameter manipulation. Fourth, the intervention can be highly discretionary with decisions made on a company-by-company basis. Fifth, credit is often the instrument around which intervention coalesces. Sixth, these discretionary decisions regularly reach the highest tiers of the administration.

The reader should not be left with the impression that this is a typical company. In fact, it is unique in having one of the worst performance records of any major Korean enterprise. It is for this reason that it has drawn such heavy government attention and allowed us to demonstrate a wide range of government intervention mechanisms in a single company. While the quantity of intervention is thus atypical, the quality is not. The characteristics of the intervention process described here are the essence of the implementation process in Korea. Discretion and command are ubiquitous.

THE EFFICACY OF DISCRETION AND COMMAND IN A "HARD" STATE

THE PARADOX OF IMPLEMENTATION IN KOREA

We have argued that field-manipulation and non-discretionary forms of intervention are generally held preferable on theoretical grounds, but we have demonstrated that Korea has relied heavily on both discretion and command. This paradox must now be explained.

Note that the question does not arise from the government's *willingness* to use discretion and command, but from its *ability* to do so effectively. LDCs around the world rely on these methods of implementation, and this is generally held to be one of their problems. Our task here is to explain why discretion and command are part of the solution in Korea.

In brief, our answer is that Korea is a "hard state." Myrdal defines a "soft state" as a country where "Policies decided on are often not enforced, if they are enacted at all . . . (and where) the authorities, even when framing policies, are reluctant to place obligations on people."[73] In contrast, he implicitly defines a "hard state"[74] in arguing that "the success of planning for development requires a readiness to place obligations on people in all social strata to a much greater extent than is now done . . . (and it) . . . requires, in addition, rigorous enforcement of obligations, in which compulsion plays a strategic role."[75]

The importance of this conclusion has not been recognized by the academic community, but it has been manifest in the revealed preferences of a generation of LDC political leaders who have shown increasing impatience with the impediments of softness. Myrdal's work is based on observations of the weaknesses of soft states, with the advantages of hardness hypothesized in the abstract. Korea under Park Chung Hee, however, provides a concrete example of hardness in action.

A label, of course, is not an explanation, however appropriate it may be. We now elaborate on two major determinants of hardness—the ability to enforce obligations via compulsion, and the ability to direct administrative discretion towards desirable ends.

COMPULSION

Compulsion is not a highly regarded virtue, and yet it is central to overcoming the problems of development. To avoid being branded a fascist for such an assertion, it is comforting to have the backing of a renowned liberal and Nobel prize winner such as Myrdal who believes:

> There is little hope in South Asia for rapid development without greater social discipline. To begin with, in the absence of more discipline—*which will not appear without regulations backed by compulsion*—all measures for rural uplift will be largely ineffective.[76]

This conclusion is by no means limited to South Asia and the rural sector. This follows from certain fundamental propositions on conditions in LDCs. To begin with, market imperfections require some form of government intervention. As indicated earlier, non-compulsory field manipulation is most desirable. Field manipulation is, however, limited in its ability to overcome many market imperfections. Command must be resorted to in some areas such as raising public revenue and enforcing standards. In many other areas, command is far quicker than field manipulation even if the latter will ultimately work.

Send an outsider to manipulate a village's field with credit and news of a magic seed that will quadruple yields. Only someone who is really crazy will believe a story like that, and the supply of such people is limited. At the end of one crop year, you will therefore have only a minute fraction of the potential area under the new grain, with a few more coming on the second year, and the bulk in the third. Discretionary command could have accomplished the same thing in one year. There is, of course, the attendant possibility of the outsider being wrong and the whole crop being destroyed by blight. Discretionary command is fast, but very risky and accordingly needs to be administered with skill or luck or both.

As more germane examples, consider the establishment of Hyundai Shipbuilding and Heavy Industries Co., Ltd., Pohang Iron and Steel Co., Ltd. and the opening up of closely held family corporations to public ownership.[77] All of these might well have happened eventually with sufficient parameter manipulation, but they occurred as early as they did as a result of command.

The question, then, is not whether or not command is necessary for rapid development, but the wisdom of the ends towards which it is directed and the degree to which it is enforced. The previous chapter discussed the policy formulation process, and here we have explained enforcement as being accomplished through either police action or partial mutuality. The former is used largely in enforcing non-discretionary commands, while the latter is the enforcement mechanism for discretionary command.

The use of police, like other scarce resources, needs to be

economized. Enforcement must therefore, of necessity, be selective but, when dramatic and well publicized, it may have a widespread deterrent effect. The selection process itself may or may not follow a random process. For example, the inspection of anti-pollution devices on diesel-engined buses was probably a random event, while the inspection of inheritance tax evasion may well be discretionary and aimed at someone who has violated an explicit or implicit discretionary command.

Partial mutuality may be defined in the articulate language of Koopmans and Montias[78] or with the pithy phrase, "You get along by going along." In any event, it is the dominant means of enforcing discretionary command and includes some combination of:

1) The controllee's expectation of possible police action to enforce previously loosely enforced non-discretionary commands (for example, tax laws).
2) Implicit threats of the withdrawal or withholding of privileges attained (or hoped for) under discretionary field manipulation.
3) Appeals to "legitimacy" in the form of patriotism or national interest.

This may be a subtle form of compulsion, but it is compulsion nonetheless.

The entrepreneurship survey provides some support, albeit weak, for our hypothesis on the importance of partial mutuality. Respondents were asked how often various compliance mechanisms were used by the government (see Table 21). "Friendly persuasion" ranked first, followed by "Moral exhortation," "Making example of one firm," "Incentives and privileges," and "Explicit threats." The first three all reflect partial mutuality, particularly "Friendly persuasion" which is the reigning euphemism. Given the biases inherent in our survey and their low statistical significance,[79] we do not wish to make too much of these results, but they are certainly not inconsistent with our hypothesis.

The effective use of compulsion in pursuit of economic goals

TABLE 21 Businessmen's Perceptions of Government Compliance Methods

Question: "If the government wishes to influence the conduct of a business, how important are the following means of insuring compliance?"

Response Scaling

Used Very Often		Sometimes Used		Never Used
1	2	3	4	5

Mean Responses (n = 118)

	All Firms	*Large*[a]	*Small*[a]	*Export*[b]	*Domestic*[b]
Incentives, privileges	3.65	3.47	3.70	3.53	3.77
Moral exhortation	3.45	3.18	3.49	3.33	3.55
"Friendly persuasion"	3.30	2.82 [c]	3.37	3.10	3.42
Making example of one firm	3.58	3.38	3.62	3.62	3.54
Explicit threats	4.17	3.69 [c]	4.26	4.18	4.20

Source: Entrepreneurship Survey, see Appendix C.

Notes: [a]"Large" companies are those in top-quintile of respondent value-added distribution.

[b]"Exporters" are those who derive more than 50% of revenue from exports.

[c]= difference significant at 5% level.

has hardly been a constant in the post-war equation. Indeed, the Rhee regime fits in perfectly to Myrdal's soft state categorization. This should be apparent from our earlier discussion, but it is worth considering the opinions expressed in our entrepreneurship survey. Table 22 gives the entrepreneurship survey responses to the question as to how effective the government was in insuring compliance with government instructions. One could not ask for a more striking confirmation of the transformation of a soft state into a hard one.[80] Under Rhee, only 3 percent said that it was impossible to avoid complying with government decisions, as opposed to 78 percent under Park.

It may be that Rhee could have enforced economic interven-

TABLE 22 "Hardness" of Implementation: Rhee Versus Park

Question: "Once the current government has made a decision affecting business, how effective is it in insuring compliance? What about the Rhee Government?"

Responses

		Percent	
		Current	*Rhee*
Always implemented: impossible to avoid complying		78.2	3.2
Almost always implemented: sometimes possible to avoid complying		16.6	17.2
Implemented with modification		1.7	50.5
Seldom thoroughly implemented		3.5	29.0
	TOTAL	100.0	99.9
		Numbers	
	Response	172	93
	No opinion	24	103
	TOTAL	196	196

Source: Entrepreneurship Survey, see Appendix C.

tion had he tried to do so and that the softness of his regime in economic matters was a result of his giving priority to other matters. The hardness of Park's Korea may thus be as much a result of his leadership commitment to growth as of his authoritarian military background. Whatever the causal factor, it seems that effective economic compulsion is a dominant characteristic of the Korean economic miracle.

THE PROBLEM OF DISCRETION

There is a problem in designing intervention mechanisms. Some degree of selectivity is required in order to identify the particular behavior which is to be promoted or proscribed. The greater the specificity, the finer the possible tuning. Privileged access to credit is one example. The government might wish to finance housing purchases by low income groups but not by the rich; or, it might wish to finance purchases of capital goods, but not land speculation. To distinguish between such groups requires specificity and selectivity. The difficulty is that this leads to administrative discretion which is subject to the abuses cited by Myrdal.[81]

One way out, suggested by Myrdal, is to rely on carefully defined legal rules which can then be automatically, though selectively, applied with a minimum of administrative discretion. That is, high legal detail can narrow the gap between discretion in principle and discretion in practice. This is not the Korean solution. Instead, rather general laws are utilized and substantial administrative discretion is allowed.

This reliance on the "rule of men" rather than the "rule of law" is not necessarily irrational. In the first place, tightly defined laws are exceedingly difficult to construct in a rapidly changing economy where intervention requirements change and where special cases abound. In many areas of industrial policy, therefore, scarce administrative talent can be better spent using general guidelines to deal with investment projects on a case-by-case basis than in framing laws which cover all possible situations, many of which will not eventuate. This is not to argue that case-by-case decision-making is ideal, but only that it is not irrational in the earlier, less complicated stages of development planning.

There is a second reason why the legalistic solution is of limited use. However specific the regulation, someone in authority must ultimately attest to the applicants meeting those requirements. In the presence of official venality, the heightened specificity can itself provide marvelous opportunities for delay and corruption. Consider the various commands involved in the name of public safety—fire, sanitation, and building codes. Throughout the world these are often spelled out in great detail, but are, nonetheless, subject to great administrative abuse precisely for that reason. In at least one Asian country, construction of industrial plants was regularly delayed several months because of the necessity to get fire department approval of construction plans, and subsequent payoffs were regularly required for construction to proceed.

Now it is, of course, perfectly legitimate, indeed mandatory, for government to enforce such standards so there will always be an ample supply of corruption opportunities in any country. If, in addition, fields are widely manipulated as in LDCs, then it is not surprising that "no major and, indeed, few minor business decisions can be taken except with the prior permission of the administrative authorities or, at the risk of subsequent government disapproval."[82] This judgment is as true for Korea as it is for other LDCs.

What is unique in Park's Korea is that the discretionary controls are administered in such a way as not to seriously impede the progress of business. This is not to say the controls are administered in a disinterested impersonal fashion according to the Western administrative ideal. On the contrary, administration is highly personalized and value is not infrequently returned for value given. The difference is that this process is not allowed to impede the processing of business documents.

The explanation for this does not lie primarily in the quality of the civil service, any particular aversion to pecuniary awards, or any specific effort at minimizing opportunities for discretion. Instead, it follows from leadership commitment to growth in a hard state where hierarchical command is rigidly enforced. Economic growth under private enterprise being well understood as the dominant system goal, officials can seldom afford to act in a manner that seriously obstructs that goal.

In sum, the lesson of the Korean case is that in a hard state with leadership commitment to growth, the Myrdalian objections to discretionary controls on economic grounds may be obviated. Just as compulsion is necessary, so also is discretion. Both mechanisms are potentially subject to great abuse, and their use constitutes a high-risk/high-gain strategy which is feasible only in a Myrdalian hard state.

BENEFITS AND COSTS

We have argued that Park Chung Hee's establishment of a hard state in Korea has been instrumental and effective in achieving a high rate of economic growth. Nothing has been said about whether the process has also been efficient in achieving these benefits at minimum cost. Hardness, after all, is a multi-edged sword which can cut in several directions, and must, at best, be considered a necessary evil.

The possible costs of the hard development model include negative effects on income distribution, concentration of economic power, and civil liberties. Available evidence suggests that by international standards Korea has actually done quite well on the income distribution side, with the income of the lowest 40 percent growing at roughly the same rate as the economy as a whole during the 1960s.[83] A few individuals at the top are obscenely rich, but this is the price the country has paid for a tripling of real income of the poor in fifteen years. The judgment on power distribution is somewhat more mixed, but we shall argue in Chapter 8 that the hardness of the state has been used to keep private economic power well below the levels it might otherwise have achieved. It is in the realm of civil liberties that the costs of hardness are clear, and this is a major, if not dominant, offset to the economic successes of the regime. Even here, however, it is not at all clear that political suppression is a necessary concomitant of hardness. Until the early 1970s, the Park regime was both hard and reasonably democratic.

Future costs must also be considered. As the economy grows increasingly complex, administrative discretion becomes proportionally more difficult to exercise intelligently. As market mechanisms develop, discretionary intervention becomes less necessary.

History's overall judgment of the Park regime will ultimately rest on the degree to which these present and future costs are minimized. For the moment, we can only make the single-dimensional judgment that effective implementation via hardness has been a major causal factor in achieving Korea's phenomenal rate of economic growth from 1961 to 1975.

FIVE

Public Enterprise[1]

THE PUBLIC-ENTERPRISE SECTOR

A minor paradox of Korean development is that an ostensibly private-enterprise economy has utilized the intervention mechanism of public ownership to an extent which parallels that of many countries advocating a socialist pattern of society. This reflects the fundamental pragmatism of Park's approach to development, which is non-ideological in the sense of being goal-oriented rather than process-oriented. In overcoming private market imperfections that impede growth, the government has selected intervention mechanisms on the basis of results rather than ideological consistency. The choice has often been public enterprise.

This chapter first traces the historical origins of the public enterprise sector (pp. 143–147) and documents its role as a leading sector in the rapid-growth period (pp. 148–155). We then evaluate the causes and consequences of the choice of this particular microeconomic tool (pp. 148–159). We begin with a bit of semantic clarification.

Public ownership is often thought of as the most thoroughgoing form of government microeconomic intervention. In practice, the public-private distinction is often blurred. On the one hand, as demonstrated in Chapter 4, the private sector is by no means immune from the manipulations of the visible hand. On the other, international experience yields numerous examples of public enterprises operating with as much autonomy as private companies.[2] Public enterprises are thus by no means unique in being subject to the government's will. They are, however, distinct in the means by which that will is imposed (a variant of discretionary command) and the behavioral consequences of that choice (for example, lessening of profit pressure and attendant lack of cost consciousness). It, therefore, forms a useful unit of economic observation, just as do the regulated industries in the United States.

A unit of observation must be distinct as well as useful. The public-private boundary is a continuum in several dimensions, so any definition is necessarily arbitrary. Boundary specification is nonetheless essential if we are to quantify the contributions of a unique sector. We, therefore, define a public enterprise as a productive entity which is owned, or controlled, or both by a public authority and which produces a marketed output. A "productive entity" is an identifiable decision-making unit with an explicit or extractable budget and which produces goods or services. "Ownership" refers to equity holdings (direct and/or indirect) of more than 10 percent. "Control" refers to the power to be involved in the internal decision-making process, most commonly through the right to appoint top management. An output is "marketable" if sales cover more than half of current costs. The aggregate of all entities thus defined constitutes the sector whose evolution we now describe.[3]

HISTORICAL DEVELOPMENT TO 1961

Public enterprise in Korea dates to the traditional period when the government ran its own establishments to produce luxury goods (such as the famous green celadon of the Koryŏ dynasty 918–1389) for the royal family and segments of the *yangban* class. The modern sector, however, dates to the Japanese period. In Chapter 2 we described the process by which private Japanese concerns were nationalized in 1945. Here we describe only the rather extensive operation of enterprises by the colonial government itself.

Among the first Japanese institutional imports were public enterprises in the form of departmental agencies. By 1908, two years before annexation, the Japanese Residency General ran both Railway and Communications Bureaus employing over 4,000 people or more than 40 percent of the total government employment.[4] The most important later addition was the honestly named Monopoly Bureau covering ginseng, salt, opium, and tobacco. Ginseng had long been an official monopoly (under either the Crown Household Department or the Finance Department) as had salt imports, but with annexation both activities were expanded and salt production added.[5] Tobacco was added to the list of monopoly products in 1921, following unsatisfactory efforts at extracting excess profits via special taxes.[6] Opium was added in the 1920s, but yielded only a few percent of total monopoly profits. Overall, the public enterprises accounted for roughly one-quarter of total government revenue in the decade following annexation, and this increased to over 50 percent from 1926 on.[7] Expenditures generally exceeded revenues prior to 1926 but were below them for the next decade, resulting in profits contributing amounts equivalent to between 5 and 35 percent of the tax bill.[8] Given the crudity of the available accounting data, it is not possible to ascertain the real subsidy by, or profit to, the government from the operation of the sector (for example, we do not know how interest and depreciation were calculated).

While the public enterprise sector was thus important under Japanese colonial rule, it was by no means dominant. The economy remained basically private, with even much of electricity production outside the government sphere. The Japanese public enterprises, however, all survive today in one public form or another (except opium). By contrast, the Japanese private enterprises that were nationalized in 1945 were largely divested, though the process was slow, as described in Chapter 2.

One seldom-noted consequence of the Korean War was a dramatic shift in the official attitude towards public enterprise. The 1948 Constitution had a decided socialist bent, specifying public ownership of a broad range of economic activity and open-ended provisions allowing nationalization of any other industries "related to the public welfare" or where "required for vital and urgent needs for national defense or the livelihood of the people" (see Table 23, column 1). The 1954 Constitution, in contrast, reserves no specific industries for public ownership and explicitly prohibits nationalization "except in cases specifically designated by law" (see Table 23, column 2).

The change is probably not explained by ideological conversion so much as by the winnowing of war; South Koreans of socialist persuasion who survived the war either went north or kept quiet. This is an important point, with ramifications well beyond the public-enterprise sector. Economic policy in many LDCs evolves through a process of conflict between competing ideological blocks with temporary accommodations upset by shifts in the political power balance. The resulting temporizing solutions are generally unstable and often internally inconsistent. Implementation may be blocked by opponents elsewhere in the system. Compromise may thus be less efficient than either polar position pursued in full. Be that as it may, the Korean War added ideological homogeneity to an already culturally homogeneous population and significantly narrowed the range of economic dialogue. This was particularly true of the attitude towards public ownership, which now seemed far more appropriate to the north than the south.

TABLE 23 Comparison of 1948 and 1954 Constitutions
Chapter VI: Economy

1948 Version	*1954 Version*
Article 84	
The principle of the economic order of the Republic of Korea shall be to attain social justice, to fulfill the basic requirements of all citizens, and to encourage the development of a balanced national economy. The economic freedom of each individual shall be guaranteed within these limits.	
Article 85	
Mineral and other important underground resources, marine resources, water power, and other economically usable natural power shall be owned by the state. A license for the development or utilization of such resources for a certain period or cancellation of the license based on public need shall be granted in accordance with the provisions of law.	Licenses to exploit, develop, or utilize mines and other important underground resources, marine resources, water power, and all other economically available natural powers may be granted for limited periods in accordance with the provisions of law.
Article 86	
Farm lands shall be distributed to farmers. The method of distribution, the extent of possession, and the nature of restrictions of ownership shall be determined by law.	
Article 87	
Important enterprises within the following industries shall be placed under state operation: transportation, communication, finance and insurance, electricity, water utilization, water works, gas, and others related to public welfare. A license for private operation or cancellation of said license based on public	Foreign trade shall be controlled by the government in accordance with the provisions of law.

TABLE 23 (continued)

1948 Version	1954 Version
needs shall be granted in accordance with the provisions of law. Foreign trade shall be under the control of the state.	
Article 88	
If required for vital and urgent needs of national defense or the livelihood of the people, privately owned enterprises may be transferred to state ownership or placed under state control or management. Such acts shall be performed in accordance with the provisions of law.	Private enterprises shall not be transferred to state or public ownership except in cases specifically designed by law to meet urgent necessities of national life; nor shall the management or operation be controlled by the state or by juridicial persons organized by public law.

This is not to say that the result was a sudden divestiture of all Japanese properties. In the first place, there are a variety of natural monopolies (for example, electricity and railways) that must either be regulated or publicly owned; second, it was arguable that there was an absence of private entrepreneurial talent capable of running the larger enterprises; third, the Office of Monopoly was a major revenue source; finally, denationalization must always deal with the inertia resulting from bureaucratic self-interest which is faced with a loss of direct power and patronage opportunities. Nonetheless, the Rhee period witnessed a steady diminution of the public-enterprise sector, with only 36 entities left by the end of the 1950s.

Under Rhee, the operation of the public enterprises maintained the (low) standard set in the turmoil of the 1945–1951 period (described in Chapter 2). A somewhat extreme statement, tainted by self-interest but, nonetheless, reflective of the situation, is made by Park Chung Hee:

> [The operation of the state-run enterprises] is convincing proof of the corruption of greedy former politicians, before whom the jackpot was thrown like a rabbit flung before the starved lion. They appointed their own managers. In other words, they appointed their own subordinates and received from them certain tributes. There was not one trace of economic reconstruction. Every time the government changed, State-run enterprises became a market place. Many scandals which cannot be condoned occurred. Comedy and tragedy were publicly repeated. The people have experienced these scandals themselves and I will not say any more.[9]

Park's own attitude towards public enterprise seems to be that it is a necessary evil: "Private ownership of production should be unconditionally encouraged except in instances where it is necessary to control it to stimulate national development and protect the interests of the people."[10] As will be seen, the "except" in his statement is to be broadly interpreted. Nonetheless, he mirrors the official position of government as reflected in the one post-1954 substantive change in the economy section of the Constitution. It its 1972 version, Article 116 reads:

> The economic order of the Republic of Korea shall be based on the principle of respect for freedom and creative ideas of the individual in economic affairs. The state shall regulate and coordinate economic affairs within the limits necessary for the realization of social adjustment and for the development of a balanced national economy to fulfill the basic living requirements of all citizens.

Other provisions of the 1954 version are retained, most notably the assertion: "Private enterprises shall not be transferred to state or public ownership, nor shall their management be controlled or administered by the state except in cases determined by law to meet urgent necessities of national defense or national economy." We shall now see how this ideological position was translated into practice.

PUBLIC ENTERISE AS A LEADING SECTOR, 1961-1972

In 1972 the public-enterprise sector consisted of slightly over 100 enterprises producing 9 percent of GDP or 13 percent of non-agricultural GDP. This is a rather high level, being similar to that of India (on the basis of non-agricultural GDP) and probably larger than that of Italy or the United Kingdom (in the late 1960s) despite substantial socialist advocacy in all three countries.

Knowledgeable Koreans are prone to explain this large public-enterprise sector in terms of the Japanese colonial heritage. In fact, the sector has grown in absolute and relative terms during the rapid growth period from 1961 to 1972, as shown in Table 24. Of the 35 enterprises in the sector as of December 31, 1960, over three-quarters were directly traceable to activities run by the Japanese Colonial Government or confiscated from private Japanese firms. By the end of 1972, however, the number of enterprises had more than tripled. Value-added estimates of the sector are possible only from 1963 on, but it seems reasonable to assume that the sector was only moderately larger in 1963 than in 1960, since most of the 17 new enterprises had not had time to enter full production. It follows that, during the period of rapid economic growth, the relative size of the public-enterprise sector increased by about a third in current prices and more than half in constant prices. Absolute size more than tripled from 80 billion wŏn in 1963 to 272 billion in 1972 (in constant 1970 prices). This implies a real average annual growth rate of 14.5 percent over a period when the economy as a whole grew at 9.5 percent and the non-agricultural economy at 12.2 percent. "Old" enterprises (those in the sector in 1960) accounted for 6.7 percent of current price GDP in 1972, while the "new" produced 2.4 percent. In sum, under Park Chung Hee, the new enterprises accounted for most of the increase in the relative size of the sector. It is thus quite misleading to view the current size of the sector as a mere passive residual of the colonial era.

TABLE 24 Growth of Public-Enterprise Sector, 1960–1972

Year	Number of Enterprises	*Sectoral Value Added (billions of wŏn)*		*Sectoral Share of Current Price*	
		Current Prices	*1970 Prices*	*GDP*	*Non-Agricultural GDP*
1960	36	N.A.	N.A.	N.A.	N.A.
1963	52	31.8	80.4	6.98	12.70
1964	54	42.9	90.6	6.49	12.56
1971	119	262.1	246.7	9.17	13.46
1972	108	320.7	271.7	9.07	13.14

Source: Leroy Jones, *Public Enterprise and Economic Development: The Korean Case* (Seoul, 1976), pp. 73–74.

The sector's role is equally impressive when considered from the financial side. Over the 1962 to 1973 period, public enterprises generated slightly more than 10 percent of savings while absorbing something like 30 percent of investment. The public-enterprise sector also performed roughly 40 percent of all financial intermediation (that is, the acquisition of financial assets beyond the level required to fund one's own physical capital formation and their reinvestment in liabilities that finance the capital formation of others).

The contribution of the sector to growth is not measured simply by the level of output and financial flows, but also by strategic importance. An introduction to the kinds of activity in the sector is given by the industrial origin of sectoral output in Table 25. Of the 11 standard U.N. categories, the sector was an important factor in 5. It accounted for seven-eighths of value added in finance; for two-thirds of electricity, water, and sanitary service; for slightly less than one-third both in mining and in transport and communications; and for 15 percent of manufacturing. Although a large number of public enterprises are engaged in providing physical facilities, most of the actual work is contracted out so that the sector counted for only 5 percent of

TABLE 25 Industrial Origin of Public-Enterprise Value Added, 1972

(%)

	Share of Public Enterprise in Industry	*Share of Industry in Public Enterprise Total*
Agriculture, forestry, and fishing	0.20	0.68
Mining	31.01	3.63
Manufacturing	15.11	34.92
Construction	5.44	2.98
Electricity, water, and sanitation	66.19	13.66
Transport and communication	30.51	18.95
Trade	2.35	4.10
Finance	86.95	19.28
Ownership of dwellings	0.40	0.09
Public administration	0.00	0.00
Services	1.70	1.72
TOTAL	9.09	100.00

Source: Jones, p. 76.

value added in construction. The public-enterprise share in each of the other industrial sectors was less than 2 percent. In terms of absolute size the manufacturing sector accounted for one-third of public-enterprise value added, with finance, transport, and communications each contributing a fifth, and electricity a further 14 percent. The remaining industries are each responsible for less than 5 percent.

A comparison of 1963 with 1972 shows no striking change in the industrial origin of sectoral product. The sector expanded by maintaining, or by slightly increasing, its share in industries that were large or rapidly growing or both, rather than by sharp expansion in a few sectors. In many industries (for example, electricity, rail transport, and communications), public-enterprise growth was "forced" in order to avoid development bottlenecks. This is not true of manufacturing, however, so it is of some interest that the public-enterprise share of this industry held its own (15.3 percent in 1963 and 15.1 percent in 1972), despite the rapid growth of the industry as a whole. Real value added by public enterprises in manufacturing increased sevenfold between 1963 and 1972. Of this increase, 60 percent was attributable to expansion of "old" industries (those in the sector in 1960) and 40 percent to "new" enterprises. Of all enterprises added to the sector under the government of Park Chung Hee, nearly half (in terms of 1972 value added) were in manufacturing.

This pattern of public-enterprise activity is not unique. In fact, the sectoral shares in India are strikingly similar to those shown above for Korea.[11] For manufacturing alone, Frederic Pryor has shown that the rank correlation of industries in Eastern and Western Europe is high.[12] The clear implication is that the pattern of public-enterprise operation is neither random nor wholly ideologically determined, but heavily dependent on certain underlying economic characteristics. We now identify these determinants of the nationalization propensity in the Korean case.

First, consider the Hirschmanian concept of linkages. Forward linkages represent sales to intermediate (rather than final) users, while backward linkages reflect purchases from intermediate producers. Industries with high linkages may thus have greater impact on other productive sectors, and might be taken as representing "the commanding heights" of the economy.[13] Figure 1 shows direct forward and backward linkages for various sectors of the Korean economy. The sector as a whole is shown to have extremely high forward linkages, but modest backward linkages relative to the entire non-agricultural economy. Most of the growth during the period, however, came from "new" industries which had very high linkages in both directions.

A second technical characteristic of public enterprises is capital intensity.[14] The data suggest that the public-enterprise sector is more than three times as capital intensive as the Korean economy, almost triple the non-agricultural economy, and more

FIGURE 1 Direct Linkages Among Sectors of the Korean Economy, 1972

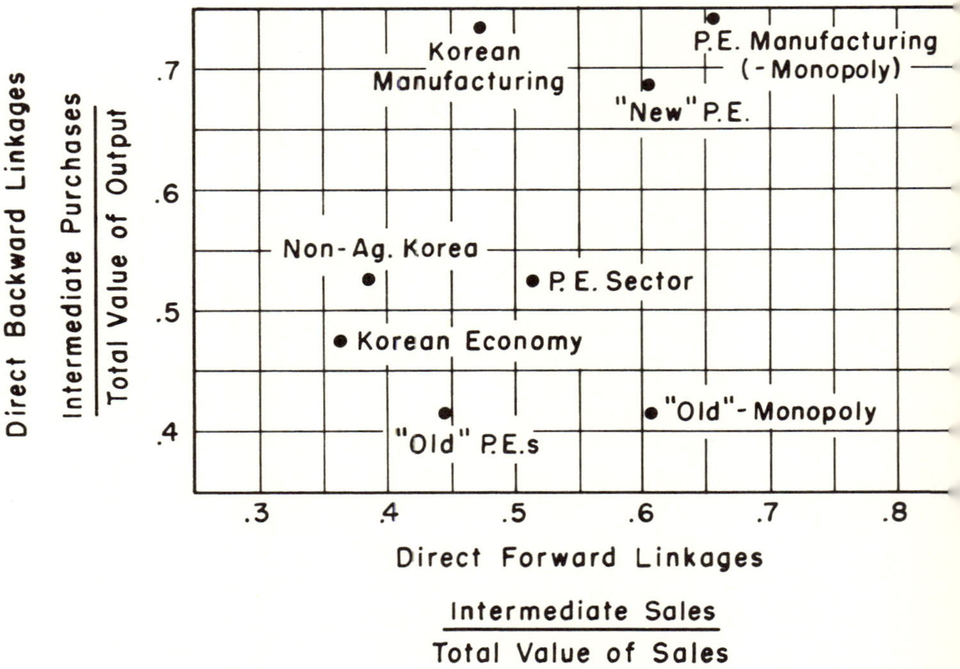

P.E. ≡ Public enterprise

"Old" P.E.s ≡ Those existing as of 5/61

"New" P.E.s ≡ Those added since 5/61

P.E. Manufacturing (– Monopoly) ≡ Public enterprises providing manufactured goods *except* for the Office of Monopoly (which is atypically consumption oriented.)

Non-Ag. Korea ≡ Korean economy less agriculture, forestry and fishing than double Korean manufacturing. Public enterprises are thus overwhelmingly capital intensive in Korea. The converse also holds, though to a somewhat lesser extent, with the capital-intensive sectors generally influenced by public operation. Of the eleven most capital-intensive sectors in the Korean economy, public enterprises produce virtually all output in four and are significant (10–50 percent of the market share) in six.

A third characteristic is output-market concentration. In 1972, 76 percent of public-enterprise value added was in markets that were egregiously imperfect (that is, monopoly, monopsony, bilateral monopoly, or regulated public oligopoly). Three-quarters of the remaining public enterprises were in manufacturing sectors with an output-weighted, ISIC four-digit, four-company concentration ratio of 0.73 compared with 0.51 for manufacturing as a whole. Public enterprises thus operate overwhelmingly in imperfect output markets with at most 10 percent of value added sold in reasonably competitive markets. The converse also holds, with public enterprise dominating highly concentrated industries. For the mining and manufacturing sector, this is readily documented. Among all four-digit industries with four-firm concentration ratios of 0.70 or greater, there is at least one public enterprise in seven sectors, that together account for 73 percent of sales in the concentrated industries. The character of those concentrated sectors without public participation is instructive. Of the fifteen concentrated industries with annual sales greater than 15 billion wŏn, there is no major public participation in sugar, beer, candies, soft drinks, dairy products, paint, watches and clocks, or meat processing. None of these, of course, is in any sense basic. Outside of manufacturing, no comparable statistics are available, but it is difficult to think of any important concentrated activity in Korea that does not have substantial public-enterprise participation.

Given this high correlation between public enterprise and imperfect competition, what is the direction of causation? One possibility is that government uses its powers to protect its enterprises from competitive pressures. This is clearly the case with the Office of Monopoly where the goal is straightforward revenue maximization. In virtually all other cases, however, enterprises may be interpreted to be in the public sector because they operated in imperfect markets rather than vice-versa.

A fourth characteristic is absolute enterprise size, as measured by total sales. This variable is of interest, both as a very crude proxy for economies of scale, and because of its relationship to the illusive concept of economic power. There are economies of scale in gaining a sympathetic government view of an enterprise's problems, and that understanding can be critical to an enterprise's success. Size is thus relevant to explaining an enterprise's behavior in the crucial, but little analyzed, market for government attention. Twenty of Korea's fifty largest enterprises are in the public sector, including twelve of the sixteen largest. Whatever the causal element, it is abundantly clear that, in absence of public enterprise, the private sector would control a far greater share of the economy's cash flow.

A fifth characteristic is foreign-exchange effects. Direct and indirect sectoral imports substantially exceeded direct and indirect exports, yielding a sectoral trade deficit representing 11.7 percent of that of the economy as a whole. However, the new enterprises were heavily import substituting, and this more than offset the explicit trade deficit. The nation's current account deficit would probably have been some 25 percent larger had the public enterprises not been operating and not been replaced by private activity.

A sixth feature of the public-enterprise sector, often claimed as being of high importance, is employment generation. In Korea, because of its capital intensity, the sector accounted directly and indirectly for only about 5 or 6 percent of increased employment from 1962 to 1973, while directly absorbing 30 percent of investment. The sector was thus a most inefficient means of employment creation.

In sum, the industries chosen for the public-enterprise sector are characterized by high forward linkages, high capital intensity, large size, output-market concentration, and production of non-tradeables or import substitutes rather than exports. These generalizations refer to sectoral averages and thus ignore many exceptions. Economic characteristics are not strictly deterministic, but they do strongly condition the probability of any given enterprise being in the public sector.

PUBLIC OPERATION: CAUSES

Given the characteristics of the enterprises in the public-enterprise sector, the government's decision to intervene is generally not surprising. Output-market concentration alone would justify intervention in enterprises producing at least three-quarters and perhaps 90 percent of sectoral value added. The size of the sector is thus largely explicable as a pragmatic government's response to the various market imperfections that are virtually synonymous with low levels of economic development. Historical inertia and political predilection do affect the outcome, but to a lesser extent in Korea than in countries less single-mindedly devoted to growth.

A rough idea of the relative importance of various market failures is given in Table 26, which assigns each enterprise or sub-unit to a single primary intervention category. Alternative categories and assignments are possible, and this morphology is presented primarily for its heuristic value.

Three basic groups are distinguished. The first, termed "basic motives," includes productive activities that provoke public intervention in one form or another in virtually all economies. This group includes the natural monopolies and producers of collective intermediates and marketed merit goods. The second group, called "developmental motives," includes reasons common to the developing economies. These all arise from a constellation of market failures involving entrepreneurial inadequacies, imperfect capital markets, shortages of information, and unwillingness to bear risk. The third group is a heterogeneous class of

TABLE 26 Market Failures and Public Enterprise, 31 December 1972

Primary Motive	*Linkages*[a] *Forward*	*Backward*	*Capital Intensity*[b]	*Trade-ability*[c]	*Share of Sectoral Value Added*
I. *Basic Motives*					0.42
Natural monopoly	2.13	1.59	15.64	NT	0.34
Collective intermediates	1.07	1.82	1.54	NT	0.04
Merit goods	1.46	1.76	1.34	NT	0.05
II. *Developmental Motives*					0.25
Entrepreneurial support	1.82	1.29	0.65	NT	0.06
Entrepreneurial substitution	2.27	1.59	8.28	T	0.11
Managerial substitution	1.73	1.77	4.26	T	0.04
Transitional	2.06	1.83	23.95	T	0.04
III. *Other Motives*					0.33
Power and control	2.44	1.79	0.96	NT	0.12
Revenue	1.11	1.63	1.64	T/NT	0.21

Source: Jones, p. 147.

Notes: [a]Direct plus indirect.
[b]Constant price capital stock over wage bill at 117 sector level.
[c]Tradeable (T) or non-tradeable (NT).

other motives including power, control, and revenue. Basic motives accounted for perhaps 42 percent of 1972 public enterprise value added, developmental motives for 25 percent, and other motives for 33 percent.

A look at individual categories reveals that natural monopolies are characterized by very high forward linkages, but modest backward linkages. They are related to development in that their expansion is necessary if bottlenecks are to be avoided, but they cannot be said to lead or initiate growth. They are characterized by increasing returns to scale over the relevant market size. The alternative to public operation is regulation, private monopoly, or, given their extremely high capital intensity, nonexistence.

Collective intermediates and merit goods have very low forward linkages, modest backward linkages, and low capital intensity. Their provision is not directly related to economic growth, but rather a component of broader social development. Since all but one of the collective intermediates are non-tradeable, the alternative to public-enterprise production is monopsonistic purchase from private producers. For the merit goods, the alternative is directly or indirectly subsidized private production.

The first two developmental motives deal with activities that are judged to be potentially profitable from a purely private point of view, but that the private sector will not undertake independently because of the magnitude of capital requirements, risk, uncertainty, technological complexity, lack of market knowledge, and so on. To compensate for this entrepreneurial failure, government may either provide technical assistance, or subsidized credit through entrepreneurial support organizations (for example, development banks), or it may itself initiate the activity taking the role of entrepreneurial substitute.

The third developmental category is termed "managerial substitution." It refers to cases where the private sector initiated activity, usually with the help of a supporting public enterprise, but then failed in the operational phase resulting in a threat of bankruptcy. Microeconomic theory suggests that the exit of these firms should be accepted in pursuit of efficiency through economic Darwinism. Governments throughout the real world, however, are conspicuously reluctant to accept this premise, particularly for firms of any size: witness Lockheed and Penn Central. This does not necessarily represent economic irrationality. It may reflect a recognition that, even where price does not cover private costs, it may well cover social costs.

The "revenue" motive category is dominated by the cigarette monopoly. Here the market failure is the existence of public goods and the resulting need for public finance. The alternatives to public ownership and control are, therefore, private ownership combined with heavy taxation.

The power and control motive is the most controversial category, but also the most interesting. The group is primarily composed of commercial banks and other financial intermediaries. A purely economic rationale for intervention in these entities' activities follows from the disequilibrium interest rate system, the opportunities for profit sharing, and the resultant necessity for close control over the temptations provided to bank officials. We suggest, however, that a much more important reason is a desire by the government in general, and Park Chung Hee in particular, to control private concentrations of economic power. Control of the banks was a central element of the Japanese zaibatsu power, and keeping the banks in public hands is a potent constraint on similar developments in Korea.

We may now summarize the use of the public-enterprise tool in Korea since 1961 by comparing the intervention motives for the old and new enterprises. The old enterprises included all but one of the natural monopolies, two-thirds of the collective intermediates, a little less than half of the merit goods, a third of the entrepreneurial support group, and the most important of the revenue activities. The new enterprises, by contrast, included all of the entrepreneurial substitution activities, the dominant share of entrepreneurial support, and slightly more than half of the merit goods, as well as virtually all the power and control category. Roughly speaking then, the old enterprises were basic (plus revenue), while the new enterprises were motivated by developmental and power considerations.

PUBLIC OPERATION: CONSEQUENCES

The prevalence of market failures provides a case for government intervention in general, but not necessarily for public enterprise in particular. In any specific case, more than one tool is usually available to achieve the desired intended deviation from unconstrained market behavior. There will then be a variety of unintended deviations associated with each intervention mechanism; for example, public operation may reduce cost consciousness; rate-of-return regulation may lead to over capitalization; and taxes and subsidies will distort relative prices. In theory, the task of microeconomic policy is to choose that mechanism that achieves the primary intended deviation at a minimum cost in unintended deviations. In practice, we know too little about the associated costs to form a judgment as to whether or not the Korean use of public enterprise has been a least-cost choice. We must, therefore, confine ourselves to rather general observations.

First, consider opportunity costs. The primary alternative to many of the Korean public enterprises is regulation and antitrust. Regulation, however, is very much a United States product which has seldom been exported; public enterprises are used to deal with natural monopolies virtually everywhere else. This may or may not represent a rational implicit cost-benefit calculation on the part of potential importers, but it is hardly surprising that the Koreans have not chosen this route. The alternative to most other public enterprises is taxes and subsidies.

A strong case for taxes as an alternative to public ownership can be made in the case of the Office of Monopoly. The goal here is revenue extraction. Scale economies are apparently small, relative to the size of the market, so that private competition is a possibility. It is thus likely that selling off the various cigarette plants to the private sector and allowing them to compete, while imposing a heavy excise tax, would increase both efficiency and government revenue. That this alternative has not been seriously considered is due to two factors. Since the operation always yields a substantial surplus, it is protected from serious scrutiny. International experience suggests that the most profitable public enterprises are likely to be the least cost efficient, since fortuitous output-market conditions eliminate pressures for cost reduction. In the absence of such attention, the second factor becomes decisive, namely bureaucratic inertia and a natural desire to retain power.

In other Korean enterprises the potential gains from divestiture are less clear, hinging on the relative efficiency of public and private operation. Around the world, it is widely believed that public enterprises are not cost efficient, so that resource wastage is a major price paid for public operation. Assessment of the situation in Korea is difficult, since we have few techniques for comparing social operating efficiency given small numbers of similar units, and even these techniques have been sparingly applied to micro units in Korea. As a working hypothesis, however, we would argue that, by world standards for public enterprise, the Korean sector does extremely well. At the crudest level, this follows from the fact that, when an economy is growing at a real rate of 10 percent annually, a sector that takes 30 percent of investment cannot be using its resources too inefficiently. At a less aggregate level, it is simply not possible to find in Korea any prolonged examples of the sorts of egregious inefficiency that characterizes many public-enterprise sectors. Indeed, preliminary work on Korean fertilizer and iron and steel industries suggests that, in at least some cases, Korean public-enterprise engineering efficiency is extraordinarily high by LDC standards and not markedly deficient when compared with similar operations in industrial nations. It is, however, widely believed that Korean public enterprises are less cost efficient than their private counterparts. We would agree with this view but would also argue strongly that the public-private gap is much smaller in Korea than in most LDCs.

If these observations are broadly accurate, then how is the relatively high level of performance to be explained? A high absolute level of public-enterprise efficiency is not surprising, given the government's dedication to growth and the skilled and energetic labor force, which have combined to make private Korean producers so competitive in world markets. What must be explained is the relatively high performance of public enterprises compared with private ones.

One way to attempt to explain the smaller public-private gap is in terms of organizational features of the control structure. Such features are often the first target of reformers, but in Korea they seem to explain very little. Consider the following:

1) Incentive System. Public enterprises are often held to be inefficient because of inadequate linkage of pecuniary rewards to performance. This is also true in Korea, with public-enterprise salaries generally below their private counterparts and little or no marginal incentives for improving performance. For example, one fertilizer company launched an ambitious and successful cost-reduction campaign and applied to its controlling organ for an increased employee bonus. This was rejected on the grounds that no other enterprise under that control unit had earned a similar profit, and bonuses had to be uniform! The Korean system of pecuniary incentives is in no sense unique.

2) Appointment Practices. Public enterprises are often held to be inefficient because managers are constantly rotated and are appointed for political reasons rather than managerial skills. In Korea two-thirds of the presidents of public enterprises (and half of the vice presidents) were formerly either military officers or civil servants. Further, 60 percent of the presidents (and 40 percent of the vice presidents) had spent less than three years with the company, and 90 percent had been there less than five years. Korean enterprises again fit the international pattern.

3) Autonomy versus Accountability. A basic problem for any organization is to decide where particular kinds of decisions should be made. Public enterprises typically fall into one of two extremes. Either all decisions are made at the enterprise level, thus ignoring social interest; or numerous minor decisions are made or approved by the bureaucracy, thus making it impossible for the enterprise to react quickly to changing market conditions. Korea comes closer to the second pole of excessive accountability, and the problem is exacerbated by multiple controlling agencies. At least on paper, the enterprises are responsible to a variety of ministries and agencies for a multitude of mundane details, and managers spend much of their time worrying about managing these bureaucratic relationships. Korea does rely heavily on holding companies—which in theory buffer the enterprise from bureaucratic involvement—but which in Korean practice seem to make little difference.

In sum, in terms of control structure there is little to differentiate the Korean public-enterprise sector from those elsewhere. When the authors conducted a separate study of the efficiency of the fertilizer industry, we were aware of these structural shortcomings and hypothesized inefficiency as the result. In the end, however, we found far greater efficiency than expected.

The relatively high performance of the sector cannot be explained by some structural gimmick which can be readily exported. Instead we would suggest that the public-enterprise sector operates relatively well for the same reasons that other forms of intervention are effective. Public enterprise is one form of discretionary command, and the potential for abuse of this form of intervention is minimized by leadership commitment to growth administered by a competent hierarchy, producing a hard state with a pragmatic non-ideological approach to choosing means.

In the public-enterprise sector this translates into a lack of tolerance for the more egregious forms of inefficiency on the part of managers and bureaucrats alike. When market restraints (via exit) on enterprise behavior are foregone, an enforceable political response to "voice" must be substituted. In Korea, while there is substantial slack before the political mechanism becomes effective, sustained and blatant inefficiency in larger entities is eventually brought to the attention of the Blue House; then things happen quickly. Public enterprises may thus be potentially less inefficient in "hard" states where political authority is able to act decisively.

Similarly, the anti-public-ownership ideological bias makes the government less tolerant of public-enterprise abuses. Throughout the world, public enterprises tend to be "unlimited liability companies" in that they are never allowed to die and are seldom divested. In Korea, there have been numerous cases of divestiture, most notably in the 1967–1969 period. Many of these supposed sales (as well as a number in the mid-1970s) were cosmetic in that government shares were sold to unrelated individuals or donated to the banks so that effective public control remained. A few real shifts of control did take place. On the negative side there is the example of Korean Machinery Manufacturing Corporation, described in Chapter 4. On the positive side there is Korean Air Lines which was a deficit operation when taken over (perhaps reluctantly) by Hanjin in 1968, but which is now highly profitable and uses international earnings to cross-subsidize low government-mandated fares on domestic flights.

No public enterprise has been actually allowed to die, but euthanasia has been seriously considered, and the threat alone proved effective. In 1972, the government became dissatisfied with the continuing operational losses of Honam Fertilizer Co., Ltd. and considered closing it down. Instead, a decision was made to give the company one more chance by seeing if new management could rectify the situation. Accordingly it was made a subsidiary of Chungju Fertilizer Co., Ltd. whose head, General Sŏn-yŏp Paek began by visiting the factory and making a speech which is vividly remembered by many of those present. The bulk of the speech was of the inspirational variety, coupling a patriotic plea by a Korean War hero with an appeal to provincial chauvinism. The conclusion, however, was a straightforward statement that, if things did not improve immediately, the plant would have to be shut down. The combination of threat and exhortation produced a sharp increase in cost efficiency as measured by capacity utilization and social profitability (in constant shadow prices). This example is illustrative of a generally intolerant government attitude towards public enterprise, and this may explain the relatively narrow public-private gap.

An alternative way of phrasing this story is in terms of non-pecuniary incentives. Carrots and sticks are not provided in cash, but in the form of the approval or displeasure of the governmental hierarchy. Since chief executives are military or bureaucratic appointees, these non-pecuniary incentives may well be more effective than pecuniary rewards. What is unique in Korea is the degree to which these non-pecuniary incentives are tied to performance.

As throughout this volume, a caveat is necessary to avoid misleading Korean readers. We have argued that the public-enterprise sector is relatively efficient by international standards. This is not to deny that it is often less efficient than Korean private enterprise, leaving ample room for improvement through reforms of the control structure mentioned above. Nonetheless, from the international point of view, the surprising feature of the sector is not its inefficiency relative to the private sector, but that the gap is as small as we believe it to be.

Public enterprise has been a "leading" sector during the period of rapid economic growth. That is, it grew significantly more rapidly than the economy as a whole, and there were identifiable mechanisms linking that growth to other sectors. This is not to be explained by historical inertia stemming from takeover of Japanese properties, since these were largely divested by 1961. Rather it was the result of a pragmatic government's willingness to use any available intervention mechanism in overcoming growth-retarding market imperfections. An antagonistic ideology obviously played no role in explaining the causes of public operation but may have been a factor contributing to its relatively efficient consequences.

SIX

Private Entrepreneurship: Sources of Expansion

ISSUES IN KOREAN ENTREPRENEURSHIP

While the role of public enterprise has been impressive, the bulk of Korean growth has come in the private sector. From 1961 to 1976, real private non-agricultural GDP grew at a compound rate of over 13 percent per annum.[1] If this is deemed the product of entrepreneurial acts, then the net volume of such activity in these fifteen years was more than six times that of all preceding Korean economic history. In world history, there are only a handful of cases of sustained entrepreneurial expansions of this magnitude. If four years are an economic sprint, and the half-century expansions of the United States and Japan are marathons, then Korean entrepreneurs may be said to be in the running for a world record in the middle distances.

The story behind this record-setting pace can be told in terms of how any of a variety of factors of production were mobilized. Entrepreneurship, termed by J. A. Schumpeter "the fundamental phenomenon of economic development,"[2] is one such factor. An argument can be made that the shortage of this talent is particularly acute in LDCs and forms one of the most intractable "bottlenecks" precluding growth. Capital can be borrowed internationally, and technology and intermediate inputs can be imported, but this leads only to debt if they are not combined effectively. This is the function of the entrepreneur.

By definition, any single-factor theory of development is myopic, but if one wishes to focus on a prime mover, then entrepreneurship is a likely candidate. With it, other factors can be found; without it, they will be squandered. This sort of consideration leads Hirschman to identify "the ability to make (development) decisions as the scarce resource which conditions all the other scarcities and difficulties in underdeveloped countries."[3] This formulation incorporates public as well as private decision-making, but justifies two chapters devoted to the role of the private entrepreneur. In Korea, despite the pervasive activity of the government's visible hand, the bulk of decisions leading to production are taken in the private sector.

Our primary purpose is not to document the successes of the Korean entrepreneurs, though this will in part be accomplished through the case studies in Appendixes A and B. Here we take the record private-sector growth rate as ample evidence of an explosion of successful entrepreneurial activity and ask what lies behind it. At the broadest level, the question may be phrased in terms of whether the observed expansion in quantity is to be explained in terms of a shift of the supply curve, a shift of the demand curve, or both. Briefly, two alternative views compete in the literature:[4]

1) Demand Primacy. Mainstream economists are prone to argue that there is no real problem of entrepreneurial supply; there is an abundant reservoir of profit-responsive

individuals in all societies, and all that is necessary to call forth the necessary talent is to alter the environment and manipulate market incentives (that is, shift demand).

2) Supply Primacy. Sociologists and psychologists, on the other hand, are likely to argue that there are real constraints on entrepreneurial supply imposed by traditional social structures and the resulting psychological motivations and inhibitions. Shifts in demand may cause reactions in deviant subordinated groups, but broad-based response will occur only with a fundamental shift in basic social values. The model here is Weber's "Protestant Ethnic" as a prime mover in the evolution of Western capitalism.

The next two chapters will examine the Korean entrepreneurial experience in terms of this supply and demand dichotomy.

The primary purpose of this chapter will be to identify the sources of expansion of Korean entrepreneurship from 1961 to 1975. Our task will be to explain the observed change in the equilibruim quantity in terms of shifts in the supply and demand curves. This is not a simple matter, since our language is imprecise, and the supply and demand functions are specified vaguely in the literature. There are in fact a number of different entrepreneurial supply and demand functions. In the course of development, many things change and shift the various curves about in a complicated way so that the change in equilibrium is not readily predictable. To clarify matters, our first step is to examine the dynamics of entrepreneurial expansion to see how much of the growth was due to entrance of new entrepreneurs, and how much to expansion of old. The result is that growth is to be interpreted primarily as a qualitative phenomenon rather than a quantitative one. To explain this, we must sharpen our conceptual tools and therefore devote a section to specifying the entrepreneurial market more carefully through disaggregation of the entrepreneurial function and a stress on the quality being demanded. With this more detailed framework, we then examine the execution of the various functions in the Korean experience. Finally, we bring the supply and demand sides together and attempt to tell an integrated story of the sources of the expansion of the equilibrium quantity of entrepreneurial acts.

In telling the story of shifts in the market, we shall emphasize the demand side and defer a detailed consideration of the supply side until Chapter 7. This is possible because what we wish to explain is a fairly rapid and discontinuous change in the equilibrium quantity in the early 1960s. Insofar as the position of the supply curve is a function of psychological motives resulting from sociological conditioning, no sudden change in the function is to be expected. What is to be explained is not so much the change in the curve as its height and slope. Chapter 7 will investigate this question by examining the social background of Korean entrepreneurs.

ENTREPRENEURIAL DYNAMICS

The simplest economic theory takes growth to be the net effect of two trends: entry of new firms—implicitly founded by new entrepreneurs—and the exit of mature companies that have outlived their usefulness in the market. In fact, the process is a bit more complicated, involving:

1) Entrance of new firms (founded by new entrepreneurs).
2) Entrance of offspring firms (founded by previously successful entrepreneurs).
3) Expansion of existing firms in new lines.
4) Expansion of existing firms in existing lines.
5) Exit of putative firms (that were never viable).
6) Exit of mature firms (that were once viable).

These distinctions are important in analyzing entrepreneurial dynamics, as the nature of the entrepreneurial act differs in each case. Most important, only source #1 requires a supply of new entrepreneurs while #2, #3, and #4 utilize the existing supply. In this section we therefore endeavor to decompose the growth of private output into these six categories. The attempt fails due to inadequate data, but comes close enough to demonstrate that the traditional entrepreneurial act—foundation of a new firm by a new entrepreneur—is of minor consequence in Korea.

First consider Table 27 which indicates trends in the size and number of manufacturing establishments. From 1962 to 1974 the number of establishments increased by less than 40 percent, while size tripled in terms of employment per establishment and rose ninefold in terms of value added per establishment. The sources of real growth in value added may thus be decomposed as follows:

Growth in average size (old firms at new size)	72%
Growth in number of firms (new firms at old size)	3%
Cross product (new firms at incremental size)	25%
	100%

This is a striking and profoundly important conclusion for an understanding of the role of entrepreneurship in economic growth. It says that net entry of entrepreneurs by itself accounted for only 3 percent of the growth of manufacturing output. What has to be explained is not how new entrepreneurs were found, but how old firms grew, and why new firms were so much larger than the old. The critical question is not net *entry*, but *expansion*. The problem is less entrepreneurial *quantity*, than *quality*.

To focus the issue more sharply, we should like to know how much of the size increase comes from expansion of existing firms and how much from replacement (exit of small firms and replacement with large ones). Some evidence on this question is provided by the corporate histories of the firms in our Entrepreneurship Survey. Firms more than one year old reported a median annual rate of expansion of productive capacity of 14 percent. Their mean employment at establishment was 97 workers, while they averaged nearly two expansion projects with a mean increase in employment per project of

114 workers. These rates of growth—extrapolated to the establishment set as a whole—could explain virtually all of the growth of manufacturing output as the product of expansion of existing firms. This is not justified, of course, since there is probably an upward response bias in our survey, and our sample represents the larger and more successful firms. Nonetheless, it is clear that expansion, rather than entry, is the dominant element in explaining the growth of industrial value added.

If the net rate of entry of firms is low, what about the gross rate? Table 28 reveals available data on entry and exit of joint-stock corporations and "other corporations" (it differs from Table 27 in excluding private proprietorships). It is woefully inadequate, with the stock series beginning in 1966 and the entry series ending in 1969, giving a complete picture for only three overlapping years. For that three-year period the gross entry flow was 2,142, while exit was 1,988, with each annual gross flow representing approximately 30 percent of the stock. While these figures are atypical in representing years with a low net flow, we take them as evidence of a very high level of turnover.

If exit is this high, is it due to the failure of putative entrepreneurs or the natural demise of mature firms? Some evidence is provided by our entrepreneurship survey samples which had a one-year exit rate of 13 percent. These firms were disproportionately young, as suggested by Table 29 which gives failure rates by year of establishment. Roughly a quarter of the companies failed within four years of founding, and this is hardly maturity. After six years, morbidity was a fairly steady 10 to 15 percent per year.[5] In addition to being young, the failed firms were extremely small, averaging one-sixth the size of the rest of the sample.

These results are further supported by casual empiricism which suggests that large firms that falter are taken over by competitors, that those which become outdated convert to other lines, and that there are large numbers of putative entrepreneurs taking a plunge with little more than hope to back

TABLE 27 Trends in Size of Manufacturing Establishments, 1958–1974

Year	*Establishments*	*Workers*	*Real Value Added*[a/b]	*Employees/ Establishment*	*Value Added Establishment*[b]
1958	12,921	260,427	62,520	20.2	4.8
1959	n.a.	n.a.	n.a.	n.a.	n.a.
1960	15,204	275,254	79,629	18.1	5.2
1961	16,028	296,585	69,892	18.5	4.4
1962	16,355	304,565	95,087	18.6	5.8
1963	18,310	401,981	140,457	22.0	7.7
1964	n.a.	n.a.	n.a.	n.a.	n.a.
1965	18,396	453,422	149,462	24.7	8.1
1966	22,718	566,665	204,389	25.0	9.0
1967	23,833	648,811	265,803	27.2	11.2
1968	24,102	748,184	358,678	31.1	14.9
1969	25,098	828,966	466,809	33.0	18.6
1970	24,114	861,041	549,793	35.7	22.8
1971	23,412	848,194	664,486	36.2	28.4
1972	23,729	973,415	759,763	41.0	32.0
1973	23,293	1,157,829	1,068,370	49.7	45.9

TABLE 27 *(continued)*

1974	22,632	1,298,384	1,158,011	57.4	51.2

Source: EPB, *Report on Mining and Manufacturing Survey* (Seoul, various years). Establishments include private proprietorships, joint-stock companies, and "other corporations."

Notes: [a]Current value added deflated using implicit GDP deflator for manufacturing sector from *National Income Statistics Yearbook* (Seoul, various years).

[b]In millions of 1970 wŏn.

TABLE 28 Corporate Entry and Exit, 1955–1974

Year	Stock (Year End)[a]	Flow: Entry[b]	Flow: Exit[c]
1955		333	
1956		373	
1957		304	
1958		231	
1959		278	
1960		206	
1961		240	
1962		374	
1963		248	
1964		289	
1965		385	
1966	2,367	601	
1967	2,285	661	743
1968	2,310	644	619
1969	2,421	737	626
1970	2,542		
1971	2,592		
1972	3,083		
1973	3,220		
1974	3,774		

Notes: [a]EPB, *Report on Mining and Manufacturing Survey* (Seoul, various years). Includes joint-stock companies and "other corporations" in manufacturing. Differs from Table 27 in excluding private proprietorships.
[b]New manufacturing corporations registered during the year from EPB, *Korea Statistical Yearbook* (Seoul, various years).
[c]Residual.

them up. We conclude that gross entry is a severalfold multiple of net entry, with the high level of exit explained disproportionately by premature disasters rather than mature burials.

The tribulations of the small and medium entrepreneur are documented further elsewhere.[6] For firms in a given size group in 1966, this source gives the percentage that has grown, shrunk, and remained unchanged as of 1969. Results, summarized in

TABLE 29 Enterprise Failure Rates

Establishment Year	Number Established	% Failed During 1975
1974 or 1975	14	7.1
1972 or 1973	73	19.2
1970 or 1971	47	8.5
1968 or 1969	33	9.1
1966 or 1967	44	11.4
1964 or 1965	21	14.2
1962 or 1963	20	15.0
1952 to 1961	44	11.4
1946 to 1951	6	14.3
Pre-1946	9	11.1
TOTAL	311	12.9

Source: Entrepreneurship Survey, see Appendix C. The level of failure is overstated, because some entries may represent a change of location which went undetected by our interviewer. However, there is no reason for this to affect the trend.

Table 30, are striking in showing that smaller firms (under 75 workers) were much more likely to shrink than grow, while the reverse was true for larger firms.

Extrapolation from Tables 27 and 28 suggests that, during the period of rapid economic growth, the net annual entry of manufacturing corporations was in the vicinity of 200 per year and that of proprietorships in the vicinity of 300.[7] How much of this net firm entrance represents new entrepreneurs? That is, how much is represented by the offspring of already successful entrepreneurs? We assume that most of the proprietorships are new entries, but this does not hold for the joint-stock companies. As detailed in Chapter 8, 46 major chaebŏl control 382 subsidiaries, and there are many smaller corporate groups as well. We lack a time series for this group, but it is not implausible that half of the new corporations each year are formed as offspring (including most of the larger ones) and many of the remainder by people stepping up from proprietorships. There has thus been an annual net flow of new entrepreneurs (mostly

TABLE 30 Growth Prospects by Size of Firm

1966 Employment	*Percentage which in 1969 were:*			*Growth Prospects*[a]
	Larger	*Smaller*	*Unchanged*	
5– 9	15.4	–	84.6	–
10– 19	19.2	40.8	40.0	0.47
20– 29	28.4	42.8	28.8	0.66
30– 49	28.3	38.0	33.7	0.74
50– 74	27.6	40.7	31.7	0.68
75– 99	42.8	35.8	21.4	1.20
100–149	47.0	27.2	25.8	1.72
150–199	53.2	31.7	15.1	1.68
200–299	46.9	27.2	25.9	1.72
300	–	15.2	84.8	–

Source: Sample size unknown from survey by: Kyŏng-ŭi Yi, "Chung so kiŏp," in *Han'guk kyŏngjeron,* Hyŏng-yun Pyŏn and Yun-hwan Kim, eds. (Seoul, 1977), p. 486.

Note: [a](Percentage of firms which grew in employment)/(percentage which shrank).

small) of an order of magnitude of 400 per year over the entire rapid growth period, with a much smaller number of entries since 1969.

Let us now summarize our interpretation of Korea's entrepreneurial dynamics. There is a vast churning at the bottom, with a high level of aspiration and gross entry leading to rapid failure. Those who survive the initial entrepreneurial act then expand rapidly. Growth in value added is due first to expansion of existing firms, second to entry of offspring firms, and only to a minor extent to net entrance of new entrepreneurs. This is equivalent to saying that, on the supply side, expansion has been the result of qualitative rather than quantitative changes. Growth in output has not come from exploiting a new supply of entrepreneurs, but from making better use of the existing stock.[8] To explain this qualitative change, we need to specify the entrepreneurial market more carefully.

THE ENTREPRENEURIAL MARKET

WHO IS AN ENTREPRENEUR?

In principle, entrepreneurship is to be clearly distinguished from management, with the former referring to the initiation of new economic activity and the latter to the operation of ongoing activities. The critical characteristic is the formation of "new combinations of means of production."[9] It should be stressed that Schumpeter interpreted "new combinations" in a much broader fashion than is commonly thought. He included:

"1) *The introduction of a new good*—that is, one with which consumers are not yet familiar—or of a new quality of good.

2) *The introduction of a new method of production*, that is, one not yet tested by experience in the branch of manufacture concerned, which need by no means be founded upon a discovery scientifically new, and can also exist in a new way of handling a commodity commercially.

3) *The opening of a new market*, that is, a market into which the particular branch of manufacture of the country in question has not previously entered, whether or not this market existed before.

4) *The conquest of a new source of supply* of raw materials or half-manufactured goods, again irrespective of whether this source already exists or whether it has first to be created.

5) *The carrying out of a new organization of any industry*, like the creation of a monopoly position . . . or the breaking up of a monopoly position."[10]

If "new" is taken to refer to newness within the Korean rather than the international economy, then two-thirds of the companies in our sample represented "new combinations" according to Schumpeter's first two criteria (see Table 31). Further, over half of the companies' expansion projects involved entrepreneurship according to the same standard, and only 12 percent were mere extensions of the firm's existing products and processes.

TABLE 31 Type of Innovation Among Sample Firms
(%)

	At Establishment	*At Expansion*
Product new to Korea	31.3	20.7
Production new to Korea	20.9	11.0
Production process new to Korea	13.4	23.2
Product new to firm (but not to Korea)	34.3	14.6
Production process new to firm (but not to Korea)		18.3
Existing product and process (within firm)	–	12.1
TOTAL	99.9	99.9

Source: Entrepreneurship Survey, see Appendix C.

Korean firms are clearly dynamic in expanding into new fields.

While it is clear that not all founders of firms are Schumpeterian entrepreneurs, we shall not make the distinction between entrepreneurial and managerial roles in reporting our survey results. There are several reasons for this. First, many of the founders who are not entrepreneurs by criteria #1 and #2 will be so by virtue of #3 to #5, particularly by their expansion in world markets. Second, many who were not strict entrepreneurs at founding became so by virtue of more innovative expansion projects. Third, an argument can be made that the mere act of binding together a new set of productive factors (regardless of newness of product, process, or market), is a significant "new combination" in LDCs. Fourth, chief executives form the observation set of virtually all studies we wish to compare our results with.[11]

For similar reasons, we shall generally make no distinction between founders and non-founders, although the latter group makes up roughly 40 percent of our sample (see Table 32). In the first place, given the rapid rate of growth of most firms in our sample,[12] most non-founders must be innovators by one or the other of the criteria. Second, we ran a variety of tests on the

TABLE 32 Relationships Between Chief Executives and Founders

(%)

Current chief executive is:	
Founder	61.4
Direct descendant of founder	7.8
Other relative of founder	12.0
Unrelated	18.8
	100.0
Where current chief executive is not the founder, the founder is:	
Deceased	8.0
Retired	16.0
Active in related company	24.0
Active in other company	16.0
Other	36.0
	100.0

Source: Entrepreneurship Survey, see Appendix C.

backgrounds and opinions of founders and non-founders and found few significant differences. In sum, then, we shall refer to all chief executives as "entrepreneurs" without deviating substantially from the original Schumpeterian concept of the entrepreneur as the creator of "new combinations."

While virtually all chief executives are therefore entrepreneurs, not all entrepreneurs are chief executives. In Schumpeter's words:

> We call entrepreneurs not only those "independent" businessmen in an exchange economy who are usually so designated, but all who actually fulfill the function by which we define the concept, even if they are, as is becoming the rule, "dependent" employees of a company, like managers, members of boards of directors, and so forth.[13]

In Korea, the function (or portions of it) is performed by a variety of individuals other than the chief executive. This is particularly true in the large chaebŏl, where various managers take charge of penetrating target markets and initiating projects. In addition, the government, domestic companies, and foreign buyers and suppliers all contribute to new combinations. It may indeed be argued that the presence of these complementary entrepreneurial contributions accounts for a substantial part of the success of Korean industry. To elaborate this proposition more fully, it is necessary to specify the functional components more carefully.

THE ENTREPRENEURIAL FUNCTION

The popular perception of the entrepreneur is of a Henry Ford type who does it all himself. Most of the academic literature follows this monistic conception and assumes that the entrepreneur is either wholly present or wholly absent. We find it more fruitful to disaggregate and argue that portions of the function are always present, and only certain missing parts need be added to expand the effective entrepreneurial supply. On this point we are in complete agreement with Peter Kilby who argues that the monistic model

> is based upon implicit assumptions about the nature of a well-functioning underdeveloped economy. These assumptions are that factors of production possess a relatively high degree of mobility; that inputs and output are homogeneous; that producers, consumers and resource owners have knowledge of all the possibilities open to them; and that there are no significant indivisibilities . . . When the assumptions are relaxed and ignorance, heterogeneity (segmented markets), impeded factor mobility, lumpiness, pervasive administrative controls, and input nonavailabilities are brought into the model, then the extraordinary qualities of the entrepreneur—and the possibility of their limited supply—become apparent.[14]

In short, monism falters on pervasive market imperfections, and we propose an alternative "lenticular" concept which we now explain.

There are a variety of functions that go into the making of an entrepreneurial bundle. These functions include:

1) Perception of a new economic opportunity, including:
   a) new products
   b) new processes of production
   c) new markets
2) Evaluation of the profitability of a new opportunity
3) Gaining command of financial resources
4) Plant design, technology, and construction supervision
5) Recruiting and training new personnel
6) Dealing with government
7) Dealing with suppliers and purchasers

In a primitive economy, the absence of skill at any of the functions is sufficient to impede seriously the entrepreneurial act. In a more developed economy, the missing item can be hired, permitting a less heroic type to successfully bring a project to fruition. In fact, as one goes down the list, it becomes apparent that not only can *any* of the functions be performed for the entrepreneur rather than by him, but in principle they *all* could. What then is left for the entrepreneur? The answer is the pure Schumpeterian function of combination. The entrepreneur takes ultimate responsibility for seeing that all the functions are carried out even though he performs few, or none, of them himself. He is like a lens that focuses the energies of others, and we therefore term this pure and unavoidable task the "lenticular" function.

Harvey Leibenstein argues that one major entrepreneurial task is "gap-filling," which refers to compensating for market deficiencies.[15] That is, information about some inputs is either unmarketable or unmarketed, and it is the entrepreneur's task to fill these gaps. If the economy provided a complete set of demand functions, a similar set of production functions, and a complete set of prices (including prices for obtaining the production and demand functions), then "perception of market opportunity" would be a trivial task easily performed by the average undergraduate with access to a computer. In fact, the market provides precious little information of this sort, and filling this gap is the entrepreneur's job and the source of his reward. In our framework, such "gap-filling" must be performed for *each* of the entrepreneurial functions with the difficulty for each function depending on the state of the market (for example, in developed economies for widely sold homogeneous commodities, "dealing with purchasers" becomes trivial). Our "lenticular" function is, then, the overview task of insuring that all relevant "gaps" are in fact "filled" and the entrepreneurial bundle completed.

The various entrepreneurial functions may be performed (the gaps filled) in one of three ways: a) by the market, b) by an agent employed by the entrepreneur, or c) by the entrepreneur himself. Where the entrepreneur steps in and does the job himself, this is then what Leibenstein refers to as "input completing." If the entrepreneur performs *all* the functions himself, then he is of the pure monistic type of yesteryear. If markets or agents or both perform all of the functions, then he is purely lenticular.

The process of entrepreneurial development may then be viewed, not so much as one of increasing the supply of the monistic entrepreneur, but as one of increasing the supply of agents and market mechanisms so as to allow success of the existing supply of lenticular entrepreneurs. Individuals with monistic capabilities are few; those with lenticular capabilities are many. As development proceeds, the requirement for a successful entrepreneurial act shifts from monism towards lenticularism, the rate of success rises, and growth accelerates. In the next section we shall examine the Korean experience for evidence of this process.

THE QUALITY OF ENTREPRENEURSHIP

Disaggregation of the entrepreneurial function allows us to specify three components of the supply of effective entrepreneurial activity:

1) The stock of individuals with lenticular intent,
2) The level of lenticular ability within that group, and
3) The availability (quantity and quality) of agents and

TABLE 33 Average Lead Time from Conceptualization to Operation of New Plants

	Months	*Number*
1962 and prior	16.5	12
1963–1968	14.1	14
1969–1975	10.2	36

Source: Entrepreneurship Survey, see Appendix C. Only new establishment projects are included, as we recorded only seven expansion projects prior to 1969.

markets that reduce the need for "input completion" by the entrepreneur.

The results of the previous section on "Entrepreneurial Dynamics" may now be rephrased by saying that the supply side of the Korean expansion has been largely due to qualitative improvements—factors #2 and #3—and only to a minor extent due to quantitative increases—factor #1.

The change in effective entrepreneurial abilities is perfectly illustrated by the development of the Korean fertilizer industry. There was a dramatic difference between the implementation of the first two plants, started in the late 1950s, and the next three, built in the mid-1960s. The first two were horror stories of inefficiency by contemporary Korean standards, but were quite typical of LDC projects in general and reflected the entrepreneurial barriers encountered in the early stages of development. Gestation periods for the first two plants were 67 and 54 months respectively; the next three, though larger and more complex, took only 17, 18, and 21 months respectively. Such experience is not limited to the fertilizer industry. As shown in Table 33, the time from conceptualization to operation of new plants declined steadily over time among our sample firms. This is particularly impressive since the later plants were, on average, larger, and more technically sophisticated. These data are not conclusive since the sample is small relative to the variance. Nonetheless, allowing for the greater size and complexity of later projects, we believe this is a fair reflection of a fundamental trend in entrepreneurial capability. This improvement in the quality of bundle supply is due to both an improvement in lenticular ability and an increase in the quantity and quality of non-lenticular entrepreneurial inputs.

THE ENTREPRENEURIAL FUNCTION IN KOREA

If it is agreed that qualitative improvements are the essence of the change to be explained, then the next step is to decompose the quality change into improvements in lenticular ability and increased availability of complementary inputs. No definitive answer is to be expected, but some insights are gained from the survey questions on the difficulty of performing various functions, the sources of assistance in solving those problems, and the nature of government assistance. We are first interested in how the answers vary across functions, in order to identify the critical tasks most often performed by the chief executive himself. Second, we are concerned with changes over time, in order to ascertain the degree to which functional differentiation evolves with development.[16] Third, we would like to examine differences related to size of firm and between exporters and non-exporters to distinguish biases in government assistance. Finally, we compare differentiation in expansion from that at establishment. The small sample size makes generalization hazardous, but some conlusions do emerge.

ENTREPRENEURIAL PROBLEMS

Responses to the question on the degree of difficulty encountered in carrying out various entrepreneurial tasks are summarized in Table 34. Despite the small sample size,[17] the following results are of interest:

1) The absolute level of perceived difficulty is low, with the modal response generally "simple" and the mean between "some problem" and "simple." This is not

TABLE 34 Businessmen's Perception of Entrepreneurial Problems

Question: In establishing your enterprise, a number of problems had to be solved. Please indicate the degree of difficulty you encountered in each.

Ranking: Very Difficult 1 — 2 — Some Problem 3 — 4 — Simple 5 — Not Applicable ( )

Results:

Problem	Establishment: All	Establishment: Pre-1968	Establishment: 1969–1975[b]	Establishment: Export	Establishment: Domestic	Expansion: All	Expansion: Pre-1968	Expansion: 1969–1975[b]	Expansion: Export	Expansion: Domestic	Managers[a]
Perception of opportunity and market identification	3.21	3.22	3.17	3.44	2.92	3.66	3.00	3.72	3.77	3.61	3.38
Obtaining financing	2.95	2.50[c]	3.17	3.44[e]	2.44	3.41	2.71	3.46	3.64	3.23	3.08
Plant design, technology, and construction	3.49	2.96[d]	3.72	3.29	3.59	3.93	2.71[e]	4.03	3.87	3.93	3.72
Obtaining technicians and training	3.15	2.73[c]	3.32	3.06	3.23	3.45	3.06	3.61	3.37	3.49	3.44
Government support and permits	3.75	3.73	4.00	3.78	4.05	4.25	4.43	4.26	4.18	4.30	4.07
Setting up organization and managing people	3.67	3.67	3.67	3.53	3.74	4.30	4.29	4.03	4.31[c]	3.75	3.57
Sample size	(74)	(27)	(47)	(36)	(39)	(84)	(7)	(77)	(39)	(46)	(101)

Source: Entrepreneurship Survey, see Appendix C. Some response categories are abbreviated here, and two are omitted.

Notes: [a]Unweighted responses on expansion projects.
[b]In comparing 1969–1975 expansions with establishments, differences in "perception" are significant @ 5% and those in "managing government" and "managing people" are significant @ 1%.
[c]t-test significant at 10%
[d]t-test significant at 5%
[e]t-test significant at 1%
([c], [d], [e]:) in comparing adjacent pairs (e.g., export and domestic)

particularly surprising, since we are dealing with largely successful entrepreneurs in a rapidly growing economy.

2) In terms of relative difficulty, "financing" is the biggest problem, followed closely by obtaining technicians, and perception of opportunity. Getting government support turns out to be the least problematical task, confirming the view of a supportative bureaucracy, and in marked contrast to what might be expected in other LDCs.

3) Over time, getting established becomes easier, though the differences are significant for only three of the six functions. Since the size and sophistication of projects increases over time, we take this as evidence, albeit weak, for the hypotheses of improved lenticular ability and increasing functional differentiation. A similar time trend is exhibited by the ease with which expansion projects are carried out.

4) Expansion projects face uniformly fewer and smaller obstacles than initial establishment, and the differences are significant (at 5 percent) in three cases. This is probably not due to greater simplicity. Only 13 percent of the expansion projects involve a mere extension of existing product and process lines, and the mean size of expansion projects is actually larger (in terms of employment) than at establishment.[18] We would instead argue that a significant role is played by learning: having gone through the process once, it is much easier the second and subsequent times. Second, and equally important, the government seems to provide more support for expansion than for establishment. This in turn is due to a combination of concern for scale economies and support for known entities.

5) Decomposition into export and domestic uses yields surprisingly little reduction in variance. To be sure, exporters have a much easier time getting financing, but that is the only "significant" difference. "Significance,"

however, is not always the final word. Note that exporters report somewhat greater ease in "perception of opportunity and market identification." Given our preconception as to the much greater difficulty of exploiting foreign markets, the absence of a statistically significant difference is striking. It shows the remarkable degree to which government field augmentation has worked to reduce the information imperfections connected with exporting.

6) Size differences by value-added decile and quintile yield no discernible pattern and are unreported. This is perhaps the result of two offsetting tendencies: smaller firms have simpler problems, but they also get less help in solving them. This absence of a size distinction is intriguing and suggests that institutional development may have been more even-handed than generally thought in providing assistance at all levels commensurate with the problems being faced.[19]

Establishing a larger firm requires more help than establishing a smaller firm, and it gets proportionately more, particularly in finance. Further, much of the extra help received by the large firm comes from foreigners and other domestic companies rather than the government (see below). It should be noted that the low size bias of government is in part due to our dealing with medium to large firms. Since our cut-off point is 50 workers, we only begin to enter the range where evidence presented in Table 30 showed growth prospects to be negative. It must be stressed that we are speaking here of assistance relative to the problems involved and not of absolute help. The same proportional assistance in, say, finance, means a much larger absolute volume of help and implicit subsidy for bigger firms.

DISTRIBUTION OF ENTREPRENEURIAL FUNCTION

The degree of perceived difficulty in performing each function depends on the magnitude of the project, the quality of the entrepreneur, and the availability of complementary entrepreneurial inputs. We now focus on the last element to see how much functional differentiation existed, and how it varied across sub-groups. Respondents were asked: Who participated in performing the various entrepreneurial functions? Percentage shares of total responses are given in Table 35.[20] Noteworthy results are as follows:

1) Overall, there is a substantial evidence of functional differentiation. Even at establishment, entrepreneurs did not act alone; they provided only from 43 to 69 percent of the total participation.
2) The greatest differentiation occurred in obtaining financing, technology, and technical training, with chief executives providing less than half the participation in each area. Note that, while obtaining financing was the most difficult task (Table 34), it is also the one in which the most help was available. Differentiation is one way in which the critical problem was solved.
3) The least differentiation occurred in conceptualization and handling government and personnel relations. These are thus the functions least often delegated by the lenticular entrepreneur.
4) Size differences are, not surprisingly, apparent. Chief executives of large firms performed a smaller share of each function than did those of smaller firms. Larger firms thus have an advantage over smaller ones in requiring less "input completion" by the entrepreneur.
5) Contrary to expectations, time differentials are not generally significant, with chief executives performing roughly similar shares of each function in pre- and post-1969 establishments.[21] This may be due to the fact that getting started in business is inherently difficult, and the change in economic environment has done much more to ease the difficulties of expansion than those of establishment. This hypothesis is consistent with evidence presented earlier on the dominance of expansion over entry as a source of growth.
6) The last hypothesis is to some extent confirmed by

TABLE 35 Performers of Entrepreneurial Functions

(%)[a]

Function[b]	*Chief Executive*	*Employees and Relatives*	*Government and Public Enterprises*	*Foreign Entities*	*Other Domestic Entities*	*Total*
Conceptualization	58.4	14.3	6.5	12.9	7.9	100.0
Financing	45.1	13.4	22.5	5.6	13.4	100.0
Technology	44.0	32.9	0.8	18.7	3.7	100.1
Construction	53.5	29.5	1.6	10.9	4.7	100.2
Technical training	43.0	39.3	0.0	12.6	5.2	100.1
Government relations	62.0	22.8	12.0	0.0	3.3	100.1
Personnel management	69.2	25.6	0.0	1.7	3.4	99.9

Source: Entrepreneurship Survey, see Appendix C. Establishment only. Response categories are abbreviated here.

Notes: [a]Respondents were asked to list up to three participants in the performance of each function. This table includes all indicated participants regardless of rank.

[b]See Appendix D for more detailed description of each function.

comparing the degree of differentiation in 1969–1975 establishments with those of 1969–1975 expansions. In the three functions identified earlier as being most often performed by the lenticular entrepreneur himself, (conceptualization, government relations, and personnel management), there is no significant difference. For the other four functions, however, the degree of differentiation is much higher for expansion than for establishment.

Thus far we have described the degree of differentiation in terms of the share of the chief executive. We now examine the distribution of differentiation by looking at who performed the remaining shares.

7) After the chief executive, the largest share in all functions, save financing, was played by employees and other individuals.
8) In obtaining financing, government (largely the commercial and special banks) played the largest supporting role with other private corporations, and employees and other individuals tied for third. Again, the most difficult function (finance) is the one where the most help is obtained. It is also clear that this is the function in which participation is most widely distributed across a variety of contributors.
9) Except for financing, foreign corporations are uniformly more helpful than domestic corporations. The advantages in being an "open" economy are not confined to access to foreign markets and exposure to the rigors of competition.

We now consider the structure of differentiation among sub-groups defined by size, age, export share, and expansion versus establishment. Caution must be used in interpreting the results, since there are cross-correlations that cannot be distinguished because of small sample size.

10) In terms of size, the only noticeable difference is that larger firms get relatively more help from government and domestic companies in obtaining financing.[22] This

is, of course, critical, and this result simply reflects the well-known higher debt/equity ratios of larger firms.

11) Exporters generally exhibit more differentiation than do domestic producers. Surprisingly, despite the export promotion policy, the extra help does not come from the government, but from foreign entities. There is a difference in this respect between expansion and establishment, with government providing relatively more help at establishment. It thus seems that in the (largely 1970s) expansions, exporters had already attained a level of international respectability and were able to obtain assistance on their own. Nonetheless, the low overall government participation rate in exporting suggests that the direct field-augmentation efforts (for example, KOTRA) may have been less important than indirect market improvement via an open economy strategy.

12) In terms of time, there is an actual decrease in the relative, though not the absolute, level of government participation in establishment. This is particularly noticeable in finance, where the government role drops precipitously from 37 percent to 15 percent.[23] A plausible explanation has two parts. First, there is increasing availability of non-governmental support as the economy diversifies. Second, the government entities find an increasing share of their resources devoted to expansion projects.

13) The last hypothesis is substantiated by the one significant difference between 1969–1975 expansion and establishment projects. In expansion, the government (again, largely through the banks) provided 37 percent of financial participation as compared with only 15 percent for new establishments.

In sum, we find that there is indeed considerable differentiation in the performance of the entrepreneurial function in Korea. There is also evidence that an increase in differentiation is a contributory factor to growth, though the change occurs in an unexpected way. There is surprisingly little support for the hypothesis that over time the assistance available to brand-new entrepreneurs has increased. Instead, the major contribution of differentiation occurs through its higher level in expansion projects (and similarly in offspring establishments). This, however, is a powerful force, given the dominant role of expansion and offspring in growth.

It is well known that large firms are favored over small firms in obtaining finance. The usual explanation is that size creates power, and this translates into being at the head of the line at the bank. While this is certainly part of the story (see Chapter 8), we would suggest that to some extent the apparent size bias may be a proxy for an underlying expansion bias. That is, there is evidence that an entrepreneur who has proven himself gets more help than one who is just starting out, regardless of size. Should this bias be rectified and the government direct more of its efforts towards supporting first-time efforts? This is a question that deserves some thought, but the answer is by no means a clear-cut "yes." Scarce resources should be directed to where they will have the highest social return, and a first-time entrepreneur—regardless of size—is an unknown quantity with a high risk factor. By contrast, an individual who has successfully put together a small-scale combination might be an excellent prospect for a medium-to-large project. Whether or not one accepts this normative justification, the fact seems to be that in Korea the first entrepreneurial act is a go-it-alone proposition. Most fail, but those who succeed are then provided with substantial support, especially financial, in subsequent acts. Since expansion creates size, this expansion bias thus leads to—and helps explain—size bias.

GOVERNMENT ASSISTANCE

The careful reader may feel he has found an inconsistency between our earlier stress on the high level of government intervention (Chapter 4) and the relatively low perception of "managing government relations" as a problem, and the modest role of perceived government support for entrepreneurs (except in obtaining finance). The first problem is resolved by bearing in mind an important distinction. The bulk of negative government intervention via command involves the conduct of ongoing operations rather than the initiation of new operations. As will become clearer in Chapter 8, the government is much more concerned with wealth utilization than with wealth accumulation. Anyone who wishes to initiate new productive combinations is contributing to the very reason for existence of the Park regime and is in no sense discouraged by bureaucratic impediments. Managing government relations in performing an entrepreneurial act is thus not a problem and is indeed a pleasure by LDC standards. Once a firm is established, however, there are real constraints on conduct in the market place. These restraints are largely enforced through partial mutuality that involves implicit threats of interference in future expansions. These threats, however, are believed, and so need seldom be actually carried out. The government is thus quite rightly perceived as a fundamental friend of business.

The second apparent contradiction is more serious. We have placed a relatively high value on the role of field augmentation in expanding the opportunity set of businessmen by making them aware of new opportunities, particularly in foreign markets. Yet, Table 35 gives a relatively small share (6.5 percent overall) to government participation in the conceptualization function. This may, in part, be attributable to response bias, with entrepreneurs begrudging recognition of government assistance in one of their fundamental functions. There may also be a time factor involved. In the pre-1969 period, the government share in conceptualization was almost four times as large as in post-1969. It may therefore be that by the 1970s, entrepreneurial capacity had improved so as to obviate the government's direct field augmentations in manufacturing. That is, the 1960s augmentation in exports having served its purpose (12 percent participation at the margin is after all quite significant), the government has now turned greater attention to supporting service exports.[24] Within the export sector it seems that government augmentation has shifted from direct gap filling (through KOTRA and the commercial attachés) to indirect horizon expansion via expanding diplomatic contacts throughout the world.

Recall, however, that there is a second element of field augmentation, namely, the reduction of uncertainty through planning and providing confidence in the government's ability to maintain a favorable business climate. As shown in Table 36, these aspects of government assistance are given "moderately important" rankings in affecting entrepreneurs' decisions to establish or expand. These field-augmentation efforts are exceeded in importance at establishment by parameter manipulations (tax and tariff privileges), but are the most important elements in the critical expansion decisions. The most counterproductive forms of parameter manipulation—tariff protection on output, exclusive licensing, and direct subsidies—are virtually irrelevant for both expansion and establishment. Exporters gain significantly more from these field manipulations in expansion, and naturally attach significantly less importance to tariff protection.

In sum, our earlier conclusion of high government intervention is not to be taken as indicative of either blindness or an anti-business bias. Intervention is structured to be supportive of entrepreneurial endeavor, with a bias towards expansion projects. Indirect field augmentation and parameter manipulation may be more important intervention mechanisms than direct performance of entrepreneurial functions. There is, nonetheless, a great deal of differentiation of the entrepreneurial function and some of this is attributable to the open-economy policy and the endogenous externalities of growth.

INTEGRATION: SOURCES OF ENTREPRENEURIAL EXPANSION

We now draw together the diverse elements of this chapter, as

TABLE 36 Types of Government Assistance

Question: "How important were each of the following types of government assistance in contributing to your final decision that this would be a profitable project?"

Ranking: Critical 1 — 2 — Moderately Important 3 — 4 — Irrelevant 5

Mean Responses:

Type of Assistance	Establishment[a] (as perceived by Chief Executives)							Expansion[a] (as perceived by)		Expansion	
	All	*Large*	*Small*	*Pre-1969*	*1969–1975*	*Export*	*Domestic*	*Chief*[b]	*Managers*[c]	*Export*	*Domestic*
Tax privileges	3.09	2.91	3.13	3.41[d]	3.87	2.59[f]	3.59	3.39	3.50	2.65[d]	3.17
Tariff privileges on inputs	3.27	2.76	3.37	3.38	3.17	2.71[f]	3.82	3.54	3.01	2.87[f]	4.10
Tariff protection on output	4.02	3.38[e]	4.18	4.07	4.02	3.89	4.11	4.46	4.09	4.16[e]	3.60
Exclusive licensing	4.34	3.86[e]	4.44	4.20	4.41	4.30	4.38	4.58	4.51	4.28	4.64
Direct subsidies	4.46	4.23	4.53	4.33	4.52	3.51[f]	4.43	4.48	4.29	4.50	4.50
Knowledge of long-run development strategy	3.19	2.78	3.20	3.41	2.98	3.25	3.11	2.76	2.75	3.03[e]	2.37
Provision of SOC	3.61	3.48	3.67	3.56	3.65	3.55	3.66	3.44	3.43	3.26	3.61
Confidence in government ability to maintain favorable business climate	3.39	3.20	3.40	3.78[e]	3.14	2.30	3.47	2.84	2.86	2.73	2.93
Sample	112	(22)	(90)	(46)	(66)	(56)	(56)	78	60	40	42

Source: Entrepreneurship Survey, see Appendix C. Response categories are abbreviated here.

Notes: [a]Comparing 1969–1975 expansion and establishments, differences were significant @ 5% on "tax privileges" and "tariff protection."
[b]1969–1975 expansions only.
[c]Unweighted.
[d]t-test significant at 10%
[e]t-test significant at 5%
[f]t-test significant at 1%
(d–f) on adjacent pairs (e.g., large vs. small, pre- and post-1969) export and domestic.

well as a variety of evidence presented elsewhere, and summarize what we see as the major sources of the expansion of Korean entrepreneurship from 1961 to 1975. Readers with a low tolerance for economic jargon will prefer to skip ahead to the summary.

THE MARKET

As an organizing framework, we use the somewhat ill-specified, but pedagogically useful, device of a market for entrepreneurship as a factor of production.[25] The market is for the entire bundle of entrepreneurial functions required to complete a new act of combination. The lenticular function is the single irrevocable role of seeing that all of the other necessary functions are carried out. Employees may design the organization, foreign consultants may provide technology, the trade-promotion board may identify the market, and government banks may provide the capital. Alternatively, some, or all, of these functions may be performed by the entrepreneur, but this is not essential. His irreducible role is to serve as a lens that focuses the various functional energies on the selected target.

Price in the market is the present value of the stream of rent accruing to the successful completion of the project. Some of this may be paid to external agents or employees, with the remainder going to the lenticular entrepreneur. In competitive equilibrium, of course, there is no rent, but neither are there any new combinations. Entrepreneurship, in fact, is the art of seeking out *disequilibrium* corners and exploiting the resulting rent-producing opportunities. Quantity in the market is man-years of (bundle) entrepreneurship of a standard quality.[26] The market is defined as a moving average to dampen short-term business-cycle fluctuations.[27] We now describe the elements of the market (see Figure 2), disaggregating to emphasize the role of market imperfections.

SUPPLY

On the supply side, we wish to distinguish between individuals

FIGURE 2 Notional Entrepreneurial Market

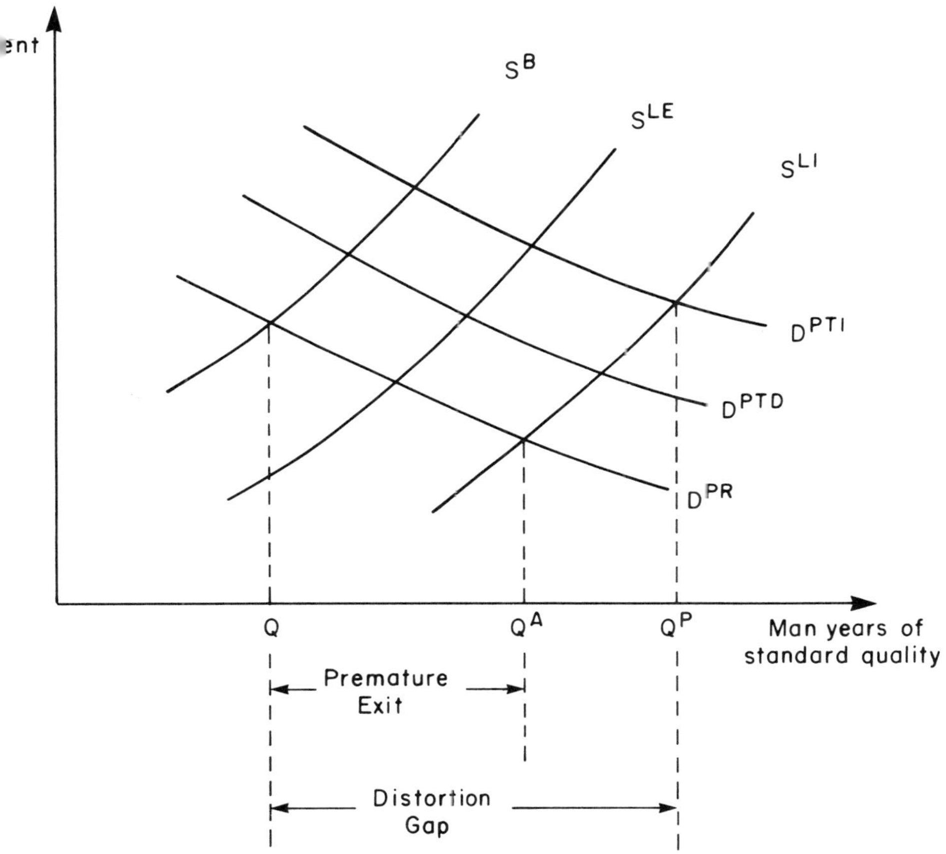

S^B ≡ Supply of the entire bundle of entrepreneurial functions
S^{LE} ≡ Supply of effective lenticular ability
S^{LI} ≡ Supply of lenticular intent

D^{PTI} ≡ Potential demand at international prices
D^{PTD} ≡ Potential demand at domestic prices
D^{PR} ≡ Perceived demand at domestic prices

Q ≡ Actual Equilibrium
Q^A ≡ Attempted Equilibrium
Q^P ≡ Potential Equilibrium

who *attempt* to perform entrepreneurial acts and those who succeed. We, therefore, specify three different supply curves. The first is the supply of entrepreneurial intent of standard quality (S^{LI}). This is a function of pecuniary and non-pecuniary returns to entrepreneurship and to alternative uses of time. Supply is a positive function of expected pecuniary return, if the other arguments are held constant. Over time, the other variables change and the curve shifts. Since non-pecuniary return must also be considered, there will be a positive supply at zero price (and perhaps even at a negative price) if prestige, power, and accomplishment yield satisfaction. We now posit a supply curve of lenticular intent in, say 1960, and ask what it will look like in the 1970s. Two factors are involved: increases in numbers of entrepreneurs and growth of average quality.

A general proposition is that quantitative supply of intent is a function of demographic variables on the one hand, and of psychological motives resulting from sociological conditioning on the other. Rising population and growing urbanization have slowly increased the pool from which entrepreneurial intent is drawn. Since from 1961 to 1974 the compound rate of growth in manufacturing establishments was only 3 percent, demographics alone can account for much of the quantitative expansion.

For a given population, the number that will attempt an entrepreneurial act depends on sociological and psychological factors. Since these change only slowly, the share of individuals involved will change only very gradually. We see no evidence of any significant movement of the curve due to this factor in the early 1960s and attribute to it no role in the early expansion. In the late 1960s, and particularly in the 1970s, however, the curve does shift as society's attitude towards the entrepreneur begins to change. Success breeds popular approval, the government's linkage of nationalistic and patriotic goals to economic achievement adds a marginal non-pecuniary incentive, and the transition from zero-sum to positive-sum entrepreneurship adds respectability.[28] We attribute a real, though probably small, role in the later expansion to such sociological factors.

The change in the number of individuals with entrepreneurial intent is thus easily explained as a result of demographic factors, possibly augmented by social change. The real problem, however, is to explain the quality change.

As lenticular ability improves, the quantity of standard-quality entrepreneurship increases and the curve shifts independently of any change in the number of individuals involved. This shift occurs largely as a result of learning by doing (or by watching). As Hirschman observes, the ability to make decisions is the only scarce resource not consumed in the process of production but actually increased by it.[29] Growth is thus a breeder reactor for entrepreneurial ability. The growth elasticity of entrepreneurial supply is, in turn, a function of the societal level of education and motivation. These factors are treated in Chapter 7 where we conclude that its cultural heritage gives Korea a much higher elasticity than other LDCs. Whatever the reason, there has been a steady and significant improvement in lenticular ability. Korea's entrepreneurs are far more finely ground lenses today than fifteen years ago.

The supply of lenticular intent, however, also includes newly aspiring entrepreneurs. Many of these fail, and this is reflected in the second supply curve of effective lenticularism (S^{LE}). This is derived from the intent function but necessarily lies to its left. At any given level of pecuniary return, only a portion of those willing to act as binding agents are capable of doing so. Available evidence suggests that in Korea the rate of increase of quality of existing entrepreneurs has outstripped the rate of entrance, so the gap between S^{LE} and S^{LI} has narrowed.

The third supply curve (S^{B}) is for the entire bundle of entrepreneurial functions. It is derived from the effective lenticular supply curve but necessarily lies above it, with the gap representing the rent accruing to the other entrepreneurial functions. With perfectly developed markets for each of the complementary functions, the entrepreneur can hire them done at their opportunity cost. No rent accrues to these other activities and the effective lenticular supply curve coincides with the bundle supply. In practice, there is a substantial gap between the two curves.

Several factors are involved here. First, there has been the rise of competent alternative sources of the complementary entrepreneurial functions. Employees, banks, consultants, research institutes, and government agencies increasingly provide assistance. A portion of this is due to exogenous government gap filling through specialized agencies. This was important in the early years of the growth spurt, but has since been subordinated to the endogenous growth-induced perfection of the markets for the complementary functions. In addition, there has been a qualitative improvement in the ability of entrepreneurs and others performing gap-filling functions. The process here is similar to the improvement of lenticular ability already described. Finally, there has been a diffuse improvement of the information markets. This again is in part due to governmental field augmentation through planning and in part to the endogenous effect of growth itself.

DEMAND

On the demand side, it is again useful to think of three distinct curves. The first is potential demand at international prices (D^{PTI}) on the assumption that domestic markets are undistorted or operating at shadow prices. It is similar to an investment function in ranking all projects in order of return. It differs in that price is not the return per unit of capital, but the rent accruing to the entrepreneur upon successful completion. The curve is a function of technology (which defines the available set of unexploited projects) and world prices (which defines the rent accruing to each). These prices are distorted by international disequilibrium market imperfections; otherwise there would be no rent.

A second curve is defined at existing distorted domestic prices (D^{PTD}). The gap between D^{PTI} and D^{PTD} is responsive to, if not solely dependent on, the level of governmental parameter manipulation. There is no necessary relation between D^{PTD} and D^{PTI}, and they may even cross.

The third demand curve is the perceived one (D^{PR}). It is derived from D^{PTD} by deleting all projects that are outside the perceived opportunity set of Korean entrepreneurs, and thus it necessarily lies below D^{PTD} and to its left. The gap between D^{PTD} and D^{PR} is a function of information imperfections and can be reduced by field augmentation.

How have these demand curves shifted over time? First, consider D^{PTI}. The stock of projects is continually changing as some opportunities are wiped out by exploitation and technical change and others added by invention. The ranking of projects, and level of rent, changes with international prices. We are in no position to specify shifts in this curve and for present purposes assume it to be more or less stable with new opportunities replacing old.

What of the relationship between D^{PTI} and D^{PTD}? As Chapter 8 will show, prior to 1962 the most egregious domestic market imperfections involved government privileges yielding exceptionally high rents to various zero-sum trading activities. Other price distortions kept the domestic rent below international rent on the majority of productive projects. The result was that D^{PTD} was above D^{PTI} at the left, and below it on the right, as shown in Figure 3. After the military revolution, the government eliminated the massive rents accruing to acquisition of government controlled inputs. This forced entrepreneurs into activities that may have yielded less private rent but which were socially more productive. In Chapter 8, we describe this loosely as a shift from zero-sum to positive-sum entrepreneurship. Project ranking was thus altered and average rents undoubtedly declined, but the impact on marginal rent is unclear. The marginal private return to entrepreneurship of standard quality may well have been reduced, but the social return increased substantially due to this substitution effect. This did not have the effect of shifting the whole curve down, but of

FIGURE 3 Korean Entrepreneurial Market, 1960–1975

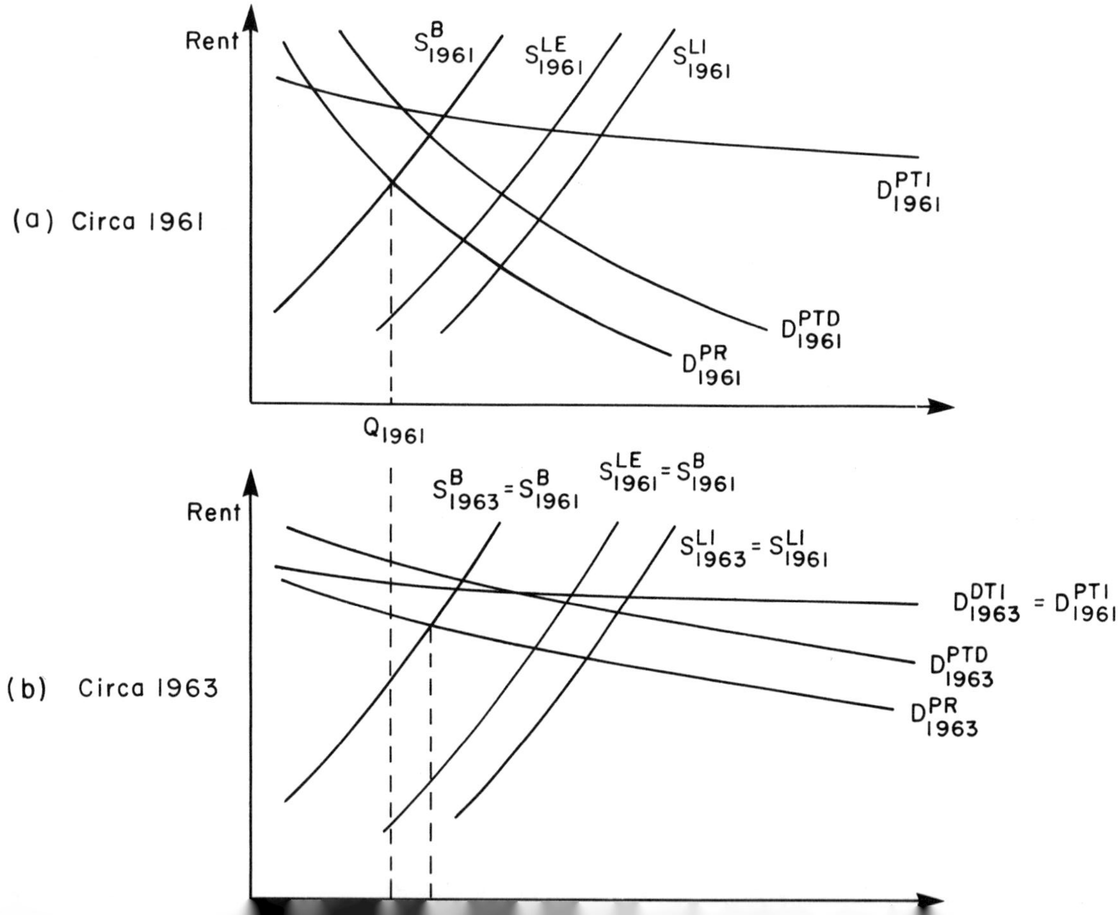

(c) Early 1970s

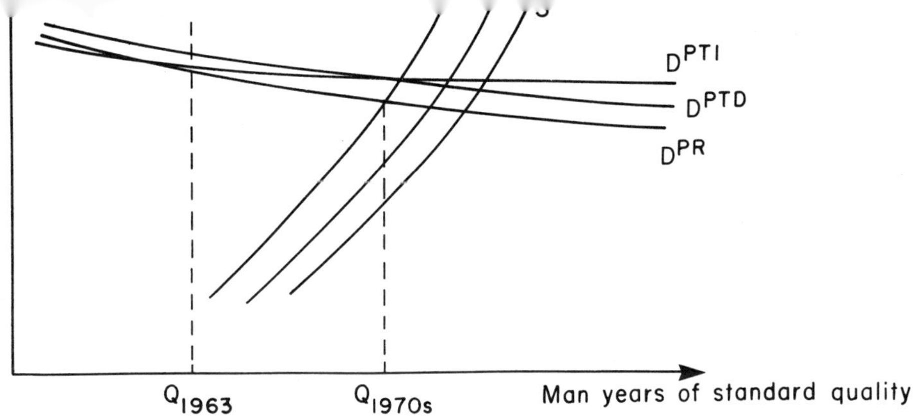

S^{B} ≡ Supply of the entire bundle of entrepreneurial functions
S^{LE} ≡ Supply of effective lenticular ability
S^{LI} ≡ Supply of lenticular intent

D^{PTI} ≡ Potential demand at international prices
D^{PTD} ≡ Potential demand at domestic prices
D^{PR} ≡ Perceived demand at domestic prices

Q ≡ Actual Equilibrium
Q^{A} ≡ Attempted Equilibrium
Q^{P} ≡ Potential Equilibrium

flattening it as the massive rents accruing to government influence were deducted at the high end. Entrepreneurial activity was thus reoriented, but not increased.

In addition to the reranking effect which flattened D^{PTD} and dropped it at the high end, there was a stability effect. Following years of political confusion if not chaos, the introduction and continuation of stability induced expectations of future stability, lengthened the time horizon, lowered the time preference discount rate, and increased the expected return on virtually all projects. The potential domestic demand curve thus shifted up, and increased equilibrium entrepreneurial supply.

Whether or not this shift in D^{PTD} left it above or below D^{PTI} is a question beyond the scope of this study. From our discussion in Chapter 4, it is clear that there remain widespread price distortions in domestic factor markets, arising from government parameter manipulation. It is also clear, however, that these manipulations are particularistic and discretionary, so that, while some projects yield a higher rent, others yield a lower one, and the net effect on $D^{PTD}-D^{PTI}$ is unclear. For present purposes we shall posit three characteristics of the relationship which we think capture the most essential features. First, the gap is relatively small by LDC standards, as evidenced by studies of international competitiveness and the low levels of shadow multipliers estimated for the economy. Second, the gap has probably been reduced slowly over time as government manipulation becomes more sophisticated and finely tuned. Third, the gap is probably positive ($D^{PTD} > D^{PTI}$) over part of its length, reflecting a subsidy which is paid by an implicit levy on other projects (for example, export projects are subsidized at the expense of domestic ones) leaving a negative gap ($D^{PTD} < D^{PTI}$) over the remainders.

With respect to perceived demand (D^{PR}), changes are more straightforward. Throughout the period, there has been a slow but steady expansion of the perceived opportunity set towards the potential. This follows in part from governmental field augmentation, in part from endogenous growth-induced reductions in information imperfections, and in part from entrepreneurial learning. Perceived demand thus converges towards domestic potential demand.

EQUILIBRIUM

We have chosen to specify a variety of supply and demand curves in order to emphasize the critical role we assign to market imperfections. Consider the relationship between three critical intersections, defined as follows:

Q^P @ $D^{PTI} = S^{LI}$ or Potential Equilibrium

Q^A @ $D^{PR} = S^{LI}$ or Attempted Equilibrium

Q @ $D^{PR} = S^B$ or Achieved Equilibrium

The point Q^A thus gives attempted equilibrium and the point Q the achieved equilibrium. The gap ($Q - Q^A$) represents premature exit. The point Q^P gives the potential equilibrium quantity of entrepreneurial acts which would occur in the absence of domestic market distortions (except unavoidable short-term adjustments). The distortion gap ($Q^P - Q$) is the loss due to various domestic market imperfections. This may be further decomposed into shares attributable to entrepreneurial market distortions and those in other factor and product markets. Entrepreneurial development is in part the process of eliminating these distortions so as to use the existing stock more effectively, and in part the process of improving the quantity and the quality of the existing stock.

THE KOREAN CASE

The initial growth spurt in the early 1960s was stimulated largely by changes on the demand side. Stability shifted D^{PTD} up and changes in parameter manipulation flattened it (compare Figure 3A and 3B). Growth was induced by the resulting increase in achieved equilibrium ($Q_{63} - Q_{61}$) and by the fact that the equilibrium quantity was now receiving rent from socially productive, positive-sum activities.

Thereafter, growth was maintained primarily through changes on the supply side.[30] These include:

1) An increase in the number of individuals with lenticular intent, resulting from demographic factors and a rise in non-pecuniary incentives, and reflected in an outward shift of S^{LI}.
2) An increase in the mean standard quality of lenticular ability (shifting S^{LE} towards S^{LI}) resulting from learning-by-doing.
3) An increase in the mean quality of performance of non-lenticular functions by entrepreneurs and others, resulting from learning and field augmentation, and reflected in the convergence of S^{B} towards S^{LE}.
4) An increase in the quantity of performance of non-lenticular functions, resulting from increased differentiation and also reflected in the convergence of S^{B} towards S^{LE}.
5) An expansion of the perceived opportunity set, resulting from experience and field augmentation, and reflected in the movement of D^{PR} towards D^{PTD}.

Each of the five shifts has both an endogenous growth-induced component and an exogenous government-induced element. The change in non-pecuniary incentives is in part the result of an explicit campaign of official praise, and in part the result of success breeding approval. The quantity of differentiation is in part an externality of growth (with a larger economy providing more complementary inputs), and in part a result of conscious government institutional development (our evidence suggests the latter was more important in the mid-1960s and now plays a minor role). The quality of lenticular and non-lenticular abilities and the expansion of the perceived opportunity set are in part the result of learning by doing, and in part the consequence of indirect field manipulation.

The result of these shifts is the steady increase in Q necessary to maintain a relatively constant rate of growth in an expanding economy. The effect on equilibrium rent is unclear. For a given D^{PTD}, the shift in supply results in a lowering of rent accruing to the marginal entrepreneur of standard quality. This is an expected result of development. In a somewhat competitive economy the entrepreneur must diligently seek out non-competitive nooks and crannies in order to slip in and grab a little rent before a competitor drives it away. In a disequilibrium LDC, the nooks and crannies become chasms and valleys, and there is less competition, so that a rental position once attained can be maintained for a substantial period of time. Development thus reduces marginal rent. On the other hand, any improvement in world technology and prices, or a rent-positive change in domestic distortions, will shift D^{PTI} or D^{PTD} and pull D^{PR} outwards. Marginal rent will then increase. It should be noted that, even if the return per unit of standard input has fallen for the marginal entrepreneur, it has undoubtedly risen for the larger entrepreneur. This is so because the number of standard units per individual has increased with ability. Also, in this market the supplier captures the whole of consumer and producer surplus so that most entrepreneurs earn substantially more than the marginal rate. Finally, we are talking here of only one year's entrepreneurial activity, but established entrepreneurs are always earning rent from previous acts as well. Pyŏng-ch'ŏl Yi will, therefore, gain an expanding rental income even as marginal returns decline.

In any event, we must remain agnostic as to whether the supply or demand shifts dominate and will leave it to others to identify the change in marginal rent that has occurred in the course of Korean growth. Our purpose has been only to explain the shift in equilibrium quantity.

SUMMARY

We began this chapter by asking what lay behind the expansion of entrepreneurship, and we phrased the question in terms of the traditional supply-and-demand dichotomy. Our first major empirical observation was that what was to be explained was not primarily an increase in the number of entrepreneurs, but the magnitude of their individual successes. That is, growth in output was not primarily due to a rise in the number of production units but to an increase in their average unit size: small units were replaced by larger units, and existing firms expanded and split to form offspring companies. This observation led us to reject (at least in their simpler versions) both the traditional competing hypotheses (supply versus demand dominance), since both focus on the *quantity* of entrepreneurs. Our primary problem, on the other hand, is to explain an exploding volume of effective entrepreneurship with only a modest increase in the number of entrepreneurs. This means we must focus on entrepreneurial *quality*.

Our interpretation is that the expansion of effective entrepreneurial supply in Korea from 1961–1975 is to be explained as follows:

1) The supply of individuals with entrepreneurial intent (those who attempt to succeed in business) increased only slightly. This supply is largely a function of demographic and sociological characteristics and its modest shift from 1961 to 1975 was largely a result of demographic change (increased population, and greater exposure to entrepreneurial opportunities through urbanization and education). There may also have been a small increase due to increased prestige for business activity.
2) The bulk of the increase in effective entrepreneurship came from qualitative improvements. Entrepreneurs' lenticular ability to combine the various entrepreneurial functions grew through learning by doing. The quality of performance of the individual functions grew with learning and functional differentiation as more and more of the entrepreneurial tasks were solved by employees, the market, government, or others.

On the demand side, there was a critical one-time shift in the early 1960s as stability and belief in government dedication to economic growth increased the expected return. Perhaps more important, the reduction of license-oriented, rent-seeking opportunities reduced the gap between private and social return and meant that a given volume of effective entrepreneurship had a greater real growth effect and hence fed the virtuous circle of learning by doing on the supply side. Thereafter, demand shifts were smaller and slower, largely taking the form of a steady reduction in the gap between potential demand (all opportunities at world prices) and effective demand (perceived opportunities at domestic prices).

On both sides, the process may be summarized as one of reducing distortions in the entrepreneurial market so as to take advantage of the existing stock of entrepreneurial aspirations. It should be emphasized, however, that these distortions are not to be conventionally thought of as price phenomena[31] but as information imperfections. The problem was not to increase the ex ante expected return to entrepreneurship, since even in the 1950s this was high enough to entice substantial entry of entrepreneurial intent. Instead, the problem was to reduce the gap between expectations and ex post actuality by improving quality in the ways we have described. Given the paucity of prior academic work in this area, definitive and detailed specifications of these changes are not possible, but we hope this analytic framework has allowed us to identify the major trends behind the expansion.

SEVEN

Private Entrepreneurship: Supply

Whether or not one accepts our theory of the workings of the entrepreneurial market, it is clear that there has been no shortage. If a real 14 percent annual non-agricultural private growth rate over fifteen years represents a world-record-class entrepreneurial performance, and if decision-making is the scarcity that underlies all others in LDCs, then it is worth examining the training methods of the contenders. This chapter therefore goes behind the supply curve to identify the distinguishing characteristics of Korean entrepreneurs. We do not, however, go very far behind the curve, confining ourselves largely to observable social background variables. Only limited reference is made to the more fundamental, but ephemeral, psychological factors.

The emergence of a thriving entrepreneurial class in Korea is particularly intriguing, since it runs counter to the traditional value system. Confucianism places commerce and industry at the bottom of the *sa, nong, kong, sang* (scholar-official, farmer, artisan, merchant) status hierarchy. A variety of authors have deplored this deep-rooted attitude as inimical to modernization in East Asia. The following Korean variant is typical:

> The traditional idea of Korean Confucianism did not have much respect for technical and physical or manual labour but rather despised this. Laboring for material production could not have the qualities of being the gentleman. Labour was the job only for a workman. Therefore, industrial techniques could never be developed . . . Trade and commerce, without being esteemed, even nominally, had been regarded as the meanest sort of work . . . Such ideas of the Korean traditional Confucianism should be thoroughly eliminated to make way for the ideological bases for democratic and liberalistic modernization.[1]

After the fact, it is evident that this value system has hardly proved an insuperable obstacle. One should remember, in considering the genesis of Korean entrepreneurs, that the choice of business was neither easy nor obvious.

We proceed in three stages. In the first, we compare the background of entrepreneurs to that of the population as a whole. Studies of many LDCs find that business leaders come from narrowly defined sub-strata of the population rather than being randomly distributed as Schumpeter would suggest.[2] Korea has had over two thousand years of unified history in roughly its present borders with no significant influxes of foreign elements. The result is one of the world's most homogeneous populations, so the definition of minority groups must necessarily be more finely drawn than elsewhere. We consider provincial origin, religion, work history, parental occupation, and education as possible differentiating factors. The last two variables also must serve as weak proxies for class, since it is impossible to distinguish traditional status classes (that is, *yangban, hyangban, t'oban, chungin, sŏŏl, sangmin* and *ch'ŏnmin*) through survey techniques.[3] We also consider birth order as one readily ascertainable component of some psychological theories.

The second stage of our search will involve an attempt to

distinguish more successful entrepreneurs from less successful ones on the basis of social background and economic variables. The third stage consists of asking entrepreneurs themselves what their distinguishing characteristics are. We conclude with a discussion of the implications of the Korean case for theories of entrepreneurial supply.

PROVINCE OF ORIGIN

There are three reasons for considering province of origin[4] as a distinguishing characteristic of the entrepreneurial set. First, Korean folklore teaches that there are profound personality differences between individuals from different provinces, and these might affect entrepreneurial behavior. Second, popular opinion holds that political favoritism conveys special advantages to those from certain provinces. Third, the group of northern refugees constitutes a highly visible candidate as a subordinated group that might find upward mobility in entrepreneurial activity.

There are indeed pronounced differences in the provincial propensity to spawn entrepreneurs. These are shown in Table 37, which compares the distribution of our entrepreneurship sample with the distribution of the male population cohort. The main results are as follows:

1) Kyŏngsang provinces (the southeastern provinces surrounding Pusan and including Taegu) dominate in absolute terms with roughly a quarter of the entrepreneurs born there. Since, however, approximately one-third of the male cohort originates in Kyŏngsang province, the province is actually underrepresented (share of entrepreneurs over share of cohort $\equiv E_P/C_P = 0.8$).
2) In relative terms, northerners are the most heavily overrepresented ($E_P/C_P = 4.93$). Within the northern provinces, there is a marked difference between Hamgyŏng and P'yŏngan ($E_P/C_P = 6.6$), and Hwanghae ($E_P/C_P = 1.8$).

3) Seoul is also heavily overrepresented ($E_P/C_P = 4.3$), while those born abroad ($E_P/C_P = 2.6$) and those from Kyŏnggi province ($E_P/C_P = 1.7$) are well above average.
4) Ch'ungch'ŏng, Chŏlla and Kangwŏn provinces are heavily underrepresented, (though the differences *within* this group are not statistically significant).

Overall, these differences are statistically significant,[5] but do they represent causality? That is, the correlations may be explained by:

1) Provincial differences in sociological or psychological propensities that lead to business success;
2) Cross-correlation with other variables (education, religion, and so on) that explain entrepreneurship; or,
3) Government biases in favor of particular regions.

No definitive answer will be attempted here, in part because of data limitations, and in part because the "other variables" might themselves be attributable to socio-psychological propensities. Some insight into the question may be gained, however, by comparing the place of birth of entrepreneurs with that of other Korean elites, and by examining the cross-correlations with other variables.

Table 38 gives the place of birth of various Korean elites (private entrepreneurs, private managers, public managers, public bureaucrats, and politicians). The first, gross result is that similar distortions appear in the distribution of all elites.[6] If bias in selection is the causal factor, it occurs across elites. It is, for example, often believed that the current regime favors individuals from President Park's Kyŏngsang province. In fact, individuals from this area are *under*represented in all elite groups by factors ranging from 0.63 to 0.88. Further, the region's representation is highest for the group where any bias should have the least effect (private managers) and lowest where bias should be most effective (public managers). In any event, contrary to expectations, there is no evidence of pro-Kyŏngsang province bias.[7] Individuals born in the north, Seoul, Kyŏnggi province, and abroad are overrepresented in all elites,

TABLE 37 Place of Birth: Entrepreneurs and Male Cohort
(%)

Location	Entrepreneurs[a]			Male Cohort[b]			Ent./Cohort		
	Total[c]	Young[d]	Old[e]	Total[f]	Young[g]	Old[h]	Total	Young	Old
South									
Seoul	16.2	22.9	14.8	3.8	4.9	2.8	4.26	4.67	5.29
Province:									
Kyŏnggi	17.0	29.3	14.5	10.3	10.1	10.5	1.65	2.90	1.38
Kangwŏn	1.0	0.0	1.2	6.0	5.9	6.2	0.17	–	0.19
Ch'ung ch'ŏng	7.5	8.9	7.3	16.4	16.1	16.6	0.46	0.55	0.44
Kyŏngsang[i]	26.1	20.2	27.3	32.2	32.6	31.9	0.81	0.62	0.86
Chŏlla	6.7	3.0	7.4	24.9	25.7	24.2	0.27	0.12	0.31
Cheju Island	1.6	3.0	1.3	1.1	1.1	1.0	1.45	2.73	1.30
North									
Province:									
Hamgyŏng	7.2	0.0	8.6	1.1	0.6	1.6	6.55	–	5.38
P'yŏngan	11.2	8.9	11.7	1.7	0.8	2.4	6.59	11.13	4.88
Hwanghae	2.7	4.0	2.4	1.5	0.8	2.0	1.80	5.00	1.20
Foreign	2.9	0.0	3.5	1.1	1.4	0.8	2.64	–	4.38
TOTAL	100.1	100.2	100.0	100.1	100.0	100.0	–	–	–
(n)	(194)	(36)	(158)						

TABLE 37 (continued)

Subtotals									
North	21.1	12.9	22.7	4.3	6.5	6.0	4.91	1.98	3.78
South	76.1	87.3	73.8	94.7	92.1	93.2	0.80	0.95	0.79

Notes: [a]Entrepreneurship Survey, see Appendix C.
[b]EPB, *1960 Population and Housing Census of Korea*, Vol. 2; 20% Sample Tabulation Report (Seoul, 1963), pp. 44–45.
[c]Born 1897–1947
[d]Born 1935–1947
[e]Born 1897–1934
[f]Born 1896–1950
[g]Born 1936–1950
[h]Born 1896–1935
[i]Including Pusan

The differences between the (total) entrepreneurship and cohort frequencies are statistically significant (after recombining northern provinces and Cheju Island plus foreign to yield adequate cell observations).

$X^2_{(0.95,7)} = 14.07 < 39.24$ (calculated)

TABLE 38 Place of Birth: Korean Elites[a]

Location	Percentage Distributions					Ratio to Male Cohorts[i]				
	Private Entrepreneurs[b]	*Private Managers*[b]	*Public Managers*[c]	*Bureaucrats*[d]	*Politicians*[e]	*Private Entrepreneurs*	*Private Managers*	*Public Managers*	*Bureaucrats*	*Politicians*
Central[f]	34.5	29.0	45.9	25.9	22.8	1.72	1.44	2.28	1.29	1.17
Southeastern[g]	24.8	28.4	20.2	23.6	24.5	0.77	0.88	0.63	0.73	0.77
Southwestern[h]	17.0	26.0	18.5	24.7	28.8	0.40	0.61	0.44	0.58	0.69
Northern	21.2	14.2	14.8	14.4	21.7	4.93	3.30	3.44	3.35	3.62
Foreign	2.6	2.4	0.6	11.5	2.2	2.36	2.18	0.55	10.45	2.75
TOTAL	100.1	100.0	100.0	100.1	100.0					
n	191	169	357	174	316					
Mean birth date	1925	1932	1924	1926	1915					

Notes: [a]The distributions of all five groups are significantly different from that of their cohort (at the 5% level, X^2 test). Pairwise differences among the elites are significant except for private enterprise versus private manager and private manager versus bureaucrat.

[b]Entrepreneurship Survey, see Appendix C. Unweighted results are reported here, since weighting yields only minor differences on this question and the tedium of weighting the management results was avoided.

[c]Hun Yu, *Konggiŏp imwŏn ŭi sahoejŏk paegyŏng* (Seoul, 1974). Survey covered presidents, vice presidents, auditors, and operating directors of 56 government enterprises. Data on place of birth was not published, but was kindly made available to us.

[d]Dong Suh Bark and Chae-Jin Lee, "Bureaucratic Elite and Development Orientations," in *Political Leadership in Korea*, edited by Dae-Sook Suh and Chae-Jin Lee (Seattle, 1976), p. 95. Sample consisted of 176 out of 203 senior central government officials who held Grade I-A positions as of January 1977.

[e]Bae Ho Hahn and Kyu Taik Kim, "The Political Leaders: Their Social Origins and Skills," in *Korea: A Pattern of Political Development*, edited by C. I. Eugene Kim (Kalamazoo, 1964), pp. 17–41. Population is diverse group of cabinet ministers, vice ministers, congressional leaders, ambassadors, service chiefs, and higher civil servants in Rhee, Chang Myon and early Military Governments. Response was 65% with 89% of this from ministers, vice ministers and congressional leaders.

[f]Seoul, Kyŏnggi province, Kangwŏn province.

[g]Pusan, Kyŏngsang provinces.

[h]Ch'ungch'ŏng and Chŏlla provinces, Cheju Island.

[i]Male cohort from Table 37. "Old" cohort for Politicans and "Total" for other groups.

while those from Kangwŏn, Chŏlla, and Ch'ungch'ŏng provinces and Cheju Island are always underrepresented.[8]

The popular opinion of pro-Kyŏngsang province bias is undoubtedly heavily influenced by the origins of the heads of the larger and more conspicuous chaebŏl (for example, Pyŏng-ch'ŏl Yi of Samsung, In-hoe Ku of Lucky, Sŏng-gon Kim of Ssangyong, Hong-je Cho of Hyosung). To examine the extent of size bias, Table 39 gives the place of birth of the founders of the forty-six largest chaebŏl. These results suggest that Kyŏngsang province is indeed more heavily represented among the largest entrepreneurs than among the entrepreneurial set as a whole. This may suggest some favoritism at the higher end of the scale, but the fact remains that Kyŏngsang province is represented almost proportionately to its share in the population. Even among chaebŏl heads it is still those from the north, Seoul, and Kyŏnggi province who are overrepresented.

To return to the individual distortion factors in Table 38, one intriguing result is the particularly large share of public managers from Seoul and Kyŏnggi province. When this rate is broken down, the distortion is higher for those entrepreneurs from government financial institutions and for presidents and (operational) directors (as opposed to auditors and vice presidents), but not by large amounts. It is difficult to escape the conclusion that there is a political bias in public enterprise appointment practices, but that these are *not* pro-Kyŏngsang province, but pro-Seoul/Kyŏnggi province.

The most striking degrees of overrepresentation are found in the northern group ($3.30 < E_p/C_p < 5.0$).[9] This is most likely attributable to one of two factors:

1) (Un)natural Selection. Those who choose to flee a Communist regime will be disproportionately educated, wealthy, and from industrial and commercial backgrounds; hence, the refugee population will be far more likely to appear in the entrepreneurial population.
2) Social Blockage. Displaced persons may be from a subordinated social group, forcing them into innovative and

TABLE 39 Place of Birth: Chaebŏl Founders

	Chaebŏl Heads	Ratio to Cohort
Central	23.9	1.23
Southeastern	32.6	1.02
Southwestern	23.8	.57
Northern	19.6	3.30
Foreign	0.0	–
	99.9	
Number	(46)	
Mean birth year	(1916)	

Source: Survey of founders of 46 largest chaebŏl; see Chapter 8. Male population cohort (older group) from Table 37. Place of birth from: Chong-gi Paek and Yŏng-jung Pak, *Chaebŏl samsimnyŏn sa ŭi tŭrama* (Seoul., 1976).

previously undesirable activity, in an effort to gain (or regain) social status. In the case of northern refugees, this motive might be enhanced by a traditionally unfavorable southern perception of northerners. To gain some insight into the northern overrepresentation among Korean elites, it is useful to compare the social origins of northern and southern entrepreneurs, as given in Table 40. The two groups are seen to be similar in the level of their own and their fathers' education, the place raised (Seoul versus city versus village, and so on), job experience and male sibling rank. Major differences occur only for fathers' jobs and religion.[10] Northerners were more heavily influenced by Christianity (30 percent versus 18 percent) and correspondingly less influenced by traditional Buddhism and Confucianism (37 percent versus 54 percent). More than one-third of the northerners' fathers had been engaged in some form of trade as opposed to only one-seventh of the southerners'. Southerners were more likely to have come from landowning backgrounds (32 percent versus 15 percent) and industry (15 percent versus 9 percent). These and other dif-

TABLE 40 North-South Differences in Social Background[a]

	Means		*t-tests*	
	North-erners	*South-erners*	*t-statistic*	*Significance level (%)*
Age (years)	51.49	48.97	1.68	9.5
Family size[b]	4.27	5.19	–2.47	1.4
Male sibling rank	1.92	1.89	0.32	74.8
Own education (years)	13.76	14.16	–0.73	46.4
Fathers' education (years)	5.43	6.13	–0.72	47.5

	Percentage Distribution		X^2 *Test*		
Former Jobs[c]	*North-erners*	*South-erners*	X^2 *Sta-tistic*		*Critical Value (5%)*
Government	17.9	20.3			
Military	10.3	10.2			
Financial institution	7.7	10.9			
Export-import	25.6	14.1	5.05	<	15.51
Domestic trade	2.6	9.4			
Korean company	56.4	54.7			
Foreign company	7.7	4.7			
Public enterprise	7.7	7.0			
Other	28.2	29.7			
(number)	(39)	(128)			
Where Raised					
Seoul	34.0	31.9			
Other city	28.8	29.1			
Small town	11.3	16.1	1.51	<	9.49
Village	20.6	16.6			
Abroad	5.2	6.4			
(number)	(45)	(147)			

TABLE 40 (continued)

	Percentage Distribution		X^2 *Test*		
Father's Job	*North-erners*	*South-erners*	X^2 *Sta-tistic*		*Critical Value (5%)*
Landowner	14.6	23.4			
Other farmer[d]	21.8	29.1			
Industry	8.8	15.4	25.56	>	14.07
Government	6.3	5.7			
Teaching	7.5	1.4			
Professional[e]	2.2	8.0			
Trade	36.7	13.6			
Other	2.2	3.4			
(number)	(44)	(149)			
Religious Influence[f]					
Buddhism	41.8	58.7			
Confucianism	31.2	48.5	7.62	≅	7.81
Catholicism	22.5	14.1			
Protestantism	36.6	21.1			
(number)	(37)	(130)			

Source: Entrepreneurship Survey, see Appendix C.

Notes: [a]Split according to father's birthplace.

[b]Number of brothers and sisters.

[c]Totals add to more than 100% since many respondents had more than one former job.

[d]Largely owner-operators, but includes a few tenants and other farmers.

[e]Including banking.

[f]Percentage responding that indicated religion had some degree of influence on them. Totals do not equal 100% since an individual could be influenced by more than one religion.

ferences are real, but even more important is that both groups had parental backgrounds decidedly atypical of the population as a whole.

In sum, there seems to be surprisingly little evidence to support the hypothesis that northerners form a subordinate class who were socially blocked thereby forcing them into industrial entrepreneurship. Instead, it appears that, if a sample of southerners were drawn with similar family backgrounds, they would be just as likely to be entrepreneurs as northerners.[11] We conclude that northern overrepresentation in the entrepreneurial set, and among elites in general, is predominantly due to (un)natural selection among those who moved south, rather than by any particular characteristics of northerners as a whole or by any special drives of displaced persons.

RELIGION

Since Max Weber stressed the role of the "Protestant Ethnic" in the development of Western capitalism, religious minorities have been examined as potential sources of entrepreneurial supply. The search has been productive: in Pakistan, Islamic subcastes representing two-tenths of a percent of the population control 44 percent of industry;[12] in Lebanon, Christians are more than four times as likely to become entrepreneurs as are Moslems;[13] in Indonesia, Clifford Geertz showed that, on Bali, enterprise was led by a ruling Hindu-Buddhist minority, while in a Javanese town it was dominated by a small group of liberal Muslims;[14] elsewhere, the role of Jains in India and Quakers in the United States has been stressed.[15]

In Korea, the major religious minorities are the Protestants and Catholics [16] who were heavily persecuted under the Yi dynasty. They have since prospered and played a prominant role in national affairs. In politics, they were particularly visible in the Rhee period (Syngman Rhee was a Christian) and have been in the forefront of protest movements from the colonial independence movement to the 1970s' civil rights effort; in education, three of today's five finest universities in Seoul are Christian sponsored. The question here is whether or not the Christian minority has played a similarly disproportionate role in industrial growth.

Unfortunately, it is surprisingly difficult to get an accurate picture of religious preference in Korea. Estimates of the Christian share of the population vary from 3.5 percent to over 13 percent.[17] This is due to the areligious proclivity of Koreans. That is, when a Westerner is asked his religion, it takes a conscious act to say "none"; for a Korean, it takes a conscious dedication to specify anything other than "none." The result is that many individuals with a strong religious upbringing nonetheless express no religious preference. Since it is religious influence rather than stated religion that affects behavior, our survey asked each respondent to specify the strength of the influence of each religion. Results are given in Table 41 and confirm the low regard for religious influence; roughly half said that even Buddhism and Confucianism were "irrelevant."

The translation of "influence" into "affiliation" for comparative purposes is a highly conjectural task that is attempted in Table 42. The results suggest the following very tentative hypotheses:

1) Christians constitute rather similar shares of the entrepreneurial and bureaucratic elites.
2) The Christian share in these elites is, if anything, higher than in the population as a whole[18] but clearly less than in the political and professional elites.

These shares may be the result of two conflicting pressures. On the one hand, Christians might be more likely to be entrepreneurs as they are less traditional, may have greater access to education, form a subordinated group, and are more heavily represented among the northern refugees. On the other hand, the moral absolutism of the churches may mitigate against participation in what was often seen to be necessarily shady business activity; further, Christians may come disproportion-

TABLE 41 Influence of Religion on Businessmen
(%)

n=174

"How strong was the influence of each of the following religions for you?"

	Very strong 1	2	*Moderate* 3	4	*Irrelevant* 5	*Total*
Confucianism	10.4	8.8	19.0	6.0	55.8	100.0
Buddhism	14.2	7.2	27.4	6.6	44.6	100.0
Catholicism	2.2	1.6	7.4	4.9	83.8	99.9
Protestantism	9.2	1.7	5.7	8.0	75.3	99.9
Other	0.0	0.0	0.0	0.1	99.9	100.0

Source: Entrepreneurship Survey, see Appendix C.

ately from lower-class social origins that are not represented in the entrepreneurial set.

In sum, neither the available data nor a priori theorizing allow us to form definitive judgements on the degree of over or under-representation of Christians in the business elite. The resulting agnosticism, however, in itself, yields a rather strong conclusion. Relative to other societies, religion plays an extremely minor role in differentiating the entrepreneurial elite from the population as a whole. In part, this is due to the religious minority's conflicting attitudes towards business. Perhaps more important, the attitudes of the Buddhist-Confucian majority have proven to be business-neutral or weakly held, so that no comparative advantage is conferred on the non-traditional religious minority.

INTERGENERATIONAL OCCUPATIONAL MOBILITY

The parental occupation of industrial entrepreneurs is of interest since it: 1) Serves as a crude proxy for class origin; 2) Is indicative of the degree of social mobility in Korean society; and 3) Suggests the degree to which entrepreneurial talent is ran-

TABLE 42 Religious Affiliations of Businessmen

(%)

	Protestant	*Catholic*	*Buddhist*	*Confucian*	*None*	*Other*	*Total*	*Sample*
I. Population								
A. Institution's claim[a]	10.7	2.5	26.8	13.7	39.3[k]	7.0	100.0	–
B. National survey[b]	2.4	1.1	4.6	0.7	91.1	0.1	100.0	–
C. Sample survey: husband[c]	6.9	2.0	15.5	75.5		–	99.9	(490)
D. Sample survey: wife[c]	10.6	2.1	21.9	65.3		–	99.9	(479)
II. Comparison Groups								
A. Political leaders[d]	32.5	8.5	13.3	17.5	27.9	0.3	100.0	(316)
B. Civil servants[e]	11.9	3.4	9.3	5.5	69.6	0.2	99.9	(1640)
C. Civil servants[f]	14.0	3.7	8.4	73.9		–	100.0	(?)
D. Professors[g]	33.4	8.6	9.4	6.6	39.7	2.2	99.9	(761)
III. Entrepreneurs								
A. Estimate #1[h]	9.9	3.0	15.7	13.9	57.5	0.0	100.0	(174)
B. Estimate #2[i]	12.4	4.6	36.5	25.3	21.3	0.0	100.1	(174)
C. Estimate #3[j]	14.8	4.7	37.6	26.0	16.8	0.1	100.0	(174)

Notes: [a]Korea Gallup Statistical Institute, *Statistical Yearbook: 1974* (Seoul, 1975), pp. 313–314. These data are apparently based on institutional claims (e.g., the "other" category includes 429,000 members of the International Moral Association).

[b]Cited in Bae Ho Hahn and Kyu Taik Kim, pp. 17–41.

TABLE 42 (continued)

[c]Bom Mo Chung, et al., *Boy Preference and Family Planning in Korea* (Seoul, 1974), p. 156. Sample consists of married couples with wives aged 45 and under from Seoul middle and lower classes and rural areas.

[d]Bae Ho Hahn and Kyu Taik Kim, p. 31.

[e]Hoon Yu, "Social Background of Higher Civil Servants in Korea," *Koreana Quarterly* (Spring 1968), p. 51.

[f]Dong Suh Bark, "The Problem of Korean Higher Civil Servants-Their Social Background and Morale," *Some Problems in Public Administration in Developing Countries* (Hawaii, 1966), pp. 1–21.

[g]Sŭng-jik Hong, *Chisigin ŭi kach'igwan yŏn'gu* (Seoul, 1972), p. 194.

[h]Assumes that the indicated religion is the affiliation of those whose highest single level of influence (from Table 41) was "1" or "2."

[i]Same as h, but "1," "2," or "3."

[j]Same as h, but "1," "2," "3," or "4."

[k]Residual.

TABLE 43 Intergenerational Occupational Mobility in Entrepreneurs' Families

(%)

Occupation	Population[d]	Entrepreneurs' Fathers	Entrepreneurs' Grandfathers	Managers' Fathers[g]	Fathers of: Young Entrepreneurs[h]	Fathers of: Older Entrepreneurs[i]
Landlord	2.9[e]	21.4	28.9	10.9	17.7	22.1
Owner-operator	9.4[e]	25.4	45.5	30.1	6.0	29.3
Other farmer[a]	67.8	2.0	3.3	0.0	0.0	2.4
Manufacturing: owner	0.4	12.4	2.5	9.0	28.6	8.5
Manufacturing: white collar[b]	0.1	3.5	0.8	6.4	6.4	2.3
Retailer: owner	} 1.6 (Retailer, Wholesale, Export-import combined)	4.9	2.5	11.5	5.9	4.7
Wholesale: owner		11.5	2.5	8.3	21.6	9.4
Export-import: owner		2.6	0.0	0.6	3.0	2.5
Government	0.5	5.9	3.5	5.8	3.0	6.5
Teaching	0.1	3.8	3.5	5.1	0.5	3.8
Professional[c]	0.2	6.7	6.1	7.0	7.4	8.4
Other	17.0	0.0	0.9	5.2	0.0	0.0

TABLE 43 (continued)

TOTAL	100.0	100.2	100.1	99.9	100.1	99.9
Sample size	6,212[f]	192	121	156	33	159

Notes: [a]Includes pure tenants, mixed owner-tenants, agricultural laborers, and other agricultural occupations.

[b]Includes engineers, managers, and clerks.

[c]Including banking, journalism, and politics.

[d]Economically active Korean males. Calculated from 1930 Census which breaks down employment into 377 categories. Chōsen Sōtokufu *Chōsen kokusei chōsa hōkoku: 1930*, pp. 246–265.

[e]The distribution between "landlord" and "owner-operator" varies with the treatment of the mixed case of those who farmed a portion of their land and rented out another portion. The population census gives 0.3% of Korean males as living wholly on land rental income and 12.0% as owner-operators, but this latter category undoubtedly includes many who were really "landlords" using hired labor to farm some of their own land. A superior breakdown is given in: Chōsen Sōtokufu, *Chōsen Sōtokufu tōkei nenpō*. As a share of Korean and Japanese agricultural household heads, pure landlords are 0.7%, mixed landlord/owner-operators are 2.9%, and pure owner-operators are 17.6%. We use these shares to roughly reapportion the population census totals. The resulting breakdown between "landlord" and owner-operator is only approximate.

[f]Thousands.

[g]Unweighted.

[h]Under 40 years of age.

[i]Forty and older.

domly distributed in society. Table 43 gives the ancestral occupations obtained from our survey as well as a matching distribution for the parental cohort taken from the 1930 census.

In absolute terms, agriculture dominates, with half of entrepreneurs' fathers and three-quarters of the grandfathers active in this sector. This is not surprising given the primitive state of the Korean economy in the 1930s. Only 16 percent of the fathers and 3 percent of the grandfathers were in manufacturing, so there is substantial intergenerational mobility into industry. This is a trivial form of mobility, however, and merely reflects the rapid structural change that has occurred in the Korean economy.

Of considerably more interest is the opportunity for movement from the masses to the "elite" (where we use "elite" to include those with high incomes or high influence as well as the traditional *yangban* occupations). In this more fundamental sense, mobility is minimal. Entrepreneurs' fathers were large-to-medium[19] landowners (47 percent), merchants (19 percent), factory owners (16 percent), civil servants (6 percent), teachers (4 percent), or professionals (7 percent). Ninety-eight percent of the fathers thus came from occupational groups representing perhaps 15 percent of the male Korean cohort. This figure actually understates the degree of concentration, since the categories are fairly broad. For example, wholesalers are more than twice as numerous as retailers in our samples but undoubtedly represent a far smaller, but wealthier, segment of the population. Similarly, in agriculture the sample owner-operator group reported an average holding of 3.3 chŏngbo whereas in 1937 only 7 percent of all farms were more than 2 chŏngbo.[20] Since 18 percent of farm households were owner-operations in 1929, it seems clear that, even within the owner-operator group, it was primarily the larger holders who produced entrepreneurs.[21] We may therefore safely conclude that very few entrepreneurs have risen from the poor masses represented by tenant farmers and rural and urban laborers. The industrial elite were recruited from the pre-industrial elite rather than from society as a whole.[22]

This result may seem to be contradicted by some of the rags-to-riches Horatio Alger stories given in our case studies of individual entrepreneurs. The paradox is resolved by recalling the general level of poverty and deprivation during the Japanese period. Even someone in the ninetieth percentile of the Korean income distribution in 1930 would be in poverty by today's standards. An individual from a relatively poor background could indeed raise himself through heroic effort to obtain the requisite education. Such cases are the exception rather than the rule, however, since under the Japanese it was difficult enough for even the upper-middle classes to obtain an education. Today's entrepreneurs indeed often came from backgrounds that were poor in an absolute sense but which were, nonetheless, well-off relative to their Korean peers.

To what extent has social background changed over time? Table 43 shows that younger entrepreneurs (under 40) come from quite different backgrounds from their elders, with nearly two-thirds having parents in trade or manufacturing (compared with just over a quarter for the older group). This is a rather more dramatic change than one would expect from the shift in industrial structure alone, and indicates that the base of recruitment is, if anything, narrowing rather than broadening. In any event, there is still little evidence of substantial recruitment from the poorer segments of society.

How does the social mobility into the industrial elite compare with that of other elites? Available evidence is summarized in Table 44.[23] Managers come from backgrounds that are similar to entrepreneurs, the only major difference being that half as many come from the landlord class. Differences between entrepreneurs and civil servants are somewhat more pronounced. For obvious reasons, entrepreneurs are twice as likely to come from industrial or commercial backgrounds and civil servants thrice as likely to come from bureaucratic origins. The landlord class has three times the representation among entrepreneurs (21 percent versus 7 percent) reflecting the conversion of agricultural to commercial capital. There are also more blue

TABLE 44 Comparative Intergenerational Occupational Mobility[a]

	Fathers of			
	Professors[b]	Civil Servants[c]	Private Entrepreneurs[d]	Private Managers[d]
Landlord	18.5	6.9	21.4	10.9
Independent farmer	22.9	40.7	25.4	30.1
Tenant farmer and other agricultural	4.2	7.6	2.0	0.0
Industry and commerce: owners	18.8	16.0	31.4	29.4
Industry and commerce: white collar	4.3	4.1	3.5	6.4
Industry and commerce: blue collar	–	2.2	0.0	1.9
Government	9.0	17.5	5.9	5.8
Teaching	6.5	2.2	3.8	5.1
Professional	9.2	2.2	6.7	7.0
Other	6.5	0.7	0.0	3.3
Total	99.9	100.0	100.1	99.9
Sample size	(761)	(583)	(192)	(156)
Mean birth date of sons	1925	1924	1925	1932

Notes: [a]The mean birth date of the civil servants (1923) is sufficiently similar to that of the entrepreneurs and professors (1925) to permit direct comparison, while the private managers are somewhat younger.

[b]Sŭng-jik Hong, p. 196.

[c]Hoon Yu, "Social Backgrounds of Higher Civil Servants," p. 39.

collar and tenant farmer backgrounds among civil servants (10 percent versus 2 percent). Professors are similar to private entrepreneurs and differ from civil servants in having a heavy landlord background (19 percent).

These differences notwithstanding, the dominant feature of all the backgrounds is their similarly narrow bases. Modern administrative, industrial, and educational elites come from somewhat different elements within the traditional elite, but all, nonetheless, recruit from a very narrow stratum of society.[24]

EDUCATION

Closely related to the narrow recruitment of Korean elites is the critical role of education in Confucian society. Internationally, business leaders are not generally thought of as paragons of academic achievement, and, in Korea, popular opinion also holds that entrepreneurs are not particularly well educated. In fact, Korean business leaders are extraordinarily well educated, in both an absolute and a relative sense. As shown in Table 45, nearly 70 percent of our sample had some college education, a level attained by less than 10 percent of the male cohort. At the other end of the scale, only 3 percent of the entrepreneurs had a primary education or less, compared with 65 percent of the cohort. Compared to the Korean norm, entrepreneurs constitute part of the minority educated elite.

Since government is the traditional occupational choice of the educated, it is of particular interest to look at educational attainment within the elite and compare entrepreneurs with civil servants. Somewhat surprisingly, Table 45 shows that there is no significant difference between the levels of education of entrepreneurs and higher civil servants of similar age. Public-enterprise managers are even better educated, with 84 percent having a college background. It should be stressed that we are here dealing largely with the first generation of entrepreneurs. The second generation is still better educated. Our admittedly

TABLE 45 Comparative Educational Attainment

(%)

Level[a]	*Entrepreneur*	*Cohort*[b]	*Higher Civil Servants*[c]	*Chaebŏl Leaders*[d]	*Public Managers*[e]
None	0.0	29.4	0.0	0.0	0.0
Primary	3.1	35.9	5.0	8.9	0.0
Secondary	27.8	26.1	32.3	40.0	15.8
College and junior college	60.8	8.6 (College and junior college and Post graduate combined)	59.1	37.8	84.2 (College and junior college and Post graduate combined)
Post graduate	8.3		3.6	13.3	
TOTAL	100.0	100.0	100.0	100.0	100.0
Sample	(194)	–	(1564)	(45)	(357)
Mean birth date	1925	–	1923	1916	1924

Notes: [a]Including those who dropped out during each level as well as graduates.

[b]Educational attainment by year of birth from: EPB, *1970 Population and Housing Census Report* (Seoul, 1972), I, 164–165. Aggregated using weights approximating age distribution of entrepreneurial sample.

[c]Hoon Yu, "Social Background of Higher Civil Servants," p. 41. This is the educational attainment at time of initial appointment, so it underestimates actual attainment, particularly at the graduate level.

[d]Sample consists of founders of leading chaebŏl groups as described in Chapter 8. Basis is "graduation" rather than "attendance," so figures are not consistent with other series. Source: Chŏn'guk Kyŏngjein Yŏnhaphoe, *Han'guk kyŏngje yŏn'gam 1973* (Seoul, 1974).

[e]Hun Yu, *Konggiŏp imwŏn ŭi sahoejŏk paegyŏng* (Seoul, 1974), p. 41.

small sample of entrepreneurs under forty have an average educational attainment of 16.2 years (versus 13.6 for older entrepreneurs), with half graduating from the elite Seoul National University.

The possibility of response bias must be considered. As one check, consider the published level of graduation for major chaebŏl leaders, also given in Table 45. Given their level of public recognition, exaggeration is more likely to be detected, and indeed they appear less well-educated than our sample. Note, however, that the reporting basis for chaebŏl leaders is "graduation" instead of the "attendance" basis used for other groups. Since a large portion of our sample would have been at the college level during the chaotic 1940–1953 period, dropouts are common, and the chaebŏl figures would be significantly higher on an attendance basis. Further, the mean age of chaebŏl founders is nine years older than that of the entrepreneurs, and this explains a further share of the gap. Even if maximum response bias is assumed and the chaebŏl figures are taken as representative, the entrepreneurs' education level remains many times that of the cohort and only marginally below that of civil servants.

Quality, however, must be considered in addition to quantity. In Korea, there are strictly held notions as to the desirability of various universities. This ranking may or may not correlate with the quality of education actually received, but we utilize it as the only available proxy for quality, however crude. Table 46 gives the institutions of higher education that each group attended. Seoul National University (SNU)—the pinnacle of the system—produced roughly 35 percent of both the civil servants and the public-enterprise managers[25] and 25 percent of the entrepreneurs. Similar shares attended Yonsei, Korea, and foreign universities, leaving entrepreneurs more heavily represented in the "other" category (44 percent versus 32 percent for civil servants). There is thus a noticeable difference in the institutional quality of the two groups. The difference, however, amounts to only having 10 percent more of the civil servants

TABLE 46 Institutions of Higher Education Attended by Korean Elites

(%)

	Entrepreneurs	Higher Civil Servants[a]	Public Managers[b]	Political Leaders Liberal Period[c]	Political Leaders Democratic Period[c]	Older Entrepreneurs	Younger Entrepreneurs
Seoul National University	25.0	34.6	31.6	8.2	14.8	20.7	50.8
Korea University	6.5	5.7	3.3	0.8	6.8	6.6	6.1
Yonsei University	5.1	5.5	2.1	2.5	2.7	6.0	0.0
Other Seoul university	23.4	19.4	19.6			21.2	37.0
Provincial university	7.9	15.0	7.1	9.8	14.9	8.2	6.2
College	12.9	–	–			15.1	0.0
Japanese university	15.2	19.7	17.1	45.9	32.4	17.8	0.0
Other foreign university	2.5		2.9	26.7	25.7	2.9	0.0
Military academy	1.3	0.0	16.2	6.6	2.7	1.5	0.0
Total	100.0	99.9	99.9	100.0	100.0	100.0	100.0
Sample	84	974	240	148	86	72	12
Mean birth date	1925	1923	1924	1906	1908		

Notes: [a]Hoon Yu, "Social Background of Higher Civil Servants," p. 46.
[b]Hun Yu, *Konggiŏp imwŏn ŭi sahoejŏk paegyŏng* (Seoul, 1974), p. 47.
[c]Bae Ho Hahn and Kyu Taik Kim, pp. 17–41.

from SNU rather than less well-known institutions. Given the bias towards civil service employment, the striking feature of the comparison is not the difference but the similarity. Korean entrepreneurs are well-educated, even by the high standards of the civil service.

Now that a correlation between entrepreneurial activity and education has been established, we must address the question of causality. This is, as always, a highly conjectural task, as demonstrated by the following range of alternative explanations. At one extreme, it may be argued that there is no causation whatsoever. Given the parental value placed on education in a Confucian society, it will be achieved by anyone with half-a-brain, a little personal drive, and a family who can afford it. Anyone with the underlying personal and family characteristics necessary for entrepreneurship will therefore acquire an education along the way. Education may thus merely be a proxy for these characteristics and makes no independent contribution.

While there is substantial truth in the foregoing view of education as a "validation" mechanism, it is, nonetheless, possible to identify several components of the educational process that might be expected to have positive marginal products.

1) Given the respect accorded education in Korea, it is extremely difficult for an uneducated man to manage educated men (unless they are of a younger generation), and hence the uneducated would have a comparatively difficult time in running an enterprise of any significant size.
2) For the reasons just given, as well as the advantages conferred by membership in the close-knit network of school ties, it is difficult for the uneducated to manage effectively the critical relationships with government.
3) Given Korea's export orientation, education is necessary to provide the breadth of perspective and urbanity necessary for dealing with foreigners.
4) While the skills formally taught in school may not be critical for small-scale enterprise, their importance increases exponentially with the size of the enterprise.

5) Even if one learns no skills in school, the Korean educational system instills values of competitiveness and diligence that are essential to entrepreneurial success. That is, until recently, the highly competitive examination system for school entrance resulted in such pressures that even elementary school children had many hours of homework per night with tutors.

In comparing these features with educational systems elsewhere, the third and fourth factors (imparting skills and breadth of perspective) are neutral in being common to education everywhere. The first two (providing status and allies in dealing with subordinates and government) are perhaps negative in comparison with an impersonal merit system. It is possible however, to argue that the fifth is critical in explaining the extraordinary Korean growth rate—the long-hours, tenacity, and competitiveness that characterize Korean expansion into world markets may be directly traceable to the values instilled by the harshly disciplinarian traditional educational system.

Even the "validation" view of education confers an advantage on the Korean system. Where putative entrepreneurs are necessarily exposed to technical skills and broadened horizons (factors three and four), the ultimate scope of their entrepreneurial endeavors is unconstricted. In comparison, where achievement-oriented individuals can drop out with impunity, business success is far more likely to be confined to small-scale domestic activity. The Korean obsession with education, reflected in the high level of education of Korean entrepreneurs, is thus an important explanatory factor underlying the rapid industrialization.

FATHER'S EDUCATION

The degree of education of entrepreneurs' fathers is of interest (together with their occupation) as a crude proxy for class background. Table 47 shows that the fathers are significantly

TABLE 47 Fathers' Educational Attainment: Entrepreneurs and Male Cohort

(%)

Level	Integrated[a] Entrepreneurs	Integrated[a] Cohort[b]	Segregated[a] Entrepreneurs	Segregated[a] Civil Servants[c]
None	37.1	72.7	37.1	9.2
Primary	25.3	18.5	18.6	24.5
Secondary	22.2	6.9	19.1	32.3
Higher	15.4	1.9	14.4	16.4
Confucian	–	–	10.8	17.6
TOTAL	100.0	100.0	100.0	100.0
Sample	194	–	194	?
Mean years	6.0	–	6.0	–

Notes: [a]"Integrated" listing incorporates those with Confucian education according to the corresponding number of years of schooling, while "segregated" listing gives Confucian separately.

[b]Same as note c to Table 46, assuming fathers are 30 years older than entrepreneurs.

[c]Dong Suh Bark, "The Problem of Korean Higher Civil Servants," pp. 1–21.

better educated than their peers, but by a substantially smaller margin than their sons. Fifty-two percent of the fathers had no education or only a primary education versus 81 percent of the male cohort. Further, entrepreneurs' fathers had significantly less education than civil servants' fathers although the sons' education levels were similar. In addition, 11 percent of entrepreneurs' fathers versus 18 percent of civil servants' fathers had the traditional Confucian education. If education is a proxy for class, it follows that entrepreneurs' families have shown significant upward mobility in two generations.

This result is consistent with Man-Gap Lee's a priori theorizing that it is not the *yangban* class that is most likely to produce entrepreneurs, but the *hyangban* (that is, the class of former *yangban* whose status has deteriorated over several generations of rural residence).[26] This group is wealthy enough to retain the essential access to education, but their fringe social status makes them more likely to take risks and enter non-traditional endeavors in an effort to move up the social scale.

WORK HISTORY

The work history of our reduced sample is generally unremarkable, as shown in Table 48. Entrepreneurs had a mean work history of some 22 years, of which 7.5 had been spent in the present company. Over the entire period, they spent a mean of 8.5 years in each of 2.5 jobs. While this is a stable occupational pattern by Western standards, it is much more mobile than in Japan, where executives typically stay with a single company for life and average 1.8 jobs in a career.[27]

As is natural, a majority of the entrepreneurs had experience in manufacturing (64 percent), or trading (23 percent) before going into business for themselves. Nearly 20 percent had previous government experience, reflecting the close government-business ties described in Chapter 4. Interestingly, less than 13 percent of the entrepreneurs had any kind of military

TABLE 48 Work History of Entrepreneurs
(%)

I. Type of Work[a]			*II. Number of Former Jobs* *Number of Jobs*	*% Entrepreneurs*
Government		19.2	0	7.7
Military		12.6	1	46.7
Officer	5.5		2	33.0
Enlisted	4.9		3	8.2
Foreign	2.2		4	3.3
Trading company		23.1	5	1.1
Domestic	7.7			100.0
Export-Import	15.4		n =	182
Financial institution		5.5		
Industrial company		63.7		
Private	51.1			
Government	7.1			
Foreign	5.5			
Professional		4.9		
Other		25.8		

Source: Entrepreneurship Survey, see Appendix C.

Note: [a]Percent of 182 respondents having previously worked in the indicated field. Total exceeds 100% as half the respondents had had more than one previous job, as shown in Part II.

service, despite the fact that the majority were of military age during the Korean War. This, however, is less a reflection on businessmen than on the elites in general, since during the 1950s (unlike the present) it was relatively easy to avoid military service.

FAMILY STRUCTURE

We have thus far examined the extent to which entrepreneurs' family backgrounds differ from those of society as a whole. We now ask whether or not entrepreneurs come from a unique position *within* the family. That is, in the West it has been shown that first children are treated differently from their siblings, producing a distinct personality type measurable in disproportionate representation in certain high-status professions. In Korea, unique treatment is accorded the first male, and it is of interest to see how this affects representation in the entrepreneurial set.

Korean custom holds that first sons should establish a base for maintaining the family line. If the parental occupation is prestigious, it should be followed; if not, the ideal is to move into traditionally respected government service. Striking out on an entrepreneurial venture of dubious repute and some risk might be fine for a second son, but not for the conservator of the lineage. This line of reasoning is further reinforced by casual empiricism (large numbers of prominent chaebŏl founders are second sons) and by geomancy, which predicts greater success for first sons in China but for second sons in Korea.[28]

Interestingly, our empirical results run counter to these expectations. Table 49 shows that, while entrepreneurs have virtually the same number of siblings as their cohort, first sons are heavily overrepresented. Fifty-two percent of entrepreneurs are first sons versus 37 percent of the cohort, and the difference in the overall distributions is statistically significant.

How is this gap between reality and popular perception to be explained? Four hypotheses may be tentatively advanced. First, at the psychological level the treatment accorded first sons may produce a personality type with an entrepreneurial bent, and this internal pressure may dominate the external pressure for more a conservative career choice.[29] Second, at the historical level it may be that blockage in traditional occupations drove first sons into a second-best solution for maintaining the family line. That is, land reform precluded the role of landed gentry and created excess demand for civil servant positions, with the surplus moving into business. Third, for the youngest entrepreneurs in the sample, there may be no

TABLE 49 Family Structure:
Entrepreneurs and Male Cohort
(%)

	Entrepreneurs	*Cohort*[a]
Mean sibling number	4.98	4.88
Male sibling rank		
1	51.58	37.02
2	27.37	28.11
3	11.58	18.39
4	5.26	9.84
5	1.58	4.40
6	2.11	1.61
7	0.53	0.62
TOTAL	100.00	99.99

Calculated[b] X^2 = 21.39
$\vee$
Critical $X^2(.95,4)$ = 9.49

Notes: [a]We know of no direct data on male sibling rank order, so we constructed an indirect estimate from data on children born by age group in: EPB, *Preliminary Report of 1975 Population and Housing Census* (Seoul, 1976), pp. 110–111. Assumes entrepreneurs' mothers are 30 years older than entrepreneurs, and that male births are 50% of total births regardless of number of children. This procedure somewhat underestimates the number of small families, since it is based on survivors and excludes mothers who die before completing child-bearing years.
[b]Based on 5 categories, collapsing ranks 5 and above.

conflict. Attitudes towards business as a career have changed dramatically over the last decade, since success has bred acceptance. Lastly, first sons are given preference in education, with the rest of the family sacrificed if necessary. Given the cruciality of education, one would expect more first sons in business, other things being equal.

As economists, we shall judiciously refrain from pushing these lines of argument any further. It is hoped that our social science brethren, (or perhaps the geomancers) will explain the causal mechanism behind our finding that entrepreneurs are not randomly selected within the family.

CHARACTERISTICS OF SUCCESSFUL ENTREPRENEURS

Thus far we have been concerned with distinguishing the background of the entrepreneurial set from that of the population as a whole. Now we wish to ascertain whether or not the same characteristics serve to distinguish more successful entrepreneurs *within* the entrepreneurial set. Since our variables are now linked to discrete observation points (as opposed to the population as a whole where we know, say, education level and family background, but not how they are associated on a case-by-case basis), we can utilize multiple regression techniques rather than partial correlation. The effort, however, will be exploratory and of a low order of sophistication, since we have little theory on which to build a model.[30]

As a dependent variable, we need a measure of entrepreneurial success. Alternatives used here are:

1) Profits (PROFITS). In the pure economic theory of the firm, the measure of success should be the absolute level of return to entrepreneurial endeavor. That is, economic rent earned by the entrepreneur, or net profit after taxes less the opportunity cost of capital plus (or minus) the surplus (or deficit) of his compensation over the opportunity cost of his time in non-entrepreneurial activity. As a very crude first approximation, we utilize available data on net profit before taxes.
2) Profitability (PROFBLE). The rate of return on assets is of interest as a popular measure of entrepreneurial success and also provides an alternative approximation to rent by crudely adjusting the profit level for the (uniform across firms) opportunity cost of capital.
3) Value Added (VALADD). In the behavioral theory of the firm, the entrepreneur may be interested in power and control rather than pure personal monetary reward. Success is then measured by size, rather than rent. Value added is the preferred measure of economic size.

4) Assets (ASSETS). An alternative measure of size.
5) Employment (EMPLOYEE). An alternative measure of size.
6) Growth (GROWTH). Success may also be construed as a trend rather than a level. As a proxy, we use annual average rate of growth of productive capacity.

As independent variables we are primarily interested in the effects on success of the social background factors already discussed. Accordingly, we utilize dummy variables for regional origin, education, religion, and father's occupation, as follows:

1) DNORTH. If father's birth place was in the north.
2) DSEOUL. If father's birth place was in Seoul or Kyŏnggi province.
3) DKYONG. If father's birth place was in Kyŏngsang province or Pusan.
4) DCOLL. If college graduate.
5) DCHRIST. If Protestant or Catholic influence was other than irrelevant.
6) DFJIND. If father's occupation was in manufacturing.
7) DFJCOM. If father's occupation was in commerce.
8) DFJLAND. If father's occupation was landlord.

Second, the degree of entrepreneurial reward should be affected by the degree of innovation in the production effort. Accordingly, we introduce a dummy variable:

9) DINNOV. If product or production process was new to Korea.

Third, success may vary with the degree of privileged access to resources. John Harris suggests this may be measured by the size of the original plant.[31] Accordingly, we include:

10) ORIEMPL. Original number of employees at establishment.

Finally, success may be affected by the industry or activity initially chosen. Accordingly, we define:

11) EXPORT2. Current share of exports in sales.
12) DTEXT. If producer of textiles or clothing.
13) DCHEM. If producer of chemical products.

TABLE 50 Entrepreneurial Success: Regression Summaries[a]

A. Linear Specification

Independent \ Dependent	PROFITS	PROFBLE	GROWTH	ASSETS	VALADD	EMPLOYEE
R^2	0.0914	0.0574	0.1190	0.2227	0.1111	0.4501
$\bar{R}^2$ [b]	0.0093	-0.0278	0.0393	0.1525	0.0308	0.4005
F [c]	1.1128	0.6735	1.4941	3.1706	1.3833	9.0597
EXPORT2			d			e
DTEXT			(-)			
DCHEM	e					
DMETAL						
DFOOD			(-)	e	e	
DWOOD			(-)			
DFJLAND	(-)			d		(-)
DNORTH						(-)
ORIEMPL		d	d	f	d	f
DSEOUL	(-)	(-)			(-)	(-)
DKYONG		(-)	(-)			(-)
DCOLL	(-)		(-)	(-)		(-) d
DCHRIST	(-)		(-)	(-) e	(-)	
DFJIND	(-)		f	(-)	(-)	(-) d
DFJCOM	(-)					(-)
Constant		(-)		(-)	(-)	

TABLE 50 (continued)

B. Log-Linear Specification

Dependent / Independent	PROFITS	PROFBLE	GROWTH	ASSETS	VALADD	EMPLOYEE
R^2	0.1651	0.0730	0.0999	0.1946	0.1302	0.3371
$\hat{R}^2$ [b]	0.0897	-0.0108	0.1852	0.1218	0.0519	0.2772
F [c]	<u>2.1890</u>	0.8712	1.2278	<u>2.6733</u>	1.6607	<u>5.6279</u>
EXPORT2	(-) d	(-)			(-)	f
DTEXT		(-)			(-)	
DCHEM						(-)
DMETAL		(-)			(-)	(-)
DFOOD		(-)		e		
DWOOD						
DFJLAND	e	(-)	d			(-)
DNORTH		(-)	(-) f			
ORIEMPL		(-)		f	f	f
DSEOUL	(-) d		(-)	(-)	(-)	(-)
DKYONG		(-)	(-) e			
DCOLL	(-)	(-)		(-)	(-)	(-) d
DCHRIST		(-)	(-)	(-)		
DFJIND	e	(-)		(-)		(-)
DFJCOM		(-) d			(-)	(-)
Constant		(-)	(-)			

Source: Entrepreneurship Survey, see Appendix C.

Notes: [a]In exploratory work such as this, little meaning is to be attached to the magnitudes of the regression coefficients. Accordingly, we report only the sign and level of significance of the coefficients.

[b]Corrected for degrees of freedom. There were 181 valid observations.

[c]Overall F-test. Equations significant at 5% level are indicated by underlining.

[d]Significance @ .10 level.

[e]Significance @ .05 level.

[f]Significance @ .01 level.

14) DMETAL. If producer of basic metals or metal products.
15) DFOOD. If producer of foodstuffs.
16) DWOOD. If producer of wood or paper products.

Since we are without priors as to the functional form of the relationship, we experimented with both linear and log-linear forms. The results, given in Table 50, are informative only for their impressive lack of explanatory power. Seven of the twelve specifications fail the F-test (5 percent level) meaning the multiple R^2 does not significantly differ from zero. Of the remaining five equations, the corrected multiple correlation coefficient ($\widehat{R}^2$) ranges from 0.09 to 0.04 with the bulk of the explanatory power (85 percent in the case of $\widehat{R}^2$=0.40) coming from the single EMPLOYEE variable. This is not informative, as it simply says that current size is correlated with size at founding. Other individual regression coefficients are never significant (at the 5 percent level) in more than three of the twelve equations and often change sign even when significant. It would be difficult to imagine a less robust set of coefficients.

It would undoubtedly be possible to alter our specification and come up with a somewhat better fit, but we believe the major point is apparent from this initial effort. That is, social background variables that distinguish entrepreneurs from non-entrepreneurs do not, in Korea, serve to distinguish more successful from less successful entrepreneurs within the set.

Upon reflection, this is not so surprising. It may well be, for example, that, compared with the U.S. population as a whole, economists have more schooling and different religious and political affiliations, but these variables do not correlate with publication records. There are two reasons for this. First, entry or validation criteria, such as education, are widely shared by all members of the set and do not serve to distinguish among them. Second, the social background factors are all intermediary rather than fundamental variables. That is, entrepreneurial success is a function of personal characteristics that may be fostered in a variety of social backgrounds. Given the proper nutritive environment, the strength of development of those characteristics is not measured by simple group variables such as father's occupation. To distinguish the characteristics of successful entrepreneurs, we must measure underlying personality variables rather than rely on proxy group variables.

SELF-PERCEPTION OF ENTREPRENEURS

While we have made no effort to measure directly the personality characteristics of the entrepreneurs, we did ask several questions designed to reveal their own perception of their species. Answers to such questions are typically self-serving and must be heavily discounted, but some of the responses are, nonetheless, informative.

The first self-perception question was specifically on the characteristics that distinguish successful entrepreneurs from their less successful brethren. Results are summarized in Table 51. The top ranking of "hard work" may be suspect relative to some of the other factors, but there can be no doubt that Koreans work long hours by international standards. Respondents report that their ordinary employees average 52 hours weekly, their senior staff 53, and they themselves 54.[32] Judging by the expressed opinions of foreign visitors, these estimates are, if anything, conservative. The long hours of entrepreneurs not only distinguish successful from unsuccessful entrepreneurs but are characteristic of the entire economic system. As one example, the regular working hours of the senior staff of the most rapidly growing chaebŏl, Daewoo, are from 8:00 a.m. to 7:00 p.m. To staff its thirty-six foreign branches, necessary language training is provided from 6:00 to 8:00 a.m. daily, with any absences "affecting promotion."

To return to Table 51, the high ranking of "scientific thinking," the bottom ranking of "good luck," and the low ranking of "government relations" would seem as much due to image building as to fact. The high ranking of "skill in handling people" is noteworthy and probably is an accurate representation of its

TABLE 51 Businessmen's Perceptions of Success Characteristics

Question: "How important do you think the following factors are in distinguishing successful Korean entrepreneurs from those who are less successful?"

Ranking:

successful have much more	some more	same	some less	successful have much less
1	2	3	4	5

Mean Responses:

	Value Added[a]			*Established*	
	All	*Large*	*Small*	*Pre-1963*	*Post-1968*
Conscientious hard work	1.49	1.50	1.45	1.30	1.54
Rational and scientific thinking	1.56	1.50	1.95	1.90	1.41
Skill in handling subordinates, peers, and superiors	1.61	1.58	1.80	1.66	1.63
On-the-job training and experience	1.94	1.96	2.20	2.10	1.94
Intelligence	2.15	2.10	2.15	2.07	2.02
Willingness to make unpopular decisions	2.24	2.23	2.10	2.00	2.35
Good network of friends	2.38	2.34	2.65	2.43	2.35
Good formal education	2.56	2.48	3.05	2.43	2.50
Skill in handling government officials	2.86	2.80	3.15	2.80	2.96
Willing to take risks	3.20	3.20	3.10	2.90	3.51
Greater personal or family capital	3.41	3.51	3.05	3.33	3.30
Good luck	3.56	3.52	3.81	3.47	3.46
Sample Size	(118)	(98)	(20)	(30)	(54)

Source: Entrepreneurship Survey, see Appendix C. There were no significant differences between the means when broken down by age or export share.

Notes: [a]"Large" firms are those whose value added placed them in the top quintile of 311 firm sample. "Small" firms are the remainder.
Single underlining ≡ t test significant @ .05 level.
Double underlining ≡ t test significant @ .01 level.

importance in Confucian society. The modest role of "formal education" reflects the fact, noted earlier, that most entrepreneurs are relatively well educated and differences in this variable do not serve to distinguish the better entrepreneurs. The low value placed on "personal and family capital" is not simply an affirmation of the "self-made" man. Rather, we take it as an accurate reflection of the ready access to capital afforded by the Korean financial system.[33] What is noteworthy in this response is that there is only a modest, though significant, difference between large and small firms in this regard. Another low-ranked item meriting comment is "willingness to take risks." The Korean entrepreneurs do not perceive themselves as risk-takers, although significantly more emphasis was given this factor by heads of pre-1963 firms than by those established after 1968. The positive ranking given "willingness to make unpopular decisions" gives some support to the notion that entrepreneurs are to some extent social deviants who are willing to disregard accepted norms in pursuit of new ends.

A second self-perception involves the degree to which various forms of formal and on-the-job training helped in preparation for the present job. As shown in Table 52, most of the responses simply reflect the diverse occupational background of the respondents. Two points are of interest, however. First, formal education is virtually tied for top place with a "moderately important" ranking. This tends to confirm our earlier conclusion that education is important in distinguishing entrepreneurs from non-entrepreneurs, though not in distinguishing degrees of success among entrepreneurs. Second, foreign language ability is accorded top place with a "moderately important" ranking. This is not too surprising given the outward looking development strategy of Korea, but it is remarkable that there is no significant difference in this respect between exporters and those producing predominantly for the domestic market. This is probably explained by the fact that foreign technical assistance, finance, inputs, and "inspiration by travel" are critical to many domestic producers. The high regard accorded foreign

TABLE 52 Businessmen's Self-Perceptions of Background Contribution

Question: "In preparing yourself for your present job, how important were each of the following factors?"

Ranking	Very Important		Moderately Important		Unimportant
	1	2	3	4	5

Mean Responses	
Foreign language ability	2.95
Formal education	2.98
Job during colonial period	4.37
Job related to allied military	4.78
Work in family business	4.14
Other work experience	3.52
Military experience	4.63
Government experience	4.31
Sample Size	(118)

Source: Entrepreneurship Survey, Appendix C.

language ability is a clear reflection of the drive for international competitiveness.

A third self-perception involves the motivation that drives entrepreneurs. To reduce bias, respondents were asked not to characterize themselves, but the entrepreneurial class in general. Results, summarized in Table 53, show that for public consumption, entrepreneurs stress altruistic motivations—nationalistic, patriotic, and community goals come first, followed by family responsibility, wealth, fame and power, and excellence. One is entitled to a good deal of skepticism at the degree to which these announcements correspond to internal drives, but it is useful to recall Schumpeter's words on the non-hedonistic motivations:

> First of all, there is the dream and the will to found a private kingdom, usually, though not necessarily, also a dynasty. The modern world really does not know any such positions, but what may be

TABLE 53 Businessmen's Perceptions of Entrepreneurial Motivation

Question: "In general, how important do you think the following factors are in motivating successful Korean entrepreneurs?"

Ranking	Very Important		Moderately Important		Unimportant
	1	2	3	4	5

Responses	*Mean*
Personal goal achievement	
Pursuit of excellence	3.39
Fame and power	3.04
Wealth	2.56
Family responsibility	2.44
Community responsibility	1.78
Patriotism: north-south conflict	1.95
Nationalism: catch the Japanese	2.28
Sample Size	(118)

Source: Entrepreneurship Survey, see Appendix C.

> attained by industrial or commercial success is still the nearest approach to medieval lordship possible to modern man . . . Then there is the will to conquer: the impulse to fight, to prove oneself superior to others, to succeed for the sake, not of the fruits of success, but of success itself. From this aspect, economic action becomes akin to sport—there are financial races, or rather boxing matches. The financial result is a secondary consideration, or, at all events, mainly valued as an index of success and as a symptom of victory . . . Finally, there is the joy of creating, of getting things done, or simply of exercising one's energy and ingenuity.[34]

In Korea, we must ask to what extent the achievement of national goals must be added to this list of non-pecuniary incentives. The government is continually stressing that the country is waging an economic war, with national survival and the welfare of the masses at stake. Entrepreneurs are the field-grade officers in this battle, and their success is praised by some significant segments of Korean Society. The skepticism of intellectuals and some journalists can be subordinated in the face of official praise and awards for entrepreneurial achievement. The inherent pecuniary and power rewards of business endeavor are thus reinforced by a certain form of social approval, and there is a convenient perceived identity of individual and social returns. In Korea, this official sanction of entrepreneurial endeavor is particularly important in helping to break down the traditional aversion to business activity.

The question is not whether or not nationalistic motivations dominate private motives, but whether official approval provides a real marginal incentive, increasing the total pecuniary and non-pecuniary returns to entrepreneurship. We believe that there is no question that these returns are significant and positive in Korea, and that the government's efforts have had a significant effect on the total output of the economic system. The impact of this appeal is reflected in the fact that community and national goals are announced as being even more important than family responsibility, the ultimate sanction in traditional Confucian society.

It is widely believed in Korea that businessmen have enjoyed not only increasing government approval, but also accelerating popular prestige (at least outside the journalistic and academic communities). This, however, is somewhat harder to document. The evidence usually cited includes a rapidly increasing share of applications to business-related departments of universities, rising quantity and quality of applications to large corporations, and an often-cited survey of marriage preference at the prestigious Ewha Womans University. At Ewha, as shown in Table 54, businessmen ranked first as desirable marriage partners from 1964 to 1971. Their share increased steadily in the mid-1960s but dropped precipitously between 1966 and 1971. The high initial level supports the notion that the *sa, nong, kong, sang* ranking was no longer operative in the period of rapid growth and had probably lost its sway over several generations, beginning with the colonial period. The 1964 and 1966 increase in

TABLE 54 Mate Preference at Ewha Womans University

Year	*Ranking of Businessmen*	*Percent selecting businessmen*
1964	1	22.2
1965	1	26.3
1966	1	31.1
1971	1	17.5

Source: Ihwa Yŏja Taehakkyo, "Haksaeng saenghwal yŏn'gu" (Study of student life) (Seoul, 1971), pp. 43–44.

the share conforms to the idea that success and government recognition breed popular approval. However, the precipitous decline between 1966 and 1971 is inconsistent with the same hypothesis. The discrepancy may be due to statistical artifact (no statistical tests are contained in the study), to the fickle nature of Ewha women, to a change in the Ewha population, or to some real value shift.

We leave this riddle to others, and for present purposes adhere to the conventional version. That is, economic success, abetted by government recognition and rising income, generated accelerating popular approval and increased the non-pecuniary return to entrepreneurship. There is thus an endogenous self-generating effect in which growth begets approval which begets growth. The importance of this, of course, depends on the weight of non-pecuniary incentives in the entrepreneur's objective function. We suspect it is real, though perhaps small, and together with nationalism and patriotism makes a noticeable contribution to entrepreneurial supply.

IMPLICATIONS FOR THEORIES OF ENTREPRENEURIAL SUPPLY

A recurring theme in studies of entrepreneurial supply is the notion of a subordinated group struggling for otherwise blocked or threatened status and providing economic leadership in the process. Geertz provides an articulate summary with four hypotheses:

"1) Innovative economic leadership (entrepreneurship) occurs in a fairly well defined and socially homogeneous group. There is on a priori grounds no reason why the entrepreneurs could not come either randomly from the general population or from several distinct social groups at once. But they do not.

2) This innovative group has crystallized out of a larger traditional group which has a very long history of extra-village status and interlocal orientation.

3) The larger group out of which the innovative group is emerging is at present experiencing a fairly radical change in its relationships with the wider society of which it is a part . . . (and) economic innovation seems in part to be a response to the status insecurity engendered by these shifts in social structure.

4) On the ideological level the innovative group conceives of itself as the main vehicle of religious and moral excellence within a generally wayward, unenlightened, or heedless community."[35]

Nothing could be farther from the Korean experience, and the reasons are instructive.

In the first place, economic leadership in Korea has not come from subordinated groups. The major candidates are northerners and Christians. While northerners are heavily overrepresented in the entrepreneurial population and Christians somewhat so, it is clear that this is the result not of subordination but of correlations with other variables. Other groups with similar occupational and educational backgrounds are similarly represented. The only way in which the theory applies to Korea is to view the entire population as subordinated by the Japanese with entrepreneurship an effort to gain international "face."

This is a little far-fetched, but does point to the (marginal) nationalistic motivation and the homogeneity of the Korean population.

A second way in which Korea differs from the Geertz model is that no role is played by moral, religious, or ideological elitism. Elsewhere, minorities prosper because the value system of the majority is inimical to growth. In Korea, minority status can convey no special advantage, because the value system of the culture as a whole has become supportive of growth. We perceive the main elements of the system to be:

1) Competitive dedication to improving the relative position of self and family.
2) Respect for education as a vehicle for improvement.
3) Inculcation of qualities of hard work, diligence, and self-discipline.
4) Absence of religious or ideological constraints inhibiting the pragmatic pursuit of ends.
5) Ability to subordinate self and participate in a hierarchical framework with a synergistic effect on output.

While the entrepreneurial elite is thus not defined by religious or ethnic status, it is emphatically not drawn randomly from the population as a whole. Instead, today's entrepreneurs come from family occupational backgrounds which represent perhaps 15 percent of the population. The industrial elite thus descended from the pre-industrial elite. The causal sequence, however, was not the capitalist equation:

$$\text{money} \rightarrow \text{physical capital} \rightarrow \text{industrial leadership}$$

but the Confucian-cum-capitalist equation:

$$\text{money} \rightarrow \text{texts, tutors, and time} \rightarrow \text{human capital} \rightarrow \text{industrial leadership}$$

The traditional value system is here again supportive of growth.

The characteristics listed above are, of course, not limited to entrepreneurs. They also lie behind the capable performance of government officials in controlling the entrepreneurial environment and the effectiveness of lower-ranking managers and workers. This is yet another virtue of cultural homogeneity. If entrepreneurs are a subordinated minority in society, as they so often are, then they must fight a constant battle against competing values in their contacts with government and workers. In Korea, by contrast, the basic value system is widely shared and conflict minimized. Our focus on entrepreneurship should not obscure the fact that growth is a joint product of the entire society.

We recognize the logical weakness in ending this chapter with a paean to the virtues of the Confucian tradition, when we began by quoting a diatribe against it. Value systems always seem useful in after-the-fact explanation (regardless of what is to be explained), but not much good in prediction. Nonetheless, it seems clear that the pro-growth virtues of the traditional heritage listed above have survived and prospered, while the major negative value—antipathy to manual labor and business—has withered away. This has not been a sudden process. Change undoubtedly began during the colonial period and continued through the 1950s. There was no sudden shift in supply in the early 1960s to explain the growth discontinuity. The initial change came from the demand side, but the resulting higher level of growth released social forces which, together with government approval, accelerated the rate of change on the supply side. These are reflected in increased non-pecuniary returns to entrepreneurship.

Much remains unexplained. The critical question is why the social system was able to selectively retain convenient facets while selectively rejecting those that were incompatible with modernity. We must leave the dynamics of value modification to others. Here we only identify the importance of the process for economic growth.

The heritage of which we speak is of course not confined to Korea. The dramatic achievements of Japan, Taiwan, Hong Kong, and Singapore confirm the potentiality of the Confucian tradition when coupled with a growth-oriented government. The high performance of the East Asian bloc also underlies a fundamental problem we have had in discussing our research with many Koreans. When we assert that some aspect of Korean entrepreneurship or government leadership is extraordinary, and we want to explain why, a typical response is: "What do you mean 'good'? Look at the United States, or Japan, or Taiwan. You're wasting your time. What you should be doing is explaining what's wrong and how we can do better!" Now this self-effacing, self-critical attitude is in itself a growth-supporting aspect of the culture, and we would not want to eliminate such a convenient social virtue. Nonetheless, from the academic point of view what is to be explained is not so much Korea's performance relative to the rest of East Asia, as its performance relative to the rest of the world.

In this respect, we believe the homogeneous Confucian heritage is a major element in explaining the high level of lenticular entrepreneurial intent. It also contributes to the rapidity of the learning process and thus lies behind much of the expansion in qualitative entrepreneurial supply.

EIGHT

Private Economic Power: Problems, Policies, and Prospects

THE CHAEBŎL PROBLEM

There are two dimensions to the problem of economic concentration. One is the share of a given number of enterprises in a particular market. The other is the share of a given number of affiliated enterprises in *all* markets. The first is conventionally termed industrial concentration, while we shall refer to the second as business concentration. While most Western economics is preoccupied with the effects of industrial concentration, the problem of business concentration has attracted particular attention in Asia—for example, the Japanese zaibatsu, Pakistan's "twenty-two families," and India's industrial houses. This is not surprising. Whereas industrial concentration confers advantage in a single product market, business concentration in an LDC may confer advantage in all product and factor markets. This follows from the following relationship: size and power beget influence which in turn produces privileged access to credit, foreign exchange, and government's complicity in a multitude of rent-creating interventions. Business concentration can thus convert the role of government in an LDC from one of overcoming market imperfections to one of creating and exploiting them.[1] In this chapter, we therefore explore the quantitative magnitude of the problem in Korea, its historical evolution, and relevant government policies.

We begin with a brief description of Korean business organization. This may be usefully done by comparing the Korean chaebŏl with the well known Japanese zaibatsu. The Chinese characters for the two are identical, and the two forms share many common features, but there are certain distinctive differences.

"Zaibatsu" has been defined as "a system of highly centralized family control through holding companies."[2] Hirschmeier and Yui identify three stages in their evolution. During the first, from the Meiji Restoration to the Sino-Japanese War (1868–1895), the "old" zaibatsu emerged under driving individual leadership and had no particular pattern of corporate control.[3] Early in the second stage (1895–1946), the "old" zaibatsu faced increasing problems of coordination and control over their expanding empires and turned to a holding-company model with heavy reliance on non-family managers selected on the basis of merit.[4] Stage three evolved during the post-World War II days where the zaibatsu were initially broken up but re-emerged as one set of nuclei[5] for modern *keiretsu*—"independent enterprises, clustered around one or several core city banks, with some coordination of policies, even some joint action, and personal regular meetings of the presidents."[6]

Contemporary Korean chaebŏl correspond most closely in structure to the stage one zaibatsu of the Meiji era. At the center of each group is the *hoejang* or "chairman," who is the dynamic and cohesive force of the group. Most typically, he is an entrepreneur, in the truest sense of the word, who founds one enterprise and then leaves its management to a relative (or, more recently, to a trusted associate) as he moves on to a new venture. Majority shares in the various enterprises are held by the *hoejang* and his immediate relatives. There is also an admixture of stage two, as a few of the groups have formed holding companies, and professional managers are playing a rapidly increasing role. Guidance and direction, however, remain highly centralized in the *hoejang*. There is no comparison with the loosely affiliated decentralized *keiretsu* of Japan's stage three. Contemporary chaebŏl are thus roughly at the stage-one to stage-two transition and are not to be compared structurally with their modern counterparts in Japan.

From the point of view of this study, there is an additional difference between Korea and Japan which is of central importance. Most pre-war zaibatsu included, and post-war *keiretsu* are centered on, their own banks and other financial institutions. Chaebŏl, on the other hand, must rely upon government-controlled credit institutions. The causes and consequences of this situation were detailed in Chapter 4. Here we only remind the reader that individual chaebŏl were dependent upon government for their credit lifeblood and consequently exercise distinctly less economic power than their zaibatsu counterparts did.

Economic power, of course, is also related to the size of the chaebŏl sector relative to the government and the rest of the economy. We therefore now consider the quantitative scope of chaebŏl activity.

QUANTITATIVE DIMENSIONS OF BUSINESS CONCENTRATION

In the absence of prior quantitative work on chaebŏl size, we constructed our own estimates. A rough list of affiliates of the forty-six largest groups was obtained from the Federation of Korean Industries and modified by informal contacts with the groups concerned. Sales and profit figures were then taken from a combination of published and unpublished sources. Value added was calculated indirectly for each company using 340 sector IO coefficients for 1973. Since profits are a major source of divergence between sectoral averages and enterprise figures in any one year, and between sectoral averages in different years, the usual procedure was modified to utilize actual profits but estimated non-profit value added. That is, for each enterprise:

$$\widehat{V} = \pi + \alpha\,(X - \pi)$$

where $\widehat{V}$ is estimated value added, π is net accounting profit, X is total sales, and α is obtained from the appropriate IO sector. Results for 1975, aggregated by chaebŏl, are given in Table 55. Given the crudity of our estimation procedure, they should be taken as indicative only of the orders of magnitude involved.

As a summary, Table 56 presents the cumulative shares of chaebŏl groups in various national accounts components. It shows that the five largest chaebŏl had a 1975 value added of 425 billion wŏn representing 5 percent of gross domestic product or 7 percent of non-agricultural GDP. In manufacturing activities alone, the five largest chaebŏl accounted for nearly 15 percent of the economy total. The forty-six largest chaebŏl accounted for approximately 13 percent of GDP, 19 percent of non-agricultural GDP, and 37 percent of manufacturing.

To provide perspective on these magnitudes, it is useful to break down the entire economy by institutional origin of GDP, as shown in Table 57. The chaebŏl sector is shown to be significantly larger than both the public enterprise and government sectors, but only one-third the size of other private non-agricultural enterprise.

How do these magnitudes compare with other Asian nations? For Japan, we have been unable to find modern data, but at the end of World War II, the four largest zaibatsu controlled one-fourth of all paid-in capital of Japanese incorporated business.[7] Comparisons with India and Pakistan are given in Table 58. Insofar as the data are compatible, the results suggest that, at all

TABLE 55 Crude Indicators of Chaebŏl Size, 1975[a]

(Million wŏn)

Rank (Value Added)	*Name of Group*	*Number of Companies*[b]	*Sales*	*Profit*	*Total Value Added*[c]	*Manufacturing Value Added*[d]
1	Samsung	22 (18)	352,819	8,599	112,751	74,774
2	Lucky	15 (11)	417,407	16,239	87,850	83,243
3	Hyundai	12 (6)	234,450	22,020	87,619	64,662
4	Hanjin	10 (9)	157,451	2,478	72,166	0
5	Hyosung	11 (10)	163,680	3,783	64,883	38,989
6	Ssangyong	12 (7)	142,883	2,760	51,281	37,324
7	Daewoo	18 (17)	109,852	12,458	43,433	24,501
8	O.B.	12 (10)	77,643	4,168	41,832	37,609
9	Dong Ah Construction	11 (10)	75,117	3,902	39,184	904
10	The Shin Dong-A	8 (6)	94,722	-2,606	36,970	29,115
11	Korea Explosives	14 (10)	147,769	2,652	31,688	22,900
12	Hanil Synthetic Fiber	5 (3)	123,453	4,098	29,784	29,784
13	Tai Han Electric Wire	16 (10)	80,233	3,941	28,370	27,713
14	Sam Yang	2 (2)	58,952	925	27,713	27,713
15	Korea Raw Silk	21 (21)	67,075	1,437	25,485	15,394
16	Kumho	10 (9)	70,375	2,876	24,843	18,677
17	Miwon	12 (12)	57,505	4,556	21,601	19,942

TABLE 55 (continued)

18	Kia	9 (6)	62,466	2,728	18,517	18,020
19	Kolon	15 (12)	75,936	−285	17,754	14,860
20	International Chemical	10 (10)	66,036	2,274	17,383	13,816
21	Korea Shipbuilding and Engineering Corporation	7 (6)	48,565	8,122	15,082	8,365
22	Sunkyung	7 (7)	50,681	−240	13,641	12,814
23	Sammisa	4 (4)	46,759	3,760	13,235	11,288
24	Lotte	11 (10)	63,398	1,432	13,167	11,859
25	Daelim	8 (7)	35,905	2,559	12,297	890
26	Chon Bang	7 (5)	36,314	719	11,698	11,402
27	Byuk San	8 (8)	35,052	1,669	11,323	8,117
28	Jinro	5 (4)	42,206	718	10,367	10,302
29	STC	7 (7)	32,524	689	10,279	3,761
30	Dong Myung	2 (2)	49,498	902	10,153	10,153
31	Dong Yang Cement	4 (4)	25,639	1,705	8,998	8,434
32	Dongkook S.R.I.	8 (8)	66,772	−3,190	8,822	8,822
33	Sung Chang	7 (6)	39,511	1,968	8,092	7,850
34	Korea Glass	3 (3)	14,170	1,074	6,899	4,790
35	Dainong	6 (6)	52,862	−8,267	6,692	0
36	Hai Tai	5 (5)	24,935	1,369	6,638	6,254
37	Il Shin	5 (5)	11,504	−305	6,498	6,455

TABLE 55 (continued)

38	Dong Boo	9 (6)	17,443	417	6,046	1,646
39	Chung Bang	7 (4)	23,234	392	5,880	5,688
40	Il Shin S.R.I.	5 (5)	41,270	-2,275	5,647	5,647
41	Shin Won	7 (4)	20,580	-986	5,318	1,294
42	Sam Yang Food	5 (4)	33,101	407	5,187	5,122
43	Kyung Bang	3 (3)	18,582	458	3,893	3,694
44	Dae Han Textile	2 (2)	16,218	-614	1,969	1,266
45	Whashin	8 (3)	9,386	251	1,892	1,388
46	Han Yang	3 (2)	387	57	266	0
	Chaebŏl TOTAL	398 (326)	3,455,050	111,794	1,111,085	757,321

Notes: [a]Basic list of companies and sales and profit figures supplied by Federation of Korean Industries. These were updated and expanded by direct contact with the relevant chaebŏl, but errors undoubtedly remain. Similar calculations were made for 1973 and 1974, but not reported here.

[b]As of Dec. 31, 1975. Figures in parentheses indicate number of companies actually included in calculations. Exclusions, in order of importance, were due to:

1) firms in pre-operational status
2) universities and "cultural funds" (a Korean form of quasi-philanthropic foundation)
3) minor companies for which no date was available.

[c]Value added was generally calculated as $V = \pi + \alpha (X - \pi)$ where α is from appropriate 340 IO and π (profits) and X (sales) are from financial statements of individual enterprise. Three exceptions involve cases where conventionally reported sales (X) are not equivalent to sales (X_{IO}) used in IO. They are:

1) Trading companies

The value added to net sales ratios were taken from the BOK's *Han'guk ŭi kiŏp kyŏngyŏng*, Seoul, 1968 as follows:

	1973	*1974*	*1975*
Foreign Trade	.107	.091	.125
Domestic Retail	.070	.154	.136

TABLE 55 (continued)

Domestic Wholesale	.047	.055	.091

These ratios were then applied to reported sales to generate value-added estimates.

2) Securities firms

The commissions earned were multiplied by the ratio of IO value added to IO sales (which is commissions earned). The ratio is 0.7970.

3) Insurance companies

$\hat{V} = \pi + \alpha\,(X_1 - \pi)$ where X_1 for each year is calculated from relevant issues of insurance yearbook as:

X_1 = direct premiums + inward premiums + *R/I* (reinsurance) claims received + *R/I* commissions received –*R/I* premiums – direct claims paid – inward claims paid – *R/I* commissions paid.

TABLE 56 Chaebŏl in the Korean Economy, 1975

Number of Chaebŏl	*Chaebŏl Value Added as Cumulative Percentage of* GDP	Non-Agricultural GDP	Manufacturing GDP
5	5.1	7.1	14.5
10	7.7	10.7	21.8
20	10.6	14.7	30.2
46	13.4	18.6	36.7

Source: See Table 55.

levels, Korea in 1975 has substantially less concentration than Pakistan in 1959 or India in 1948, 1958, and 1968. For example, the four largest Korean groups accounted for 13 percent of manufacturing versus 23 percent in India; the sixteen largest Korean groups accounted for 26 percent versus 34 percent in Pakistan.

A portion of these international differences in business concentration is attributable to the relative size and structure of the economies concerned. A small country with a few hundred manufacturing establishments might be naturally expected to have higher business concentration than a large country with several thousand firms. In terms of structure, of two countries with the same absolute volume of manufacturing output, the more advanced economy with larger-scale plants would be expected to have greater business concentration. How do these two factors affect our comparisons? In terms of size, Korea's 1975 manufacturing value added was certainly smaller than that of India in 1968, similar to India in 1958, and larger than Pakistan in 1959. In terms of structure, Korea in 1975 was certainly far more advanced, so a larger share of manufacturing output was in large scale plants and a higher degree of concentration might be predicted. Structural conditions thus make Korea's low level *more* remarkable in all four comparisons,

TABLE 57 Crude Institutional Origin of GDP, 1975
(%)

Government and other non-profit institutions	10
Public enterprise	9
Chaebŏl enterprise	13
Other private enterprises	40
Agriculture, forestry, and fishing	28
	100

Source: Calculated from: BOK. *Economic Statistics Yearbook, 1976* (Seoul, 1977).

while size considerations make it less remarkable in two, more remarkable in one, and neutral in one. Though the comparisons may be crude, it is at least clear that, across these countries, differences in business concentration remain to be explained even after allowing for differences in the size and structure of the economy,

The relatively low level of business concentration in Korea runs contrary to popular opinion, but is not surprising given the fact that everyone started from a near zero base in 1951. Concentrations of power have thus evolved over only twenty-five years in Korea versus three to four times that period in Japan and South Asia. As with income distribution, the crucial question is not so much the absolute level as the rate of change. Unfortunately, we have been able to put together a consistent time series only for the most recent years, as shown in Table 59. The results are striking, however, showing a substantial increase in concentration at all levels in only three years. While there is no justification for extrapolating a similar rate of increase over the entire rapid-growth period, we would argue that these figures reflect a long-term rise in the level of business concentration. This follows from the evidence in Chapter 6 on the dominance of expansion over establishment as a source of growth, and the fact that chaebŏl founders are by definition the most

TABLE 58 Manufacturing Shares of Business Groups in India, Pakistan, and Korea

(cumulative percentage)

Number of Groups	*Korea 1975*	*Pakistan 1959*	*India*		
			1948	*1958*	*1968*
4	13	–	24	30	23
7	18	21	–	–	–
9	21	–	31	36	28
16	26	34	–	–	–
20	30	–	46	62	39
24	32	40	–	–	–
37	36	47	–	–	–
46	37	–	–	–	–
50	–	–	60	71	50
60	–	53	–	–	–

Sources: Gustav Papanek, *Pakistan's Development: Social Goals Private Incentives* (Cambridge, Mass., 1967), p. 68. Arabind Ghosh, "Role of Large Industrial Houses in Indian Industries," *The Indian Economic Journal,* April–June, 1974, pp. 317–345.

Note: Korean figures are shares of chaebŏl manufacturing value added in total manufacturing value added, while Indian and Pakistani data cover group "assets" as a share of "industrial assets." The comparison is therefore valid only insofar as:
1) value added is proportional to "assets" and
2) "industrial assets" refer to the entire manufacturing sector.

TABLE 59 Trends in Chaebŏl Concentration, 1973–1975

(cumulative percent of non-agricultural GDP)

Number of Chaebŏl	*1973*	*1974*	*1975*
5	5.2	5.6	7.1
10	7.9	8.5	10.7
20	10.9	11.8	14.7
46	15.0	15.3	18.6

Source: Same as Table 55.

accomplished expanders. This is further supported by casual empiricism, since the largest chaebŏl have clearly grown at rates far outstripping the economy as a whole, and there have been only a limited number of cases of declining chaebŏl.[9]

In sum, available evidence suggests that the problem of business concentration in Korea is relatively low by historic Asian standards, but increasing at a rapid rate.

THE SOURCES OF CHAEBŎL ACCUMULATION

THE ISSUE

If Korean chaebŏl have expanded rapidly, what is the source of their growth? How is it that a very small number of individuals have accumulated wealth at a rate even faster than that of the economy as a whole? Within the Korean academic-journalistic community, there is a wide consensus that the answer is "political connections."[10] As a representative example of this view, Kyong-Dong Kim refers to the chaebŏl leaders as "political capitalists" who

> accumulated capital mainly through such "non-rational" processes as speculation, price-fixing, tax evasion, and taking advantage of cumulative inflation. More crucial to this process, however, was that they played on political connections to gain economic favors in exchange for political contributions.[11]

Our own view is that, while the consensus holds a substantial element of truth when applied to the Rhee period, it is misleading (if not simply wrong) as a description of the dominant features of the Park era.

Before outlining the accumulation process in the two periods, it is useful to follow Leibenstein in distinguishing between "zero-sum" and "positive-sum" entrepreneurship.[12] Traditional microeconomic theory holds that all voluntary exchange and production are "positive-sum" in leading to mutual gain (or at least no loss) for all parties. Leibenstein, on the other hand, argues that in the real world, there is "zero-sum" activity when entrepreneurs

> spend their time and energy in any of the following ways that may directly or indirectly increase the personal wealth and income of some of them but which involve activities that add little or nothing to the productive capacity of the economy. (1) They may spend their time in *non-trading* activities in order to secure for their interests a greater monopolistic position, increased political power, more prestige, etc. Such activities can conceivably lead to greater financial gains for some of them than the alternative of engaging in investment activities that lead to increases in national product. (2) They may engage in *trading* activities that may secure for some of them a greater monopolistic position or simply what they believe to be better ways in which to hold their wealth so that such activities will not increase aggregate resources in any way. (3) They may use their talents and marshal wealth in order to engage in speculative trading which, in turn, need not increase aggregate resources or aggregate income. Such activities, even when they do not use up savings, do waste rare entrepreneurial resources. (4) Finally they may engage in activities that do use up net savings, but the investments involved are in enterprises of such a nature that their "social value" is either zero, or their social value is very much lower than their private value.[13]

The question of chaebŏl accumulation may thus be posed in terms of the extent to which it resulted from zero-sum trade and speculation.

THE PREVAILING VIEW OF CHAEBŎL ACCUMULATION

We now present a sampling of academic-journalistic descriptions of the methods of chaebŏl growth, reserving our comments until later. One observer summarizes the process under Rhee as follows:

> Before the Liberation, there were only a few Korean entrepreneurs in a modern sense. Wealthy men at the time were mostly landlords, local brewery owners, or mill owners. Therefore, most Korean entrepreneurs were created during the 20 years after the Liberation. During the same period, there was not much new saving and investment. *Therefore, these newly created entrepreneurs and their wealth accumulation must indicate redistribution of existing national wealth and/or foreign wealth transferred through aid rather than new wealth accumulated through their productive activities.* It is well known that Japanese properties and aid dollars were distributed at ridiculously low prices. Even these acquisitions were made with cheap bank loans under the existing hyper-inflationary situation. And cheap bank loans were mostly concentrated on a few chaebŏl. Hyper-inflation, shortage of supply, high import tariff, import restrictions, protected chaebŏl's monopoly prices and the domestic tax structure were all favorable for chaebŏl. These types of privileges were concentrated on a few chaebŏl since an inter-locking mechanism was in operation. For example, once a businessman acquired Japanese property, he usually also received working capital or reconstruction loans from banks and foreign exchange for importing equipment and raw materials. As their production began, imports of foreign products were restricted on the excuse of protecting domestic firms and at the same time, various tax privileges were also provided. As this example illustrates, most chaebŏl in Korea were created in a short period of time with the help of the government privileges provided.[14]

The italicized passage clearly reflects the prevailing view that accumulation was the result of zero-sum transfers.

The major sources of chaebŏl accumulation during the Rhee period are thus thought to be:

1) Non-competitive allocation of import quotas and import licenses.
2) Bargain price acquisition of former Japanese properties.
3) The selective allocation of aid funds and materials.

4) Privileged access to cheap bank loans.
5) Non-competitive award of government and U.S. military contracts for reconstruction activities.

Examples of each source of accumulation follow.

One of the better known examples of improper foreign exchange allocation was the "Tungsten Dollar" incident of 1952. Three million dollars in earnings from tungsten exports were allocated to privileged firms for the import of grain and fertilizer. A combination of monopoly sales practices and a disequilibrium exchange rate resulted in "enormous profits. The government was then offered a large contribution in return for the favor, which was allegedly used in Rhee's Liberal Party campaign for a constitutional amendment that permitted his re-election as president."[15]

With regard to the privileged acquisition of Japanese properties, one writer describes a spinning mill sale in 1954.[16] The "market price" of the particular mill was said to be ten times as high as the purchase price. Further, the purchase price was to be paid off on an installment basis over fifteen years, and this in turn was financed by low-interest bank loans. During the subsequent fifteen-year period, however, the price level increased almost 260 times, making the factory a virtual gift. This illustrates how a chaebŏl could be created with virtually no equity base of its own.

Even those who had their own, or Japanese derived, factories destroyed during the Korean War had a head start in accumulation. The war was indeed a major economic leveling force, but certain individuals were in a better position to take advantage of the post-war disequilibria. One group was the Kyŏngsang province businessmen in Taegu and Pusan whose plants were not destroyed. In addition, all pre-war owners were given a competitive edge in taking advantage of the U.S. aid for reconstruction after the war. As they gained privileged accesses to aid allocation, either in dollars or raw materials, they again could take full advantage of a rapid inflation and undervalued exchange rate. ICA and AID allowed beneficiaries to build plants if they put up only 15 or 25 percent of their own funds, and even this could be financed via a low-interest, long-term loan.

An even more important source of distortion in aid allocation was the favoritism said to have been shown to members of Rhee's Liberal Party. Joungwon Kim reports that by 1960, the Controller of the Liberal Party "was estimated to have large interests in twenty-nine projects, and the party was believed to have a large interest in at least 50 percent of all private projects receiving American aid."[17]

Domestic credit seems to have been likewise distributed to the advantage of the Liberal Party. It is reported that, just prior to the 1956 election, the Commercial Bank of Korea made loans of 17 billion hwan (the pre-1961 currency unit) to twelve industries which then kicked back as much as 100 percent of the loans to party campaign coffers.[18]

Kyong-Dong Kim also emphasizes the role of non-competitive bidding for government construction contracts, leading to the emergence of the "Five Men" of the construction industry.[19] The same group of transportation companies also benefited from U.S. military contracts. This to some extent resulted from a simple ability to do the job but was certainly enhanced by various formal personal contacts with military non-coms and officers.

In the Park period, four of the five sources of zero-sum accumulation were largely eliminated by policy or circumstance. The remaining element, domestic and foreign credit, is the dominant target of zero-sum accumulations under Park.[20] It is somewhat more difficult to document post-1961 aberrations in the credit allocation process, so we simply present a typical scenario of chaebŏl growth via credit access in the 1960s.[21]

Suppose one privately held company "luckily" gets governmental approval for an industrial project. It will typically be financed by one-fifth equity and four-fifths foreign and domestic loans. So the project starts with a meager equity base but with substantial external debt and other government-provided privileges (notably tax advantages). The privately held firm may then grow rapidly if the project becomes successful. The firm then starts a new line of business with the profits accumulated from the first venture. Of course, once again the firm will not usually put up much equity but will rely heavily on external debt. The extension of this process leads to a group of firms, or chaebŏl. Profits earned from the group may be extracted for distribution to stockholders, usually family members, through legal or illegal methods, or both. This is particularly likely for a weak firm that might be bled. This process gives rise to a popular saying that, "even when business goes bankrupt, businessmen survive." Even for the far more numerous prosperous firms in the group, the financial structure remains weak.

The point of this scenario is that a very small initial equity base can be pyramided into a substantial empire. This is a common phenomenon as was demonstrated by our finding in Chapter 6 that growth of Korean output is more often due to expansion (or founding of "offspring" firms) by existing entrepreneurs than to entry of new entrepreneurs. A second, and far more questionable, contention that is popularly derived from this scenario is that, since credit is controlled by the government, credit-based expansion derives from political influence and implies zero-sum activity. We now evaluate the zero-sum argument.

EVALUATION

It is necessary to exercise some discretion in evaluating the foregoing, since the mere existence of high profits in government-controlled markets is far from sufficient to prove zero-sum activity. In the first place, accounting profit must be broken down into normal economic profit and economic rent. The former is the minimum return necessary to draw a given bundle of capital and entrepreneurship into a particular activity, while the latter is any return beyond that minimum. It is only economic rent that is to be associated with zero-sum activity, and this can indeed be minuscule even with high accounting profit.

Consider the sale of the factories confiscated from the Japanese. As explained in Chapter 2, the political and economic instability of the interwar years and the inexperience of domestic entrepreneurs gave rise to a great deal of uncertainty about the future stream of earnings to be gained from ownership. Had the factories been auctioned off in a perfectly competitive fashion, the price would accordingly have been quite low, and appropriately so. The minimum return necessary for a nascent entrepreneur to bring his talents to bear was high, and the low sales value was to some extent the price paid by society to get, and keep, the factories operating. The crucial question, then, is not whether the price was "low" and the return "high," but whether the price was lower than the minimum necessary to get the factory operating. A qualitative answer to this question can be found by looking at the sales process itself. If bidding was competitive, then any return, however high, was "normal" in being the minimum society had to pay to get things running. If, on the other hand, the bidding was rigged so that a privileged few were able to obtain the properties at below the competitive price, then there was a zero-sum transfer involved. Even so, it would be incorrect to treat the whole transaction as zero-sum, since jobs were created and real output produced.

Further, while rent is necessary for zero-sum activity, it is not sufficient. In addition, the rent must be "unnatural" rather than "natural." Natural rent accrues as a result of information imperfections or unanticipated shifts of supply and demand, while unnatural rent is the result of government intervention or private collusion. Natural rent accrues to the entrepreneur who discovers and fills a disequilibrium gap, while unnatural rent accrues to whoever fills the desires of the government official who maintains and protects a gap. Exploitation of a natural rent opportunity is positive-sum (for example, in filling a hitherto unperceived desire of the consuming public), while acquisition of unnatural rent is zero-sum (for example, in getting an import license where the market is known to all, the only question being who will be granted the boon of collecting the unnatural rent). Hyundai may have earned rent on its shipyard, but there was hardly a multitude clamoring for the opportunity. Had Hyundai not acted, the shipyard and its jobs might not have existed. To this extent, the rent was natural and the entrepreneurial act positive-sum. In contrast, if entrepreneur *A* had not gotten a particular import license under Rhee, then it would have gone to individual *B* (or *Z*, or the state); society's value added is not affected, but the distribution of the rent is.

With these distinctions in mind, it is clear that the earlier academic-journalistic indictment is somewhat overdrawn. Just how "overdrawn" is, of course, impossible to estimate with precision, but we are convinced that, in the move from the Rhee to the Park periods, there has been a shift away from zero-sum activity and towards positive-sum.

This follows from two major trends—in market access and in the character of the privileged markets. With regard to the former, it is only a modest exaggeration to say that, whereas under Rhee political and bureaucratic connections were necessary *and* sufficient for privileged access, under Park bureaucratic (not political) contacts are only necessary. Under Park it is sufficient that a convincing argument can be made to the bureaucracy that the privileges thus conferred will be used productively. To make such an argument effectively, it is also necessary that one be well connected with the bureaucracy. This condition clearly provides an advantage for those who are already wealthy and for those with backgrounds that parallel those of the bureaucrats. Nonetheless, the stock of those entrepreneurs so endowed is sufficiently large that the bid price is reasonably competitive, and the positive-sum "minimum return" dominates pure economic rent. Under Rhee, in contrast, privileged access seems to have been limited to those with much more narrowly defined political affiliations.

The second difference between the two periods is in the

nature of the dominant privileged markets. Under Rhee, the most important source of zero-sum transfers was for foreign exchange and aid, with privilege leading to massive profits with no further effort than a bit of paper work in ordering imports. Under Park, the dominant form of privilege is industrial credit, which leads to profits only if combined with the various entrepreneurial functions to create productive activity. Here zero-sum transfers may still exist, but are necessarily combined with positive-sum behavior.

In both periods, of course, there was a mix of both sorts of activity. Consider the case of Pyŏng-ch'ŏl Yi (see Appendix B). Under Rhee, the bulk of his early capital accumulation came from windfall profits in imports; given prevailing conditions, these were undoubtedly predominantly zero-sum. Some of these, however, were ploughed back into the nation's first large-scale sugar and woolen textile mills, a positive-sum achievement of no small magnitude, given the unsettled conditions of the time. In the 1960s, by contrast, Samsung's accumulation came overwhelmingly from production and competitive export trade. An effort at zero-sum importing in connection with the construction of a fertilizer factory led to forfeiture of equity in the plant. This shift by Pyŏng-ch'ŏl Yi from a mixture of zero- and positive-sum to predominantly positive-sum activity is reflective of the major change between the two periods.

Zero-sum activity, of course, remains under Park. One example of contemporary zero-sum activity involves the use of industrial credit for speculation in land. More broadly, there is no doubt that the dynamics of discretionary allocation result in economic rents beyond the minimum necessary to extract entrepreneurial effort. Just how much beyond the minimum is an empirical question that we leave to others. The critical point is that it now occurs largely as an add-on to some productive positive-sum entrepreneurial act.

In sum, a major difference between Rhee and Park is that, under the latter, zero-sum activities were substantially reduced relative to positive-sum efforts. In part this followed from an elimination of some zero-sum incentives by a shift to nondiscretionary allocation of foreign exchange. There nonetheless remained abundant opportunities for discretionary allocation of underpriced resources, most notably credit. Here, however, leadership commitment to growth ensured that bureaucratic discretion was now exercised so that these resources were allocated to reasonably productive users. The result is that while zero-sum transfers still exist, they occur largely as frosting on basically positive-sum ventures.

Our view, then, is that under Rhee much, if not the bulk, of chaebŏl accumulation took place as a result of government-controlled transfers that produced relatively few compensatory benefits for society as a whole. Under Park such transfers remain, but are decidedly ancillary to accumulation resulting from socially beneficial growth of productive activity. This change is not to be attributed to any consciousness-raising on the part of entrepreneurs. Businessmen may not strictly maximize profits, but they are certainly out to make a buck, and will take the path of least resistance in doing so. Under Rhee, this path led to zero-sum activity; under Park, the rules changed, and the Keynesian "animal spirits of the capitalists" were channeled into predominatly positive-sum ventures.

GOVERNMENT POLICIES TOWARDS CHAEBŎL

Two periods of notable activity stand out with respect to Korean government policies towards chaebŏl expansion. The first was the "illicit wealth accumulation" measure designed to punish the zero-sum entrepreneurs at the fall of the Rhee regime. The second is the series of actions taken in the early 1970s to begin to put brakes on the expansion of positive-sum entrepreneurs. These measures will be discussed in detail below, but we begin with an overview.

ACCUMULATION VERSUS UTILIZATION

It will be obvious to even the most casual reader of this volume that the Park Government has put no serious restraints on the rate of chaebŏl accumulation. Growth has come largely through expansion of existing groups rather than entry of new participants, and the chaebŏl have almost certainly grown much more rapidly than the economy as a whole. While income and property taxes are progressive, and the inheritance tax is probably more ambitious than is common in LDCs, there has been no serious effort at income redistribution by placing heavy levies on the very wealthy. Instead, the government has indirectly promoted business concentration by its single-minded devotion to growth and its credit allocation policy. Credit and other advantages are provided to those thought most likely to use it productively, and this has meant those with a proven track record. Reducing project gestation periods has taken precedent over improving the Gini coefficient.

While there has therefore been implicit encouragement of chaebŏl wealth accumulation, it is important to note that there have been real restraints on its utilization. These are of three sorts. First, wealth has not been translated into political influence. Second, a high proportion of the wealth has been reinvested and remarkably little diverted to conspicuous consumption. Third, there have been limitations on the utilization of wealth to acquire certain forms of economic power—most effectively in precluding chaebŏl control of banks, and more recently in a variety of restraints on chaebŏl asset use.

The first constraint—breaking the link between economic and political power—was discussed earlier in this chapter and need not be considered further. The second constraint—limitation of conspicuous consumption—is a subjective and relativistic observation which requires some elaboration. The life-style of the chaebŏl rich varies from conspicuous frugality to moderately conspicuous consumption. Casual empiricism suggests, however, that by Southeast Asian standards the mean level is on the conservative side. While the Korean rich live indecently well by Korean standards, their homes, cars, and entertainments appear to us to be decidedly frugal in comparison to their counterparts elsewhere in Asia (except Japan and Taiwan).

If the foregoing generalization is correct, then there are four causal elements. First, Korean wealth is largely first-generation, and this is naturally more conservative in its consumption habits than profligate second-generation inheritors. Second, there may be in operation a Korean ethical asceticism that frowns on overt manifestations of wealth. Third, government policies clearly discourage luxury consumption. The taxes on "luxury" vehicles (more than four cylinders) in 1974 totaled more than 500 percent (of c.i.f.) at purchase and ran from 50 percent to nearly 100 percent per year thereafter. Fourth, the pecuniary and non-pecuniary returns to successful entrepreneurship are so great that the opportunity cost of consumption is higher than elsewhere. All of this serves to channel a high proportion of profits back into investment of one form or another.

The third constraint on utilization—precluding certain forms of economic activity—is of particular interest. The abolition of private control over banks and the reduction of opportunities for zero-sum forms of speculation and trade have already been stressed. In the mid-1970s, however, there has been a marked upsurge in government attention to the chaebŏl problem. This is not surprising, since, as our quantitative measures have indicated, chaebŏl size relative to the economy is small, but seems to have recently been expanding at a rapid rate. The new government concern has manifested itself in a series of measures aimed at opening the chaebŏl to public ownership and control, lowering their debt/equity ratios, and prohibiting real estate speculation. These measures will be discussed in detail, after considering the earlier "illicit wealth accumulation" episode.

THE "ILLICIT WEALTH ACCUMULATION" EPISODE

One of the last acts of the short-lived Chang Myon regime was the passage of a Special Law for Dealing with Illicit Wealth Accumulation. This had the stated objective of punishing those who "accumulated wealth illicitly by taking advantage of their positions and power."[22] One of the first measures of the new Park Military Government was the issuance of the following guideline:

> The purpose of this guideline is in accordance with administrative procedures and criminal laws to deal with those who illicitly accumulated wealth. They include civil servants, politicians, and high-ranking government officials who took advantage of their positions and their power in their private fortune-making. They also include those businessmen and profiteering commercial agents who accumulated wealth illicitly by associating with above-mentioned government officials or politicians.[23]

Based on this guidance, the Park Military Government immediately arrested most of the nation's leading businessmen. A new law was legislated in June 1961, and it defined illicit profiteers as those who during the period of July 1, 1953, to May 15, 1961, had:

1) Illicitly earned profits totaling more than 100 million hwan by either purchasing or renting publicly owned properties (largely those confiscated from the Japanese).
2) Obtained loans or purchases of more than 100,000 dollars worth of government- or bank-owned foreign exchange.
3) Provided political funds of more than 50 million hwan in return for bank loans.
4) Earned profits of more than 200 million hwan in the process of contracting or bidding for public works or commodity trade in an illegal way.
5) Earned profits of more than 200 million hwan by monopolizing the purchase or allocation of foreign exchange.
6) Avoided taxes of more than 200 million hwan.
7) Illegally transferred their wealth abroad.

This list illustrates the popular perception of the scope of zero-sum activity during the Rhee period.

In the end, as already described in Chapter 3, a compromise was worked out whereby criminal sanctions were abolished, and the accused businessmen were to build factories and turn them over to the government. The matter was closed in December 1964 with most paying their fines in cash. Altogether the government collected about four billion wŏn (about $16 million).[24] Some will view this episode as a "sell-out," while others will agree with us that it reflects the government's dominant commitment to growth coupled to a belief that entrepreneurs were an essential scarce commodity to be utilized in pursuit of that goal. In either case, a pattern was established whereby substantial assistance was given to established businessmen who proved themselves capable of initiating new manufacturing and export activity. Those who fulfilled these qualifications were allowed to expand largely unchecked until the mid-1970s.

THE MAY 29 PRESIDENTIAL SPECIAL DIRECTIVES OF 1974

In 1974 a set of Presidential Special Directives were issued which may represent a turning point in the government's attitude towards the chaebŏl. At this writing, the ramifications are not entirely clear, but a new era may have been initiated.

The background to the May 29 Directives was the effort that began in 1972 to force privately held business firms to open themselves to public participation by selling their shares on the stock market (see Chapter 4). Few chaebŏl firms responded, and the May 29 Directives were issued with the following objectives:

1) Family-oriented management should be modernized.
2) The scale of enterprises should be enlarged to enable them to become internationally competitive.
3) The managerial and financial capacities of families are limited so privately held firms should go public.
4) The accumulation of business assets in the hands of a few individuals or family groups should be prevented.

To accomplish these objectives, the following measures were to be taken:

1) Induce corporations to go public by means of appropriate privileges to "well-managed" publicly held corporations.
2) Establish a system of overseeing and controlling credit

allocations and tax records of privately held corporations (especially large chaebŏl firms).

3) Reduce the debt/equity ratio of large corporations by managing the bank loan system appropriately, and by instructing indebted businessmen who want to start new projects to sell all or part of their existing equity and use the proceeds to finance the new project.
4) Reinforce tax surveillance and the outside audit system for corporations and large shareholders to increase the creditability of corporations.

In accordance with these directives, the Ministry of Finance prepared Measures on Bank Credit and Business Concentration. Business groups with outstanding credit of more than 5 billion wŏn (including bank payment guarantees but excluding export credits) were put into two categories according to whether their financial structure was weak (Group A) or strong (Group B). Group B firms were to be ordered to go public, while Group A firms were to be directed to first improve their financial structure.

In the meantime, Group A firms were prohibited from:

1) Receiving new foreign loan guarantees.
2) Establishing or acquiring additional businesses.
3) Investment in stock.
4) Acquisition of non-operating real estate.

In addition, the main companies of each chaebŏl were required to file a three-year financial structure-improvement schedule using the following means to reduce their debt/equity ratios:

1) Going public.
2) Increasing paid-in capital.
3) Selling off subsidiaries (proceeds to be used for debt retirement or equity increase).
4) Public offering of debt instruments in the securities market.
5) Merger and rationalization.
6) Other means.

If these firms do not proceed as they are supposed to, or are slow in implementing the annual plan, the Financial Normalization Committee established under the Office of the Prime Minister will examine these cases, and the government or Bank Audit Board will notify banks not to extend low-interest loans to these firms.

Subsequent actions have strengthened these efforts. In August 1975, an additional measure was taken to extend coverage of the May 29 Directives to the main chaebŏl holding companies. In August 1974 a land bank was established "for the purpose of channelling otherwise idle capital invested in unutilized land into industrial uses, improving the financial structure of business firms, and improved utilization of lands by publicly facilitating land transactions and utilization."[25] This was done to facilitate liquidation of firms' non-operating land holdings in the spirit of the May 29 Directives. According to the law,[26] the Minister of Finance can order those business firms that have bank loans and bank guarantees above a given level[27] to sell their non-operating real estate to the bank. In case those firms or individuals do not follow the order, the minister can direct financial institutions to limit the provision of credit.

Thus far the only clear impact of the May 29 directives has been the decimation of the Shinjin Group—the chaebŏl which had been by far the slowest in converting to positive-sum activity.[28] Overall, however, we can now only outline the kinds of effect that the measures might be expected to have on the more solid chaebŏl. Initially there is only a constraint on wealth utilization as they are forced to reshuffle their portfolios, exchanging one form of asset for another. In the long-run, however, the rate of accumulation may be reduced since:

1) The reduction in the debt/equity ratio reduces leverage earnings.
2) It becomes more difficult to use low-interest industrial credit to finance zero-sum land speculation.
3) The public offerings are made at well below recognized market value, giving an immediate transfer to middle- and upper-class buyers. Insofar as the market undervalues

current offerings, there will be a further transfer as economic rent from earlier entrepreneurial acts accrues to new equity holders.

On the other hand, the rate of accumulation may be enhanced to the extent that

1) Openness improves managerial practices.
2) The cost of public-equity funding via dividends proves to be less than that of debt via interest payments.

If, as seems highly likely, the negative distributional effects outweigh the positive from the point of view of the chaebŏl, there will be a further negative-incentive effect leading to reduced chaebŏl entrepreneurial effort and thus to a further lowering of the rate of accumulation.

Sorting out these various effects would require a research effort well beyond the scope of the present study. Here we only note that the government has once again shown its dominance over the business community and has finally taken a set of measures that could conceivably lead to a reduction in the rate of chaebŏl accumulation.

NINE

Summary

We began this volume by asking if there was any causal connection between the coincidence of economic and political turning points in Korea in the early 1960s. That is, to what extent was the government of Park Chung Hee in some sense "responsible" for the decade-and-a-half of 10 percent real growth? This is not the sort of question with which economists are comfortable. Not only are many of the relevant variables unquantifiable, but we lack the scatter of observations that would allow us to identify the effect of various aspects of "government" in a multivariate framework under *ceteris-paribus* conditions. As a result, hypotheses cannot be "tested" but only "examined"; they are never "proven," but at best "survive." Any conclusions are thus necessarily subjective and leave one professionally vulnerable.

We, nonetheless, believe this sort of question to be important and now summarize our more important results by presenting a series of propositions that have survived our examination. Since the issues are inherently slippery, and since most have not previously received serious attention in the Korean context, it is to be expected that some will fail to survive further scrutiny. We only hope that our formulation will serve to stimulate additional work.

THE COLONIAL HERITAGE (CHAPTER 2)

While our focus is on the Rhee and Park periods, we begin with a summary of the historically imposed initial conditions.

1) The Japanese colonial period (1910–1945) brought rapid industrialization, with real manufacturing NCP growing at an average rate of 10 percent per year to a level of roughly 20 percent of total NCP in the early 1940s.
2) This impressive achievement in potential contribution to post-war growth was minimized by three factors: first, the colonial enclave industrial structure; second, the dominant role of Japanese owners, managers, and technicians; and third, the location of heavy industry in the north.
3) Nonetheless, at Liberation, South Korea was left with a substantial set of productive facilities, a large work force familiar with at least low-level manufacturing tasks, and a group of entrepreneurs exposed to the demonstration effects of modern technology and organization.
4) This heritage proved of little use to the new nation, however, as the physical capital was largely dissipated by a combination of administrative chaos (1945–1950) and war (1950–1951). The human capital was not destroyed but diverted into largely non-productive activities by incompetent government economic management.

GOVERNMENT AND GROWTH

A return to our main theme gives rise to three propositions:

5) The government of Park Chung Hee has in no sense pursued a laissez-faire strategy towards the economy; rather, it has been heavily interventionist in attempting to influence the microeconimic decisions of productive units either through direct government participation in public enterprise or through stimulating, forcing, or cajoling private enterprises.
6) These intervention efforts have been effective in actually altering private decisions, resource allocation, and economic outcomes.
7) The effective intervention has had a positive net impact on growth.

We are quite confident that the first two propositions can be substantiated to the satisfaction of most readers, and we shall elaborate upon them presently. The third proposition, however, is somewhat more controversial. At first, this may seem surprising. If the Korean economy has achieved a world-record growth rate over a fifteen-year period, and if the government has intervened effectively, then how can its role have been anything but positive? It is, nonetheless, possible to find foreign visitors who, having stayed in Korea long enough to be both impressed by the economic dynamism and aware of the pervasive intervention, make statements of the form: "My God, just imagine what these people could do if the government didn't stick its nose into everything!"

Since some knowledgeable Koreans take a similar view, it would be a mistake to dismiss this position as purely facetious. Two forms of the argument are possible—marginalist and structural.

The marginalist version would run as follows:

> We know that certain policies have had a negative effect on growth, that the bureaucracy sometimes processes paper too slowly (and

> other times acts too rapidly), that the public enterprises are not as efficient as they could be, and so on; if these demonstrable deficiencies were corrected then the economy could clearly have grown even more rapidly; Q.E.D.

We can hardly quarrel with the substance of this position, but would ask just how much perfection can reasonably be expected of human beings in a world of uncertainty.

In any event, the critical question is not whether a slightly different intervention mix could have yielded slightly higher growth rates, but whether a fundamentally non-interventionist strategy would have yielded significantly higher rates. Assessing this structuralist variant of the argument would require a counterfactual exercise of substantial dimensions. Suppose that in 1961 the government had adopted and pursued a Friedmanesque hands-off policy; where then would the economy have been fifteen years later? Consider the single issue of bank ownership. Under a laissez-faire policy, Pyŏng-ch'ŏl Yi would have owned half of the banking system with the remainder held by other major chaebŏl. The non-interventionist would have to argue: 1) that competitive pressures would have led to a dilution of this control; or 2) that pressures in other markets would have led even a concentrated banking sector into a basically competitive allocation of resources; or 3) that the costs of private oligopolistic allocation would have been less than the costs associated with a government-run sector. While the first two positions are palpably absurd, the third is at least arguable. Unfortunately, a systematic comparison of the relative costs (including the possibility that the resulting power concentration would provoke a revolution) over fifteen years lies well beyond the scope of this study. A similar effort for the economy as a whole is even further beyond our means.

In sum, we would readily agree with the marginalist position that a somewhat different pattern of intervention could have added a point or even two to the growth record. We do not pursue this further since, from an international point of view, the fundamental question is not how Korea might have done a little better, but how she achieved a 10 percent rate of growth in the first place. While we attribute part of this achievement to the interventionist government, we cannot disprove the structural hypothesis that a laissez-faire pattern would have been superior. For the present, we only offer the following deductive theorizing:

8) The economic theory of government intervention implies that, for a developing economy sunk in the depths of an interlocking web of disequilibria, the theoretically optimal escape path involves substantial government intervention in order to achieve even a crude approximation to the Pareto efficient resource allocations that would prevail in the absence of such distortions (Chapter 1).

9) Since Korea has the best sustained non-resource-based growth record of any LDC, it is therefore not only unsurprising, but actually expected, that the level of government intervention is high and has a positive net impact.

The reason that positive intervention seems surprising is that a generation of development economists have become accustomed to working in LDCs where misguided intervention has been part of the problem rather than part of the cure. The intriguing question is, then, not why Korea is interventionist, but why intervention works. We now consider some propositions as to why this might be the case.

GOVERNMENT ECONOMIC DECISION-MAKING PROCESS (CHAPTER 3)

Planning, in the broadest sense, is the laying out of a set of means-ends chains. The highest tier in this set, and thus the apex of the decision-making process, is the establishment of national priorities. In Korea:

10) The first and perhaps most important difference between the Rhee and Park regimes was the degree of leadership commitment to growth. Rhee was an independence leader

who devoted his attention to politics and national integration while largely ignoring economics. Park's orientation could not be more different, with economic growth having priority second only to national and personal political survival. Since only the higher goals are seen as being furthered by growth, economic affairs have been enshrined as the dominant operational system objective.

For leadership commitment to make a difference, it must alter the behavior of others. The first step is to affect bureaucrats, and the second—discussed in the next section—is to influence production units.

11) Park's commitment to growth is manifested in part in the allocation of his own time, but even more important in his influence on the behavior of the entire bureaucracy. As a military man, he is trained in using a staff. The Korean civil service, with its high selection standards and inculcation of the Confucian hierarchical tradition, is admirably equipped to respond. As a result, virtually the entire executive branch has been mobilized to make decisions based on expected economic outcomes. To do otherwise brings shame on oneself and one's immediate superiors and subordinates.

Bureaucratic decision-making is manifested both in formal medium-term planning exercises and in short-term day-to-day policy making.

12) Formal Korean planning has relatively little to distinguish it from its counterparts in a multitude of LDCs with undistinguished growth records. It has been only partially successful in charting a detailed path for the economy, but has served to map the economic terrain, educate officials, provide a focus for dialogue, and announce government commitment to business. The educational aspect was particularly important, as it helped bureaucrats make the short-term decisions that really drive the economy.

We have stressed that Korea's economic growth performance is remarkable not only for its rate but also for the length of time over which it has been sustained. In 1976, Park Chung Hee presided over an economy that was more than four times as large as the one he inherited in 1961. The accompanying structural changes were even greater, and the nature and sophistication of government policy has had to adjust at a corresponding rate. That one man has proven capable of overseeing such disparate economies is remarkable. It is as though Calvin Coolidge were called upon to deal with the economy of the United States as faced by Jimmy Carter. One aspect of the problem is how Park was able to maintain his discipline and dedication in the absence of any effective internal threat via election or coup.

13) Internationally, there is a common pattern of strong LDC leaders who take office with great dedication to the national welfare, but who over time deteriorate into corruption in pampered and isolated splendor. Despite the absence of an effective internal threat, this trend is not yet apparent in the economic sphere in Park's case. This may be due to personal character or to the substitution of an external threat from the north.

The second aspect of the problem is how—given continued leadership dedication—the administrative structure was able to respond to change.

14) That the bureaucratic decision-making structure has been able continually and successfully to adapt to rapidly changing conditions is due in part to the following characteristics of the short-term policy formulation process: executive dominance, speed, flexibility, pragmatism, particularism, and openness.

15) Executive dominance. The legislative and judiciary branches have become nearly irrelevant under Park.

16) Speed and Flexibility. Government policy response to changing conditions is typically closer to the alacrity of a crack air-force unit scrambling to the attack than to the lethargy usually associated with bureaucracy. This has costs in that the first decision may prove misguided, but such costs are minimized by flexibility in changing direc-

tion as the effects of the initial decision become apparent. The Korean policy-making style is not so much a deliberate one of careful planning and debate, but more one of diving in, getting started, observing results, adjusting policy, and repeating the process until the appropriate mix is found.

17) Pragmatism. The selection of instruments to deal with a particular economic problem is not constrained by any ideological predilections. The test is what works, and the Koreans are perfectly willing to try anything from public ownership to free markets to coercion.

18) Particularism. Policies are often made with low levels of generality; for example, for application to a single firm. This allows fine-tuning of policy with attendant risks of corruption and uncertainty.

19) Openness. Economic policy-making is open to a wide range of opinion inputs, even though the final decision process itself is closed. There is virtually unlimited freedom of economic expression with various levels of government quite receptive to the opinions of businessmen, academics, and foreigners. The influence of labor unions, however, is negligible.

The question of business influence is particularly interesting, since it raises the question of whether there is a "Korea, Inc." We argue that

20) Given economic growth as the legitimizing goal of the Park regime, there is a clear harmony of interest between government and business, and this is reflected in close working relationships of a sort that might be crudely characterized as "Korea, Inc." The analogy with "Japan, Inc." is misleading, however, in that the Korean government is clearly and unquestionably the dominant partner.

The reasons for the dominance of government can be seen by considering the mechanisms whereby government controls business.

IMPLEMENTATION OF GOVERNMENT POLICY (CHAPTER 4)

Implementation in a narrow sense is the translation of an administrative abstraction into concrete action by a production unit. We believe that

21) Korea is distinguished from less successful LDCs, not so much by the wisdom of the policy abstractions generated by its planners, as by its ability to implement these policies.

This can be explained by examining the lower—but perhaps most crucial—level of government planning; that is, the set of mechanisms whereby individual or enterprise compliance is stimulated, forced, or cajoled. These compliance mechanisms are central to understanding any mixed economy.

22) Despite our emphasis on the role of government, Korea is in no sense a command economy. Rather it is "mixed" both in terms of ownership and in the distribution of decision-making power. In such an economy, the critical point in the decision-making hierarchy is the gap between public influence and private decisions. This gap is bridged by compliance mechanisms.

Selection of compliance mechanisms involves a two-dimensional choice between non-coercive field manipulation and command on the one hand and between discretionary and non-discretionary administration on the other. Of the four possible sets of behavioral mechanisms, one—non-discretionary parameter manipulation—is generally held to be superior on theoretical grounds. This is reflected in the popular dictum that, where intervention is necessary, it should be accomplished by "getting the prices right." However:

23) In Korea, non-discretionary parameter manipulation has by no means been eschewed, but it has been heavily supplemented by the illiberal compliance mechanisms of command and administrative discretion. Korea is thus interventionist in the broad sense of altering decisions of productive entities, but also in the narrower sense of using compulsion and discretion in doing so.

The dominant uses of each compliance mechanism are as follows:

24) The single most important realm of non-discretionary field manipulation is the foreign exchange market. On the supply side, both Rhee and Park used this device to a surprisingly similar extent to stimulate exports. The export boom thus does not seem to be attributable directly to "getting the price right" in terms of constant wŏn-per-dollar return to foreign sales.

25) On the demand side, foreign exchange was allocated to importers via discretionary command under Rhee but via non-discretionary field manipulation under Park. This had the important result of driving entrepreneurs out of zero-sum arbitrage activity and into positive-sum production and thus contributing indirectly to exports.

26) Credit allocation is the most important example of discretionary field manipulation. There is no discernible difference between Rhee and Park in the degree of discretion exercised by government officials over the allocation of credit. There is, however, a major difference in the principle guiding discretion. Under Rhee, political and personal gain seem to have played a major role. Under Park, such considerations are by no means absent but are clearly subordinate to economic priorities.

27) Non-discretionary command prevails in tax administration and consumption bans, while discretionary command occurs in price controls and in both "informal guidance" and formal directives in a plethora of areas.

The critical question with both variants of command is not so much why it is attempted, but why it succeeds. Field manipulation carries its own reward for compliance, but command must be enforced. Two methods are available: straightforward legal police action and informal "partial mutuality" (for example, the implicit threat of withdrawing a privilege previously conferred under discretionary field manipulation). In Korea:

28) Partial mutuality is the dominant means of enforcing discretionary command, while selective police action is

typically used to ensure compliance with non-discretionary command.

29) Discretionary credit allocation is the fulcrum upon which partial mutuality rests. The critical importance of credit to the enterprise, and its virtually complete control by the government, make this a powerful tool for ensuring private compliance with almost any command the government wishes to give. Government control of the banks is thus the single most important economic factor explaining the distinctly subordinate position of the private sector.

The use of discretion in implementing government policy has been widely criticized as a source of corruption and inefficient resource allocation in other LDCs. In Korea:

30) Under Rhee, all the evils normally associated with bureaucratic discretion were abundantly apparent. Under Park, discretion remained, but the negative effects were reduced, and the advantages of flexibility under a "rule of men" rather than a rigid "rule of law" were reaped. The difference follows from leadership commitment to growth imposed on a rigid hierarchical structure in which no official can afford conspicuously to make decisions that run counter to the goals of economic efficiency and growth.

The efficacy of discretion and command under Park may be summarized in terms of Myrdal's distinction between "hard" and "soft" states.

31) The second critical difference between the Rhee and Park periods (after leadership commitment to growth) is in the efficacy of implementation. Under Rhee, Korea was the familiar "soft" LDC in which economic regulations were seldom enforced. Under Park, it became a prototype of the "hard" development model with the ability to impose obligations via compulsion and the ability to direct administrative discretion towards economically desirable ends.

The examination of the governmental apex of the economic decision-making triangle leads us to consideration of its base in the productive units. We first briefly consider the public enterprises and then turn to the quantitatively more important private sector.

PUBLIC ENTERPRISE (CHAPTER 5)

Korea is widely, but mistakenly, regarded as being among the most capitalistic of LDCs. In fact:

32) A minor paradox of Korean development is that, despite a rhetorical commitment to private enterprise, public ownership has been used to an extent that parallels that of many countries advocating a socialist pattern of society.

33) The relatively large public enterprise sector is not to be attributed to the heritage of Japanese properties confiscated at Liberation. Most of these enterprises had been divested by 1961.

34) During the period of rapid economic growth, public enterprises constituted a "leading sector" in the sense that they grew substantially more rapidly than the economy as a whole, and there were identifiable linkages whereby that growth was transmitted to other sectors.

35) Enterprises chosen for public operation are characterized by output-market concentration, high forward linkages, high capital intensity, large size and production of nontradeables or import substitutes rather than exports.

Given these characteristics of the public enterprises:

36) The alternative to the imperfections of public control is usually not the ideal of perfect competition, but the imperfections of private monopoly (or oligopoly) or outright nonexistence.

The paradox of Korean reliance on public ownership is thus resolved:

37) The size and growth of the sector is explicable in terms of a growth-oriented government's pragmatic response to some of the market imperfections that must be overcome

in the course of development. Public enterprise is simply one tool for dealing with these problems.

What are the consequences of this choice? Public enterprises elsewhere are widely held to be "inefficient." Based on partial evidence, we believe that

38) Korean public enterprises are generally more cost efficient than their counterparts in most LDCs, but much of this is due to the general competence of the labor force and the externalities of a well-run economy. More important, while the public enterprises are less efficient than comparable private Korean firms, we believe the public-private gap is smaller than in most other LDCs.

39) The relative efficiency of the public-enterprise sector is not to be explained in terms of novel organizational features of the control structure. These seem to be as inimical to efficiency as elsewhere. Instead, it may be due to the same features that make other forms of discretionary command effective. Leadership commitment to growth, as administered by a competent hierarchy, precludes major prolonged inefficiencies.

PRIVATE ENTREPRENEURSHIP: SOURCES OF EXPANSION (CHAPTER 6)

The importance of government's visible hand and the scope of the public-enterprise sector notwithstanding, the quantitative bulk of decisions leading to growth are taken in the private sector. If decision-making is the scarcest of the scarce factors that must be mobilized in order to develop, then to understand Korean growth we must understand the sources of expansion in the quantity of successful entrepreneurial acts. This may be phrased in terms of how much of the expansion in the equilibrium quantity of entrepreneurship is due to demand shifts and how much to supply shifts. We argue that

40) The initial growth spurt in the early 1960s came from

demand side effects, but thereafter expansion is explicable largely in terms of shifts in supply.

A first look at the important changes on the demand side reveals that

41) After years of political and economic confusion, the imposition of the military regime in 1961 brought stability and promises of economic support. This induced expectations of future stability, lengthened entrepreneurs' time horizons, lowered the time preference discount rate, and increased the expected return on virtually all projects.

42) The military regime also took steps to eliminate the massive rents accruing to recipients of various government privileges, notably foreign exchange. This had the effect of reordering the project yields that constitute the demand curve. The net effect on private return is not clear, but social returns increased substantially as the existing quantity of entrepreneurship shifted from zero-sum to positive-sum activities.

On the supply side, we distinguish between "lenticular" and "bundle" entrepreneurship. There are a variety of entrepreneurial functions that must be fulfilled if a project is to succeed. However, the entrepreneur need not perform all (or any) of these "bundle" functions himself. He need only perform the combinatorial or lenticular function of insuring that they are all carried out by someone. There are therefore three entrepreneurial supply curves:

a) Lenticular intent: individuals who are willing to try to provide a standard unit of the lenticular function at a given price.

b) Effective lenticularism: those who are able to provide a unit of standard lenticularism.

c) Bundle entrepreneurship: those who are able to provide a standard lenticular unit *and* find (or supply) complementary entrepreneurial imputs.

We argue that the major shifts in these curves have been as follows:

43) Lenticular intent is a function of sociological characteristics that change only slowly, so shifts in this curve play only a minor role. There may, nonetheless, have been some outward shifts as the non-pecuniary returns expand with increasing societal approval.
44) Learning by doing has progressively and substantially reduced the gap between intended and effective lenticularism.
45) Bundle supply has progressively shifted outward (towards effective lenticular supply) as gap filling has become easier. This occurs due to learning by doing, growth externalities, increased functional differentiation, and government field augmentation.

A major implication of the foregoing is that

46) The expansion of entrepreneurial acts seems to be due more to the qualitative improvement of the existing stock of entrepreneurs rather than to an increase in the quantity of active entrepreneurs.

This is supported by an examination of entrepreneurial dynamics which suggests that

47) There is substantial churning at the bottom of the entrepreneurial ladder with a high level of aspiration and gross entry leading to rapid failure. Those who survive the initial entrepreneurial act then expand rapidly. Growth in value added is due first to expansion of existing firms, second to entry of offspring firms, and only to a minor extent to net entrance of new entrepreneurs.

This has major implications for business concentration, a topic to which we shall return after looking more carefully at the sources of entrepreneurial supply.

PRIVATE ENTREPRENEURSHIP: SUPPLY (CHAPTER 7)

A recurring theme in studies of entrepreneurial supply is the notion of a subordinated group struggling for otherwise blocked or threatened status and providing economic leadership in the process. Korea has an exceptionally homogeneous population, but there are two important minorities—northerners and Christians—which must be considered as candidates for subordinated group status.

48) Northerners are indeed heavily overrepresented in the entrepreneurial population, and Christians somewhat so. However, examination of cross-correlations with other variables—notably parental occupation—make it clear that this is not due to subordination.

49) Northern overrepresentation is to be explained in terms of natural selection—those who chose to flee a Communist regime are disproportionately educated, wealthy, and from industrial and commercial backgrounds. Social blockage does *not* explain their overrepresentation, as southerners from similar family backgrounds would seem to have an equal probability of representation among the entrepreneurial elite.

If the sociologists' subordination theories do not work in Korea, neither does the notion of a random distribution of entrepreneurial energy:

50) The entrepreneurial elite is emphatically not drawn randomly from the population as a whole. Rather, today's entrepreneurs came from a narrow selection of family occupational backgrounds—large to medium landlords, merchants, factory owners, civil servants, and professionals. Since these occupations were confined to at most 15 percent of the parental cohort, it is clear that the industrial elite has been derived from the pre-industrial elite (though not necessarily from the traditional *yangban* elite).

51) The link between traditional and industrial status does not seem to be primarily capital or influence, but education. That is, the traditional elite had disproportionate access to the education which correlates highly with a

position within the entrepreneurial elite. Seventy percent of entrepreneurs have some college education compared with only 10 percent of the male cohort. Further, there is surprisingly little difference between the entrepreneurs and the renowned civil servants.

Since education is not widely regarded as a determinant of entrepreneurial success, it is worth asking why the situation may be different in Korea. One possibility is that

52) In the Confucian system, education has such a high value that it serves as a validation mechanism for anyone with higher aspirations and makes it difficult for an uneducated man to manage relations with subordinates or with government. Even if education yields few useful technical skills, it nonetheless provides social prerequisites that are useful for entrepreneurial success.

It is widely believed that the government discriminates in favor of entrepreneurs from Park Chung Hee's Kyŏngsang province. However, our results show that

53) While Kyŏngsang province dominates in absolute numbers, its citizens are actually underrepresented relative to the population as a whole. If there is any discrimination, it operates in favor of those born in the north, Seoul, or Kyŏnggi province. Even this, however, is probably due to differences in education and parental occupation rather than discrimination.

Finally, consider the question of the generally high quality of lenticular entrepreneurial supply. One set of reasons may be that, in common with other high-growth East Asian societies:

54) The Confucian heritage emphasizes certain virtues that are supportive of growth. Among these are: competitive dedication to improving the relative position of self and family; respect for education as a vehicle for self-improvement; inculcation of qualities of hard work, diligence, and self-discipline; absence of religious or ideological constraints inhibiting the pragmatic pursuit of ends; and ability to subordinate self and participate effec-

tively in a hierarchical structure yielding a synergistic effect on output.

The notion that the Confucian heritage is growth supporting is, of course, open to the charge of "ex-postism," since twenty years ago it was viewed by many as the curse rather than the cure. The question is why the growth-negating elements withered away, while the growth-accentuating elements have prospered; for example, why the "empty" classical education has yielded to the modern, but the traditional drive and respect for education has (if anything) increased. A superficial answer is that one element was compatible with modernity and the other not, but such cultural Darwinism must itself be explained. We leave this puzzle to others, and only suggest that the nontheistic flexibility of Confucianism may be a factor.

Social homogeneity may also play a role in explaining the high level of entrepreneurial supply. Elsewhere, minorities prosper because the majority faith is inimical to growth. In Korea:

55) The basic Confucian values are widely shared, even among those who profess some other religious faith. This means that minority status confers no special advantage, and that the entrepreneurs' contacts with workers and civil servants are less likely to be marred by competing values.

PRIVATE ECONOMIC POWER (CHAPTER 8)

One problem of capitalistic or mixed patterns of development is the tendency towards an increasing concentration of economic power in a small number of hands. This business concentration has spawned both academic research and corrective government policy towards such manifestations of the phenomenon as the Japanese zaibatsu, India's industrial groups, and Pakistan's twenty-two families. In Korea, the term for such groups is chaebŏl.

56) The Korean chaebŏl are similar to the early Meiji zaibatsu

in that control is centralized in a single dynamic individual who founds one enterprise, gets it running, passes management to a relative or associate, and moves on to something new. A major difference is that the chaebŏl do not hold their own banks.

Our quantitative estimates suggest that

57) The forty-six largest chaebŏl produce roughly 13 percent of GDP or 37 percent of value added in manufacturing. This level of business concentration is surprisingly low in comparison to available Japanese, Indian, and Pakistani data.

However, since most Koreans started from a near-zero base in 1951, the *level* of business concentration is perhaps less important than the *trend*:

58) The trend in business concentration seems to be rapidly upward. This follows both from empirical data on the brief 1973–1975 period and from our earlier conclusion that expansion dominates entry as a source of entrepreneurial growth.

If so, then how is this rapid growth to be explained?

Journalistic opinion in Korea holds that chaebŏl accumulation is largely the result of political connections. We argue that

59) Under Rhee, a major source of chaebŏl growth was privileged access to government controlled markets, and the resulting transfers produced relatively few benefits for society as a whole. Entrepreneurs were thus largely involved in zero-sum activity.

60) Under Park, zero-sum transfers remain, but largely as add-ons to productive positive-sum ventures. In part this followed from elimination of some zero-sum opportunities (for example, the shift to non-discretionary allocation of foreign exchange). More important, it follows from insuring that bureaucratic discretion is exercised so that resources are allocated to reasonably productive users.

The result, however, has not been egalitarian:

61) Underpriced resources—notably credit—have nonetheless been channeled predominantly into the hands of a relatively small number of chaebŏl. This is not necessarily due to political favoritism but may simply reflect the fact that they have a proven track record that shows them to be capable of using the resources most efficiently.

This last point is certainly not gratuitous, probably not trivial, and deserves some elaboration. We begin with the proposition that all entrepreneurs are not created equal. In the mid-1960s, Pyŏng-ch'ŏl Yi oversaw the construction of a 300,000-MT fertilizer factory in 18 months; in the early 1970s, Chu-yŏng Chŏng built both a shipyard and two world class tankers in thirty months; during the 1970s, U-jung Kim has been discovering new export markets at a rate of increase of over 70 percent a year. What if these and other chaebŏl leaders had been denied credit on the grounds that it was time to give someone else a chance? How many Koreans could have done as well? What if the counterfactual set of allocations went to entrepreneurs who were merely good rather than great, and this meant longer project gestation periods, greater lags in identifying and exploiting foreign markets; lower cost efficiency, and so on? It does not require a very heroic set of assumptions about the magnitudes involved to demonstrate a significant negative effect on the growth rate. The point is simply that "X-efficiency," as well as allocative efficiency, must be considered in making allocation decisions. Economists devote much time to getting resources to the right *industry*, whereas getting them to the right *individual* may be far more important.

In any event, whatever the rationale for the government policies actually pursued, it is clear that

62) While there have been no serious government attempts to control the rate of chaebŏl asset *accumulation*, there have been two sets of major constraints on asset *utilization*. First, by the international standards of mixed economies, wealth has purchased a minimum of political influence. Second, there have been restraints on certain

forms of asset acquisition–most important, in the prohibition of bank ownership.

While the historical record thus shows implicit government support of largely unlimited chaebŏl accumulation:

63) In the mid-1970s, the government has shown increasing concern with the rate of chaebŏl expansion and has begun to take measures that might constrain their future growth. The seriousness of this effort remains to be seen.

DECISIONS AND GROWTH IN A "HARD" STATE

We have taken a somewhat unconventional view of the dynamics of development. Instead of focusing on factors of production and policies, we have emphasized the behavior of the individuals and structures that produce economic decisions: that is, on the economic system. This approach would find favor with the architects of Japan's Meiji reform who argued:

> If we assign weights to these three factors with respect to their effectiveness (in building Japanese industry), the spirit should be assigned five parts, laws and regulations four, and capital no more than one part.[1]

The major thing wrong with this statement is that it overemphasizes the role of capital. If one could somehow quantify "spirit" and "regulation" and use them together with capital as independent variables explaining growth, one might come out with the coefficients specified above. The results would, nonetheless, be erroneous and suffer from multicollinearity, since the equation is misspecified–the behavioral and structural variables lie deeper in the causal chain and themselves explain the level of capital accumulation.

"Spirit" presumably has something to do with the latent energy and ability of the population. Important as this is, it cannot have changed dramatically between the Rhee and Park periods. There was, however, a major change in the structure of the economic system, allowing the tapping of the potential. We characterize this change as the imposition of a hard growth-oriented state.

Consider the economic decision-making hierarchy running from the president through the bureaucracy, chaebŏl leaders, enterprise chief executives, and workers. In a hard state, decisions at one tier in the hierarchy result in a change in behavior at lower levels. In a soft state they do not. In moving from Rhee to Park, several major changes occurred in this structure. First, economic growth was given top emphasis. Second, that priority was effectively transmitted to the forefront of bureaucratic consciousness and made to strongly condition their decisions. Third, the crucial discontinuity in the hierarchy—between government and enterprise—was breached by a set of compliance mechanisms that selectively, but effectively, guided the behavior of entrepreneurs and managers. The modifier "selectively" is important, for we are in no sense describing a highly centralized command economy. Where the market yields reasonable prices, fine; where it does not, prices are manipulated, information provided, or commands imposed. Scarce decision-making talent is further conserved by concentrating on large-scale industry. Even there entrepreneurs are allowed substantial latitude within bounds set by the government, and subject to intervention at the government's discretion even within those bounds. Finally, decision-making talent has been further conserved within the private sector by providing a disproportionate share of resources to a limited number of chaebŏl leaders who have proven themselves able to stimulate their subordinates to use those resources efficiently.

CONCLUDING CAVEATS

To avoid misunderstanding, it is necessary to reiterate several caveats that should be borne in mind when interpreting our work. First, we have summarized our results in a series of propositions that should be taken as hypotheses that have survived a first cut rather than conclusions that have been proven. While some of the assertions are solidly based in empirical evidence (for example, those on the social background of entrepreneurs), most are open (and indeed designed to provoke) alternative interpretations and revision based on further research. We are acutely conscious that we have only scratched the surface of an underdeveloped area and have had to sacrifice depth of primary work to the breadth of an overall story of how economic decisions are made.

A second major concern is that our generally positive view of the economic role of the government of Park Chung Hee should not be extended beyond the limits intended. It should be obvious that approval of economic policies in no sense implies endorsement of developments on the political side. We believe this factoring is possible, since authoritarianism is neither necessary nor sufficient for hardness. Recall that hardness refers to a government's ability to translate decisions into action, and this ability may vary from decision to decision. A "hard-state" designation is thus the result of a subjective weighting of various functional areas. Idi Amin may be able to enforce any decision where he can mobilize sufficient troops, but in the absence of more subtle compliance mechanisms and a basically supportive population, the range of decisions that he can in fact implement is extremely limited. Iran (prior to the 1978 revolution) and Burma are but two conspicuous examples of states that are highly authoritarian but extemely "soft" when it comes to making a variety of decisions stick. In marked contrast, Norway and Sweden would seem to qualify as non-authoritarian states that are, nonetheless, "hard." Further, even if authoritarianism should be chosen as the means of initiating hardness in an LDC, there is no necessity that it take on its more brutal forms. For these reasons, we feel approval of the Park regime's economic policies can be divorced from its more controversial political actions.

Third, our stress on hardness and hierarchy is relative. Compared with the Rhee period and with most LDCs, the Park regime has been able to enforce its desires. This is not to say that the structure is monolithic, that pluralism is absent, or that there is no slack in the enforcement mechanisms.

Fourth, while the "hard" development model has served Korea well, it must be remembered that it is a risky strategy, potentially subject to great abuses. The fact that discretion and command *can* work—and *have* worked in Korea—is not to say that they necessarily *will* work elsewhere. We have stressed that the Confucian culture and the homogeneous population are particularly well suited to the discipline of the hard state. To imply that it would serve equally well in a consensus-oriented society such as Indonesia, or with a heterogeneous population such as India, would be unwarranted.

Fifth, our analysis of the factors behind Korean growth in no sense implies a universally applicable model of rapid development. It may be true that growth of capital stock is strictly necessary for substantial growth, but if we wish to go deeper and explain that growth in terms of institutions and decision processes, then there are no necessary conditions, only sufficient ones. South Korea has grown rapidly with an open market economy, but North Korea has (in some periods) not done badly with a closed command system. South Korea prospers with a single strong leader, while Hong Kong does well without. We submit that these, and other, counter-examples do not disprove our analysis of what drives the Korean economy. Rather, they suggest that there are alternative institutional paths to capital accumulation, and all that can be said is that some combinations work in certain historical contexts and others do not.

Finally, our emphasis on decision structure should not be taken as disparaging the importance of economic policies. While these policies have not been nearly as close to the laissez-faire model as sometimes supposed, they have obviously been instrumental; for example, one price which has been more or less "right" is that of foreign exchange, and this has been critical in subjecting entrepreneurs to the discipline of the international market place. Our point has simply been that it is far easier to find someone to *give* good advice than to find someone to *take* it. The surprising thing about Korea is not so much that particular policies have worked, but that they came to be adopted in the first place.

In sum, we have argued that, if we are seriously concerned with explaining economic results, we must ask inconvenient questions as to how and why decisions are made. For example, consider the economic outcome of growth. It can be explained at one of three levels. At the shallowest level, growth is a function of the expansion of the quantity and quality of factor inputs—notably capital. The second level involves the policies or strategies that lead to, say, capital accumulation. The third is the process whereby political entities make decisions that lead to the policies, and whereby productive entities respond to policies in a way that produces a particular level of accumulation and, for that level, a particular rate of growth. Thus, one might "explain" part of the difference between Korean and Indian growth rates in terms of differential investment (level one); this is further partly explained by interest rates and the interest elasticity of investment (level two). Growth is not really understood, however, until one moves to level three and asks why one country chooses an interest-rate policy that "works," and why, for a given rate, entrepreneurs in different countries produce markedly different effects on output. Level-three questions thus lie deeper in the causal chain. They are inherently more complex but concomitantly more fundamental in explaining economic outcomes. It is to such issues of political economy that this volume has been addressed.

Appendixes

Appendix A
Case Studies of Small and Medium Enterprises

by

Vincent S. R. Brandt

This chapter summarizes the results of a brief anthropological study of Korean entrepreneurship in small and medium industry that my wife and I carried out during the spring and summer of 1976. We conducted extended interviews with the presidents (and founders) of 11 firms and we collected whatever additional information we could from employees or knowledgeable outside observers about the experience, personality, and business performance of our principal informants.

With such a small number of firms, it was impossible, of course, to obtain a representative sample. Nine companies were chosen because we had personal ties with, or good introductions to, the owner, while in 2 cases we simply walked in cold off the street. Nevertheless, because our initial contacts were with people of extremely varied background and social status, there is a good spread in terms of these factors.

Six of the firms were small (20–50 employees), while the other 5 all had between 100 and 400 workers. The industries represented were: textiles (4), machinery (3), aluminum-foil products (1), deep-sea fishing (1), plastics (1), and buttons for export (1).

In addition, we talked at length, both informally and in more or less structured interviews, about entrepreneurship with 17 other Koreans, including some who started out with small firms but now run large companies, others who were bankers, corporation lawyers, and professors of business administration, and one man engaged in the speculative lending of risk capital to small but promising and innovative firms.

BRIQUETTE-MACHINE FACTORY

This company, located in the eastern suburbs of Seoul, manufactures two products: 1) a massive briquette-making machine, and 2) a device for increasing the efficiency of crude-oil burners. The plant with its equipment seemed impressive for only 25 workers. It was obviously much more capital intensive than any of the other establishments we looked at. Six briquette machines were in various stages of construction. We didn't see the place where the oil-burner attachment is made, but there were about 50 of them crated and stacked for shipment, with several destined for Southeast Asia.

The person we talked to, Mr. Cho, is a mechanical engineer and inventor. He developed a coal-crushing and briquette-making device in 1960 with 3 mechanics and a capital of 8,000,000 wŏn. He is more interested in his new inventions than in their production and sales and, once a workable and economically feasible invention has been patented, he turns the production over to someone else; he claimed that about 20 of his inventions are being produced in Korea at several other small factories, some of which he started himself. In this case, however, although he introduced another man to us as the company president, Mr. Cho was very much in charge; the titular president plays a definitely subordinate role—that of a hired manager. We weren't able to find out just what Mr. Cho's stake in the business is, though. In response to fairly persistent questioning, he said the company has assets of several billion wŏn, and ownership is shared. He also said the company would probably go public in the near future. He claimed that his briquette-making machines are far superior to others being manufactured in Korea but also more expensive. He also claimed that his crude oil-burner device greatly improves efficiency, and he predicted that export sales should increase rapidly, unless the idea is stolen or improved on by the Japanese, who might then export a better and cheaper model.

PERSONAL BACKGROUND

Mr. Cho's father, who lived in North Ch'ungch'ŏng province, had been a minor local official, a small landowner, a *yangban* (really *hyangban*), and a practitioner of Chinese medicine. His education was in the Chinese classics at a local *sŏdang* (a village school).

Mr. Cho, who is an eldest son with many brothers and sisters, has been interested since childhood in any new mechanical device, and he has always enjoyed tinkering with and repairing machinery. As a youth he dropped out of college in order to earn money and engage in more practical activities.

He described himself as having more vision and accomplishing things more quickly than others. After several years as managing director of a fuel and oil company, he decided in 1960 to go on his own as an inventor. In spite of his lack of formal education, he has been asked recently by Korea University to teach a course at its engineering college. He drove his own car, which was not at all new, however.[1]

Mr. Cho was only a private during the Korean War, because he did not have a college degree. A friend of mine, who was a lieutenant colonel and at that time Private Cho's superior officer, told me recently that Cho's energy and intelligence were quickly recognized, and he was soon performing staff jobs at battalion headquarters that were usually assigned to a captain or a major. His superiors were already predicting that he would be extremely successful after the war.

ENTREPRENEURSHIP

Mr. Cho asserted that all of the usual qualities that are cited as necessary for entrepreneurial success, such as the ability to utilize new technology, manage a firm effectively, supervise employees, sell at a profit by riding herd on costs through efficient accounting procedures, and so on, really amount to only about 60 percent of what is needed. He labeled this 60 percent, "intelligence and action," while the other 40 percent is "timing and luck." By timing he meant perception of an opportunity within the context of contemporary possibilities, both for production and sales.

Entrepreneurs and managers, he thinks, should have a vision of an improved society through technological achievement, and they have a responsibility to produce better quality products. He stressed the importance of free-market competition in promoting this process. On the one hand, he praised government initiative in providing capital, know-how, and export market information to help industry, while on the other he criticized the kind of favoritism that resulted in the enrichment of inefficient producers and other distortions. He indicated that government administration was becoming more efficient and more impartial, at least with regard to small industry, and that personal connections with government officials were now much less crucial than in the past.

Mr. Cho is a man of great energy and self-confidence. He likes to delegate anything routine to others in order to retain his independence and freedom to work on his own inventions. He doesn't speak much English, but he seemed to be thoroughly westernized in his outlook, both in terms of his own uncompromising individualism and in his evaluation of Korean industrial capacity. He said that the distaste of Koreans for hard, dirty, manual labor is a major problem, and that technicians with education and skills want to keep their hands clean. Uneducated laborers, although most of them have plenty of native intelligence, do not function well under contractual wage relationships; they do not recognize the priority of technological precision, efficiency, and merit promotions within a factory, expecting rather that seniority and connections are enough to entitle them to permanent employment at good wages.

Finally, Mr. Cho said that, although he does not consider himself primarily an entrepreneur, he has been involved in helping start and in nursing along several small companies, so he is something of a judge of entrepreneurship. He feels that, while a factory head must begin by presiding effectively over his employees in a traditional paternalistic way, he must gradually introduce rational scientific attitudes and operations into his organization in order to succeed competitively today. It is much better, he thinks, to have a small number of intelligent, rational, highly motivated employees than to hire a lot of cheap labor.

He was highly critical of what he called the temporary, emergency, guesswork approach to management decisions characteristic of much Korean medium and small industry. There is little long-range planning, and most important decisions are made on the basis of hunches in order to deal with short-term crises. Another problem is that all responsibility and decision-making power is usually concentrated in one man, who, as he gets older, is unlikely to maintain the necessary adaptability to new challenges and the flexibility to adopt needed innovations. In contrast to traditional practice, he said, leaders should train younger men, give them adequate material rewards, and then delegate authority.

In addition to careful, systematic planning, he advocates a highly structured organizational setup with extensive functional specificity. In spite of the Korean emphasis on hierarchy in personal relationships, he has found a great deal of sloppy informality in the way most small manufacturers operate; they try to get by on personal influence, connections, or through offering bribes, rather than by a determination to achieve planned objectives through systematic organization.

KNITTING FACTORY IN TAEGU

The present owner and president, Mr. Choi, started his knitting enterprise in 1966 with 4,000,000 wŏn of his own money. At first there was just one machine and 3 machine operators. He and his wife were the main skilled technicians, and he had 15 employees all together. In 5 years he had 170 workers; today there are 300. It is still a small, family-style operation, however, with everyone crammed together in old buildings and a minimum of office space for administration. In producing knitted clothing, his factory performs three operations: 1) spinning yarn; 2) knitting material; 3) designing, cutting, and making clothes. Mr. Choi said that, while the first two operations are fairly routine, his particular talent and the reason for his rapid, independent success in his flair for design and color. In Taegu we heard from other sources as well that Mr. Choi not only has a good personal sense of design, but he keeps close track of fashion trends in Japan and the United States. He seems to know what consumers want and to have a good sense of timing in introducing new styles. Everything he makes is bought up quickly, he said, and there is never any trouble with large unsold stocks. In his reception room (which is a kind of anteroom to the factory with all sorts of people passing through) there is this framed motto:

1) Let's make the utmost effort to produce high quality products.
2) Let's make new products that the consumer wants, and that fit the time.
3) Let's work with trustworthiness for our common bright future.

Mr. Choi touched on, or rather emphasized at some length and with evident sincerity, all three of these points in talking to us. He said that, unlike many other textile plants, he is more concerned with establishing his new company's reputation for trustworthiness and quality products than he is with making large profits. He claimed to be scrupulous about maintaining quality and meeting contract deadlines. He said he wants to become really big, and it is just a question of time, because his reputation in the field is already so high.

PERSONAL BACKGROUND

Mr. Choi had a difficult childhood. His father, having graduated from "middle" (now high) school, was under the Japanese a relatively well-educated farmer in a village near Taegu. Mr. Choi's mother was Christian, and as a small boy he attended Sunday School. His father got into financial trouble before the Liberation and became further impoverished in the post-Liberation period. He died during the Korean War, having sold all his land to pay off debts and feed his family. Mr. Choi spent several years of his childhood peddling things on the streets of Taegu and as a result was obliged to miss several months of elementary school each year. When he applied for the entrance exam to middle school, the teacher refused to accept his application, saying that, because of his prolonged absences, he would never be able to pass. The boy went to his principal and obtained permission to take the examination. Then he studied at home night and day for one month, sleeping only three or four hours a night. According to the exam results, his work was equivalent to that of a third-year middle school student. Mr. Choi told this story, not only to illustrate his determination and ability, but also to show how strong his reaction was when he felt he had been unfairly treated or slighted. This early feat gave him great self-confidence, so he feels he can do anything if he wants it badly enough.

His mother was constantly supportive, urging him to get as good an education as possible and trying to make it possible for him to do so. He feels, however, that his dominant motivation during his school years was to achieve business success and escape poverty rather than to distinguish himself academically. Formal education has had little to do with his own success, he said. Rather it is due to the experience of petty commerce and industry he acquired as a boy and later on as a small factory manager, combined with great determination and diligence.

During the period 1958–61, he was a *Katusa* (a Korean enlisted soldier assigned to an American unit). He worked in a personnel office for 16 months, learned a fair amount of English, and was fascinated by what was to him a completely novel way of thinking. It was clear that, although he admired the American way of doing things and tried to imitate it, he resented the patronizing way in which the U.S. military treated Koreans. He often wanted to show the Americans that he was as intelligent and civilized as they and should not be treated as a simple barbarian.

After finishing his military service, Mr. Choi got a job in a small knitting factory through a friend's introduction. The method of manufacture was backward and inefficient, "since no one connected with it had any education." (He explained the apparent contradiction with his previous remark about education by saying that constant inquiry and self education are necessary for success in business.) He did his best to improve the system and in a few months became manager of the factory because of his hard work and good ideas. But although profits increased, his salary remained low. The owners thought the business success was due mainly to their own good luck and failed to give Mr. Choi credit.

In 1966 he started on his own with money saved during the previous three years. The contacts he had made and the reputation he had established for himself during the previous years in the knitting industry were very helpful, particularly in arranging for the distribution of the products of his new factory. He pointed out, however, that, while such connections are important in getting started, they are only useful the first time around. After that it depends on the quality and price of the product. Further, he said, knowing useful people is far more crucial to the very small businessman. As the volume of business gets larger, such ties, while still of some help in facilitating transactions, are much less important.

Mr. Choi described himself as the careful systematic type who plans ahead, trying to foresee every possibility. He admitted that the bold investor who takes big risks sometimes makes a killing but added that when he (Mr. Choi) makes a mistake, it is usually a minor one and doesn't cost him his business as happens so frequently with others. During the late 1950s and early 1960s the bold-gambler approach was often suitable, he thought, but now there is more stability and keener competition, so that knowledge, experience, and rational calculation are necessary.

He has completed two five-year development plans for his company, and so far things have gone pretty much as expected, although the pace of expansion has been a little faster than originally anticipated. Now that he has established his firm's reputation for trustworthiness and high quality, he believes he can attract capital and expand still more rapidly.

He said that he knows as much about the technical side of the business as anyone in Korea. He knows just how much each machine is capable of producing according to international standards, and he makes sure his supervisors and workers know this too. They then feel a strong personal obligation to do as well as workers in other countries. Mr. Choi said he pays his 15 supervisors well (as much as they would get in the big textile mills) and keeps in close and constant touch with them.

With regard to accounting, he admitted that the way he does it is pretty simple and sloppy—more like a family system than a business firm. Whatever income there is goes into one account; then he pays his employees, his material costs, and his own expenses from that. In the past, somewhat more elaborate books were kept, but they were phony and used only to dodge taxes. Now, with the recent crackdown by tax officials, this kind of evasion is impossible, he said. In the near future he expects to incorporate his business and sell shares to the public. Then he will have to hire a professional accountant, which he thinks would, in spite of the additional cost and nuisance, help him keep better track of his expanding business.

With regard to motivation, Mr. Choi stressed that, because of his deprived life as a child, his goal was to attain financial security and live in luxury. He wondered if his children (who are now small) would share his attitude towards conscientious hard work. Most young people, he said, are more interested in having a good time now than in preparing for the future. They are suspicious of the advice of all those over forty who "have never learned how to enjoy life." Choi's last point was that the girls who work in the factory today are more independent and less docile than they were ten years ago. The company can no longer take the same kind of paternalistic attitude—scolding and exhorting employees—as in the past. Instead it is less troublesome and more profitable to keep them contented by making sure conditions and wages are adequate.

ALUMINUM-FOIL PLANT IN PUSAN

The company is a medium-sized manufacturer of aluminum foil for cigarette and chewing-gum wrappers, for other industrial uses, and for the home. The owner and president, Mr. Kim, aged 50, started the company in 1960 with 12 employees and an ICA loan of $60,000. Now he has 304 employees. His products were all new in Korea when he started making them, although other competitors have now entered the field. The technology—both know-how and machinery—was all imported. He received the original ICA loan because of the policy of fostering import-substitution industries.

The idea originally came to him when, while working for a paper company in the 1950s, he found out how much the government tobacco monopoly was spending to import the inner foil wrapping for cigarettes. Also his company sent him to Germany in the late 1950s to study technology connected with other aspects of paper making, but while there he was able to learn a good deal about making aluminum foil for packaging. On returning to Korea, he spent several months carrying out his own informal but, nevertheless, thorough study of production costs and potential markets before launching his firm.

His most serious problem has been acquiring enough capital for expansion and technological improvements but, since his company went public three years ago, the supply of capital has been adequate. There have been no major problems with regard to personnel supervision or accounting, and he said he has no trouble finding intelligent, hard-working technicians to maintain and repair the machinery. Technology is not a problem, since he himself has a thorough knowledge of the technical aspects of the business.

Mr. Kim claimed that he is in close communication not only with his supervisors but with other employees as well. There is a constant exchange of ideas that plays an important part in major decision-making.

PERSONAL BACKGROUND

Mr. Kim's father was a small businessman from South Ch'ungch'ŏng province, who moved to Seoul as a young man. He had a classical education in the local rural *sŏdang*. The family was never well off ("lower-middle" income), but they managed to send their son to the best schools—Kyŏnggi High School and Seoul National University. Mr. Kim called himself an atheist and his father a Buddhist (Confucian would be more appropriate from a social science perspective).

Mr. Kim graduated from Seoul National University in 1950 just before the Korean War and then went to Pusan as a refugee. If there had been no war, he thinks that he probably would have gone on to graduate school and become a college professor. He worked in Pusan for a newspaper for 6 months, then an import-export firm for 6 months, another import-export firm for 3 years, and finally for a paper company for 5 years before starting on his own.

ENTREPRENEURSHIP

Mr. Kim said he prefers the careful systematic approach to business leadership. Although he carries out Confucian rituals at home, he does not think traditional values and ways of thinking are of any use in industry and commerce. He insisted that Western techniques and ideology based on scientific rationality and impersonal contractual relations must replace old-fashioned Korean ideas. On the other hand, when Mr. Kim talked about his style of leadership, it all sounded very much like the typical paternalistic form of industrial organization.

Mr. Kim gives an impression of quiet scholarly dignity—of being an intellectual entrepreneur. Also, he talked as though diligence, competence, and technical know-how are the only qualities needed for success. Nevertheless, he received his early training and experience in the "export"-import field (there were no exports) in Pusan during the Korean War period, so that he is thoroughly familiar with the seamy side of doing business in Korea. In the 1950s and early 1960s, he said, it was relatively easy to get started, provided one had access to some capital and was willing to study and work hard. Today it is much tougher. All the easy niches have been filled, and the technology of most new industries is much more complex and expensive. Also, it may take several years for a new product to gain widespread market acceptance, so that, unless there is some sort of guaranteed (by the government) profit, which is extremely rare in small and medium industry, the risks are high. He pointed out that, in fact, the number of business turnovers and bankruptcies is large.

Mr. Kim said there have been no official pressures on his company or troublesome outside interference of any kind. Because the government is interested in promoting exports, he has received some encouragement to expand his facilities with the objective of promoting sales overseas, but there has been very little offered so far in the way of concrete incentives. With regard to domestic operations, Mr. Kim believed he had exerted influence on the government rather than the other way around. Because of his independent thinking, he sometimes differs sharply with the opinions of officials of the Ministry of Commerce and Industry, and, in some cases, he has been able to use his official connections to persuade the bureaucracy to change its regulations and outlook, not just for his own company's benefit, but for the good of the industry as a whole.

Mr. Kim thinks many Koreans are motivated to work hard by their experience of deprivation and hardship; as a result they try to make the most of any available opportunity. There is also a strong and persistent desire to catch up with the Japanese and show them what Koreans can do.

My assessment of Mr. Kim was that, although he appears to be gentle, unassuming, and have a quiet manner, he is actually extremely tough and knowledgeable. We attended a meeting of several company presidents who have an informal coffee break together each morning and, although Mr. Kim made less noise than the others, he commanded evident respect among his peers.[2] Whatever his actual performance may have been in terms of bold decision-making, Mr. Kim's style was the antithesis of the heroic, risk-taking, intuitive genius.

AUTOMOBILE REPAIR SHOPS IN INCH'ŎN AND SEOUL

Mr. Lee, who is only 29 and a country boy from a small, isolated farming-fishing village of South Ch'ungch'ŏng province, started with nothing and now owns 3 car repair shops in the Seoul-Inch'ŏn area.[3] One of these has a small machine shop attached for manufacturing hard-to-get parts. All together he employs 32 people.[4]

The first repair shop was acquired in 1973 in partnership with 2 other young men, one of whom is now in jail; the other has returned to his native village. The partner who is in jail obtained his capital by dealing in TV and Hi-Fi sets, typewriters, and other valuables stolen from private homes. The other partner, who is from the same village as Mr. Lee, has returned to farming. He had previously made a good deal of money as a lucky and capable fishing-boat captain out of Inch'ŏn.

Although Mr. Lee's capital was mainly derived from real-estate speculation in the suburbs of Inch'ŏn, his original stake had come from the profits made by stealing auto parts when he first came to Seoul as a migrant and worked in a repair shop.

The two other shops were acquired by Mr. Lee alone, using his profits from a variety of sources, including the first shop (which now also sells gas), further real estate deals, investments in sleazy Inch'ŏn restaurants and bars, and a taxi venture. Mr. Lee estimated his current income from his various investments at a little more than 600,000 wŏn per month ($1,300).

He is living very inconspicuously in Inch'ŏn in a small room with the woman who runs one of his sailors' bars, but he is starting to invest money in rice land near his native village.

PERSONAL BACKGROUND

Mr. Lee's parents were farmers from North Korea. During the war his father died as a refugee when Mr. Lee was four years old. His mother, as a not-too-young widow with two small children, was lucky to obtain an arranged marriage with a poor, widower fisherman in South Ch'ungch'ŏng province. The fisherman, a jovial, hard-drinking, second son with no schooling, maintained his family at the subsistence level through working on other people's boats and with the grudging assistance of his more prosperous relatives.

When the boy was 19, he left the village for Inch'ŏn where, after a year or so working on the fishing boats, he joined a gang of youths engaged in petty thievery, street peddling, pimping, and any other available "hustling" activities. His mother visited him in Inch'ŏn and was so horrified by his lifestyle and associates that she found (through North Korean connections) an apprentice job for him at an automobile-repair shop and made him promise to go to work. As a devoted son he did as she asked him, but within six months he was using his job as a base for illegal earnings. The transactions in auto parts were complex. On the one hand, he connived with his boss to replace good-quality parts on late-model cars with old but still serviceable parts, then the parts acquired in this manner were sold as new to other customers. In addition, he stole parts both from the shop and from customers on his own, using his underworld contacts in order to dispose of them.[5]

He left his job just in time to avoid the inevitable investigation and hid out in the Inch'ŏn slums for six months. During this period he lent out some of his money at high interest rates and bought some cheap suburban lots. Many migrants from his village were working on Inch'ŏn-based fishing boats; he was able to utilize their contacts in order to learn a good deal about the waterfront entertainment industry. When apartment buildings were built in 1972 on the area where he had bought land, he made large windfall profits, and decided to invest in a repair shop.

ENTREPRENEURSHIP

Mr. Lee's experiences are similar to those of a great many other petty capitalists who are constantly involved in a variety of investments, many of which are illegal or on the fringes of normal legitimate commercial or industrial activity. The ups and downs of such people are usually meteoric, and Mr. Lee is unusual in that he has pyramided a series of successes into a fairly substantial financial position.

Although he has only a primary-school education, his earnest, convincing manner, and a fast flow of glib conversation give him the qualifications of a first-rate con man. He told me that the secret of success is gauging people. He knows how to inspire confidence in others, and he can usually predict how reliable his "associates" will be in any given situation. The other essential, he said, was to know a business really thoroughly through personal participation before risking one's own money.

There is no shortage of skilled mechanics, according to Mr. Lee, and his main problem in the repair business is obtaining parts and supervising his employees. There is a rapid turnover of personnel in the business, and he must guard against the likelihood that his employees and the chauffeurs of private cars or taxis will get together in order to defraud him as well as the owners of the cars. He added that his experience in the business helped him devise effective measures of control.

Mr. Lee seemed to be still hiding out from official scrutiny, using two front men to handle most of his business and bureaucratic contacts. Nevertheless, he was also concerned about establishing a respectable public position. The purchases of rice land would give him a more solid rural base, he thought, and periodic attendance at night school would eventually provide a high school diploma.[6] In the future he expected to buy more land on the outskirts of Seoul for speculation, but he was undecided about expanding his automobile repair business. "I have as much money as I need now," he said, "and it's a dirty business."

He attributed much of his skill at judging others' characters and motives to his mother's intelligent advice. They had been low-status outsiders in the village, and he had always dreamed of succeeding in the city, so he could return home as someone important.

HANDWOVEN-SILK FACTORY

Mr. Ham, aged 44, is founder and president of a company manufacturing high quality, handmade silk, mostly for export. He started in 1959 with a small amount of capital (he declined to say how much), some of which came from his former employers, the USAID Mission in Korea (then called Office of the Economic Coordinator, OEC). The remainder was obtained from his family. In the beginning there were only 4 looms and 15 employees. He himself knew nothing about the textile business, but he had read about Thompson's success with Thai silk in *Life* magazine. Also, his office at the USAID Mission had recently sponsored a craft center at which foreign designers were paid by the U.S. government to come to Korea and advise craftsmen on how to improve their products for sale in the international market. He had heard from them that good opportunities existed, if really attractive hand-woven silk could be produced in Korea.

Mr. Ham was able to recruit a few old, professional silk-weavers in order to get started. But since they had not worked for many years and had never used wide looms, there was a difficult breaking-in period, during which quality was irregular. Also, the old weavers had trouble maintaining high export standards, because a considerable number of imperfections in the cloth had always been tolerated in the past; they saw no need to be so precise. Eventually he replaced them all with younger men trained on the job. The other major technical problem at the start was getting the dyes right, both in terms of shade of color and fastness. They experimented and eventually obtained good results through trial and error.

Another problem was getting hold of silk yarn at reasonable prices. One large Korean filature dominated the business and, because of close connections with the Korean government, it was able to export all its production to Japan (a high-cost producer of silk) at prices above those in the world market. Mr. Ham, who had to compete with low-cost silk producers in the American market, needed cheap yarn but was at the mercy of his monopolistic supplier. As a result, the company was struggling in the early 1960s trying to find buyers for its silk, and it was only bailed out when the Far East Post Exchange system of the U.S. Army started selling their silk. The result was an almost unlimited market, and by 1970 Mr. Ham was operating 40 looms, still on a craft basis.

In 1971 his company merged with another silk-weaving firm that had been started and supported lavishly by a foreign investor. Mr. Ham said that under his general direction the operations of the combined firm were rationalized, so that it was possible to reduce the number of workers while increasing production. As a result of firing nearly half the work force, however, there were serious troubles with the local (enterprise) labor union. These were dealt with in a somewhat high-handed manner. Through persuasion, threats, and other incentives, the plant manager was able to obtain a vote from a majority of the remaining workers in the firm dissolving the union on the grounds that it was causing needless trouble and wasting their dues. Later he rehired some of the leading troublemakers, and gave them responsible, well-paid positions. Morale is now high, Mr. Ham said, and his plant has a reputation for having the best labor-management relations in the region.

We heard other accounts of the merger and subsequent labor troubles that contrasted somewhat with this story, particularly with regard to the amount of credit due Mr. Ham for resolving the firm's problems. But these comments came from informants connected with the other company. In any case, the combined firm is thriving today.

PERSONAL BACKGROUND

Mr. Ham's father, the second son of a fairly well-to-do farmer (not *yangban*), was from North Korea and was educated both at a *sŏdang* and at a Japanese middle school He was determined and ambitious, and at the age of 20 he left home, obtaining a job in the far north as an apprentice in a Japanese-owned sawmill. After several years, he was able to start a prosperous business making railroad ties with the patronage and help of his former Japanese employer. Subsequently he moved to Ch'unch'ŏn (Kangwŏn province) and set up a good sized sawmill.

Although he had thrived in the colonial period in close association with the Japanese, Ham's father was unable to function in the conditions of chaotic instability that followed Liberation. He was taken in again and again by sharp operators, each time bewailing the loss of the atmosphere of mutual trust and honesty that had prevailed under Japanese rule.

Mr. Ham was in high school when the Korean War broke out and escaped to Taegu just ahead of the North Korean troops. Eventually he went to officers candidate school, ending up as an interpreter with the U.S. 2nd Division in combat. After the retreat from North Korea in the winter of 1950, he spent three years at Fort Benning, Georgia. After getting out of the army, he worked for OEC (USAID) in Seoul until starting his own business.

ENTREPRENEURSHIP

I heard Mr. Ham referred to twice as "the reluctant entrepreneur," once by a Korean businessman who had invested money in his firm and once by a foreigner in the import-export business. He was criticized for his extreme conservatism and caution in financial matters and for his unwillingness to expand his firm and adopt mass-production methods. The importer said he had been willing to guarantee overseas markets and financing on favorable terms, but Mr. Ham was reluctant to borrow the substantial amounts necessary for expansion, and he was extremely jealous of any hint of control or interference by outsiders in his firm.

The Korean critic pointed out that, in the 1960s, Mr. Ham had run into a lot of trouble through delegating authority within his company to a couple of dishonest relatives. These in turn had hired their own cronies, and the company had been on the verge of bankruptcy in spite of steadily expanding sales. He added that the 1971 merger had finally enabled Mr. Ham to get rid of nearly all his administrative personnel and build up a much more efficient organization.

The following comments by Mr. Ham regarding the management of his firm are revealing in the context of this background information. He contrasted the situation in a well-run factory under strong leadership such as his own with that of many Korean companies where the directors or managers are in a weak position, because they have made bad mistakes or engaged in illegal activities. Others on the office staff find out about such weaknesses, and the vulnerable executive is obliged to keep them happy for his own survival. It may be necessary for him to grant unwarranted promotions, hire relatives, or increase salaries. He, in turn, is then involved in covering up their failures and incompetence so that a kind of reciprocal intrigue of conspiracy is established among the top employees, whereby they protect each other, while placing increased pressure on workers to make up for their own errors and extravagance. An inevitable result is greater hostility and a sharper separation of interests between workers and management.

Mr. Ham feels strongly that, with the exception of two key men, his office staff is more expendable than the workers, and he occasionally tells them so. He attributes much of his success in dealing with employees to his production manager, a Mr. Kim, who, although a former military officer and strict disciplinarian, is greatly respected by the workers. Mr. Ham said it was necessary that he show a constant interest in the welfare of the workers but retain a certain social distance. When he goes to the factory or participates in company recreation and ceremonies, however, he rides the same bus, wears the same kind of clothes, and eats the same food. He thus tries to give the impression of sharing a common existence as well as participating in a common enterprise. Nevertheless, various kinds of protocol, including respectful forms of speech and behavior, are always observed and reinforce his status.

AWNING FACTORY IN KUNSAN AND TEXTILE PLANTS IN PUSAN

An awning factory, that was formerly Japanese, was acquired in 1950 by Mr. Pyun (now aged 65). He invested his own money in this and some small factories in the Pusan area that manufacture *kimonos* and towels for the Japanese market. With these textile plants, he was able to take advantage of an extensive network of personal relations and resume the export business engaged in by his father and older brothers during the colonial period.

Mr. Pyun said the awning factory with 50 employees is reasonably efficient and profitable, but there seems to be little prospect of further expansion. Therefore he has delegated much of the responsibility for running it to trusted local personnel, and concentrates most of his efforts on the companies producing cheap textiles for export to Japan. In addition to modern weaving plants in the city, he has organized a cottage industry, employing small groups of farm wives in a number of nearby rural areas. The total assets for all of Mr. Pyun's companies are substantial, but no single plant is very large.

PERSONAL BACKGROUND

Mr. Pyun comes from a wealthy, landowning, *yangban* family based originally in Pusan. His father was one of the relatively few Koreans to establish a successful industrial firm on his own under Japanese rule. Although the family business was entirely dependent on the Japanese market, and extensive collaboration with the colonial regime was necessary, the atmosphere within the family group was strongly nationalistic.

Mr. Pyun was involved twice in anti-Japanese agitation as a student, spending 40 days in jail. On the other hand, he received a thorough Japanese education, eventually studying economics at two universities in Japan. On his return to Korea, he entered the intensely bureaucratic atmosphere of Japanese colonial banking, where he worked until Liberation. His indoctrination at home as a child had been one of strict traditional Confucian ethics and, despite his anti-Japanese bias in political terms, this native Confucianism seems to have been strongly reinforced by Japanese puritanism.

At one point in his youth he was determined to be a "man of culture and the arts" but, after trying to paint for a year, he realized that his talent was mediocre.

After the Korean Liberation in 1945, he became an economics professor at Pusan University. Then, during the Korean War he worked at a large machinery factory in Inch'ŏn, while continuing to draw his salary at the University in Pusan. At the same time he was investing extensively in local industry. By 1953 he was devoting himself full time to managing his companies.

ENTREPRENEURSHIP

Mr. Pyun believes that Korea's recent history, while tragic, has taught valuable lessons. During the Japanese period, Koreans were indoctrinated with the ideals of loyalty, faithfulness, and hard work. The Korean War showed them the evils of communism. Now, he said, under the orderly stable leadership of Park Chung Hee, native Korean ability at last has the opportunity to flourish. But, according to Mr. Pyun, Koreans have one critical flaw which is their desire for immediate wealth with its temptations to corrupt unethical business behavior. Mr. Pyun's recipe for correcting the evil seems to be strong paternalistic political leadership and the reinvigoration of the traditional family system. He said that Koreans do not perform well if there is too much individualism and lack of discipline.

The exceptional ability of Koreans lies in their intelligence, imagination, and capacity for hard work. But they do not have the innate conscientiousness and loyalty of the Japanese. Therefore effective strong leadership by the government, in industry, and in the family is crucial. There is no shortage of skills and competence either among workers or managers. The problem is to get everyone working together and maintain morale over a period of many years.

Entrepreneurial success, according to Mr. Pyun, does not require a special or rare talent. Anyone can do the job provided he has honesty, faithfulness, and sufficient determination. He pointed to himself as an example—a plain college teacher who was running several companies profitably (the fact that Mr. Pyun grew up in an industrial family, studied economics in Japan, and had many years experience in banking and company management was glossed over at this point). He did say, however, that theoretical learning at school is of little use to the businessman, who needs practical experience.

Mr. Pyun pointed out that, while political connections can be useful, politicians and officials in Korea eventually always lose their power; and those who are too closely associated with them are usually dragged down too.

PLASTIC-CONTAINER FACTORY

Mr. Shin, aged 49, is the founder and president of a small company located on the outskirts of Seoul that makes plastic medicine and cosmetic containers. He started in 1965 with 250,000 wŏn, 7 workers and 2 simple machines. Each machine required 3 men to operate it. Now he employs 25 workers, and he has installed 10 more or less automatic machines during the past 6 years. With only one worker per machine, productivity is, of course, much higher than before, but because of the cost of the machines, he has a heavy debt burden. Mr. Shin said the industry is very competitive, and he would not have been able to survive without modernizing his system of production. The new machinery was purchased with loans from the Small and Medium Industry Bank, The Tong Hwa Pharmaceutical Co. (his principal customer), and from relatives. He believes his business is in good shape at present, but he pointed out that, since the marketing of his product depends largely on his own personal connections with the buyers, there is a good deal of uncertainty concerning future prospects.

With regard to technological innovation, Mr. Shin said that fairly frequent seminars are held by the Korea Institute of Science and Technology (KIST) or by the Korean Plastics Industry Association, at which there is an opportunity to learn about new products and processes. But in any case the demand for current production seems to be increasing, so there is no immediate pressure for technological change.

Two men from the original company group are still working for Mr. Shin. They are his key assistants, and he shares profits with them on an almost equal basis, he said. One of these men takes care of the installation, maintenance, and repair of the machinery; the other provides detailed day-to-day supervision of the employees and product quality.

Mr. Shin thinks sometimes of enlarging and further modernizing his plant, but he is also a little reluctant, because there are advantages to a small operation. In particular, he emphasized the importance of maintaining a family atmosphere among the workers. He pointed out that, because of this, his workers are conscientious and obedient, often putting in longer hours than their pay really warrants. He is also reluctant to share ownership with outsiders, feeling that, because of his lack of higher education and his South Chŏlla province origins, his position might be undermined.

PERSONAL BACKGROUND

Mr. Shin's father was a small shopkeeper in Kwangju (South Chŏlla province) who had attended only primary school. As a child Mr. Shin remembers that they were not as poor as most other Koreans, and there was always plenty to eat. He attended a primary school for Japanese colonial children, and he still has bitter memories of their discrimination. Also, he admired and envied the more luxurious lifestyle of his classmates. At the time of Liberation in 1945, Mr. Shin had just graduated from a vocational middle school, an education that he regarded as superior to contemporary high-school instruction. Training under the Japanese was extremely thorough, providing both practical knowledge and skills and a disciplined moral indoctrination that produced respectable, hard-working people. Mr. Shin thought that if the colonial regime had not pushed emperor worship and Japanese superiority so hard, it would have been able to win over the respect, and even the loyalty, of a great many Koreans. As it was, Koreans hated the Japanese, even while becoming half Japanese themselves.

After 1945 Mr. Shin worked at home for a while and then got a job with a glass-bottle maker nearby. During the Korean War he was a noncommissioned officer and was wounded twice. In 1956 after his father's death he sold the shop and land in Kwangju and invested all his money in a bottle-making plant. But lack of good connections with Rhee's Liberal

Party's local hierarchy and a crooked partner resulted in failure and impoverishment. His family moved to Seoul, where for a while his earnings as a laborer and those of a sister in a "service" job (presumably a bar, nightclub, or restaurant) were all that kept them going. Mr. Shin's mother and his other relatives often reproached him for not having continued the family store in Kwangju. Previously his parents had urged him to invest his money at home, and there had been considerable conflict as a result of his determination to go off on his own. After his failure, it had been painful for him to have to listen to their reproaches. Mr. Shin was vehement in describing how difficult it had been to resist family pressures. But he insisted that a man must do as he feels right. In his case, he didn't like the merchant's role and wanted to produce something, rather than just trade on other people's work and money. He thinks that most Koreans follow the safest and easiest course to ensure their own economic security, and that only those who have the courage to take risks and defy the opinions of others can succeed in business.

Under the Chang Myon regime (1960–1961), he was hired as a clerk by an import-export firm engaged in trading with Japan. Although such jobs were scarce then, he was hired because of his superior skills in doing arithmetic calculations in Japanese. The firm prospered during the few months before the Military Revolution, and Mr. Shin made so much money, mostly through "side deals" that he was able to carry out on his own, using company channels. The trading firm was eliminated and the owners arrested for profiteering following the coup, but Mr. Shin was not important enough for official notice. Subsequently he got a job in the sales department of a pharmaceutical company, where he was able to learn a lot about the business as well as to establish the personal ties that have been essential for the development of his own business. He joked that, if he had stayed with the company, which was now much larger, he would probably be a director and have a luxurious office and a big black car. During this period (1961–1965), he had lent out his money on the informal curb market at very high interest rates, and by 1965 he had enough capital accumulated to start his own business. At present, Mr. Shin said, he lives reasonably well, but he is not yet able to afford a car and driver.

Confucian rituals were always regularly carried out in his family, and he continues the practice today. Mr. Shin gives an impression of toughness and strong will without much social grace. His remarks were blunt and stated aggressively, as if he had something of a grudge against a hostile world. One of his managers, with whom we talked separately, said that he was fair but very demanding.

ENTREPRENEURSHIP

Mr. Shin derided the idea that special talent or brilliance had anything to do with his accomplishment in starting his own business. He pointed around to the drab dirty office and to the tiny factory, asking rhetorically if such a result after a lifetime of hard work indicated genius.

Instead he stressed the importance of faithfulness, diligence, and stubborn determination. One must not pamper the employees, he said, but one must show kind heartedness, respect for their feelings, and occasional generosity. Then the right kind of person will respond with hard, devoted work; the others can leave. He added that a company as small as his could not give a substantial bonus—just a little extra at New Year's. Thus, the key factors, he feels, in managing the firm are maintaining close ties with his customers and recruiting good (docile, hardworking) personnel.

There are no serious problems in the areas of technology, quality control, or financial management, according to Mr. Shin. Supervision of the product is very strict, both within the factory and by outside inspectors. Mr. Shin emphasized the need for a company president to be on his guard in order to avoid being cheated. He feels fortunate having two absolutely trustworthy assistants who, so far, have been able to get rid of any other employees whose behavior was at all questionable. In general he thinks it is better to deal with big companies, both in obtaining raw materials and in marketing his products, because their business ethics are somewhat better.

Mr. Shin said that representatives of official agencies have usually been helpful, although he does not deal with them often, and he credited the government with a positive, supporting role towards business. Tax officials are increasingly nosy and insistent, and he has had to make some changes in his bookkeeping methods in order to satisfy them. More effective and impartial tax collection would be helpful in the long run to his company, he thinks, because his competitors are evading their taxes much more than he is.

DEEP-SEA FISHING

Mr. Moon, who is now 50, started his fishing business in 1970 with a loan of $150,000 from a Japanese trading company. He also received various kinds of assistance from one of his wife's close relatives who was a high-ranking Korean government official. During the first year of operation (1970) with just one boat, he landed fish with a value of $350,000. In addition to the 30-man crew, there were 4 office workers. By 1975 he had 9 boats that caught fish worth $2,500,000. His office staff has grown to 9. Because of the decreasing numbers of tuna due to over-fishing, he does not expect his business to grow in the future, and there is some concern that the fish catch may decline. He estimated his firm's current assets at 15 billion wŏn ($30,000,000). Mr. Moon lives very well. He has a late-model car with a radio telephone; he belongs to the most prestigious clubs and frequents the most expensive places of entertainment in Seoul.

PERSONAL BACKGROUND

Mr. Moon comes from a devout Presbyterian family who lived in North Korea. His father graduated from middle school under the Japanese and was an elder of the church. Mr. Moon was still a high school student just after the Liberation when he left Communist North Korea and fled south. He worked for the Customs Bureau from 1948, when South Korea was still under the U.S. Military Government until the outbreak of the Korean War in 1950. As a refugee, he was seized by the Korean military police, drafted into the army and participated in the invasion of North Korea with American troops. At the time of the retreat in the winter of 1950, he was evacuated to Japan with the help of a friendly American officer who got him a job in Tokyo as a civilian employee of the U.S. Forces. Mr. Moon also attended college for two years in Japan during this period, but he became impatient and dropped out, never obtaining a degree. Next he worked for a Korean firm engaged in engineering construction and foreign trade during the period 1953–1963. He eventually became a branch manager, learning all aspects of the business.

In 1963 he formed a construction business of his own with an American partner. They contracted with the U.S. Army to build barracks and bachelor officers' quarters in Japan, sub-contracting the actual construction to several smaller firms. The business was profitable, and he learned a great deal about construction materials, machinery, and purchasing procedures. This business was dissolved abruptly in 1967, when the American partner was jailed for large-scale black market dollar transactions.

With the help of his well-placed Korean relative, Mr. Moon next got a job in Japan with the Korea Shipping Corporation as a consultant. He utilized this position to learn about the shipping industry and to develop close personal ties with many Japanese businessmen. One of these was the vice president of Mitsui Bussan Kabushiki Kaisha. In 1969 this friend became Mitsui's president, and Mr. Moon, now assured of financial support from Mitsui and convinced that the time was right for a deep-sea fishing venture, started his own company.

Mr. Moon is tall, handsome, articulate, and extremely likeable. He has a flair for personal relationships, constantly creating a mood of confidence, expansiveness, and excitement.

ENTREPRENEURSHIP

Mr. Moon represents a sophisticated variant of the flamboyant gambler-speculator type that has sometimes been regarded as the characteristic Korean businessman. His explanation of the entrepreneurial personality was straightforward.

> Most men have the personality of a clerk, and they will remain clerks all their lives, no matter how much brains or ability they have. The entrepreneur, on the other hand, must have bold ideas and the daring to back them up with action. The game with all its picayune, boring details isn't worthy playing unless it's for big stakes. There are thousands of good opportunities available in the world, but they have to be seized and exploited. The more different ventures a man tries, the greater will be his experience, skill, and chance of success. But because luck too is important, he must be willing to keep on trying even though he fails.
>
> Establishing and running a business should not be a matter of agonizingly slow, careful decisions. It is necessary to be able to act forcefully and confidently on the basis of a quick assessment of the situation. Too much caution can never meet the challenges of a rapidly changing economic and political situation.
>
> If a serious mistake has been made, one must have the resilience to shrug it off and bounce back. There is always a way out of every difficulty, even if it involves humiliating dependence on others or temporary poverty. Everyone should expect to go through bad times in his life as well as good.

Mr. Moon's business activities fit in with these opinions rather well. He is constantly traveling in order to settle crew problems in the Caribbean, to negotiate fishing rights in Saudi Arabia, or to sell his tuna in New York. He travels alone, making major decisions out of his briefcase, while manipulating and expanding the network of personal relations that constitutes one of his greatest assets.

Mr. Moon also pointed out that most successful businessmen of any stature have received favors from the government. For this it is necessary to pay bribes, even when everything is perfectly legal. He criticized such practices, since they amount to a heavy informal tax on businessmen without rewarding efficiency and productivity. On the other hand, he thought the government's policy of encouraging foreign direct investment through tax and other incentives has been beneficial. Koreans have been able to observe and learn many of the techniques of foreign businessmen first hand; also, they are increasingly obliged to compete with foreign firms, so that traditional, inefficient ways of doing things have to be abandoned.

BUTTON-MANUFACTURING PLANT

Mr. Song, aged 47, founded his button factory in 1971 with 10 workers and 5 million wŏn (3 million of his own and 2 million borrowed from the bank). Of his 10 initial workers, 4 were experienced button-makers whom he had hired away from other small firms. He claims to be the first in Korea to get into the business of producing standard-grade buttons for export goods. As the volume of exported clothing rapidly increased in the 1970s, the demand for his buttons rose as well. Today he has 35 workers and a lot of relatively complicated machinery that can fabricate buttons out of 5 different raw materials. Now that Korea is exporting more expensive clothes, Mr. Song plans to improve the quality of his buttons in order to supply the new demand.

He said that, while there are many button manufacturers in Korea, only one is large enough to be a threat to him competitively; so far he has had no difficulty marketing his products, however. Eventually he expects to diversify, making belt buckles and other accessories for clothing.

Before starting to manufacture buttons, Mr. Song spent several months talking to people in the import-export business in an effort to find a product that could be easily produced in Korea, and that would compete successfully with imports. Once he had decided on buttons, he spent a year as a button broker, taking orders from exporters and then contracting with local suppliers for delivery. Although he was able to make money, he decided he could do better with his own factory.

PERSONAL BACKGROUND

Mr. Song, the youngest of 6 brothers and sisters, is from one of the most prominent lineages of Korea. For hundreds of years his family has produced high officials. An uncle was briefly President of the Republic of Korea. Another uncle was president of Seoul National University. A grandfather, who held high office under the Japanese colonial administration, insisted on a modern education for his children and grandchildren, emphasizing military training, political science, and engineering over the humanities.

In spite of this modernizing influence, Mr. Song grew up in a traditional *yangban* family atmosphere. His family was poor compared to other branches of the lineage, however, and he had been determined since his youth to improve its financial position. As it turned out, he was the first person among all his relatives to enter business; curiously, he seemed proud that his family retained the traditional *yangban* prejudice against merchants and commercial activity. Some 150 of his relatives are now living in the United States, where most are active in the professions.

Apparently his lineage publishes such statistics along with the regular genealogies.

After graduating from the College of Foreign Languages, where he majored in Russian, Mr. Song started raising cattle for milk production in 1961 near Ch'ungju. This was one of the first attempts to produce milk by modern methods on a large scale, and he obtained a 4,000,000-wŏn loan from the National Agricultural Cooperative Federation (NACF). After ten years, during which he was elected president of the Korean Milk Producers Association, Mr. Song became so frustrated by the failure of the Ministry of Agriculture and Fisheries to support farmers with consistent, effective policies that he sold his farm and moved back to Seoul in 1971. He denounced the incompetence and corruption of officials of that period in the Ministry of Agriculture and Fisheries and the NACF. Also, he criticized the government's support of low food prices to benefit the urban population at the expense of farmers.[7]

Although he had been unable to make a profit producing milk, the increase in land values during the ten-year period provided him with a substantial amount of capital when he sold his farm in 1971.

ENTREPRENEURSHIP

Mr. Song said that self-confidence, determination, and detailed knowledge or experience are all more important to the entrepreneur than extraordinary brilliance or intuition. A man must have a definite goal and a carefully worked out plan of how to reach it. Then he must pursue that goal doggedly without being swayed by all the rumors and opinions that he hears from day to day. He should study the situation carefully and make up his mind only after long deliberation. But, once his decision is made, he must follow through with all his energies. The producer's mentality is quite different from that of the broker who is constantly looking this way or that for a chance to make money by participating in a transaction. Many Korean entrepreneurs have been diverted from concentrating on production by the temptation to speculate in land prices, exchange rates, or the value of commodities. It is true, of course, that the economic environment has often provided greater rewards in the past for such activities.

According to Mr. Song, the small entrepreneur who starts out on his own must have enough faith in his own ability and destiny to resist the advice of those (usually relatives) who caution him against taking risks. On the other hand, he should not try to exceed his real capacity and potential; he must reject the advice of those who urge him on to impossibly grandiose schemes.

With regard to government control and intervention, Mr. Song thinks bureaucrats are increasingly performing service functions for commerce and industry instead of arrogantly throwing their weight around as in the past. He thinks that the larger firms are manipulating the administration rather than the other way around. Except for a few outrageous cases the principles of merit and accomplishment are predominant. In general Mr. Song, while extremely critical of the government's previous agricultural policy, spoke favorably of the administration's role in support of business.

Mr. Song said he is able to hire men with technical and financial skills without any difficulty. In his company he has two key men whom he pays well, providing them with health insurance and retirement benefits. The rest of his workers receive low pay but, since there are plenty of applicants for jobs at such wages, he is able to choose fairly well-educated, conscientious workers. Usually they are young, live near his plant, and work to supplement the earnings of the household head rather than to support themselves independently.

Mr. Song thinks the company president's role is crucial in that he must handle relations between the company and its suppliers and customers as well as with the bureaucracy on the one hand, and he must establish and supervise the internal organization and environment on the other. Because there is plenty of cheap, docile labor, the latter job is relatively easy. He added, however, that worker satisfaction is important, and young people no longer will accept the authoritarian-paternalistic manner of the past.

TEXTILE MILL IN TAEGU

Mr. Hwang, aged 59, formed a company producing cheap cotton cloth in 1965. He invested about 2 billion wŏn (1965 prices) and employed 200 workers. The company's assets have doubled in value since then, he said, and he is now employing more workers. Most of the capital came from a cotton yarn mill he had been operating until 1965; the rest was borrowed from a bank. During the middle 1960s, according to Mr. Hwang, it was not too hard for small entrepreneurs to obtain loans (although there were informal costs involved), but in recent years the government has favored large industry, and as a result it is much harder to borrow money. In the winter of 1975–1976 he bought another cotton-cloth mill also employing about 200 workers for an undisclosed amount.[8] The business had been owned jointly by 16 Koreans resident in Japan, and Mr. Hwang stepped in when they failed. He attributed the failure to lack of experience, shortage of capital, and the inability to provide unified, forceful leadership. He has turned the management of his other mill over to a younger brother, and he is now devoting himself full time to making the new acquisition profitable. He seemed to be confident that this could be done without too much difficulty.

PERSONAL BACKGROUND

Mr. Hwang's father was a small shopkeeper with only a primary school education; the family was poor. The second of 4 brothers, Mr. Hwang was brought up in a Confucian household, but he no longer performs any family rituals. The family must have had some money, because he graduated from middle school (the equivalent of high school today), and at the time of Liberation in 1945 he was working in his older brother's small cotton-batting factory. In 1955 he and his older brother started producing cotton yarn; a younger brother took over the cotton-batting plant. So far none of his business ventures has failed.

ENTREPRENEURSHIP

Mr. Hwang does not want to expand his business further. He prefers to operate small companies, acquiring them and disposing of them whenever it is to his advantage. He said that it is important to understand one's limitations, and that he does not have the qualifications to operate a large factory, although he is thoroughly experienced in all aspects of the textile business. Also, a small firm can avoid involvement in politics, which requires a quite different kind of skill than entrepreneurship.

With regard to personal qualities, he thinks the entrepreneur must be diligent, forceful, and stubborn or determined. He must "desire to live well."[9]

As far as the entrepreneur's functions are concerned, he rated the political aspects involving personal relationships with suppliers and customers as the most crucial; next comes internal management and the supervision of employees; technology, innovation, and the quality of the product provide relatively few problems. It is always easy to find technicians (or hire them from other firms) who can furnish whatever information or instruction is required.

Mr. Hwang said that strong leadership and forcefulness are essential because Koreans, unlike the Japanese or Americans, will not work well together unless there is firm direction. "Koreans are like grains of sand; they will not stick together."

Mr. Hwang's manner was relaxed and confident. He made no effort at formality or even good manners; he joked and used an occasional crude expression. This is unusual in Korea in relations with strangers and seemed to betray low-class origins rather than a modern egalitarian attitude. Another textile executive in Taegu said that Mr. Hwang does in fact have difficulty dealing with Seoul bureaucrats because of his lack of social competence. Within the "textile world," however, his style is very effective.

SMALL MACHINE SHOPS IN SEOUL

We had no introduction to Mr. Kim (aged 49), who owns several small machine shops in the Chongno borough of downtown Seoul. By chance we walked through a part of Chongno borough at night where rickety old Korean-style buildings housed big lathes, drill presses, and other complicated machine tools. Work was going on under bright, naked light bulbs in rooms that opened right onto the alleys. The atmosphere was one of relaxed, noisy informality, with numerous other men and boys gathered around the machines in addition to those who were operating them. Usually one room was just big enough for one or—where a partition had been knocked out—two machines. Everything was cluttered and dirty; bits of metal, rags, grease, and other refuse were scattered around.

After being rebuffed at two places, we asked a teen-aged apprentice where the boss was; he led us several houses down the street to a somewhat larger shop that had living quarters attached. Mr. Kim was willing to talk and asked us into his house, eventually providing hospitality in the form of a mixture of *soju* (an inexpensive hard liquor) and cider (lemon soda). We subsequently saw him on two more occasions and returned the hospitality.

After failing and losing everything in 1960, Mr. Kim bought a lathe for 600,000 wŏn (1963 prices) with earnings from his new wife's wine shop. Mr. Kim did fairly well after that and entered into a kind of partnership with two other expert machinists. He furnished the site, some of the capital, and the sales outlets, while they provided additional money towards the purchase of two more machines. Since Mr. Kim had a close ex-army friend in the automobile parts business, most of their work at first consisted of manufacturing spare parts to keep Seoul's ancient fleet of taxis running. Their debts from high interest rates were heavy, however, and they could never have gotten through the early 1960s without periodic capital infusions from the wife's flourishing entertainment business. By 1966 the volume of orders had increased substantially, and Mr. Kim was able to get a bank loan of several million wŏn. He bought 4 more machines and hired men to operate them while continuing his special profit-sharing relationship with the two original "partners." Business continued to improve, although there were some difficult years as well, and at present Mr. Kim has 22 machines scattered about the neighborhood with a work force of 49 men and boys. He has not taken on any more partners and would like to buy out the 2 that now exist, despite their long and successful relationship. Some of the apprentices from several years before are now machinists.

Mr. Kim said he has recently gotten in touch with officials of the Ministry of Commerce and Industry about the possibility of relocating his scattered shops in a single small plant outside the city. There has been a lot of official talk about governmental promotion of the small-scale machine-tool industry, and he hoped to obtain financial help for the move. Although the officials were receptive, they wanted him to leave the Seoul area and move to South Kyŏngsang province. Mr. Kim recognizes that he will eventually be forced out of his present location by Seoul city planners, but he is determined to stay in the metropolitan region.

PERSONAL BACKGROUND

Mr. Kim's father, a farm boy without education from North Ch'ungch'ŏng province, left his village to work on the railroads during the colonial period. He became foreman of a track gang and was able to send both his sons to vocational middle (high) school. Mr. Kim, the second son, graduated just before Liberation in 1945 and obtained an apprentice position in the Inch'ŏn Machinery Company. He had become a full-fledged machinist by 1950, when, after the retreat to Taegu, he was drafted into the army. He also worked in military machine shops during the war and left the army as a sergeant in 1956. Through his experience and connections and the "informal" payment of a large sum of money, he was able to obtain two high-quality machine tools of U.S. manufacture as military surplus; he then set up shop in Seoul with the friend who had supplied the money. This "friend" absconded in 1960 with all the partnership's assets, leaving large debts for which the machines were collateral. Mr. Kim was wiped out.

He recouped two years later by marrying the prosperous owner of a nearby wine shop where he had been a regular customer. Today Mr. Kim appears to be living well below his means. He owns valuable property in the heart of Seoul in addition to the machines, and he has bought a large residential lot south of the Han River. His wife still owns her business, but she now delegates the day-to-day operation to a younger cousin.

Mr. Kim has a breezy, confident, almost overbearing manner; he is also a thoughtful and intelligent man.

ENTREPRENEURSHIP

Mr. Kim thinks life was so hard for ordinary Koreans under the Japanese regime, with so few opportunities for advancement, that there was an enormous pent-up desire among all Koreans for material success. They had learned about the importance of hard work and productivity under the Japanese, and many, like himself, had learned useful skills; but until the Japanese left, there was nothing for them but low rank and low pay. Then division of the country, the war, and bad leadership had resulted in economic chaos, so that only within the last 10 or 15 years had there been a chance to gain real rewards from one's own labor. Until fairly recently it was only the smugglers, brokers, speculators, bureaucrats, and politicians who could make money, but now anyone who was willing to work hard and learn could get by. Except for those who are lazy or crooked, most Koreans, Mr. Kim thinks are eager to get ahead through hard work, and anyone who can provide a place to work and reasonable incentives will get all the good labor he needs. Of course, his own workers always complain that they are not paid enough, and after several years some may become discontented and move on to another shop. But Mr. Kim sees this as a kind of natural restlessness that can only be cured by a change of scene.

Because of the temptation for some workers to make extra money on the side, he keeps close—although indirect and informal—watch over the machinists, and all financial matters connected with buying raw materials, paying maintenance costs, and selling the product are in the hands of two close relatives whom he knows he can trust.

Mr. Kim feels that no amount of brilliant business sense is worth much without an intimately detailed knowledge of a particular industry. A man's hunches will be right only if they are based on such "dirty-handed" participation. Se far he feels he is not at a disadvantage in dealing with college-educated businessmen or bureaucrats, even though he occasionally has to react fairly sharply against their assumptions of pervasive and superior wisdom.

With regard to risks, he said he has much more to lose now than when he was young, and he is therefore more careful in making additional investments. In particular, he is suspicious of plausible, profit-making schemes proposed by charming and likeable people. He contrasted his wariness with the gullibility of many others who get taken in again and again because of their greed and susceptibility to flattery. On the other hand, he said sometimes it is necessary to act forcefully and quickly on impulse when the right opportunity comes along. The skill lies in judging both the situation and the person correctly. Everyone, himself included, who wants to be more than a clerk or a laborer, must be good at winning over people by giving an impression of sincerity, trustworthiness, and good will. To succeed, one must sustain a reputation for these qualities. In Mr. Kim's opinion, the combination of these skills (in personal relations) plus detailed practical knowledge and hard work make the successful entrepreneur. He does not think that an austere lifestyle or a penny-pinching emphasis on savings is a particularly useful attribute.

Mr. Kim is confident that he can make the transition from a collection of loosely organized, scattered downtown machine shops to a conventional factory system without much trouble. A year ago he had hired his first accountant, a niece who had just graduated from commercial college, and he was pleased with the results. He realizes that many savings should be possible through more rational procedures; his oldest son would eventually study business administration, and he expects they would make many changes together in the future.

Mr. Kim complained that some of his machinists tended to be rather independent, insisting as they got older on discussing their work as if they were fellow-owners of the business. He would like eventually to replace all but the most skilled with younger men who are better trained, both in terms of schooling and, where possible, as apprentices in his own shops.

In his opinion most government officials now seem to be more concerned with promoting industry rather than with extracting personal advantage from it, but Mr. Kim thinks that too much assistance is being given to large firms.

Appendix B
Chaebŏl Case Studies

In this appendix we sketch the evolution of five of Korea's leading chaebŏl. The goal is not in-depth critical analysis but a fleshing out of the dimensions of Korean growth by decomposition into individual entrepreneurs and companies.

The groups presented have been selected to illustrate the diversity that characterizes Korean entrepreneurial success. We begin with one of the oldest chaebŏl, Sam Yang, and trace its origins to the colonial period We then consider three groups that started during, or immediately following, the Korean War and prospered during the Park regime: Samsung, the largest chaebŏl which produces largely consumer goods; Hyundai which concentrates on producers' goods; and Hanjin which deals in the transportation sector. Finally, we consider Daewoo, one of the "new generation" groups which was founded in the late 1960s and has since enjoyed phenomenal success.

SAM YANG: CHAEBŎL FORMATION DURING THE COLONIAL PERIOD

Sam Yang is today only the fourteenth ranked chaebŏl,[1] but it is, nonetheless, of considerable interest as one of the nation's oldest groups. Its history illustrates the conversion of traditional aristocratic landowners into modern industrialists; their prosperity under the Japanese; the tribulations during the chaos of 1945–1951; the political nature of entrepreneurship under Rhee; and the devolution of power as control was passed to the "second generation."

ENTREPRENEURIAL BACKGROUND[2]

Sŏng-su Kim and Yŏn-su Kim were brothers who came from a traditional *yangban* family. Their father was a wealthy landlord who had also once been chief administrator of a county and had edited a 17-volume national history. Sŏng-su Kim was the fourth son and Yŏn-su Kim the fifth, but their three older brothers had died in infancy. In keeping with Confucian tradition, Sŏng-su Kim was adopted by his father's elder brother who did not have a son. The adoptive father was also, of course, a wealthy landlord, who had also been a chief county administrator and had established a private school.

Sŏng-su Kim was born in 1891. When he was seventeen years old, he left home without his parents' permission. Together with a friend, Chin-u Song, the famous patriot, he traveled to Japan where he majored in political science at Waseda University and eventually graduated in 1914. In Japan, he was also very active in extracurricular activities. He was once the president of the Korean Student Association in Japan and made good friends with many of his contemporary expatriots.

Yŏn-su Kim was born in 1896. He majored in economics and graduated from Kyoto Imperial University in 1921.

ENTREPRENEURIAL HISTORY: SŎNG-SU KIM

After returning to Korea in 1915, Sŏng-su Kim first showed his interest in education by taking over the Chungang School which was in financial trouble. Then in 1917 he entered the industrial world by acquiring a failing textile venture, and in 1919 he founded a modern spinning factory—Kyŏngsŏng Spinning Co. (now named Kyungbang Limited).

It is often argued that Mr. Kim's motive for engaging in entrepreneurial activities was nationalism. For example, Ki-Zun Zo maintains that Mr. Kim established Kyungbang Limited as part of a movement to develop domestic enterprises and thus make the nation economically independent.

Zo thus sees the establishment of the Kyungbang Limited as a part of the March 1st Independence Movement of 1919.[3]

Mr. Kim's involvement in the textile industry was influenced by one of his friends who had majored in textile weaving in Japan and who persuaded him to take over the financially troubled Kyŏngsŏng Chigyu. This firm had been the first Korean joint-stock textile company in the nation. It had been organized by two earlier Korean entrepreneurs who integrated scattered small-scale owner-operators. The company made various cotton, jute, or silk products such as belts, hair ribbons, and small bands for hats. The production method was still not really modern and mostly hand-operated, though there was some electrification. The company's plant space as of 1913 was 237.5 p'yŏng and was equipped with 67 pedaled textile sewing machines and one motor generator of five horsepower. The company encountered financial difficulties, in part because it had started producing traditional products in large quantities just as the process of modernization reduced the demand for old-style hairdos, clothing, and accessories.

When Mr. Kim took over the company, he was not interested in producing those same products but wanted to move into cotton fabrics, which were at that time largely imported from Japan. Mr. Kim imported 40 Japanese power textile weaving machines, but found he could still not compete with Japanese cloth. He therefore decided to establish a new large-scale textile company, the Kyungbang Limited.

Selling shares of the company at the time was not an easy task. Mr. Kim traveled all over the country to emphasize the national need for establishing such a company. Even though the concept of a joint-stock company was new, many people bought shares as a gesture of patriotism, since the timing was immediately after the 1919 anti-Japanese uprising. Most of those who actively participated in founding the company were provincial landlords who were influential in their regions and who had become interested in the nation's modern enterprises. These promoters together bought 3,790 shares, and the rest (or 16,210) shares were sold to the public.

Those who see nationalism as a primary motive in establishing the company also see a similar influence in its operation.[4] For example, its employment advertisement usually specified "Koreans only," paralleling the "Japanese only" designations of some Japanese-run companies. The company also appealed to the public with promotional catch phrases such as "Koreans with Korean cotton clothes."[5] The marketing strategy also took full advantage of the company's use of traditional Korean symbols for its trademark (see below). It concentrated its marketing effort in the north, especially in P'yŏngan province where nationalism was well established.

The company also benefited from the Chosŏn Mulsan Changyuhoe (Korean Products Promotion Group), established in 1920 in P'yŏngan province by a famous patriot. This nationalistic movement stressed industrial development, promotion of domestic products, reduction of luxurious consumption, and frugality.

An episode involving the company's *t'aegŭksŏng* trademark is famous. *T'aegŭk* is the symbol used in the Korean national flag, and the trademark also included eight stars to indicate the eight Korean provinces. Japanese police allegedly asked the company to explain the trademark, because it was politically sensitive. Since trademark control was handled in Japan, rather than by the colonial administration in Korea, the company was able to get away with a nonsense explanation.

In 1928, when the Kyungbang Limited celebrated its tenth anniversary, Sŏng-su Kim retired from business activities to devote himself to journalism and education. He had established today's *Dong-A Ilbo* (Dong-A daily newspaper) in April 1920 and had expanded the Chungang School to the middle-school level in 1921. Stimulated by a visit to America and Europe, he decided to establish a private college. In 1933, he took over the financially troubled Posŏng Professional School with the intention of developing it into a university. His effort was interrupted by World War II, but he founded today's Korea University in 1946.

Sŏng-su Kim was also active in politics, becoming Vice President of the country in 1951, but resigning in 1952 due to a feud with Syngman Rhee. He died in 1955.

ENTREPRENEURIAL HISTORY: YŎN-SU KIM

When Yŏn-su Kim returned to Korea after his graduation, he became the managing director of Kyŏngsŏng Chigyu under the presidency of his brother. He was then appointed executive director of the newly founded Kyungbang Limited and became its president in 1935.

Yŏn-su Kim also paid much attention to his family land in Chŏlla province. These holdings were so extensive that it was said that "one can't go anywhere in Chŏlla province without walking on Mr. Kim's land."[5] In 1924, he began to regroup and consolidate his holdings, and in 1927 he established Samsu Sa to manage his agricultural efforts. In 1931, Samsu Sa was renamed Sam Yang and became a limited partnership in 1934. The company then acquired management control of Kyungbang Limited but continued land reclamation projects in Chŏlla province.

In 1933, Kyungbang Limited participated in an industrial exhibition in Manchuria and in 1934 established a branch there. In 1936, Kim established the Sam Yang in Manchuria in an effort to resettle Koreans on six farms that he owned there and to promote other business interests in Manchuria. In 1939, he established the Nam Man Spinning Company and in 1940 took over Samch'ok Kiŏp, a logging venture. With all these activities, Mr. Kim was one of the best known entrepreneurs in Manchuria.

With Liberation in 1945, Mr. Kim lost all of his business interests in North Korea and Manchuria, as well as an office in Osaka. His ventures in the south also encountered difficulties. Immediately after the Japanese left the country, workers of most Japanese-owned companies took over management. Kyungbang Limited, being the only major company in the textile industry run by Koreans, remained under family control, but soon ran afoul of the labor unrest of the period. The employees went on strike, accused the management of being "capitalist exploiters," and demanded inventory distribution and wage increases. Workers sometimes confined managers and harassed Mr. Kim at his residence. Similar revolts occurred on his farms, and tenants also came to Seoul to confront him. To meet these demands, Mr. Kim decided to pay employees a "special bonus to celebrate the nation's independence," amounting to 20 percent of annual sales. The bonus per employee was equivalent to 100 times the monthly wage. Conditions nonetheless continued to deteriorate, and in December 1945 he decided to retire from Kyungbang Limited and all of his other businesses.

In 1948, the new National Assembly passed a law on the punishment of anti-nationalistic behavior during the colonial period, and Yŏn-su Kim was detained the following January. He was accused of having:

1) been elected as the Kyŏnggi Province Representative by the colonial government;
2) been appointed as an Honorary Counsellor in Manchuria;
3) been selected as a member of colonial government advisory body;
4) served as a staff member of an agency designed to cooperate with the Japanese war effort;
5) encouraged Korean students in Japan to take part in the war.

His trial ended with dismissal of the charges. The reasons given were:

1) In managing the Kyungbang Limited, he always fought against Japanese capital.
2) He always made efforts to establish a national economic foundation.
3) Kyungbang Limited's use of the *t'aegŭk* trademark should be taken into consideration.
4) It was proved that his taking colonial government offices or honorary offices were mostly involuntary and the result of pressure.
5) A few hundred Korean students were supported by him as a part of his effort to educate more Koreans.

The Land Reform Act delivered a further blow. According to Mr. Kim's memoir, he had to hand over 6 big farms producing 150,000 sŏk (bushels) of grain. In return, he got land bonds worth 100,000 sŏk. As explained in Chapter 2, the value of these bonds decreased drastically in the ensuing years and, when sold in 1953, brought returns of only 30 to 70 percent.

Proceeds from the bond sale were used to finance his return to the industrial sphere. In 1953, he established Sam Yang Tong Sang Co., Ltd. (Sam Yang Trading Co.) to replace Sam Yang which had become little more than a personal real estate holding company. He decided to move into food and textiles, so he submitted an application for government permission to establish a sugar mill in 1953, at about the same time that Samsung submitted its application (see below). Samsung received permission immediately, and two other firms were similarly entitled before Sam Yang got its permit in December 1954. Mr. Kim thinks that this was due to his being identified with the major opposition party. Even after receiving approval, Sam Yang could not get a government dollar loan for importing equipment at the privileged exchange rate of sixty to one. Instead, it got FOA (Foreign Operations Administration) funds at a 320 to one exchange rate.

As his sugar mill in Ulsan started its operation, the Sam Yang Tong Sang Co., Ltd. changed its name to Sam Yang Co., Ltd. in June 1956. In the late 1950s, the Rhee administration became more open in suppressing businesses related to the opposition party. The Sam Yang Group was one of the first targets, and it was often subjected to tax investigation. This was believed to have been done primarily to prevent political funds from flowing into the opposition Chang Myon party. With the Student Revolution of 1960 this party came into power, and Yŏn-su Kim emerged as president of a newly formed business federation.

Despite the change in its political fortunes, Sam Yang Co., Ltd. did not prosper in the 1960s. At the time of the April Student Revolution, Yŏn-su Kim was already sixty-four years old, and a process of devolution of control—begun in the 1950s—continued. In 1955, the salt division of Sam Yang Co., Ltd. had become an independent company. It separated from the group in 1956, with Yŏn-su Kim's eldest son as president. Kyungbang Limited separated from the Sam Yang group in 1958 when Sam Yang's shares were sold. It is now under the leadership of Yŏn-su Kim's brother-in-law and is itself the nation's forty-third ranked chaebŏl. The *Dong-A Ilbo* is controlled by one of Sŏng-su Kim's sons, while another of Yŏn-su Kim's sons is President of Korea University.

The main branch of Sam Yang Co., Ltd. acquired a financially troubled textile firm in 1963 and built it into the Sam Yang Woolen Textile Co., Ltd. More recently, it has acquired 56 percent of a heavy equipment company and 33 percent of a grape sugar company. It is currently headed by Yŏn-su Kim's third son.

The centralized first-generation control has thus been heavily decentralized in the second generation. Descendants still control the original businesses, but have to some extent gone their independent ways. It remains to be seen whether the newer chaebŏl will follow this or a more centralized inheritance pattern.

SAMSUNG: THE LARGEST CHAEBŎL[6]

Pyŏng-ch'ŏl Yi is widely regarded as the richest man in Korea, and our value-added calculations confirm that his Samsung group is the largest chaebŏl in Korea. The group's 1975 sales amounted to over 700 million dollars and its exports to over 200 million dollars (see Table B-1 for these and other quantitative indicators).[7]

Yi got his start as a provincial businessman under the Japanese but prospered in the import trade before, during, and immediately after the Korean War. In the mid-1950s, he moved into import substitution of consumer goods such as sugar, flour, and textiles and from there into a wide range of services and products (see Table B-2 for a complete listing).

Yi has often been criticized as "profiteering" from his early concentration on the so-called "three whites"—sugar, flour, and cotton yarn. While it is certain that there was a substantial zero-sum element in these early activities, it is equally clear that the group has since prospered in fundamentally positive-sum ventures. Yi has proven adept at taking the fullest advantage of the economic opportunities offered by the government and the environment. While he was a leader in the consumer-goods import substitution of the 1950s and the export expansion of the 1960s, he has been a follower in the basic industries. This can be interpreted as a simple reflection of his personal style, which is known to be meticulous, cautious, and "steady as you go." This had led him to operate in markets where demand was assured, comparative advantage clear, and the risks small. His strength had been in early recognition of these opportunities and rapid mobilization of resources to fill the perceived demand. When followers begin to enter one market, he has typically moved on to something new, one step ahead of the crowd. Where demand and comparative advantage have not been clear—as in the heavy and chemical industries—he has moved slowly. In his memoirs he attributed this to a desire "to avoid trial and error" in areas where mistakes are terribly costly.[8] His entrepreneurial style has thus been basically conservative and in marked contrast to the

TABLE B-1 Samsung Group: Quantitative Indicators

	1975			1974			1973		
	(a) Nation	(b) Samsung	$\frac{b}{a} \times 100$	(a) Nation	(b) Samsung	$\frac{b}{a} \times 100$	(a) Nation	(b) Samsung	$\frac{b}{a} \times 100$
Number of companies[c]		17			16			16	
Number of companies in non-agriculture[c]		17			16			16	
Number of companies in manufacturing[c]	22,787[a]	9		22,632[a]	8		23,293[a]	8	
Total sales[d]		352,819			197,461			91,056	
Total manufacturing sales[d]	7,994,143[a]	175,405	2.19	5,438,104[a]	139,345	2.56	3,450,879[a]	61,606	1.79
Value added at factor cost[d]	8,259,280[b]	112,751	1.37	6,307,740[b]	77,889	1.23	4,515,830[b]	39,367	0.87
Non-agricultural value added at factor cost[d]	5,965,570[b]	112,751	1.89	4,625,600[b]	77,889	1.68	3,263,970[b]	39,367	1.21
Manufacturing value added at factor cost[d]	2,088,710[b]	74,774	3.58	1,603,060[b]	60,195	3.76	1,105,300[b]	26,925	2.44
Employment	11,830[e]	21,541	0.18	11,586[e]	18,741	0.16	11,139[e]	17,711	0.16
Employment in manufacturing	2,205[e]	14,405	0.65	2,012[e]	12,462	0.62	1,774	13,050	0.74
Export[f]	5,081,016	349,346	6.88	4,460,370	108,728	2.44	3,225,025	85,140[g]	2.64

Notes: [a]Source: EPB, *Report on Mining and Manufacturing Survey*, 1973–1975.

[b]BOK, *Economic Statistics Yearbook, 1977.*

[c]Corporations existed but not in operation at the time were excluded from the calculation (e.g., there were 21 entities in 1975, but 4 entities were excluded from the calculation).

[d]In current million wŏn.

[e]In thousands of workers.

[f]In current thousand U.S. dollars.

[g]Samsung Corning Company's export is included even though the company is excluded from other calculations.

TABLE B-2 Samsung Group: Affiliated Companies

Company	Year
Textile and Paper	
Cheil Wool Textile Co., Ltd.	1954, est.
Cheil Synthetic Textile Co., Ltd.	1972, est.
Chonju Paper Manufacturing Co., Ltd.	1965, acq.
Food	
Cheil Sugar Co., Ltd.	1953, est.
Electronics	
Samsung Electronics Co., Ltd.	1969, est.
Samsung Electric Co., Ltd.	1969, est.
Samsung Electron Devices Co., Ltd.	1970, est.
Samsung Corning Co., Ltd.	1973, est.
Samsung Electrical Parts Co., Ltd.	1973, est.
Petrochemical and Machinery	
Samsung Petrochemical Co., Ltd.	1974, est.
Samsung Heavy Industries Co., Ltd.	1974, est.
Daesung Heavy Industries Co., Ltd.	1977, acq.
Samsung Precision Equipment Co., Ltd.	1977, est.
Samsung Shipbuilding Co., Ltd.	1977, acq.
Trade	
Samsung Co., Ltd.	1952, est.
Shinsegye Department Store Co., Ltd.	1962, acq.
Real Estate and Construction	
Joongang Development Co., Ltd.	1966, est.
Samsung Construction Co., Ltd.	1977, acq.
Finance	
Ankuk Fire & Marine Insurance Co., Ltd.	1958, acq.
Dongbang Life Insurance Co., Ltd.	1957, acq.
Mass Communication	
Joongang Daily Newspaper Co., Ltd.	1965, est.
Tongyang Broadcasting Co., Ltd.	1963, est.
Other	
Hotel Shilla Co., Ltd.	1973, est.
Korea General Hospital, Inc.	1966, est.
Yongin Farm	1975, est.
Samsung Cultural Foundation	1965, est.
Sung Kyun Kwan University	1965, acq.

adventuresome risk-taking pattern of Hyundai's Chu-yŏng Chŏng, described in the subsequent section.

ENTREPRENEURIAL BACKGROUND

Yi was born in 1910 in South Kyŏngsang province in a small village of about 300 households. He was the second and youngest son of a wealthy landlord. His early education was in a *sŏdang*, or traditional Confucian school that taught largely Chinese literature and philosophy. Yi wanted, however, to go to a modern school, and his parents finally allowed him to do so at the age of ten. He first went to a primary school in Seoul and eventually entered the Chungdong Middle School. Although he did not graduate from middle school, he proceeded to Japan and enrolled in the Political Science-Economics Division of Waseda University. However, due to "poor health" he dropped out after a couple of semesters and returned to Korea. He then spent a couple of years wandering around Seoul doing nothing in particular.

ENTREPRENEURIAL HISTORY

Pyŏng-ch'ŏl Yi's entrepreneurial activities began in 1936, when he established a local rice mill with funds inherited from his parents. He recalls that his decision was rather hasty, and he is today not really sure why he chose this career. He nonetheless did quite well and by 1945 had expanded into trucking, real estate, domestic trading,[9] milling, noodle-making, and brewing. These activities were largely confined to Taegu, but were of sufficient magnitude to make him one of the biggest taxpayers in the province.

After Liberation, Yi became interested in starting a new line of business in Seoul, using funds accumulated primarily from his brewery profits. He moved to Seoul in 1947 and decided to engage in international trade. His decision was based on his assessment of the prevailing economic environment in which demand for daily necessities was increasing rapidly, although the nation lacked domestic production capabilities. Yi established the Samsung Mulsan Company in Seoul in November 1948. Within two years, his import activities were successful enough for his trading company's sales to rank in the nation's top ten. This venture was devastated by the Korean War, but was reestablished in Pusan in January 1951. The success of this company laid the foundation for the chaebŏl's subsequent rapid expansion. Concentrating on import activities, this company is claimed to have grown 17-fold in the first year of its existence—a substantial achievement, even after allowing for inflation.[10] Yi admits that windfall gains of this magnitude were only possible because of the abnormal circumstances of the war.

With his substantial trading profits in hand, he started thinking about establishing a manufacturing firm and decided the best prospects were in import substitution of daily consumer necessities. In pursuit of this philosophy, he established the Cheil Sugar Company in Pusan in 1953. The company was initially a monopolistic supplier and reaped the natural benefits of this status. The resulting profits were put into another import-substitution consumer product when he established the Cheil Wool Textile Company, Ltd. in 1954. This company became very profitable as it gradually replaced foreign-made woolen textiles and became the backbone of today's Samsung Group.[11]

With this foundation established in the early 1950s, the Samsung Group emerged as a formidable chaebŏl in the late 1950s and took over numerous firms, including financial intermediaries. He actually purchased almost half of all commercial bank shares in the later years of the Rhee regime.[12]

With the inception of the Park Military Government, Yi became a major target of the illicit-wealth-accumulation investigation discussed in Chapter 8. The official calculation gave his illicit wealth as 800 million wŏn or about 19 percent of the national total.[13] He was also accused of providing political funds of 64 million wŏn and evading taxes amounting to 451 million wŏn.[14] Yi was in Japan at the time of the military coup and so initially avoided arrest. When he returned to Korea, he participated in the meeting with Park Chung Hee that led to the compromise described in Chapter 3. He emerged as the leader of the new entrepreneurs, served as the first president of the association that became FKI, and headed the businessmen's economic mission to the United States.

Yi had explored the possibility of entering the fertilizer field in the late 1950s but had been deterred by the April Student Revolution. Now, as part of the compensatory entrepreneurship program, he committed himself to constructing a fertilizer plant whose shares would be turned over to the government. The government's permission to build the plant, however, was abolished in December 1963,[15] and Yi finally paid his fine in cash. Less than a year later, in August 1964, he founded the Han Kook Fertilizer Company, one of the largest industrial projects of the period. The plant was completed in record time and commenced production in early 1967. Even before the plant was in operation, however, the company was plagued by the "saccharin smuggling" scandal. In September 1966, it was discovered that some of Pyŏng-ch'ŏl Yi's staff—including one of his sons—had illegally profiteered by smuggling saccharin when they imported raw materials from Japan. This became a controversial social issue and undoubtedly contributed to the unfavorable public image of Samsung and Yi himself. The President himself ordered a full investigation, and in the end Yi decided to "donate" 51 percent of the company's shares to the government.

The fertilizer setback, however, was hardly fatal, and throughout the 1960s, Samsung continued to expand into new fields such as department stores, securities brokerage, educational institutions, real estate, paper mills, and mass media. In the early 1970s, the group moved into electronics and, in the mid-1970s, they began to enter the "heavy and chemical industries" emphasized by the nation's Fourth Five-Year Economic

Development Plan, establishing or acquiring ventures in petrochemicals, heavy equipment, precision machinery, construction, and shipbuilding.

Samsung thus promises to maintain its prominence, if not its pre-eminence, for the foreseeable future. Though Pyŏng-ch'ŏl Yi was sixty-five years old in 1975, the group as yet shows no signs of dissolution.

HYUNDAI: AGGRESSIVE ENTREPRENEURSHIP IN PRODUCERS' GOODS[16]

Hyundai's evolution has been markedly different from that of Samsung, even though it is the second or third largest chaebŏl.[17] In the first place, Samsung concentrated on consumer goods, while Hyundai has focused on producers' goods—construction, shipbuilding, machinery, cement, engineering, and one consumer durable, automobiles (see Table B–4 for a complete listing). Second, and more important, Hyundai has been the leader in the 1970s effort to move the economy into a stage of industrialization that is higher in the product cycle. The uncertainty of success in this effort has meant that Hyundai has taken far more risks and had to be far more innovative—witness its construction of a world-class shipyard, efforts to export automobiles, and successful competition with established American and European giants for Middle Eastern construction contracts. Hyundai also is viewed much more sympathetically by the Blue House than Samsung, since heavy industry development is a long-run government objective; risky endeavors require implicit government contingency insurance, and the personal style of the chairman of the group is more compatible with that of the President.

ENTREPRENEURIAL BACKGROUND

The chairman and founder of the Hyundai Group is Chu-yŏng Chŏng. He was born in a village of Kangwŏn province in November 1915, the first son of an average farmer. He attended a traditional Confucian *sŏdang* for a few years before entering a modern primary school from which he graduated at the age of fifteen. His parents naturally wanted him to follow his father in the ancestral occupation of farming, but the boy was not satisfied with this idea. Early one morning, he left home with another village boy and headed towards Ch'ŏngjin where he had heard job opportunities were available. On the way, they got jobs as laborers on a road building crew in order to earn travel expenses. There, Chŏng's father caught up with them and took the boy back home. He then worked on his father's farm for about two years before again deciding to leave home with one of his friends. This time he went to Seoul, where he first worked

TABLE B-3 Hyundai Group: Quantitative Indicators

	1975			1974			1973		
	(a) Nation	(b) Hyundai	$\frac{b}{a} \times 100$	(a) Nation	(b) Hyundai	$\frac{b}{a} \times 100$	(a) Nation	(b) Hyundai[c]	$\frac{b}{a} \times 100$
Number of companies		6			6			5	
Number of companies in non-agriculture		6			6			5	
Number of companies in manufacturing	22,787[a]	5		22,632[a]	5		23,293[a]	4	
Total sales[d]		234,450			136,221			63,509	
Total manufacturing sales[d]	7,994,143[a]	179,950	2.25	5,438,104[a]	104,742	1.93	3,450,879[a]	31,982	0.93
GDP at factor cost[d]	8,259,280[b]	87,619	1.06	6,307,740[b]	47,313	0.75	4,515,830[b]	23,045	0.51
Non-agriculture value added at factor cost	5,965,970[b]	87,619	1.47	4,625,600[b]	47,313	1.02	3,263,970[b]	23,045	0.71
Manufacturing value added at factor cost[d]	2,088,710[b]	64,662	3.10	1,603,060[b]	35,747	2.23	1,105,300[b]	11,764	1.06
Employment	11,830[e]	29,329	0.25	11,586[e]	22,742	0.20	11,139[e]	20,531	0.18
Employment in manufacturing	2,205[e]	26,345	1.19	2,012	21,655	1.08	1,771[e]	19,616	1.11
Export[f]	5,081,016	120,710	2.38	4,460,370	163,733	3.67	3,225,025	71,213	2.21

Notes: [a]Source: EPB, *Report on Mining and Manufacturing Survey*, 1973–75.
[b]Source: BOK, *Economic Statistics Yearbook, 1977.*
[c]Hyundai Shipbuilding and Heavy Industries Co., Ltd., was excluded from the 1973 calculations except for employment.
[d]In current million wŏn.
[e]In thousands of workers.
[f]In current thousand U.S. dollars.

TABLE B-4 Hyundai Group: Affiliated Companies[a]

Construction and Real Estate	
Hyundai Construction Co., Ltd.	1950, est.
Keum Kang Development Co., Ltd.	1958, est.
Shipbuilding	
Hyundai Shipbuilding & Heavy Industries Co., Ltd.	1973, est.
Automobile Industry	
Hyundai Motor Company	1967, est.
Machinery	
Hyundai Industrial Co., Ltd.	1962, est.
Cement and Ceramics	
Hyundai Cement Co., Ltd.	1969, est.
Keum Kang Co., Ltd.	1958, est.
Engineering	
Hyundai Engineering Consultant Co., Ltd.	1974, est.
Repair Service	
Hyundai Mipo Dockyard Co., Ltd.	1975, est.
Hyundai Motor Service Co., Ltd.	1974, est.
Marine Transportation	
Asia Merchant Marine Co., Ltd.	1976, est.

Note: [a]Besides these firms, there are a few more small-scale firms in the group, e.g., Korea Urban Development, Korea Pavement Construction, and Dong Suh Industrial Co. We could not gather data on these firms.

briefly as a port laborer in Inch'ŏn and then became an errand boy for a small rice mill. The owner of the mill was impressed by his hard work and sincerity and, after about a year, made him a bookkeeping clerk.

ENTREPRENEURIAL HISTORY

After three years at the mill, he had learned enough about the rice trade to open his own retail shop. He was then twenty-two years old. His shop became prosperous and expanded into the wholesale business, but his success was brought to a quick halt by the colonial government control of the rice trade which accompanied the Sino-Japanese War. In 1940 he acquired a small auto-service shop. The shop burned down once but reopened with personal loans. He also provided transportation services in a mining region. After the nation's Liberation, Chŏng established the Hyundai Motor Company—and auto repair shop—in Seoul in 1946 and the Hyundai Construction Company, Ltd. in 1947, with the two merging in 1950.

With the onset of the Korean War, Chŏng and the company moved to Pusan. With the assistance of one of his brothers[18]—who possessed the requisite fluency in English—the company got contracts for U.S. Army barrack construction and airport expansion projects. Throughout the war, he continued to obtain extensive contracts from both the Korean government and the U.S. Army. This activity provided both the profits for later expansion and the contacts that allowed later contracts in Vietnam and Thailand.

After the war, the construction industry was understandably in demand for reconstruction of the facilities destroyed by the war. The Hyundai Construction Company, Ltd., took full advantage of the boom, expanding into unloading, warehousing, and international trade. Its growth rate was even faster during the rapid national expansion of the 1960s. Hyundai constructed many of the large-scale infrastructure projects undertaken under Park, including the Soyang Dam, Ch'unch'ŏn Dam, Kyŏngin Highway, Ulsan Thermal Plant, the six Han River bridges, Yŏŭi Apartment complex, Chosun Hotel, and National Assembly building. By 1965 the company's contract volume was already the highest in the nation.

A striking feature of Hyundai's growth has been its expansion into international construction markets. Its initial contracts were with the U.S. Government for work in Thailand and Vietnam. These were in part due to the contacts made through successful completion of similar contracts in Korea, but the subsequent expansion into the Middle East demonstrates the importance of the entrepreneurial spirit—as one opportunity dries up, a new one is developed.

Hyundai's first overseas contracts were in 1966—the Pattani-Narathiwat Highway[19] in Thailand and dredging work in Vietnam. The company acquired a reputation for completing projects successfully and on time and won further contracts with the expansion of the U.S. war effort. The experience thus earned was transferred to the Middle East, where in 1976 alone Hyundai was awarded $1.4 billion worth of contracts, including a $931 million industrial port at Jubail, Saudi Arabia.[20]

One of the more impressive entrepreneurial feats in Korea, and indeed, the world, was the creation of a world-class shipbuilding firm by Chu-yŏng Chŏng. This venture seemed quixotic to most Koreans, with the notable exceptions of Chairman Chŏng and President Park.[21] Not only had Hyundai had no previous experience in shipbuilding, but Korea itself had never produced a vessel larger than 10,000 tons, and no nation anywhere near Korea's level of development had ever built world-class tankers. International financiers and shipbuilders were no doubt bemused at the pretensions of someone soliciting funds with little more to show than a picture of a lovely sandy beach where the proposed Hyundai dry dock was to be built. It is no wonder that the first year's efforts at finding financing led to failure, and Chŏng persevered only because of the urgings of President Park. Finally, in April 1972, an agreement was reached with a Greek shipowner whereby two vessels—of 240,000 and 260,000 tons—were to be delivered in two-and-a-half years (July and December 1974). While the terms of the contract are not known, one may assume that the Greek was not risking a great deal in the event of failure. He may indeed have been astounded that the contract was honored and the dry dock built, workers trained, supplementary facilities completed, and the ships completed. Actual construction of the first vessel was begun in March 1973, and it was delivered nineteen months later in November 1974.

The contribution of government is of course crucial in an effort of this magnitude. In the first place, without the personal urging of President Park it is virtually certain that the project would have been shelved. In the second place, without efficient and energetic bureaucratic support the project could not have been completed on time—there are many countries in the world where one could not complete the necessary paper work in the allotted time, let alone build a shipyard and deliver ships. Finally, for risky ventures of this sort, partial mutuality comes into play through the government's provision of implicit contingency insurance. When the 1975 world shipbuilding slump led to the cancellation of orders for three virtually completed tankers, the company faced a potentially enormous loss as the vessels sat at their moorings. At this point, the government happened to decide that it would be a good idea if the Korean oil refineries started to ship crude from the Middle East in Korean-owned bottoms. Though the companies were reluctant to comply, given the prevailing tanker surplus and attendant low shipping rates, the government's view prevailed. After a year of discussions, the Korea Oil Corporation (a government-Gulf joint venture—began leasing the services of the three tankers from the newly created Hyundai Shipbuilding and Heavy Industries Company, Ltd. This is a perfect example of the practical operation of partial mutuality.

HANJIN: SUCCESS IN THE SERVICE SECTOR[22]

Hanjin is the fourth largest chaebŏl in Korea (see Table B–5 for quantitative indicators). It is similar to Hyundai in that U.S. military contracts during and after the Korean War provided its initial accumulation, and Vietnam contracts provided further impetus to its growth. It differs sharply from the other chaebŏl considered thus far in that its activities are largely confined to transportation and ancillary services (see Table B–6 for a complete list).

ENTREPRENEURIAL BACKGROUND

Chung-hun Cho was born in Seoul in 1920, the second son of a middle-

TABLE B-5 Hanjin Group: Quantitative Indicators

	1975			1974			1973		
	(a) Nation	(b) Hanjin[c]	b/a x 100	(b) Nation	(b) Hanjin[c]	b/a x 100	(a) Nation	(b) Hanjin[c]	b/a x 100
Number of companies		8			8			7	
Number of companies in non-agriculture		8			8			7	
Number of companies in manufacturing	22,787[a]	0		22,632[a]	0		23,293[a]	0	
Total sales[d]		157,451			98,779			63,113	
GDP at factor cost[d]	8,259,280[b]	72,166	8.74	6,307,740[b]	41,366	0.66	4,515,830[b]	31,741	0.70
Non-agricultural value added at factor cost[d]	5,965,970[b]	72,166	1.21	4,625,600[b]	41,366	0.89	3,263,970[b]	31,741	0.97
Manufacturing value added at factor cost[d]	2,088,710[b]	0	0	1,603,060[b]	0	0	1,105,300[b]	0	0
Value added factor cost (Transportation & Storage)[d]	375,470	63,667	16.96	295,650	36,247	12.26	219,780	29,402[g]	13.38
Employment	11,830[e]	10,161	0.09	11,586[e]	8,144	0.07	11,139[e]	7,776	0.07
Employment in manufacturing	2,205[e]	0	0	2,012[e]	0	0	1,774[e]	0	0
Export	5,081,016[f]	214,793	0.04	4,460,370[f]	149,841	0.03	3,225,025[f]	113,853	0.04

Notes: [a]Source: EPB, *Report on Mining and Manufacturing Survey*, 1973–1975.

[b]Source: BOK, *Economic Statistics Yearbook, 1977.*

[c]Units not in operation were excluded from the calculation.

[d]In current million wŏn.

[e]In thousands of workers.

[f]In current thousand U.S. dollars.

[g]Hanjin Tourist Co., Ltd. was acquired in 1973 but excluded from the calculation of value added at factor cost.

TABLE B-6 Hanjin Group: Affiliated Companies

Transportation	
Korean Air Lines Co., Ltd.	1969, acq.
Hanjin Transportation Co., Ltd.	1945, est.
Daejin Shipping Co., Ltd.	1967, est.
Korea Airport Co., Ltd.	1968, est.
Construction	
Hanil Development Co., Ltd.	1968, est.
Sightseeing	
Hanjin Tourist Co., Ltd.	1973, acq.
Livestock	
Jaedong Industrial Co., Ltd.	1973, est.
Securities and Insurance	
Hanil Securities Co., Ltd.	1973, est.
The Oriental Fire & Marine Insurance Co., Ltd.	1966, acq.
Education	
Inha University	1968, acq.

class business family. His education was curtailed at the middle school level when his family's business failed during the world depression. He left home for Japan when he was about 17 years old. Because he was fond of mechanics, he became an apprentice in a shipbuilding plant where submarines and warships were constructed. He then worked as a ship's mechanic for about three years, widening his perspective through visits to various Southeast Asian cities such as Hong Kong, Shanghai, and Singapore. He returned to Korea toward the end of World War II and opened a small machinery shop in Seoul. This venture did not prosper, thanks to the Japanese colonial control of mechanical and engineering firms.

ENTREPRENEURIAL HISTORY

With the nation's Liberation in 1945, Cho went to Inch'ŏn and opened the Hanjin Transportation Company, Ltd. with one truck. His company grew quite fast, and by the Korean War he owned a fleet of about 30 trucks and 20 small ships. The war took all his property, and afterwards he had to start all over again. He managed to get service contracts for transporting military supplies and became a supply agent for the U.S. Army in Korea. He established his creditability with the U.S. Army authorities, and this became critical for his future involvement in Vietnam. He also saw the inseparable relation between war and transportation, and this led him to look for business in Vietnam before others did. He believes his successful involvement in Vietnam was due to the creditability established in Korea among U.S. Army officers, some of whom were again serving in Vietnam. His company in Vietnam started to engage in land transportation with trucks imported from Japan and the United States, and sea transportation using barges imported from Hong Kong. Hanjin's performance was such that the U.S. Army asked them to take over complete operation of the important port of Qui Nhon, and they did so. It is estimated that the Hanjin's total dollar earnings in Vietnam amounted to $10 million in 1966 and $28 million in 1968.

The dollars earned in Vietnam allowed further expansion of his domestic ventures, which had expanded to 150 trucks in 1965. Chung-hun Cho established an airline and a marine transportation company in 1967, largely to carry necessary equipment and workers to Vietnam. With this experience he bought the government's Korean Air Lines in March 1969. It is said that the government urged Cho to take over the deficit-ridden Korean National Airlines, and he complied despite advice to the contrary from some of his major subordinates. In the end, the venture proved quite profitable, and the purchase price was paid off in five years instead of the contracted ten. By 1977, KAL routes covered much of the world with a fleet of 5 jumbo jets, 4 DC–10s, 6 air buses, and 17 other planes.

DAEWOO: A "NEW GENERATION" CHAEBŎL[23]

In 1975 Daewoo was the seventh largest chaebŏl in terms of value added (see Table B–7 for selected quantitative indicators). It is of particular interest for two reasons. First, it is in all probability the fastest growing chaebŏl of the 1970s. Second, and more important, it is one of the "new generation" of business groups. Unlike the entrepreneurs discussed previously, Daewoo's founder grew up in an independent Korea (he was eight years old at the time of Liberation) and did not get a start in business until the high-growth years of the 1960s. The group's initial success came in the export trade but soon expanded into export production and, in the mid-1970s, diversified into a variety of areas including construction, electronics, and heavy machinery (see Table B–8 for a complete list).

ENTREPRENEURIAL BACKGROUND

U-jung Kim was born in December 1936 to a family of educators. Both his parents were among the limited number of college graduates during the colonial era. His brother, Tŏk-chung Kim, also entered academia as a professor of economics before joining Daewoo in the mid-1970s.

U-jung Kim himself was quite active in extracurricular activities and showed leadership capabilities during his school days. He was the head of

TABLE B-7 Daewoo Group: Quantitative Indicators

	1975			1974			1973		
	(a) Nation	(b) Daewoo	$\frac{b}{a} \times 100$	(a) Nation	(b) Daewoo	$\frac{b}{a} \times 100$	(a) Nation	(b) Daewoo	$\frac{b}{a} \times 100$
Number of companies		16			15			10	
Number of companies in non-agriculture		16			15			10	
Number of companies in manufacturing	22,787[a]	9		22,632[a]	8		23,293[a]	7	
Total sales[d]		109,852			69,089			70,885	
Total manufacturing sales[d]	7,994,143[a]	88,213	1.10	5,438,104[a]	58,647	1.08	3,450,870[a]	62,128	1.80
GDP at factor cost[d]	8,259,280[b]	43,433	0.53	6,307,740[b]	21,741	0.34	4,515,830[b]	22,123	0.49
Non-agriculture value added at factor cost[d]	5,965,970[b]	43,433	0.73	4,625,600[b]	21,741	0.47	3,263,970[b]	22,123	0.68
Manufacturing value added at factor cost[d]	2,088,710[b]	24,501	1.17	1,603,060[b]	15,062	0.94	1,105,300[b]	15,970	1.44
Employment	11,830[e]	24,244	0.21	11,586[e]	14,386	0.12	11,139[e]	11,130	0.10
Employment in manufacturing	2,205[e]	23,022	1.04	2,012[e]	13,624	0.68	1,774[e]	10,772	0.61
Exports[f]	5,081,016	223,871[c]	4.41	4,460,370	153,536[c]	3.44	3,225,025	95,164[c]	2.95

Notes: [a]Source: EPB, *Report on Mining and Manufacturing Survey*, 1973–1975.

[b]Source: BOK, *Economic Statistics Yearbook, 1977.*

[c]The Daewoo Group produces most of the products that it exports. In 1975, 90% of the group's exports were produced by group members, compared with 85% in 1974 and 80% in 1973.

[d]In current million wŏn.

[e]In thousands of workers.

[f]In current thousand U.S. dollars.

TABLE B-8 Daewoo Group: Affiliated Companies

Trading	
Daewoo Industrial Co., Ltd.	1967, est.
Shinsung Tongsang Co., Ltd.	1973, acq.
Textile and Leather Products	
Daewoo Textile Co., Ltd.	1974, acq.
Shinwon Textile Co., Ltd.	1975, acq.
Koryo Leather Industrial Co., Ltd.	1972, acq.
Sambon Incorporated	1976, acq.
Financing	
Korea Capital Corp.	1973, acq.
Orient Investment & Finance Corp.	1973, est.
Dongyang Securities Co., Ltd.	1973, acq.
Daihan Education Insurance Co., Ltd.	1975, acq.
Construction	
Daewoo Development Co., Ltd.	1973, est.
Machinery and Its Sales	
Daewoo Heavy Industries Co., Ltd.[a]	1973, acq.
Daihan Boiler Industrial Co., Ltd.	1976, acq.
Daewoo Machines Sales Co., Ltd.	1976, est.
Electronics	
Daewoo Electronics Co., Ltd.	1974, est.
Engineering	
Daewoo Engineering Co., Ltd.	1976, est.
Cosmetics	
Peeres Cosmetics Co., Ltd.	1975, acq.

Note: [a]Korean Machinery Manufacturing Corp. was acquired in 1976 and merged into this company.

the high school student body's disciplinary division and the president of Yonsei University's student body. Upon graduation he went to work for a trading company.

ENTREPRENEURIAL HISTORY

In 1967 Kim teamed up with three of his close business friends to form their own trading company—Daewoo Industrial Company, Ltd. Kim initially dealt with foreign buyers he knew from his previous job, but rapidly expanded his contacts. The company's growth was impressive. Over the nine-year period, 1967–1976, real Korean exports grew at a simple annual average rate of 35 percent, whereas Daewoo grew at 122 percent (see Table B-9). By 1976, it was exporting over $300 million worth of goods representing about 4 percent of the nation's total exports. This success is in part attributed to a policy of paying employees extremely high wages but demanding comensurately long hours.

TABLE B-9 Daewoo Industrial Co., Ltd.: Growth of Real Exports[a]

	(a) Korea[b]	Annual Growth Rate	(b) Daewoo[c]	Annual Growth Rate	b/a in %
1967	327.4		593		0.18
		38.0		488.0	
1968	451.8		2,894		0.64
		43.8		42.7	
1969	649.8		4,130		0.64
		28.5		106.7	
1970	835.2		8,536		1.02
		29.4		186.9	
1971	1,080.6		24,493		2.27
		50.4		115.7	
1972	1,625.7		52,834		3.25
		58.3		28.2	
1973	2,573.1		67,752		2.63
		8.2		14.5	
1974	2,784.3		77,581		2.79
		23.0		48.3	
1975	3,423.9		115,066		3.36
		35.9		67.1	
1976	4,653.4		192,306		4.13
Average		35.0		122.0	

Notes: [a]Current dollars deflated by export unit value index.
[b] In million 1970 U.S. dollars. Data from BOK, *Economic Statistics Yearbook, 1976.*
[c] In thousand 1970 U.S. dollars. Data from Daewoo Industrial Company, Ltd.

In its first year the company engaged only in trade, but in 1968 it established its own textile plant and added four more by 1972. With its foundation in textiles and trade, the group expanded into finance, construction, electronics, and cosmetics. In 1976 the group took a major new direction when it acquired the infamous Korean Machinery Manufacturing Corporation (Han'gi: see Chapter 4, pp. 127-132). Leaving the group's other operations in the hands of his brother, Kim devoted himself to "turning around" the new acquisition. There is some evidence of success, as Han'gi stock nearly doubled in price in the following year. In 1977 Daewoo took over the financially troubled Shinjin Automobile Manufacturing Company from the same group that had held Han'gi.

Overall, the group's growth has been phenomenal, even by Korean standards. In less than ten years it has grown from a miniscule base to 23 companies with 30 foreign branches and 35,000 employees. Its 1975 sales were nearly a quarter of a billion dollars, and its rate of growth is, if anything, accelerating.

Appendix C
Entrepreneurship Survey

The KDI/HIID "Modernization" studies were conceived on the premise that extensive primary research had already been conducted, and the primary need was to synthesize existing work. The topic of "Government, Business, and Entrepreneurship in Economic Development," however, had heretofore attracted little scholarly attention in Korea, and the gaps dominated the explored areas.

To partially fill this lacuna, a two-part research effort was initiated. First, case studies were made of selected small entrepreneurs, and large conglomerates.[1] Since we could not hope to carry out enough case studies to yield generalized conclusions, it was decided to administer an "Entrepreneurship and Management" questionnaire in a random sample of Korean industries. The depth of the case study approach was thus to be complemented by the breadth of the survey.

Appendix C

SURVEY DESIGN

QUESTIONNAIRE

An initial draft questionnaire was prepared by the two principal authors. Because the comparative disadvantage of economists in such an endeavor was recognized, the participation of a sociologist—Man-Gap Lee—and an anthropologist—Vincent Brandt—was solicited. These two individuals, both with extensive field experience in Korea, assisted in revising the initial questionnaire and added the sections on "Values, Attitudes, and Management Philosophy." Following a field test in 25 firms, a revised and shortened final questionnaire was prepared. Questions cover 5 sets of topics, as follows:

1) Company Characteristics (for example, size, location, product mix): to allow exploration of the extent to which the type of economic activity affects responses to other questions.
2) Entrepreneurship (problems faced in founding or expanding the enterprise, and how they were overcome): to identify the various economic factors which contributed to fulfilling the entrepreneurial function.
3) Social Background (for example, place of birth, family background, job experience, education): to identify any unique social subsets that contributed disproportionately to entrepreneurial success.
4) Government-Business Relationships (opinions on the nature of government-business interaction): to identify extent and techniques of government influence on business and vice versa; and a comparison of the Rhee and Park administrations in this respect.
5) Personal Values and Attitudes (for example, motivation, success criteria, and management philosophy): to suggest attitudinal concomitants of successful entrepreneurship.

There are two versions of the questionnaire—one for "entrepreneurs" and the other for "top managers." Because the latter is a shortened and slightly reworded version of the former, only the entrepreneurs' questionnaire is reproduced below as an appendix. Top managers were added for two reasons: 1) to add perspective on questions such as government-business relations and contributions to enterprise expansion; 2) to provide a control on certain social-background questions where comparable society-wide data is not available.

SAMPLING PROCEDURE

The universe was defined as all manufacturing enterprises listed in the *Han'guk kiŏp ch'ongnam* (Directory of Korean business)[2] as employing more than 50 workers as of June 30, 1975. This resulted in a population of 1,867 firms.[3] Application of a one-in-six equal probability of selection procedure resulted in a sample size of 311 enterprises (after eliminating wholly government-owned enterprises). Table C–1 gives sample characteristics in terms of asset size, location, industry, and year of establishment.

The sample size was determined by a resource constraint rather than by optimal sampling theory. Had we been interested in estimating a single parameter for which we held reasonable priors as to the variance and mean of various subsets, then we would have applied a stratified random-sampling procedure with different probabilities for different strata. This was inappropriate here, however, because we were generally without priors and interested in many different questions whose response distributions would vary independently across strata. Further, we hoped to allow for cross-strata correlation (for example, if northerners were disproportionally represented in the entrepreneurial population, was this explicable in terms of education, class, and/or religious background?) To "fine-tune" our answers in this fashion requires multiple stratified cell observations large enough to be statistically significant. Because we were beginning in ignorance of just how much cross-correlation would be required, it was, therefore, clear that, the larger the sample size, the better. Constraints on interviewer availability and funding made 300 firms the largest feasible level.

SURVEY EXECUTION

Interviews were conducted by 15 sociology students from Ewha Womans University, most of whom had had prior survey interview experience.[4] Training began with a one-day seminar on interviewing techniques. Each interviewer then pre-tested the draft questionnaire in two enterprises outside the sample. A half-day session was then held to discuss problems encountered and, after questionnaire revision and shortening, an additional instructional seminar was held to insure common interpretation of the questionnaire. Interviews were then conducted during February 1976.

All sample firms were sent three letters—from the Deputy Prime Minister, KDI, and HIID. These explained the purpose of the survey, stressed the national interest in the results, and guaranteed anonymity. Enterprises that were initially reluctant were subjected to repeated visits by interviewers and telephone calls from the KDI staff.

Despite these measures, the success rate was poor, amounting to only about 40 percent of the sample in the case of the entrepreneurship version. The problem was gaining access to chief executives; once this was attained, the 45-minute interview generally went smoothly. Managers were much easier to interview.

Appendix C

TABLE C-1 Sample Characteristics

(%)

1. *Location*[a]	
Seoul	56.9
Pusan	8.0
Seoul vicinity	3.9
Kyŏnggi province	12.9
Kangwŏn province	0.6
S. Ch'ungch'ŏng province	4.2
N. Ch'ungch'ŏng province	1.9
S. Chŏlla province	2.9
N. Chŏlla province	1.6
S. Kyŏngsang province	4.8
N. Kyŏngsang province	2.0
Cheju Island	0.3
TOTAL	100.0

2. *Asset Size*[b]	
0– 0.1	31.2
0.1– 0.2	17.0
0.2– 0.4	17.4
0.4– 0.8	10.3
0.8– 1.5	6.1
1.5– 3.0	7.7
3.0– 5.0	2.2
5.0–10.0	2.9
10.0–20.0	4.2
20.0–50.0	1.0
TOTAL	100.0

3. *Industry*	
Foodstuffs	6.1
Beverages	1.9
Fibers and textiles	13.8
Clothes and leather	7.4
Lumber and wood	2.3
Paper and publishers	6.1
Petroleum, coal and chemicals	13.2
Medicine and medical instruments	4.5
Cement, glass, and clay	4.8
Basic metals	3.5
Fabricated metals	6.1
Machines	7.4
Electrical and electronic products	13.5
Transport equipment	2.6
Miscellaneous	6.8
TOTAL	100.0

4. *Establishment Date*	
1975	0.6
1974	3.9
1973	14.2
1972	9.4
1971	7.8
1970	7.5
1969	5.5
1968	5.2
1967	7.4
1966	6.8
1965	4.5
1964	1.9
1963	2.3
1962	3.9
1952–1961	14.2
1946–1951	1.9
Pre–1945	2.9
TOTAL	99.9

Source: Data from Han'guk Saengsansŏng Ponbu, *Han'guk kiŏp ch'ongnam* (Seoul, 1975).

Notes: [a]Main plant only. Some readers may be surprised at this distribution, particularly the very low representation of North Kyŏngsang province. A check against the entire population in the *Han'guk kiŏp ch'ongnam* shows that our sample does not differ from the population in a statistically significant way. The population is 2.7% from North Kyŏngsang province whereas our sample is 2.0%.

[b]Billion wŏn as of June 1975.

To improve the response rate, two additional steps were taken. First, it was thought that a foreigner might gain access where a college student failed. Accordingly, a pilot group of 11 recalcitrant firms were visited by an interviewer, a KDI research assistant, and the American researcher. The results were: 1 additional interview ultimately compelted; 6 assurances from junior executives of support that never materialized; 3 chief executives too "ill" to be interviewed; and 1 failure to get past the guard at the door. This was deemed an unproductive use of time.

In the second stage of response upgrading, we accepted the fact that we could not gain direct access to all chief executives and lowered our sights to a "reduced questionnaire" distributed by mail.[5] The primary aim was to attain a statistically significant response to the more straightforward empirical questions. A secondary purpose was to ascertain the extent to which the original respondents differed from the non-respondents, in order to see whether or not we could safely generalize from our limited number of full respondents. This effort, coupled with additional telephone prodding, yielded an additional 74 observations.

The final results were as given in Table C-2. While the final response rate was thus 63 percent of the sample as a whole, it amounted to 74 percent of the "effective" sample (after eliminating the "could not respond" category). The reliability of the resulting response pattern will now be evaluated.

SURVEY RELIABILITY

The results of our survey may be biased in three ways. First, there is a "no-response" problem, since the omitted firms may differ from the included ones. Second, there is a "partial-response" problem, since those chief executives which were willing to submit to an interview may differ from those who were only willing to fill out a reduced questionnaire. Third, there is a "distorted response" problem, since the recorded answers may deviate from the actual circumstance or opinion. These possibilities will be evaluated in turn.

TABLE C–2 Survey Response Categories

		Number	Percent
Response		196	63
Full	(122)		
Reduced	(74)		
Would not respond		69	22
Could not respond		46	15
Misclassified[a]	(6)		
Failed[b]	(40)		
Total		311	100

Notes: [a]Trading organizations misclassified in source as engaged in manufacturing. [b]Enterprise failed between mid-1975 date and early 1976 interviewing. Includes 11 known failures and 29 failures assumed on grounds that enterprise was no longer at listed address, no address could be found, and neighbors knew nothing about the firm. Some of these cases no doubt reflected a change of name and location rather than strict failure, but the firms were probably at the margin of existence.

NO-RESPONSE PROBLEM

We can generalize from our survey results only to the extent that the omitted firms are similar to the included firms. For the no-response firms we have data only on assets, sales, profits, value added,[6] and location. The greater the similarity of the "response" and "would not respond" sets in these variables, the greater the chance that the other responses would be similar.

Tables C–3 and C–4 give comparative data on the available indicators. First, consider the various size comparisons of the response and "would not respond" sets as given in Table C–3. For assets, sales, profits, and value added, the *t* values (from 0.09 to 0.15)[7] are such that we accept the null hypothesis that the two sets have the same mean.[8]

A look at the location differentials in Table C–4 reveals that the opposite conclusion holds. Again comparing the "response" and "would not respond" sets, Chi^2 values are large enough that we reject the null hypothesis of no difference in location. This is an expected result of interviewer assignment bias. For obvious reasons of transport efficiency, companies were assigned to interviewers on a geographic rather than a random basis. Interviewer success rates varied from 30 percent to 95 percent, and this produced different geographic success rates (for example, Seoul is over-represented and Pusan is underrepresented). There is every reason to believe that these differences reflected variable interviewer tenacity and the difficulties of transport rather than the differences in provincial willingness to cooperate. With differential response thus a function of the survey procedure rather than the response set, then it is appropriate to eliminate

TABLE C-3 Size Differences of Sample Sections

		Assets		*Sales*		*Profits*		*Value Added*	
	n	$\bar{x}$	*t*	$\bar{x}$	*t*	$\bar{x}$	*t*	$\bar{x}$	*t*
Would not respond	69	2,916		2,496		131		600	
			>0.77		>0.10		>0.09		>0.15
Response	196	2,193		2,600		139		637	
			>2.07*		>1.68		>1.65		>1.88
Could not respond	46	414		712		7		152	
Full response	122	1,266		1,912		58		413	
			>2.93**		>1.64		>2.72**		>2.33*
Partial response	74	3,722		3,733		273		1,005	

Notes: $\bar{x}$ ≡ mean in million wŏn
t ≡ absolute *t* value
* ≡ significant at 95% value
** ≡ significant at 99% value

TABLE C-4 Location Differentials of Sample Subsets
(%)

	Would not respond	*Response*	*Full Response*	*Partial Response*
Seoul	47.8	56.1	58.2	52.7
Pusan	14.5	6.1	5.7	6.7
Seoul vicinity	4.4	4.6	3.3	6.8
Other Kyŏnggi province	20.3	9.7	5.7	16.2
Ch'ungch'ŏng province	2.9	7.7	9.0	5.4
Chŏlla province	1.5	6.6	8.2	4.0
Kyŏngsang province	8.7	7.7	8.2	6.8
Kangwŏn province and Cheju Island	0.0	1.5	1.6	1.4
TOTAL	100.1	100.0	99.9	100.0
Number	69	196	122	74
Chi^2 value	15.278		8.885	
	V		Λ	
Critical value (0.95,7)	14.070		14.070	

the bias by weighting the responses to compensate for variable non-response rates. This is explained below.

PARTIAL-RESPONSE PROBLEM

We can compare the "full" and "partial" response sets on many more dimensions than the "response" and "would not respond" sets. Consider first the various measures of size already presented in Table C–3. It would be possible to report that "in terms of sales, the full and partial response sets are not significantly different at the 95 percent level; and in terms of value added, the differences are not significant at the 99 percent level" and go on to accept the null hypothesis. However, for profits and assets, the two sets are significantly different even at the 99 percent level; at the 90 percent level, all variables are significantly different. We must therefore in conscience admit the probability of size bias and adjust by reweighting as explained below. The adjustment is critical, since many answers vary with firm size.

Tests were also done on location (Table C–4), establishment date, export share, founder/chief-executive relationship, birthplace, number of male siblings, and father's job. In all cases *t* and Chi^2 values were low enough to not reject the null hypotheses at the 95 percent level, although a few were rejectable at 90 percent. We feel that these divergences are acceptable and make no attempt to adjust by reweighting along any of these dimensions.

DISTORTED RESPONSE PROBLEM

Recorded responses may be misleading if the question is ambiguous or if the interviewee feels it is in his best interest to be less than candid. The first problem was hopefully minimized by our pre-test and training procedures, but the second possibility must be borne in mind throughout.

The problem of distorted response is most conspicuously reflected in the absence of any question on class origin. In the United States, entrepreneurs are quick to stress their humble origins and project the image of a self-made man. In Korea, the reverse is true—today, everyone usually pretends to come from the elite *yangban* class. Following the pre-test, we dropped the class-origin question and instead must rely on loose inference from ancestral occupation.

Distorted responses are particularly likely in sections dealing with government relationships; our "guarantee" of anonymity was not uniformly accepted as ironclad. "Values-and-attitudes" questions are suspect, since "effective" values may differ from the "image" values a manager wishes to project and may even differ from the conscious self-image of the manager.

All of these problems must be dealt with on a question-by-question basis. In the most problematic cases, we have not even reported the results; this is particularly common in the values-and-attitudes area. Basically, however, our solution is to stress comparative rather than absolute responses, (that is, the role of government under Rhee as opposed to Park; the opinions of managers versus those of founders; and support of large versus small firms or exporters versus domestic producers). This comparative device adds a measure of respectability to our interpretations, but in the end it is very much a subjective effort. Other readers will no doubt attach different meanings to our results. This is as it should be, for a major purpose of the survey is to stimulate research into a neglected area of Korean economic history.

REWEIGHTING

The weights for each group i are calculated as follows:

$$w_i = \frac{n_i^s / n_\Sigma^s}{n_i^a / n_\Sigma^a}$$

where n is the number of enterprises, and s and a subscripts designate the originally drawn sample and the actual achieved sample respectively. Applying the weights to the achieved sample produces a weighted sample with the same distribution as the originally drawn sample, but of the same size as the achieved sample. The effect is similar to that of replacing missing observations with the mean of similar achieved observations, except that in this case, the size of the weighted sample would be that of the drawn sample. Note that we are weighting *observations* rather than *responses* so that, for example, the standard deviation is:

$$s = \sqrt{\frac{\Sigma\,(x_i-\bar{x})^2 w_i}{n-1}} \qquad \text{and } not \qquad s = \sqrt{\frac{\Sigma\,(w_i x_i-\bar{x})^2}{n-1}}$$

Two different weighting systems were used:

1) For questions on the "reduced-form" questionnaire, we have an achieved sample of 196 firms which differs from the drawn sample only in location (see pp. 370–371). Accordingly, when dealing with these questions, we use a 196-firm sample weighted by location only.
2) For questions on the "reduced-form" questionnaire, we have an achieved sample of 122 firms, which differs from the drawn sample in both location and size (see pp. 371–372). Accordingly, when dealing with these questions, we used a 122-firm sample weighted by both location and value added. That is, w_i are calculated for each of $i = 80$ cells of an eight location by ten value-added decile matrix.

Unless otherwise noted, all results reported in the text are based on these weighted samples.

Appendix D
Survey Questionnaire

This is an English translation of the questionnaire used in the Entrepreneurship Survey described in Appendix C. Questions indicated by a box around the number (for example, [1]) were included in the "reduced-form" version.

Enterprise I.D. No. ☐

Interviewer ______________________

Date ____________ Time: from ____________

to ____________

Name of respondent: ______________________

Name of company ______________________

Name of chief executive ______________________

Date established ______________________

Address: Main office ____________ Phone ____________

Plant(s) ____________ Phone ____________

____________ Phone ____________

	1973	1974	1975
Total assets	______	______	______

Total sales	______	______	______
Net profits	______	______	______

I. *Company History*

[1.] a. When was the company established?

Date ______

Location ______

b. If the plant was not established by the present owner, when was it acquired?

1) Date ______

2) Location ______

3) From whom?

a. Japanese, directly ( )

b. Japanese, via government ( )

c. Korean, going concern ( )

d. Korean, failing or bankrupt ( )

e. Other (specify) ______

4) If the present location of the company is different from that of establishment (or acquisition), when did the company move here?

2. a. Have you had any expansion projects?

Yes ( ) No ( )

b. If so, when and where?

	Date	Location
1st expansion started	______	______
2nd expansion started	______	______
3rd expansion started	______	______
4th expansion started	______	______
5th expansion started	______	______

[3.] [a.] What was your 1975 average employment of regular workers?

______

[b.] At establishment-acquisition? After each major expansion?

Establishment	______	1st expansion	______
Acquisition	______	2nd expansion	______
		3rd expansion	______
		4th expansion	______
		5th expansion	______

[4.] What are your major products? How has their production capacity grown? (100 = acquisition, establishment, or initial production under expansion program).

	1	2	3	4	5
Product	______	______	______	______	______
Acquisition-Establishment	______	______	______	______	______
1st expansion	______	______	______	______	______
2nd expansion	______	______	______	______	______
3rd expansion	______	______	______	______	______
4th expansion	______	______	______	______	______
5th expansion	______	______	______	______	______
Present	______	______	______	______	______

5. What is the composition of those major products?

Product	1	2	3	4	5	Other	Total (%)
Acquisition-Establishment							100
1st expansion							100
2nd expansion							100
3rd expansion							100
4th expansion							100
5th expansion							100
Present							100

[6.] What is the domestic-export sales composition for each of your major products?

Unit: %

Product	1		2		3		4		5	
Market	Dom	Exp	Dom	Exp	Dom	Exp	Dom	Exp	Dom	Exp
Time										
Acquisition-Establishment										
1st expansion										
2nd expansion										
3rd expansion										
4th expansion										
5th expansion										
Present										

7. What is the present financial structure of your company? At establishment-acquisition?

	Est. or Acq.	Now
Debt	____%	____%
Equity (paid-in capital plus retained surplus)	____%	____%
Total	100%	100%

8. a. Is your enterprise a member of any industrial trade association?
   Yes ( ) No ( )

   b. If so, when did you join? Was membership voluntary or compulsory?

Trade association	Year joined	Voluntary	Compulsory
1) ____	____	( )	( )
2) ____	____	( )	( )
3) ____	____	( )	( )
4) ____	____	( )	( )
5) ____	____	( )	( )

II. *Entrepreneurship*

[9.] Is the current chief executive of the firm:
a. founder (first generation) ( )
b. second generation (son or other relative) ( )
c. unrelated manager ( )
d. others (specify) ____

10. If the current chief executive is not the founder, is the founder:
a. deceased ( )
b. retired ( )
c. active in parent or related company (specify) ____
d. active in another field (specify) ____

e. other (specify) ______________________________

(Note to interviewers: questions 11 thru 16 for founders only)

11. When you began production, which of the following statements applied?

a. The major product was new to Korea	( )
b. Production was new to Korea (but the product had been sold here before)	( )
c. The production process was new to Korea (but the product had been made here previously)	( )
d. Production process had been used previously in Korea	( )

12. How did you first get the idea to get into this business?

a. previously employed in company producing same product	( )
b. previously trader of same product	( )
c. previously user of this product	( )
d. saw local use of imported product and decided I could produce it	( )
e. saw other local producer and thought I could do better	( )
f. suggested by foreigners	( )
g. suggested by government	( )
h. saw during foreign travel	( )
i. other (specify) ______________________________	

13. From the time you began actively pursuing the idea until operations began, how long did it take?

______________________ months

14. In *establishing* your enterprise, a number of problems had to be solved. Please indicate the degree of difficulty you encountered in each.

	Very difficult		Some problem		Simple	Not applicable
a. perception of opportunity and market identification	1	2	3	4	5	( )
b. obtaining financing	1	2	3	4	5	( )
c. plant design, technology, and construction	1	2	3	4	5	( )
d. getting technicians and training	1	2	3	4	5	( )
e. government support and permits	1	2	3	4	5	( )
f. recruiting personnel, setting up an organization, and managing people	1	2	3	4	5	( )
g. importing capital equipment	1	2	3	4	5	( )
h. importing intermediates	1	2	3	4	5	( )
i. other (specify) ____________	1	2	3	4	5	( )

15. In solving these problems, you may have had help from others. Please indicate all significant participants (if you had 2 or more, please rank).

		DOMESTIC										FOREIGN				
		1	2	3	4	5	6	7	8	9	10	11	12	13	14	15	16
		self	employee(s)	friends and relatives	other individuals	commercial and special banks	other financial institutes	other private companies	government proper	government agency	military	other (specify)	private companies	government	banks or financial institutes	military	other (specify)
a.	perception of business opportunity and market identification	☐	☐	☐	☐	☐	☐	☐	☐	☐	☐	____	☐	☐	☐	☐	____
b.	obtaining financing	☐	☐	☐	☐	☐	☐	☐	☐	☐	☐	____	☐	☐	☐	☐	____
c.	production process choice and plant design	☐	☐	☐	☐	☐	☐	☐	☐	☐	☐	____	☐	☐	☐	☐	____
d.	plant construction	☐	☐	☐	☐	☐	☐	☐	☐	☐	☐	____	☐	☐	☐	☐	____
e.	getting technicians and training	☐	☐	☐	☐	☐	☐	☐	☐	☐	☐	____	☐	☐	☐	☐	____
f.	government support and permits	☐	☐	☐	☐	☐	☐	☐	☐	☐	☐	____	☐	☐	☐	☐	____
g.	recruiting personnel, setting up organization structure and managing people	☐	☐	☐	☐	☐	☐	☐	☐	☐	☐	____	☐	☐	☐	☐	____

16. How important were each of the following types of government assistance in contributing to your final decision that this would be a profitable project?

	Critical		Moderately important		Irrelevant
a. direct tax reductions-exemptions	1	2	3	4	5
b. tariff reductions-exemptions on imported inputs	1	2	3	4	5
c. tariff protection on output	1	2	3	4	5
d. exclusive licensing privileges	1	2	3	4	5
e. direct government subsidies	1	2	3	4	5
f. knowledge of long-run government development strategy	1	2	3	4	5
g. government provision of social overhead capital (that is, transport, communications, utilities)	1	2	3	4	5
h. confidence in government's ability to maintain favorable business climate	1	2	3	4	5

(Note to interviewer: questions 17 to 23: founder; Answer for *recent* expansion project. non-founder; Answer for *early* expansion project.)

17. When was your most recent (or earliest) expansion?

____

18. When you began production:
    a. Was your major product new to Korea? ( )
    b. Was production new to Korea? ( )
    c. Was the production process new to Korea? ( )
    d. Was the product new to your firm? ( )
    e. If the product was not new, was the process new to your firm? ( )
    f. Existing product and process ( )

19. How did you first get the idea to initiate the expansion project?
    a. previously employed in company producing same product ( )
    b. previously trader of same product ( )
    c. previously user of this product ( )
    d. saw local use of imported product and decided we would produce it ( )
    e. saw other local producer and thought I could do better ( )
    f. suggested by foreigners ( )
    g. suggested by government ( )
    h. saw during foreign travel ( )
    i. other (specify) ______________________________ ( )

20. From the time you begin actively pursuing the idea until operations began, how long did it take?

______________________________ months

21. In your expansion, a number of problems had to be solved. Please indicate the degree of difficulty you encountered in each.

	Very difficult		Some problem			No problem
a. perception of opportunity and market identification	1	2	3	4	5	( )
b. obtaining financing	1	2	3	4	5	( )
c. plant design, technology, and construction	1	2	3	4	5	( )
d. getting technicians and training	1	2	3	4	5	( )
e. government support and permits	1	2	3	4	5	( )
f. recruiting personnel, setting up an organization, and managing people	1	2	3	4	5	( )
g. importing capital equipment	1	2	3	4	5	( )
h. importing intermediates	1	2	3	4	5	( )
i. other (specify) __________	1	2	3	4	5	( )

22. In solving these problems, you may have had help from others. Please indicate all significant participants. (If 2 or more, please rank.)

		DOMESTIC										FOREIGN				
		1	2	3	4	5	6	7	8	9	10	11	12	13	14	15	16
		self	employee(s)	friends and relatives	other individuals	commercial and special banks	other financial institutes	other private companies	government proper	government agency	military	other (specify)	private companies	government	banks or financial institutes	military	other (specify)
a.	perception of business opportunity and market identification	☐	☐	☐	☐	☐	☐	☐	☐	☐	☐	____	☐	☐	☐	☐	____
b.	obtaining financing	☐	☐	☐	☐	☐	☐	☐	☐	☐	☐	____	☐	☐	☐	☐	____
c.	production process choice and plant design	☐	☐	☐	☐	☐	☐	☐	☐	☐	☐	____	☐	☐	☐	☐	____
d.	plant construction	☐	☐	☐	☐	☐	☐	☐	☐	☐	☐	____	☐	☐	☐	☐	____
e.	getting technicians and training	☐	☐	☐	☐	☐	☐	☐	☐	☐	☐	____	☐	☐	☐	☐	____
f.	government support and permits	☐	☐	☐	☐	☐	☐	☐	☐	☐	☐	____	☐	☐	☐	☐	____
g.	recruiting personnel, setting up organization structure, and managing people	☐	☐	☐	☐	☐	☐	☐	☐	☐	☐	____	☐	☐	☐	☐	____

23. How important were each of the following types of government assistance in contributing to your final decision that this would be a profitable project?

	Critical		Moderately important		Irrelevant
a. direct tax reductions-exemptions	1	2	3	4	5
b. tariff reductions-exemptions on imported inputs	1	2	3	4	5
c. tariff protection on output	1	2	3	4	5
d. exclusive licensing privileges	1	2	3	4	5
e. direct government subsidies	1	2	3	4	5
f. knowledge of long-run government development strategy	1	2	3	4	5
g. government provision of social overhead capital (that is, transport, communications, utilities)	1	2	3	4	5
h. confidence in government's ability to maintain favorable business climate	1	2	3	4	5

(Note to interviewer: there is no question 24. Question 25 is to be answered only in the case of acquisition.)

25. How important were each of the following types of government assistance in contributing to your final decision that acquisition would be profitable?

	Critical		Moderately important		Irrelevant
a. direct tax reductions-exemptions	1	2	3	4	5
b. tariff reductions-exemptions on inputs	1	2	3	4	5
c. tariff protection on output	1	2	3	4	5
d. exclusive licensing privileges	1	2	3	4	5
e. direct government subsidies	1	2	3	4	5
f. knowledge of long-run government development strategy	1	2	3	4	5
g. government provision of social overhead capital (that is, transport, communications, utilities)	1	2	3	4	5
h. confidence in government's ability to maintain favorable business climate	1	2	3	4	5

III. *Social Background*

[26.] What is your age? ____________ years

[27.] What was your place of birth? Your father's?

	Self	Father
a. Seoul	( )	( )
b. Pusan	( )	( )
c. Kyŏnggi province	( )	( )
d. Kangwŏn province	( )	( )
e. Ch'ungch'ŏng province	( )	( )

	Self	Father
f. Kyŏngsang province	( )	( )
g. Chŏlla province	( )	( )
h. Hamgyŏng province	( )	( )
i. P'yŏngan province	( )	( )
j. Hwanghae province	( )	( )
k. Cheju Island	( )	( )
l. Other (specify)	________	________

28. What is your family origin (*pon*)? ____________________

[29.] Were you primarily raised in:

a. Seoul ( )
b. Other city or province (*to*) capital ( )
c. Town where county office (*kunch'ŏng*) is located ( )
d. Rural village or place where district office (*myŏnsamuso*) is located ( )
e. Japan ( )
f. Other foreign country (specify) ____________________

[30.] a. How many sons and daughters did your parents ever have (including self)?

____

b. What is your male sibling rank (*myŏttchae adŭl*)?

No. ____________________

[31.] What was the primary occupation of your father? Your paternal grandfather?

	Father		Grandfather (Paternal)
a. Farming			
1) Landowner	( )	______Chŏngbo	( )
2) Independent owner-operator	( )	______Chŏngbo	( )
3) Mixed owner-tenant	( )	______Chŏngbo	( )
4) Tenant	( )	______Chŏngbo	( )
5) Other (specify)	________		________
b. Fishing			
1) Large owner	( )		( )
2) Small owner-operator	( )		( )
3) Laborer			
c. Industry	( )		( )
1) Large owner (over 200 employees)	( )		( )
2) Small and medium owner-operator	( )		( )
3) Manager			
Foreign firm	( )		( )
Korean firm	( )		( )
4) Technician	( )		( )
5) Clerical	( )		( )
6) Worker	( )		( )
d. Government			

Time		Yi Dynasty	Japanese Colony	Liberal Party	Post 5.16
Ranking	Father Grandfather				

	Father	Grandfather
e. Teacher		
1) Traditional Confucian	( )	( )
2) Primary school	( )	( )
3) Middle school	( )	( )
4) College or university	( )	( )
f. Politician	( )	( )
g. Journalist	( )	( )
h. Trade	( )	( )
1) Domestic trade		
a) self-employed: retail	( )	( )
b) self-employed: wholesale or large retail	( )	( )
c) employee (foreign-owned firm)	( )	( )
d) employee (Korean firm)	( )	( )
2) Foreign trade (import and export)		
a) self-owned	( )	( )
b) employee (foreign-owned firm)	( )	( )
c) employee (Korean firm)	( )	( )

i. Military

Position / Relation	Enlisted		Officer	
	Ranking	Branch of the Service	Ranking	Branch of the Service
Father				
Grandfather				

	Father	Grandfather
j. Laborer (urban)	( )	( )
k. Financial institution employee	( )	( )
l. Professional (lawyer, doctor, etc.)	( )	( )
m. Money lender	( )	( )
n. Craftsman	( )	( )
o. Other (specify) _________	( )	( )

[32] How strong was the influence of each of the following religions for you?

	Very strong		Moderate		Irrelevant
a. Confucianism	1	2	3	4	5
b. Buddhism	1	2	3	4	5
c. Catholicism	1	2	3	4	5
d. Protestantism	1	2	3	4	5
e. Other (specify) _________	1	2	3	4	5

IV. *Education*

[33] How many years of formal education have you completed? Your father?

self: ________years father: ________years

34. Under what system was most of your pre-college education? Your father?

	Self	Father
a. Traditional Confucian	( )	( )
b. Japanese colonial school	( )	( )

	Self	Father
c. Modern Korean school after Independence	( )	( )
d. Foreign (specify)	( )	( )

35. If you graduated from a higher educational institution:
    a. institution ______________________________
    b. major field ______________________________
    c. the institution was
        1) technical college ( )
        2) junior college ( )
        3) college ( )
        4) university ( )
        5) military academy ( )
        6) graduate school ( )
36. How was your higher education financed?
    a. parents ______%
    b. relatives ______%
    c. self ______%
    d. scholarship ______%
    e. other (specify) ______%
37. How many months have you spent in special training programs related to your profession (in addition to your formal education)?
    a. domestic ______ months
    b. Japan ______ months
    c. other foreign (specify) ______ months
    d. nothing

V. *Work Experience*

38. How long have you been with this company?
    ______ years ______ months
39. How long have you held your current rank?
    ______ years ______ months
40. Excluding the company you now work for, how many years have you spent in each of the following lines of work?

	years	months
a. government		
b. military: officer		
c. military: enlisted		
d. financial institution		
e. trading company (export-import)		
f. domestic trading company		
g. private Korean-owned industry		
h. private foreign-owned industry		
i. government-owned enterprise		
j. professional		
k. employee of foreign military or government		
l. other (specify)		
* total employment outside present company		

41. In preparing yourself for your present job, how important were each of the following factors?

	Very important		Moderately important		Unimportant
a. formal education	1	2	3	4	5
b. job during colonial period	1	2	3	4	5
c. job related to allied military	1	2	3	4	5
d. work in family business	1	2	3	4	5
e. other work experience	1	2	3	4	5
f. military experience	1	2	3	4	5
g. government experience	1	2	3	4	5
h. foreign language ability	1	2	3	4	5
i. other (specify)___________	1	2	3	4	5

VI. *Government-Business Relationships*

[42.] To what extent can you (or your company) influence government policies affecting your business?

a. can get anything ( )
b. can frequently affect ( )
c. can sometimes affect ( )
d. seldom affect ( )
e. affect not at all ( )
f. other (specify)______________

43. If you can have some influence on government economic policy, how frequently are the following methods used?

	Used very often		Sometimes used		Never used
a. direct formal impersonal appeal to government	1	2	3	4	5
b. direct informal personal appeal to government officials	1	2	3	4	5
c. indirect appeal through business association	1	2	3	4	5
1) Industrial Trade Association	1	2	3	4	5
2) Chamber of Commerce	1	2	3	4	5
3) Small and Medium Industrial Association	1	2	3	4	5
4) Federation of Korean Industries	1	2	3	4	5
5) Korean Traders Association	1	2	3	4	5
6) Other (specify)__________	1	2	3	4	5
d. indirect personal appeal through politician	1	2	3	4	5
e. indirect impersonal appeal through political party	1	2	3	4	5
f. indirect impersonal appeal through newspaper	1	2	3	4	5
g. other (specify) ___________	1	2	3	4	5

44. Once the current government has made a decision affecting business, how effective is it in insuring compliance? What about the Rhee Government?

	Current	Rhee
a. Always implemented; impossible to avoid complying	( )	( )
b. Almost always implemented; sometimes possible to avoid complying	( )	( )
c. Implemented with modification	( )	( )
d. Seldom thoroughly implemented	( )	( )
e. Don't know	( )	( )

45. If the current government wishes to influence the conduct of a business, how important are the following means of transmitting the request?

	Used very often		Sometimes used		Never used
a. general impersonal law	1	2	3	4	5
b. specific regulation for one firm	1	2	3	4	5
c. personal request	1	2	3	4	5
d. request via industrial association	1	2	3	4	5
e. other (specify)__________	1	2	3	4	5

46. If the government wishes to influence the conduct of a business, how important are the following means of insuring compliance?

	Used very often		Sometimes used		Never used
a. incentives, privileges	1	2	3	4	5
b. moral exhortation	1	2	3	4	5
c. "friendly persuasion"	1	2	3	4	5
d. making example of one firm	1	2	3	4	5
e. explicit threats	1	2	3	4	5
f. other (specify)__________	1	2	3	4	5

47. How often do you meet personally with government officials at different levels concerning business matters?

	Never	Once a year	Several a year	Once a week	Daily
a. President, Prime Minister	1	2	3	4	5
b. DPM and minister	1	2	3	4	5
c. Vice minister/assistant minister	1	2	3	4	5
d. Bureau director	1	2	3	4	5
e. Division head or below	1	2	3	4	5
f. Local government officials	1	2	3	4	5

48. The government affects your operations in many ways. In each of the following areas, would you rate their involvement as having a positive, negative, or neutral effect on your business? If you were in business under the Rhee Government, please rate them on the same items.

	Very positive		Neutral		Very negative	Rhee Govern-ment
a. establishing business	1	2	3	4	5	( )
b. conducting ongoing operations	1	2	3	4	5	( )
c. expanding business	1	2	3	4	5	( )
d. foreign marketing	1	2	3	4	5	( )
e. domestic marketing	1	2	3	4	5	( )
f. obtaining foreign financing	1	2	3	4	5	( )
g. obtaining domestic financing	1	2	3	4	5	( )
h. stimulating general level of economic activity	1	2	3	4	5	( )
i. controlling prices	1	2	3	4	5	( )
j. providing long range planning	1	2	3	4	5	( )
k. controlling unfair competition	1	2	3	4	5	( )
l. key industry rearing and social overhead capital formation	1	2	3	4	5	( )
m. other (specify)	1	2	3	4	5	( )
n. don't know.						( )

[49.] Please list the two important ways in which the current government is an improvement over that of the Rhee Government in contributing to the economic development of Korea.

a. ______________________

b. ______________________

[50.] Please list the two most important things you think the government should change in order to further improve the business climate.

a. ______________________

b. ______________________

VII. *Questions on Managerial Practices*

51. In order to invest in a new project, what return on equity do Korean entrepreneurs in companies of your size generally expect (after paying all expenses including tax)? What about in 1960?

Now ______________% 1960 ______________%

52. Do your employees ever play an important role in innovative decision-making?

	Often		Some-times		Never
a. developing new products	1	2	3	4	5
b. identifying new markets	1	2	3	4	5
c. introducing new process of production	1	2	3	4	5
d. introducing cost reducing modification of production process	1	2	3	4	5
e. change in management organization	1	2	3	4	5
f. other (specify)______________	1	2	3	4	5

53. In general, in Korea *today*, how important are the following in attaining a high ranking job in a company? How about under the Rhee Government?

	Today					Rhee
	Very important		Moderately important		Unimportant	
a. merit	1	2	3	4	5	( )
b. personal ties within company	1	2	3	4	5	( )
c. outside influence	1	2	3	4	5	( )
d. school prestige	1	2	3	4	5	( )
e. experience within firm	1	2	3	4	5	( )
f. experience in previous job	1	2	3	4	5	( )
g. government experience	1	2	3	4	5	( )
h. military experience	1	2	3	4	5	( )
i. other (specify) ________	1	2	3	4	5	( )

54. On the average, how many hours per week are worked in your company by:

a. ordinary workers
   1) technicians _______hrs.
   2) administrators _______hrs.

b. high-ranking staff _______hrs.

c. the chief executive _______hrs.

55. In country A, employees are hired on a merit basis and fired whenever they perform below expectations. In country B, employees are hired for life, become part of a business family, and are seldom released. Is your country closer to A or B?

	Life employment				Fired quickly
a. managers, technicians, executives	1	2	3	4	5
b. workers	1	2	3	4	5

VII. *Values, Attitudes, and Opinions*

56. In general, how important do you think the following factors are in motivating successful Korean entrepreneurs?

	Very important		Moderately important		Unimportant
a. personal goal achievement					
1) pursuit of excellence	1	2	3	4	5
2) fame and power	1	2	3	4	5
3) wealth	1	2	3	4	5
b. family responsibility	1	2	3	4	5
c. community responsibility	1	2	3	4	5
d. patriotism					
1) originating from the fact the south is in confrontation with the north or in a semi-war situation with north.	1	2	3	4	5
2) originating from the Japanese colonial-imperial experience.	1	2	3	4	5
3) other (specify)__________	1	2	3	4	5

57. What do you think the general opinion among your entrepreneurial peers is on each of the following statements?

	Strongly agree	Agree	Neutral	Dis-agree	Strongly dis-agree
a. You should not accept the idea of your boss if you think it is wrong.	1	2	3	4	5
b. You should not accept an under-the-table request by the government even if failure to comply will have a unfavorable impact on your business	1	2	3	4	5
c. To achieve an objective, one sometimes has to take certain measures which might be considered somewhat questionable legally.	1	2	3	4	5

58. How important do you think the following factors are in distinguishing successful Korean entrepreneurs from those who are less successful?

	Successful have much more	Some more	Same	Some less	Successful have less
a. conscientious hard work	1	2	3	4	5
b. willing to take risks	1	2	3	4	5
c. intelligence	1	2	3	4	5
d. skill in handling people	1	2	3	4	5
e. skill in handling government officials to get support	1	2	3	4	5
f. good formal education	1	2	3	4	5
g. greater personal or familial capital (inheritance)	1	2	3	4	5
h. on-the-job training and experience	1	2	3	4	5
i. rational and scientific way of thinking	1	2	3	4	5
j. good luck	1	2	3	4	5
k. good network of friends	1	2	3	4	5
l. willingness to make unpopular decisions	1	2	3	4	5
m. other (specify) ________	1	2	3	4	5

Notes
Bibliography
Index

Notes

ONE *Introduction*

1. The real annual compound rate of GNP growth was 4.2% from 1953 to 1962 and 9.8% from 1962 to 1975. Further, the variance was nominal: the highest rate of growth in the pre-1962 period (7.7% in 1957) was lower than all but two of the rates (6.1% in 1965 and 7.0% in 1972) in the post-1962 period. BOK, *Economic Statistics Yearbook: 1976* (Seoul, 1977).

2. Including "size of traditional sector, extent of dualism, degree of urbanization, character of basic social organization, size of the indigenous middle class, extent of social mobility, extent of mass communication, crude fertility rate, and the degree of modernization of outlook." Irma Adelman and Cynthia Taft Morris, *Society, Politics and Economic Development: A Quantitative Approach* (Baltimore, 1967), pp. 151, 152, 170.

3. Gilbert T. Brown, *Korean Pricing Policies and Economic Development in the 1960's* (Baltimore, 1973), p. 265.

4. The "enterprise" sector sells its output, while the "institutional" sector, largely government, does not. The "unorganized" sector loosely refers to small production activities such as agriculture, petty commerce, and handicrafts.

5. John Maynard Keynes, *The End of Laissez Faire* (London, 1927), p. 40.

6. For a more comprehensive survey in a similar spirit, see Edward S. Mason, *Economic Planning in Underdeveloped Areas* (New York, 1958).

7. Eli F. Heckscher, "Mercantilism" in ***Revisions in Mercantilism,*** ed. D. G. Coleman (London, 1969), p. 32.

8. Keynes, pp. 46–47.

9. Adam Smith, *The Wealth of Nations* (New York, 1937).

10. William J. Baumol, *Welfare Economics and the Theory of the State* (Cambridge, Mass., 1969), p. 51.

11. For a succinct summary, see Kenneth J. Arrow, "The Organization of Economic Activity: Issues Pertinent to the Choice of Market versus Non-market Allocation," in *Public Expenditure and Policy Analysis,* eds. Robert H. Haveman and Julius Margolis (Chicago, 1970), pp. 59-73.

12. Kenneth J. Arrow, "Uncertainty and the Welfare Economics of Medical Care," *American Economic Review,* (December, 1963), p. 947.

13. Albert O. Hirschman, "Ideology: Mask or Nessus Shirt?", in *Comparison of Economic Systems,* ed. Alexander Eckstein (Berkeley, 1971), p. 294. For a contrasting view on the role of ideology, see Alexander Gerschenkron, "Ideology as a System Determinant," in *Comparison of Economic Systems,* pp. 269-288.

14. Talcott Parsons, "Some General Theories in Sociology," in *Theoretical Sociology*, ed. John McKinney and Edward Tyriakian (New York, 1970).

15. Bert Hoselitz, "Economic Policy and Economic Development," in *The State and Economic Growth*, ed. Hugh J. Aitken (New York, 1959), pp. 325-352.

16. Keynes, p. 31.

17. Ibid., p. 47.

18. For example, Alexander Eckstein, "Individualism and the Role of the State in Economic Growth," *Economic Development and Cultural Change* (Vol. 6, 1957 & 1958), pp. 81-87.

19. A particularly strong exposition of this view is found in Harry Johnson, "Planning and the Market in Economic Development," in *Economic Development: Readings in Theory and Practice*, eds. Theodore Morgan and George Betz (Belmont, Calif., 1970), pp. 289-299.

20. Hugh Patrick and Henry Rosovsky, eds., *Asia's New Giant: How the Japanese Economy Works* (Washington, D.C., 1976).

21. Tjalling C. Koopmans and John Michael Montias, "On the Description and Comparison of Economic Systems," in *Comparison of Economic Systems: Theoretical and Methodological Approaches*, ed. Alexander Eckstein (Berkeley, 1971), pp. 27-78.

22. Benjamin Ward, "Organization and Comparative Economics: Some Approaches," in *Comparison of Economic Systems*, pp. 103-133.

23. The Korean chaebŏl is equivalent to the Japanese zaibatsu. See Chapter 8.

TWO *The Colonial Heritage*

1. The following is our interpretation and synthesis of several sources:

Ho Chin Choi, *The Economic History of Korea* (Seoul, 1971), pp. 139–187; Daniel Sungil Juhn, "Entrepreneurship in an Underdeveloped Economy: The Case of Korea, 1890–1940" (PhD dissertation, George Washington University, 1965), pp. 12–62; Woo Keun Han, *The History of Korea* (Seoul, 1970), pp. 229–255, 298–315.

2. Ho Chin Choi, *Economic History of Korea*, p. 197; Paul W. Kuznets, *Economic Growth and Structure in the Republic of Korea* (New Haven, 1977), p. 19.

3. There were also 4 Chinese-owned factories with 42 workers. Juhn, p. 30.

4. Juhn, pp. 33–34; Ki-Zun Zo, "Types of Enterpreneur in Modernization Process of Korean Economy," in *Report of International Conference on the Problems of Modernization in Asia* (Seoul, 1966), pp. 618–619.

5. Ki-Zun Zo, p. 619.

6. Ki-jun Cho, *Han'guk kiŏpka sa* (Seoul, 1973), pp. 17–20.

7. For a summary, see Kozo Yamamura, "A Reexamination of Entrepreneurship in Meiji Japan (1868–1912)" in *Entrepreneurship and Economic Development,* edited by Peter Kilby (New York, 1971), pp. 267–286.

8. Sang-Chul Suh, *Growth and Structural Changes in the Korean Economy, 1910–1940* (Cambridge, Mass., 1978), p. 119, (Table 56).

9. Juhn, p. 47.

10. Ibid., p. 48.

11. Ki-Zun Zo, "Types of Entrepreneur," p. 618.

12. Juhn, pp. 68–71.

13. Sang-Chul Suh, p. 100.

14. For a detailed discussion of the group, see Appendix B, pp. 344–349.

15. Sang-Chul Suh, p. 106.

16. Ibid., p. 194.

17. Ibid., p. 180.

18. Ibid., p. 193.

19. Ibid., p. 185.

20. George M. McCune, *Korea Today* (Cambridge, Mass., 1950), p. 332.

21. Table 1, and Sang-Chul Suh, p. 50, Table 21. Change is overstated, since 1910 figures are for household heads.

22. McCune, pp. 332–333.

23. See Table 5.

24. Juhn, p. 122.

25. Calculated from Sang-Chul Suh, pp. 196, 246.

26. Juhn, pp. 131, 140.

27. Gregory Henderson, "Japan's Chosen: Immigrants, Ruthlessness and Developmental Shock," in *Korea Under Japanese Colonial Rule* (Kalamazoo, 1973), pp. 268–269. See Chapter 7 for a reflection of the Japanese experience in the motives of modern entrepreneurs.

28. Sang-Chul Suh calculates trade dependency (exports plus imports over GNP) at approximately 55% in 1938–1939. Suh, p. 120, Table 57. Modern trade ratios were 22% in 1961, 40% in 1970, 47% in 1972, and leapt to 67% in 1973. Computed from BOK, *Economic Statistics Yearbook, 1976*.

29. Kyŏng-nam Yi, *Han'guk ŭi kiŏpka* Vol. 2, (Seoul, 1976), pp. 113–114.

30. To our knowledge, no serious study has been made of this critical feature of Korean economic history. An excellent exploratory survey has been made by Harold Koh, upon whom we rely throughout this section. Harold Koh, "The Early History of U.S. Economic Assistance to the Republic of Korea, 1945–1955," (Mimeo., Harvard Institute for International Development, Cambridge, Mass., September 1975). Available statistics are highly inconsistent, befitting the chaos of the period. For additional coverage, see Myŏng-su Hwang, *Kiŏpka sa yŏn'gu* (Seoul, 1976), pp. 316–321. Ch'ang-hwan Sŏng, *Han'guk kyŏngjeron* (Seoul, 1959), pp. 80–104.

31. Sung Hwan Ban, Pal Yong Moon, and Dwight H. Perkins, Studies in the Modernization of the Republic of Korea: 1945–1975, *Rural Development*, (Cambridge, Mass., 1980), pp. 283–297.

32. Kwang Suk Kim and Michael Roemer, "Macroeconomic Growth and Structural Change in Korea," (Seoul, KDI Working Paper 7705, April 1977), p. 40.

33. Ch'ang-hwan Sŏng, p. 82.

34. See Chapter 5 for the fate of these public enterprises.

35. U.S. Armed Forces in Korea, *South Korea Interim Government Activities* (No. 28, January 1948), p. 10. Another source says that only 17% of the plants were shut down in June 1948. This may in part reflect an increase over the intervening 6 months, but probably is largely attributable to a distinction between plants that were open and those that were producing. Also, the army figure is much more consistent with the levels of production actually achieved. See Ch'ang-hwan Sŏng, p. 84.

36. E. Grant Meade, *American Military Government in Korea*, (New York, 1951), p. 49. Meade himself had 9 months of civil affairs training but only a one-hour lecture on Korea.

37. See Joungwon A. Kim, *Divided Korea: The Politics of Development, 1945–1972*, (Cambridge, Mass., 1975), pp. 47–85.

38. McCune, p. 98.

39. Meade, pp. 67, 203–212.

40. Ibid., p. 204. The People's Committee was the local branch of the "People's Republic of Korea" which took de facto control of the government upon surrender and later jousted with the occupation forces for control.

41. Ibid., p. 210.
42. McCune, p. 100.
43. Joungwon Kim, p. 84.
44. W. Reeve, *The Republic of Korea: A Political and Economic Study* (London, 1963), p. 103.
45. Ibid., p. 103.
46. Roy W. Shin, "The Politics of Foreign Aid: A Study of the Impact of United States Aid in Korea from 1945 to 1966" (PhD dissertation, University of Minnesota, 1969), p. 51.
47. United Nations Command, Office of the Economic Coordinator, "Fiscal Year 1955 Congressional Presentation," (Seoul, March 1954), p. 20.
48. Moon Hwan Choi, "A Review of Korea's Land Reform," *Koreana Quarterly* (Spring 1960), p. 67.
49. According to one study of 11 plants, sales price ran between 38% and 82% of the "government estimated price." How this price was determined is not explained. Myŏng-su Hwang, p. 319.
50. For a somewhat similar position stressing the failure of the government to utilize the vested properties, see Ho-jin Ch'oe, "Kwisok chaesan purha wa kongŏphwa ŭi chwajŏl, 1945–1953" in *Han'guk kyŏngje chŏng-ch'aek samsimnyŏn sa* (Seoul, 1975).

THREE *Government Economic Decision-Making Process*

1. Economic growth, of course, need not be considered a primary end. It may be valued for its contribution to human happiness, which in turn may be valued as service to some theistic principle.
2. Adelman and Morris, pp. 237–238.
3. Ibid., p. 246.
4. Ibid., p. 246 and the correlation matrix on p. 290.
5. David C. Cole and Princeton Lyman, *Korean Development* (Cambridge, Mass., 1971), p. 27.
6. Ibid., p. 166.
7. Ibid., p. 167.
8. Park Chung Hee, *The Country, the Revolution and I* (Seoul, 1970), p. 26.
9. Park Chung Hee, *Our Nation's Path* (Seoul, 1970), pp. 39–40.
10. Maeil Kyŏngje Sinmun Sa, *Pak Chŏng-hŭi taet'ongnyŏng ŭi chido inyŏm kwa haengdong ch'ŏrhak* (Seoul, 1977), p. 42.
11. Park Chung Hee, *The Country, the Revolution and I*, p. 31. Also

see the section entitled "Foreign Aid with Emphasis on Consumer Goods and its Consequences," pp. 36–38.

12. Joe Won Lee, "Planning Efforts for Economic Development," in Joseph S. Chung, ed., *Patterns of Economic Development: Korea,* (Detroit, 1966), p. 2.

13. Ibid., p. 5.

14. David C. Cole and Young Woo Nam, "The Pattern and Significance of Economic Planning in Korea," in *Practical Approaches to Development Planning*, edited by Irma Adelman (Baltimore, 1969), p. 32.

15. Article One of Puhŭngbu chojikpŏp (the Ministry of Reconstruction Organization Law), Presidential Decree Number 1001, February 17, 1955.

16. W. Arthur Lewis, *Development Planning: The Essentials of Economic Policy*, (London, 1966), p. 245.

17. Sŏk-chun Cho, "Kyehoek," in Han-bin Yi, et al., eds., *Han'guk haengjŏng ŭi yŏksajŏk punsŏk, 1948–1967* (Seoul, 1969), p. 409.

18. Hahn-Been Lee, *Korea: Time, Change, and Administration* (Honolulu, 1968).

19. In 1956, the Ministry of Reconstruction did prepare a Five-Year Reconstruction Plan, but this plan was hurriedly put together to be shown to the visiting U.S. Secretary of State, Mr. Dulles. See, Sŏk-chun Cho, "Han'guk kunsa chŏngbu ha e issŏsŏ ŭi tugaji haengjŏng kaehyŏk e kwanhan pigyo yŏn'gu" in *Han'guk haengjŏng nonch'ong* 6.2:97–98 (1968).

20. Hahn-Been Lee, p. 91.

21. Ibid.

22. David Cole and Young Woo Nam, p. 33.

23. Ibid., p. 100.

24. Sŏk-chun Cho, "Han'guk kunsa chŏngbu."

25. Hahn-Been Lee, p. 123.

26. Sŏk-chun Cho, "Chojik," in *Han'guk haengjŏng ŭi yŏksajŏk punsŏk, 1948–1967* (Seoul, 1969), p. 428.

27. This operates to the advantage of large businesses as well as government. See Chapter 7.

28. ROK, "Chŏngbu chojik kaep'yŏn e kwanhan pŏpkyu," July 22, 1961.

29. The Ministry of Reconstruction was replaced by the Ministry of Construction in May 1961 and made responsible for long-range planning, resource budgeting, national construction work, regional development, etc. The Economic Development Council was absorbed into the Ministry.

30. This group of civilian advisers contacted government officials, BOK staff, and business associations for inputs of data and opinions. At the same time, they made use of the previously prepared but unimplemented

plan of the Chang Myon regime. For details, see Sŏk-chun Cho, "Han'-guk kunsa chŏngbu," p. 103.

31. The Military Revolution took place on May 16, and the directives were handed to the government by civilian advisers on July 18. Ibid., p. 105.

32. David Cole and Young Woo Nam, p. 34.

33. Consideration of alternative planning models began nearly two years before the plan was finalized. Ibid., p. 19.

34. See ROK, *The Second Five-Year Development Plan, 1967–1971*, pp. 122–128.

35. This proposal was not implemented immediately, but deferred until the end of the plan period when the Korea Development Institute was established.

36. Working committees can be classified into two broad categories—those committees dealing with macro aspects of the plan and those dealing with specific industrial projects. Members included government officials, scholars, businessmen, bank staff, researchers, and foreign advisers.

37. This council was established in December 1963 to advise the President regarding important policy decisions on economic development and the promotion of science.

38. See David Cole and Young Woo Nam, pp. 36–37.

39. ROK, *The Third Five-Year Economic Development Plan, 1972–1976*, p. 1.

40. David Cole and Young Woo Nam, p. 35.

41. Lawrence Westphal and Irma Adelman, "Reflections on the Political Economy of Planning: the Case of Korea," in Sung Hwan Jo and Seong Yawng Park, eds., *Basic Documents and Selected Papers of Korea's Third Five-Year Economic Development Plan (1972–1976)* (Seoul, 1972), p. 24.

42. This committee was established in March 1969 to advise the DPM. It consists of vice ministers and heads of government agencies, representatives of national banking institutions, representatives of business associations, and scholars. It included a USAID official as an observer. The committee is chaired by the vice minister of EPB. The committee can organize working groups when necessary to work out details of the plan. Actually, these working groups formulated plans which were finally adjusted by the Coordinating Committee.

43. This committee was established to assist the prime minister in setting basic directions and taking important policy measures in the formulation of the plan. The committee consists of all ministers, heads of national banking institutions, business association heads, scholars, representatives of journalists' associations, labor associations, etc.

44. In February 1970, this committee was established to coordinate and

adjust plans prepared by the Working Committee. Members consist of ministers of economic affairs and a few scholars. A few foreign observers were also invited.

45. Westphal and Adelman, p. 18.

46. Ibid., p. 17.

47. Ibid., p. 20.

48. ROK, *Second Five-Year Economic Development Plan, 1967–1971* (Seoul, July 1966), p. 122.

49. For documentation, see the section entitled "Executive Supremacy" in Chitoshi Yanaga, *Big Business in Japanese Politics* (New Haven, 1968), pp. 103–107.

50. Ibid., p. 105.

51. Data provided by Secretariat of the National Assembly. By period, the share of passed legislation initiated by the executive branch is:

Rhee regime (May 1948–April 1960)	62.5%
Chang Myon regime (July 1960–May 1961)	57.1%
December 1963–June 1967	46.4%
September 1967–June 1971	65.6%
July 1971–October 1972	84.6%

The government-initiated share of economic legislation after 1972 was unattainable, but presumably was even higher.

52. For an analysis along these lines, see Tong-sŏ Pak, "Haengjŏng kwa chŏngch'i," in *Han'guk haengjŏng ŭi yŏksajŏk punsŏk, 1948–1967* (Seoul, 1969), pp. 61–71.

53. Chitoshi Yanaga, pp. 100–101.

54. For example, see *Sŏul Kyŏngje Sinmun*, June 10, 1977.

55. We cannot vouch for all the details of this story, but feel it is a plausible reflection of the way things are done. See *Sŏul Kyŏngje Sinmun*, January 16, 1974.

56. The magic number of 10 is said to have been decided on the "objective" grounds that it was the number of such leading companies in Japan.

57. Translation based on article reported in *Sŏul Kyŏngje Sinmun*, August 31, 1977.

58. Gregory Henderson, *Korea: The Politics of the Vortex* (Cambridge, Mass., 1968).

59. Philip Trezise and Yukio Suzuki, "Politics, Government and Economic Growth in Japan," in *Asia's New Giant: How the Japanese Economy Works*, (pp. 753–812), ed. Hugh Patrick and Henry Rosovsky (Washington, 1976), p. 756.

60. For a summary, see Patrick and Rosovsky, pp. 48–49.

61. Ibid., pp. 48–49.

62. For example, see "Korea, Inc.—'Volcano With the Lid On,'" *Busi-*

ness Week August 1, 1977. Reprinted in: *Asian Wall Street Journal*, August 4, 1977.

63. Chitoshi Yanaga, p. 70.

64. Eugene Kaplan, *Japan: The Government-Business Relationship* (Washington, 1972), p. 16.

65. Ibid., p. 15.

66. For one version of the meeting, see Yong-wan Kim, "Kuttăe kŭ ildŭl" (Memoirs), *Dong-A Ilbo*, May 12, 1976.

67. Ando, Yoshio, "Zaikai no Chii to Yakuwari," *Ekonomisuto* (December 1957), p. 16. Quoted in: Chitoshi Yanaga, p. 32.

68. Han'guk Muyŏk Hyŏphoe, *Muyŏk yon'gam* (Seoul, 1974).

69. For a description of the Japanese manifestation, see Chitoshi Yanaga, pp. 12–13.

70. Contrary to expectations, "direct formal impersonal appeals" rank much higher than "direct informal personal appeals." This may be due to response bias.

71. Small firms rate the government more favorably only on controlling prices and competition, which is natural, since it is the larger firm whose prices and practices are subject to control.

72. Exporters rate the government higher on "domestic financing" because the prime source of export credit is via domestic financial institutions.

FOUR *Implementation of Government Policy*

1. Eli F. Heckscher, *An Economic History of Sweden* (Cambridge, Mass., 1954), p. 10.

2. Jawaharal Nehru, quoted in Albert Waterston "A Hard Look at Development Planning" in *Economic Development: Readings in Theory and Practice*, eds. Theodore Morgan and George Betz (Belmont, California, 1970), p. 403.

3. For a summary and a bibliography, see Hans-Helmut Taake, "The Implementation of Development Plans: Organization and Policies," in *The Developing Economies*, March 1975, pp. 22–36.

4. Gunnar Myrdal, *Asian Drama: An Inquiry into the Poverty of Nations* (New York, 1968), p. 935.

5. E. S. Kirschen, et al., *Economic Policy in Our Time* (3 vols., Amsterdam, 1968), pp. 15–16.

6. Robert A. Dahl and Charles E. Lindbloom, *Politics, Economics, and Welfare: Planning and Politic-Economic Processes Resolved into Basic Social Processes* (New York, 1953); Koopmans and Montias, "Description and Comparison."

7. Dahl and Lindbloom, pp. 99–109.

8. Our usage diverges somewhat from that of Dahl and Lindbloom, resulting in our attributing a much larger role to command. See Dahl and Lindbloom, pp. 106–109.

9. Koopmans and Montias, p. 58.

10. The penalty can, of course, be psychological: i.e., loss of "face" and public esteem if non-compliance is exposed. In the event that social control has progressed to the point where an individual receives positive pleasure from paying his taxes, then the instrument becomes field manipulation. We ignore this possibility.

11. Myrdal, p. 903.

12. Ibid., p. 904.

13. Ibid., p. 904.

14. Ibid., p. 933.

15. Ibid., p. 905.

16. Albert O. Hirschman, *The Strategy of Economic Development* (New Haven and London, 1958), p. 145.

17. Myrdal, p. 904.

18. EPB, *Major Statistics of the Korean Economy: 1977* (Seoul, 1977), p. 7.

19. Ibid.

20. Ibid.

21. The distortion premia are estimated from the "thin" market for the limited free foreign exchange sold at auction. It is thus an overestimate of the price that would have obtained had all exchange been freely sold.

22. For details, see Charles Frank, Kwang Suk Kim, and Larry Westphal, *Foreign Trade Regimes and Economic Development: South Korea* (New York, 1975).

23. Frank, Kim, and Westphal, pp. 36–37, 44–45, 48–49, 58–63.

24. Ibid., p. 44.

25. Ibid., p. 61.

26. A non-discretionary intervention may be structured with varying degrees of particularism; e.g., a tariff may be levied on all goods, on all manufactures, or on cement of a particular quality in particular size bags from a particular company.

27. Official rate plus premia were above 300 constant 1965 wŏn per dollar in the late 1950s and fell to 213 in 1970. See Table 14, columns A, D, and F.

28. Wontack Hong, "Trade, Distortions and Employment Growth in Korea," (Seoul, 1977).

29. The omissions, however, may be even greater in the 1950s than in

the 1960s, because data on tax and tariff exemptions were not available until 1962.

30. For a similar story of the "push" effects of exchange-rate reform, see Gustav F. Papanek, *Pakistan's Development: Social Goals Private Incentives* (Cambridge, Mass., 1967).

31. In other circumstances, rate unification would have a further benefit (independent of the rate itself) if the premia and subsidies were discretionary. In the Korea of the 1950s, however, premia dominated and these were essentially non-discretionary.

32. Most notably in 1955 and 1959. Brown, p. 132.

33. Export Day was established on November 30, 1964, when Korea celebrated the first 100 million dollar export mark in its history.

34. The first 100 million award went to Hanil Synthetic Fiber in 1973. The first 200 million award went to Samsung Mulsan Co. in 1975. The first 300 million awards went to Samsung Mulsan Co., Hyundai Shipbuilding and Heavy Industries Co., Ltd. and Daewoo Industrial Co., Ltd. in 1976.

35. Section 2, Article 26 of the Corporate Tax Law.

36. ROK, Office of National Tax Administration, *Statistical Yearbook of National Tax*, 1976.

37. *Chosŏn Ilbo*, July 24, 1976.

38. Brown, p. 101.

39. For evidence of the electricity subsidy, see Yŏng-sik Chang, *Han'guk chŏllyŏk suyo mit kagyŏk ŭi punsŏk* (Seoul, 1977). For grain and fertilizer, see P'ar-yong Mun and Pyŏng-sŏ Yu, *Nongsanmul kagyŏk punsŏngnon* (Seoul, 1975).

40. Liabilities over Net Worth. BOK, *Economic Statistics Yearbook, 1976*, pp. 128–129. For a detailed discussion, see Il SaKong, "An Overview of Corporate Finance and the Long-Term Securities Market" in *Planning Model and Macroeconomic Policy Issues*, edited by Chuk Kyo Kim (Seoul, 1977).

41. BOK, Ibid., p. 179.

42. Decomposition into 1960s and 1970s yields no discernible trend in the savings/equity/debt flow breakdown. Within the debt category, however, there is a clear shift towards domestic financial institutions and away from "other" domestic sources. This is in part a result of institutionalization of financial intermediation functions and in part a result of increased accuracy in flow-of-funds accounting.

43. In 1976, the government's shares in the Commericial Bank of Korea were entirely divested, and this was hailed as a step in "privatization." The buyer, however, was the Korean Traders Association, which is hardly an independent body and, in any event, has no ties to any particular chaebŏl group.

44. In-sang Song, "Anjŏng kuch'uk kwa sŏngjang ŭi mosaek," in *Han'-guk kyŏngje chŏngch'aek samsimnyŏn sa*, edited by Chŏn'guk Kyŏngje Yŏnhaphoe, (Seoul, n.d.), p. 113.

45. See Chapter 8 for a more detailed treatment.

46. Article 2 of the Law of April 17, 1961.

47. Joungwon Kim, p. 153.

48. Chin-hyŏn Kim, "Pujŏng ch'ukchae ch'ŏri chŏnmalso," *Sindonga*, December 1964, p. 160.

49. This measure was taken together with the interest rate reform of October 1965.

50. The council is chaired by the Minister of the Economic Planning Board (DPM) and consists of various economic ministers, governors of special banks, and other private members designated by the President. See Article 49 of The President's Emergency Measure Regarding Economic Stability and Growth, August 3, 1972.

51. Ibid., Article 50.

52. Ibid., Article 51.

53. Ibid.

54. Until nationalization in both countries in the first half of the 1970s.

55. Jorgen Lotz and Elliot Morss, "Measuring 'Tax Effort' in Developing Countries," in *I. M. F. Staff Papers*, November 1967, pp. 478–499.

56. For a more sophisticated measure of tax effort, see Roy W. Bahl. "A Regression Approach to Tax Effort and Tax Ratio Analysis," in *I. M. F. Staff Papers*, November 1971, pp. 570–612.

57. Raja J. Chelliah, "Trends in Taxation in Developing Countries," in *I. M. F. Staff Papers*, July 1971, pp. 254–331.

58. *Chosŏn Ilbo*, July 24, 1976.

59. *Sŏul Kyŏngje Sinmun,* September 12, 1976.

60. Our description of non-tariff barriers is based on Frank, Kim, and Westphal, pp. 37–38, 48–49, 58–63.

61. Ibid., p. 59.

62. See Appendix B, p. 353.

63. *Dong-A Ilbo*, September 16, 1974.

64. See Appendix B, pp. 354–357 for a wider treatment of this episode and the Hyundai Group as a whole.

65. The Law for the Promotion of the Capital Market, Article 1.

66. Hyŏng-yun Pyŏn, "Inp'ŭlle angjin kwa anjŏnghwa kiban ŭi siryŏn" in *Han'guk kyŏngje chŏngch'aek samsimnyŏn sa*, edited by Chŏn'guk Kyŏngjein Yŏnhaphoe (Seoul, 1975).

67. Soon Chough, "The Economics of Price Supervision," *Seoul National University Economic Review*, December 1968, pp. 51–70.

68. Ibid., p. 59.

69. *Choson Ilbo*, February 7, 1974.
70. Kyu-ŏk Yi, *Sijang kujo wa tokkwajŏm kyuje* (Seoul, 1977).
71. *Sŏul Sinmun*, July 1, 1977.
72. Appendix B, pp. 361–365.
73. Myrdal, p. 66. See also pp. 891–900.
74. Myrdal uses the term "strong state" as the antonym to "soft state" (ibid., p. 898), but we prefer "hard state" as more direct and accurate.
75. Ibid., p. 67.
76. Ibid., p. 895 (emphasis added).
77. See Appendix B, pp. 357–358, and Chapter 8, p. 234.
78. See Chapter 4, pp. 82–83.
79. The mean difference between the response on "Friendly persuasion" and "Incentives and privileges" is statistically significant at the 95% level, but narrower pairings (e.g., "Moral exhortation" versus "Incentives and privileges") are not. Large firms, not surprisingly, report greater use of all mechanisms, but the differences (large versus small) are significant in only two cases. Similarly, export firms generally report a higher level of compliance effort, but the differences (export versus domestic) are in no case significant.
80. It is pedantic to report that these differences are statistically significant, but it is worth noting that this is one of the few opinion questions on our survey in which "eyeballing" confirmed significance. Compare the responses to the question on the helpfulness of various government policies (Chapter 3, pp. 74–77) where the present government is shown superior to the Rhee regime, but only by a statistical test. Responses to the implementation question are similar for large and small firms, exporters and domestic producers, and Seoul and provincial enterprises.
81. See Table 22.
82. Myrdal, p. 921.
83. Montek Ahluwalia, "Income Inequality: Some Dimensions of the Problem," in *Resdistribution with Growth* (pp. 3–37), ed. Hollis Chenery, (London, 1974), p. 14.

FIVE *Public Enterprises*

1. This chapter is largely a summary of another book by one of the co-authors. Extracts are often taken verbatim without citation, and factual information not footnoted here is generally from this source. See Leroy P. Jones, *Public Enterprise and Economic Development: The Korean Case* (Seoul, 1976).

2. Indeed, in extreme cases, such as Indonesia's Pertamina, the size of the public enterprise and the political power of its chief executive may make it even *less* subject to government control.

3. We exclude local government enterprises—largely water works—which contribute only about three-tenths of one percent of GDP. We also omit defense industries run by the military, since no published information is available.

4. Residency General plus regular Korean government. From 1905–1910, Korea was administered by the Residency General which, after 1910, was called the Government General.

5. Government General of Tyosen, *Annual Report on Administration of Tyosen: 1936–37* (Keizyo (Keijō), December 1937), pp. 56, 59.

6. Ibid., p. 57.

7. Ho Chin Choi, *Economic History of Korea*, p. 304.

8. Ibid., pp. 301–304.

9. Park Chung Hee, *The Country, the Revolution, and I*, p. 47.

10. Park Chung Hee, *Our Nation's Path*, p. 218.

11. See Indian Institute of Management at Bangalore, *Overview of Public Enterprise Sector in India* (Bangalore, 1976), Appendix Table 4.

12. Frederic Pryor, "Public Ownership: Some Quantitative Dimensions," in *Public Enterprise* (pp. 3–22) edited by William G. Shepherd (Lexington, 1976).

13. Direct plus indirect domestic linkages are theoretically superior measures, but at this level of generality yield similar results, and present purposes do not warrant the greater expository detail.

14. As measured by the ratio of capital stock to wage bill at the 117 sector level in 1977.

SIX *Private Entrepreneurship: Sources of Expansion*

1. Gross domestic product in constant 1970 prices less shares originating in agriculture, forestry, fisheries, government, and public enterprise. Public enterprise data as in Chapter 5, extrapolated from 1974/1975 to 1976 and from 1963/1964 to 1961. Other figures from: EPB, *Major Statistics of Korean Economy, 1977*, pp. 26, 29.

2. J. A. Schumpeter, *The Theory of Economic Development* (Cambridge, Mass., 1934), p. 74.

3. Hirschman, *Strategy of Economic Development*, p. 27.

4. For a more elaborate exposition of the supply versus demand formulation, as well as an excellent survey of the literature, see Peter Kilby,

"Hunting the Heffalump," in *Entrepreneurship and Economic Development*, ed. Peter Kilby (New York, 1971), pp. 1–40.

5. This is probably an overstatement, since there was a recession in 1975. It was, however, a *Korean* recession, meaning a real growth rate of 8.3%. This is not a dramatic deviation from the long-run 10% mean growth rate, but the resulting profit squeeze would be much more dramatic. Note that the 13% exit rate for our sample in 1975 is much lower than the rates implicit in Table 28 of 30% in 1967 (a recession year) and 25% in 1968 and 1969. Part of the difference might be due to a time trend (with a higher exit rate expected in the more fragile economy of the 1960s), but we believe most of the gap is explained by differences in the size of sampled firms. Table 28 covers *all* corporations and joint-stock companies, while Table 29 includes only those with more than 50 workers. As will be shown below (Table 30) smaller firms are much more vulnerable than larger firms and their exit rate is probably much much higher.

6. See Kyŏng-ŭi Yi, "Chung so kiŏp," in *Han'guk kyŏngjeron*, eds. Hyŏng-yun Pyŏn and Yun-hwan Kim (Seoul, 1977), p. 486.

7. Note that this average conceals a much higher rate of increase in proprietorships through 1969 and an actual decline thereafter.

8. There are, of course, many new young entrepreneurs replacing older ones. The point, however, is that the *net* addition to the stock has been only a minor source of growth.

9. Schumpeter, p. 34.

10. Ibid., p. 66 (emphasis added).

11. See Kilby, p. 3.

12. The mean annual reported growth of productive capacity of our 196 sample firms (less those 6 established in 1974) was 32%, while the median was 16%.

13. Schumpeter, pp. 74–75.

14. Kilby, p. 26.

15. Harvey Leibenstein, "Entrepreneurship and Development," *American Economic Review* (May 1968), pp. 72–92.

16. This is the major area in which the "no-response" problem is serious (see Appendix C). We have relatively few observations on early establishments and very few on early expansions. Accordingly, we are unable to cross-correlate by size and date, and often unable to distinguish pre-1962 from 1963–1968 events.

17. This sample is even smaller than those reported elsewhere in this section, as this question was inadvertently left off the "reduced form" questionnaire.

18. See Table 31 and pp. 177–178.

19. For additional discussion of size bias, see Chapter 3. pp. 75–77, and this chapter, pp. 190–192.

20. In aggregate, for establishment only. Expansion data and breakdown by size, locus of sales, and time are discussed, but are not presented in tabular form for lack of space.

21. Note that we have few observations in the Rhee period, so that what is being compared is early and late Park. Comparing Rhee and Park would presumably yield quite a different time trend.

22. The larger role of private companies is not just a function of the advantage of size, but also reflects the greater likelihood of large companies being members of chaebŏl groups and thus receiving cross-financing.

23. Here again, it is unfortunate that we cannot distinguish between the pre- and post-1962 periods.

24. It is regrettable that our sample was too small to test changes within the pre-1962 period. We had originally broken our data down into pre-1962, 1963–1969 and post-1969, to correspond to stagnation, growth-initiation and sustained-growth periods. Too few pre-1962 observations forced us to merge the first two periods.

25. For an early suggestion of this approach, see F. Harbison, "Entrepreneurial Organization as a Factor in Economic Development," *Quarterly Journal of Economics*, August 1956, pp. 364–379. For a more recent application, see John Harris, "Industrial Entrepreneurship in Nigeria" (PhD dissertation, Northwestern University, 1967). We also draw heavily on Kilby, "Hunting the Heffalump,"; Leibenstein "Enterpreneurship and Development"; and Leibenstein, *Economic Backwardness and Economic Growth* (New York, 1963), pp. 112–143.

26. The specification of a "standard unit" of entrepreneurial time is cumbersome, but is identical with that necessary in any labor market where quality changes. For an alternative specification of quantity, see Leibenstein, *Economic Backwardness and Economic Growth*, pp. 122.

27. These are further dampened by the definition of rent as the present value of a future stream, but these will be affected by expectations so the moving average concept is necessary.

28. See Chapter 7.

29. Hirshman, *Strategy of Economic Development*, p. 7.

30. Strictly, we should say changes in the entrepreneurial market rather than changes in prices in other markets. The perception gap (D^{PTD}-D^{PR}) is on the demand side, but is narrowed by events within the entrepreneurial market. We say "supply side" in the text for rhetorical convenience at the summary stage.

31. Except in the formalistic sense of the price duel of the quantity of information.

SEVEN *Private Entrepreneurship: Supply*

1. Jai Hi Choi, "Traditional Values of Korea and Problems of Modernization," in *Report of International Conference on the Problems of Modernization in Asia*, (Seoul, 1966), p. 82.

2. For a summary, see Everett Hagen, *The Economics of Development* (Homewood, Illinois, 1968), pp. 221–227. Schumpeter, n.1, p. 81.

3. In an interview, response bias renders meaningless answers on parental class. Class can be obtained for a given individual by geneological investigation techniques, but this is well beyond the scope of our current effort. See Appendix C for elaboration.

4. When Koreans speak of province of origin, they generally refer not to place of birth but to *kohyang* which can mean place of birth, ancestral origin, or place where one was raised. This, however, is a vague and imprecise term, and for comparative purposes we follow other Korean sociological studies in using place of birth.

5. See note h to Table 37.

6. The distribution of each elite is significantly different from that of its cohort (5% level, X^2 test).

7. Note that, since we are dealing with stocks rather than flows, it is possible that the current regime has appointed a disproportionate number of Kyŏngsang natives. A breakdown of our entrepreneurial sample by year of establishment provides little support for this view. Firms established prior to 1962 were 24% from Kyŏngsang province; those from 1963–1968, 31%; and from 1969–1975, 25%. Also note that 31% of the vested properties from the Japanese period were in Kyŏngsang province (Chapter 2, Table 7).

8. It would be desirable to push the analysis one step deeper by comparing the distribution of the elites to that of the college-educated population. Unfortunately, we can find no data on the place of birth of college graduates. Given the results of our education section below, we would expect a high correlation between provincial representation in elites and the degree of educational attainment.

9. We ignore the foreign-born group where the number of observations is too small for the distortion factors to be significant.

10. There are also significant differences in age and family size. The former is small enough to be ignored (2.5 years), and we are at a loss to explain the latter.

11. We say "appears," because we have had to rely on sequential partial correlation analysis rather than simultaneous multiple regression. A more rigorous test of the hypothesis would require a larger sample size as well as linked observations on the set of non-entrepreneurs.

12. Gustav F. Papanek, "The Development of Entrepreneurship," *American Economic Review, Supplement*, May 1962, pp. 45–58.

13. Y.A. Sayigh, *Entrepreneurs of Lebanon* (Cambridge, Mass. 1962).

14. Clifford Geertz, *Peddlers and Princes* (Chicago, 1965).

15. Balwant Nevaskar, *Capitalists Without Capitalism* (Westport, Conn., 1971).

16. There are, however, numerous minority sects founded by charismatic leaders whose followers operate sometimes substantial business ventures. The workers receiving little or no compensation, substantial profits accrue to the benefit of the faith or the leader, or both. Internationally, the best known of these groups is the Reverend Sun Myung Moon's Unification Church, whose substantial Korean holdings produce ginseng-based consumer goods and textiles. Much larger is T'ae-sŏn Pak's Changno sect which operates 2 industrial parks producing textiles, candy, and other consumer goods.

17. See top of Table 42.

18. Note that males are much less likely to report religious influence than females (compare lines I-C and I-D of Table 42) so that the relevant base group is males rather than the population as a whole.

19. By "medium" landowner we mean those respondents who classed their fathers as "owner-operators" holding an average of 3.3 chŏngbo (a chŏngbo is a little less than one hectare).

20. Ban, Moon and Perkins, p. 294.

21. Ki Hyuk Park et al, *A Study of Land Tenure System in Korea* (Seoul, 1966), p. 58.

22. There are two sources of bias in this result. The first arises from use of the 1930 cohort as the basis of comparison. Given the rapid change during the 1930s, using 1940 data would have yielded a higher share of the cohort in these occupations. Since only a truncated version of the 1940 census was printed (giving occupation by industry but not by function), no exact figures are available, but the distortion is undoubtedly small, particularly since tenancy increased during the period. It would be most surprising if the 15% figure in 1930 grew to 20% in 1940, and our basic story is not materially affected. A more serious source of bias is respondent exaggeration. This is likely primarily in the "owner-operator" class. No respondent claimed a parent in the mixed tenant/owner-operator group (which represented 8% of the population), and it is possible this is due to exaggeration. Taking outside estimates of both sources of bias, our statement could be modified to "98% came from groups representing up to 25% of society." The limited social mobility remains apparent.

23. A number of other studies have inquired into parental backgrounds,

but most do not publish results with sufficient detail to be useful (e.g., listing simply "farming" as a category).

24. It should be noted that this conclusion applies only to medium- and large-scale industrial entrepreneurs. Hagen Koo's study of petty traders, shopkeepers, and small manufacturers in Chŏnju led into the conclusion that "small business constitutes the most significant avenue of upward social mobility opening the greatest opportunities for manual workers to move into non-manual occupations." Hagen Koo, "Small Entrepreneurship in a Developing Society," (Memphis State University, mimeo, 1976), p. 15.

25. Only 32% of public-enterprise managers were actually from SNU, but 38% of the non-military academy managers came from there.

26. Man-Gap Lee, "Sociological Implications of Modernization in Korea" (Seoul, undated mimeo).

27. Hiroshi Mannari, *The Japanese Business Leaders* (Tokyo, 1974), pp. 85–86.

28. Chong-gi Paek and Yŏng-jung Pak, *Chaebŏl samsimnyŏn sa ŭi tŭrama* (Seoul, 1976), p. 30.

29. This would be further supported if it could be shown that a disproportionate number of the first sons were also first children. We failed to ask this question, as we initially accepted the prevailing stereotype that only male birth order mattered.

30. John Harris has taken the first step in developing the framework for a maximization-based model of entrepreneurial supply. However, the model requires specification before testable hypotheses can be derived from it. Nonetheless, the present effort was stimulated by Harris's work and follows him in spirit. John Harris, "Entrepreneurship and Economic Development," (Cambridge, MIT, Economics Department Working Paper 69, April 1971). Reprinted in *Essays in Honor of Harold F. Williamson*, edited by L. Cain and P. Uselding (Kent State University Press, 1973).

31. Ibid., p. 23.

32. Larger companies' chief executives reported working an average of 57 hours versus 55 for smaller firms, and the difference was significant at the 10% level. Other differences were not significant for export versus domestic, young versus old, etc.

33. See Chapter 4, pp. 101–104 for a discussion of the capital market and leveraging.

34. Schumpeter, p. 93.

35. Geertz, pp. 149–151. A fifth hypothesis deals with the nature of the entrepreneurial function.

EIGHT *Private Economic Power: Problems, Policies, and Prospects*

1. A second problem with business concentration is that technical and allocative efficiency may be reduced by intermarket exploitation (e.g., through transfer pricing, and extending the scope for oligopolistic collusion). We leave this aspect of the problem to others. For a path-breaking approach to this question, see Richard Caves and Masu Uekusa, *Industrial Organization in Japan* (Washington, 1976), especially Chapter 4, "The Role of Intermarket Groups".

2. Yanaga, p. 38.

3. Johannes Hirschmeier and Tsunehiko Yui, *The Development of Japanese Business: 1600–1973* (Cambridge, Mass., 1975), p. 187.

4. Ibid., p. 187.

5. The others coalesced around the large banks. For a survey of *keiretsu*, see K. Bieda, *The Structure and Operation of the Japanese Economy* (Sydney, 1970), pp. 210–221.

6. Hirschmeier and Yui, p. 264.

7. Caves and Uekusa, p. 2. The only vaguely quantitative statement we could find on the contemporary scene is Bain's assertion that "Mitsubishi, Mitsui and Sumitomo control about 40% of Japan's big business, even excluding loosely affiliated firms." With "control" and "big business" undefined, this is of no help. Joe Bain, *International Differences in Industrial Structure* (New Haven, 1966), p. 88.

8. 1960 GNP in constant 1975 dollars was about $10 billion in Pakistan and $48 billion in India compared with $20 billion in Korea in 1975. (From IBRD, *World Bank Atlas*. Washington, 1977). Manufacturing was 28% of GNP in Korea in 1975, and we assume a share of 10 or 15% in India and Pakistan.

9. One conspicuous exception is the Sam Ho Group that was one of the three largest chaebŏl in the early 1960s but now does not even appear on our list of the top 45.

10. For example: Yŏng-nok Kim, "Han'guk Kiŏpka chŏngsin ŭi pansŏng," *Sasanggye* (August 1964); Sŏng-du Kim, *Chaebŏl kwa pin'gon* (Seoul, 1965); Wan-hyŏk Pu, "Chaebŏl kwa ogaenyŏn kyehoek," *Sasanggye* (August 1966); Chang-nyŏl Yi, "Chaebŏl iran muŏt in'ga?" *Sindonga*, November 1966; Man-gi Yi, *Han'guk kyŏngjeron* (Seoul, 1973); and Pyŏng-yun Pak, "Han'guk ŭi chaebŏl," *Sindonga*, December 1975.

11. Kyong-Dong Kim "Political Factors in the Formation of the Entrepreneurial Elite in South Korea," *Asian Survey* (May 1976), p. 469.

12. Leibenstein, *Economic Backwardness and Economic Growth*, pp. 111–119.

13. Ibid., pp. 117–118.
14. Yŏng-nok Kim, pp. 37–38. Emphasis added.
15. Kyong-Dong Kim, p. 468.
16. Sŏng-du Kim, pp. 23–24.
17. Joungwon Kim, p. 152.
18. Ibid., p. 157.
19. Kyong-Dong Kim, p. 464.
20. For a more detailed development of this process and its policy implications, see KDI, "Kiŏp chŏngch'aek ŭi kibon panghyang," (Seoul, March 1974).
21. For example, see Kyong-Dong Kim, p. 473.
22. The Special Law for Dealing with Illicit Wealth Accumulation of April 17, 1961.
23. Issued on May 28, 1961.
24. At the 1962 demand price from Table 12.
25. Article 1 of the law. According to the bank's estimate, A and B groups together own 648 pieces of non-operating real estate amounting to 18,290,000 p'yŏng (one p'yŏng is approximately equivalent to 4 square yards). Its estimated value is 42 billion wŏn or 87 million dollars. Reported in *Sŏul Kyŏngje Sinmun*, December 28, 1975.
26. Article 50 of the law.
27. According to the Presidential Implementation Order for the law, the level was set as follows: in case of business firms, the amount is 1 billion wŏn, and in case of individuals, it is 100 million wŏn. (Article 38 of the Implementation Order).
28. See Chapter 4, pp. 130–132.

NINE *Summary*

1. *First Economic White Book* of 1884 as reported in Hirschmeier and Yui, p. 77.

APPENDIX A *Case Studies of Small and Medium Enterprises*

1. *First Economic White Book* of 1884 as reported in Hirschmeier and the additional cost (100,000 wŏn/month) of a driver is part of the normal expense of operating a car.
2. Ethnographic note: Although many Koreans, particularly successful

ones, are noisy, flamboyant, and inclined to arrogance, the Confucian ideal of restraint, dignity, and inner integrity is still widely respected.

3. Although this case perhaps does not strictly qualify as small industry, it is included because I have a great deal of accurate information about Mr. Lee, and in a very general sense his path to success is not atypical of the whole period since the Korean War.

4. In Korea such shops are *heavily* manned, with a couple of young apprentices for every mechanic.

5. Most of this "sensitive" information was told to me by age mates of Mr. Lee from the same village who had also migrated to Inch'ŏn or Seoul.

6. His reputation at home was not high, because he had gotten into trouble for cutting firewood on other people's land and poaching fish from others' traps.

7. This policy was changed in the late 1960s.

8. Mr. Hwang was generally vague and evasive about money amounts.

9. This phrase is heard fairly frequently as a description of ambition or the motivation to succeed. It contrasts with the resigned acceptance of one's assigned role in society or before the misfortunes dealt out by fate or circumstance. It is not entirely praiseworthy under traditional Confucian canons of behavior.

APPENDIX B *Chaebŏl Case Studies*

1. In terms of 1975 value added. See Table 55.

2. References used for this company are as follows: 1) Yŏng-gu Cho, ed., *Kyŏngsŏng Pangjik osimnyŏn, 1919–1969* (Seoul, 1969); 2) Ki-jun Cho, *Han'guk kiŏpka sa*; 3) Yŏn-su Kim, "Chaegye hoego" reported in *Sŏul Kyŏngje Sinmun* during the period of January 8–July 31, 1975; 4) *Samyang osimnyŏn* (Seoul, 1974); 5) Kyŏng-nam Yi, *Han'guk ŭi kiŏpka,* vol. 1 (Seoul, 1973); and 6) various newspaper articles.

3. Ki-jun Cho, p. 257.

4. Ibid., pp. 261–267.

5. His family owned about 900 chŏngbo of rice paddy and 380 chŏngbo of dry land.

6. Information included in this section comes from a variety of sources including: 1) interview with Pyŏng-ch'ŏl Yi; 2) Yi's memoir reported in *Sŏul Kyŏngje Sinmun* during the period of April 7–July 26, 1976; 3) Kinji Yajima, *Challenge of Korean Economy* (Tokyo, 1977); 4) Kyŏng-nam Yi, *Han'guk ŭi kiŏpka,* Vol 1; 5) company-provided data; and 6) "Samsŏng Kujung," *Hyŏndae Kyŏngyŏng*, March 1977.

7. Internationally, the group would rank 293rd in *Fortune's* list of

"the 500 Largest Industrial Corporations Outside the U.S." based on sales. *Fortune*, August 1976, p. 237.

8. Yi's memoir reported in *Sŏul Kyŏngje Sinmun*, July 26, 1976.

9. The domestic trading was carried out by the Samsung Sanghoe established in 1938. A part of the trading was sales of Korean products, e.g., fruits and dried fish to Manchuria.

10. The wholesale price index increased 150% from 1951 to 1952 and 217% from 1952 to 1953.

11. In 1976, Cheil Wool Textile Co., Ltd. and Cheil Synthetic Textile Co., Ltd.–its sister company established in 1972–together exported U.S. $53 million worth of textile products.

12. He purchased 85% of Hŭngŏp (today's Hanil), nearly 50% of Cho-Heung, and 30% of Commercial Bank of Korea.

13. Chin-hyŏn Kim, p. 172.

14. There was another person whose illicitly accumulated wealth was higher than Mr. Yi, but that was largely the result of illegal foreign exchange flight.

15. The official reason was the difficulty of getting foreign loans.

16. Various sources were used for this section. They include: 1) interviews with Chu-yŏng Chŏng; 2) data provided by the group; 3) Kyŏng-nam Yi, *Han'guk ŭi kiŏpka*, Vol. 2, (Seoul, 1976); and 4) various newspaper reports.

17. Table 55 gives Lucky as slightly larger than Hyundai, but, given the crudeness of our estimates, the difference is hardly significant. See Table B–3 for detailed quantitative estimates of Hyundai's activities.

18. The brother remains the number-two man in the group as of this writing.

19. Ninety-nine kilometers in length, including 39 bridges.

20. Based on Hyundai projects reported in *Application for Prequalification* (Seoul, Hyundai Construction, Co., Ltd.).

21. See Chapter 4, pp. 119–120 for President Park's role.

22. Sources of information for this section include: 1) interviews with Mr. Cho; 2) data provided by the group; 3) Kyŏng-nam Yi, *Han'guk ŭi kiŏpka*, Vol. 1; and 4) various newspaper articles.

23. Data sources include: 1) company-provided data; 2) "Taeu kurup" in *Hyŏndae Kyŏngyŏng*, May 1977; 3) interviews with Tŏk-chŏng Kim, Co-President of the group; and 4) various newspaper articles.

APPENDIX C *Entrepreneurship Survey*

1. Appendixes A and B.

2. Han'guk Saengsansŏng Ponbu (KPC), *Han'guk kiŏp ch'ongnam* (Seoul, 1975).

3. There is undoubtedly some under-enumeration in the KPC data, but we know of no reason to expect it to be substantial. The Economic Planning Board's *Report on Mining and Manufacturing Survey, 1973* lists 3,291 manufacturing establishments with more than 50 workers. If 1 in 7 enterprises consists of an average of 3 establishments, then the results are consistent.

4. Except Chŏlla provinces which were covered by two KDI research assistants.

5. The questions included in this questionnaire are indicated in Appendix D.

6. Value added was calculated indirectly by using reported profits, non-profit value added, and sales coefficients from the 340-sector BOK IO table for 1973.

7. The somewhat higher asset *t* value (0.77) is discounted because of vintage pricing distortions.

8. By way of contrast, compare the "response" and "could not respond" sets. Here we also cannot reject the null hypothesis, but the differences in the means are so palpable and the *t* value so high that neither do we accept it.

Bibliography

Adelman, Irma and Cynthia Taft Morris. *Society, Politics and Economic Development: A Quantitative Approach*. Baltimore, Johns Hopkins University Press, 1967.

Ahluwalia, Montek. "Income Inequality: Some Dimensions of the Problem," in *Redistribution with Growth*. Edited by Hollis Chenery et al. London, Oxford University Press, 1974.

Arrow, Kenneth, J. "Uncertainty and the Welfare Economics of Medical Care," *American Economic Review 53* (December 1963).

——. "The Organization of Economic Activity: Issues Pertinent to the Choice of Market versus Non-market Allocation," in *Public Expenditure and Policy Analysis*. Edited by Robert H. Haveman and Julius Margolis. Chicago, Markham, 1970.

Bahl, Roy W. "A Regression Approach to Tax Effort and Tax Ratio Analysis," in *International Monetary Fund Staff Papers*, November 1971.

Bain, Joe. *International Differences in Industrial Structure*. New Haven, Yale University Press, 1966.

Ban, Sung Hwan (Pan, Sŏng-hwan), Pal Yong Moon (P'ar-Yong Mun), and Dwight H. Perkins. *Rural Development*, Studies in the Modernization of the Republic of Korea: 1945–1975. Cambridge, Council on East Asian Studies, Harvard University, 1980.

Bank of Korea (Han'guk Ŭnhaeng). *Han'guk ŭi kiŏp kyŏngyŏng* (Financial statement analysis). Seoul, 1968.

——. *Economic Statistics Yearbook*, various years. Seoul.

——. *Flow of Funds Accounts in Korea: 1963–1975*. Seoul, 1976.

——. *Monthly Economic Statistics*, various issues. Seoul.

——. *National Income in Korea*, various issues. Seoul.

——. *Survey of Business Financing and Unorganized Money Markets*, various quarterly issues.

Bark, Dong Suh. "The Problem of Korean Higher Civil Servants—Their Social Background and Morale," in *Some Problems in Public Administration in Developing Countries*. Honolulu, East-West Center, 1966.

—— and Chae-Jin Lee (Ch'ae-jin Yi). "Bureaucratic Elite and Development Orientations," *Political Leadership in Korea*. Edited by Dae-Sook

Suh (Tae-suk Sŏ) and Chae-Jin Lee. Seattle, University of Washington Press, 1976.

Baumol, William J. *Welfare Economics and the Theory of the State*. Cambridge, Harvard University Press, 1969.

Bieda, K. *The Structure and Operation of the Japanese Economy*. Sydney, John Wiley and Sons, 1970.

Brown, Gilbert T. *Korean Pricing Policies and Economic Development in the 1960's*. Baltimore, Johns Hopkins University Press, 1973.

Caves, Richard and Masu Uekusa. *Industrial Organization in Japan*. Washington, The Brookings Institution, 1976.

Chang, Yŏng-sik. *Han'guk chŏllyŏk suyo mit kagyŏk ŭi punsŏk* (A study of the demand for and price of electricity in Korea). Seoul, Korea Development Institute Press, 1977.

Chelliah, Raja J. "Trends in Taxation in Developing Countries," *International Monetary Fund Staff Papers*, July 1971.

Cho, Ki-jun (Zo, Ki-Zun). *Han'guk kiŏpka sa* (History of Korean entrepreneurs). Seoul, Pagyŏng Sa, 1973.

Cho, Sŏk-chun. "Han'guk kunsa chŏngbu ha e issŏsŏ ŭi tugaji haengjŏng kaehyŏk e kwanhan pigyo yŏn'gu" (A comparative study of two administrative reforms under the Korean military government). *Han'guk haengjŏng nonch'ong* (Korean journal of public administration), 6.2 (1968).

——. "Chojik" (Organization), in *Han'guk haengjŏng ŭi yŏksajŏk punsŏk, 1948–1967* (A historical analysis of Korean public administration, 1948–1967). Seoul, Han'guk Haengjŏng Munje Yŏn'guso, 1969.

——. "Kyehoek" (Planning) in *Han'guk haengjŏng ŭi yŏksajŏk punsŏk, 1948–1967* (A historical analysis of Korean public administration, 1948–1967). Edited by Han-bin Yi (Hahn-Been Lee) et al. Seoul, Han'guk Haengjŏng Munje Yŏn'guso, 1969.

Cho, Yŏng-gu, ed. *Kyŏngsŏng Pangjik osimnyŏn, 1919–1969* (Fifty years of the Kyŏngsŏng Spinning Company). Seoul, Kyŏngsŏng Pangjik Chusik Hoesa, 1969.

Ch'oe, Ho-jin (Choi, Ho Chin). "Kwisok chaesan purha wa kongŏphwa ŭi chwajŏl, 1945–1953" (The divestiture of vested enterprises and the failure of industrialization, 1945–1953), in *Han'guk kyŏngje chŏngch'aek samsimnyŏn sa* (A thirty-year history of Korean economic policy). Edited by Chŏn'guk Kyŏngjein Yŏnhaphoe (Federation of Korean Industries). Seoul, Sahoe Sasang Sa, 1975.

Choi, Ho Chin (Ch'oe Ho-jin). *The Economic History of Korea*. Seoul, Samsŏng, 1971.

Choi, Jai Hi, (Ch'oe, Chae-hŭi). "Traditional Values of Korea and Problems of Modernization," in *Report of International Conference on the Problems of Modernization in Asia*. Seoul, Korea University, Asiatic Research Center, 1966.

Choi, Moon Hwan, (Ch'oe, Mun-hwan). "A Review of Korea's Land Reform," *Koreana Quarterly*, Spring, 1960.

Chŏn'guk Kyŏngjein Yŏnhaphoe (Federation of Korean Industries). *Han'guk kyŏngje yŏn'gam, 1973* (Economic yearbook of Korea, 1973). Seoul, 1974.

Chōsen Sōtokufu (Japanese Government General in Korea). *Chōsen Sōtokufu tōkei nenpō: 1909, 1910, 1930, 1931* (Statistical yearbook of the Government General of Korea: 1909, 1910, 1930, 1931).

Chōsen Sōtokufu (Japanese Government General in Korea). *Chōsen kokusei chōsa hōkoku: 1930* (Report on the Population Census of Korea: 1930).

Chough, Soon (Cho Sun). "The Economics of Price Supervision," *Seoul National University Economic Review*, December 1968.

Chung, Bom Mo (Chŏng, Pŏm-mo) et. al. *Boy Preference and Family Planning in Korea*. Seoul, Korea Institute for Research in the Behavioral Sciences, 1974.

Cole, David C. and Princeton Lyman. *Korean Development: The Interplay of Politics and Economics*. Cambridge, Harvard University Press, 1971.

Cole, David C., and Young Woo Nam (Yŏng-u Nam). "The Pattern and Significance of Economic Planning in Korea" in *Practical Approaches to Development Planning*. Edited by Irma Adelman. Baltimore, The Johns Hopkins University Press, 1969.

Dahl, Robert A. and Charles E. Lindbloom. *Politics, Economics and Welfare: Planning and Politic-Economic Processes Resolved into Basic Social Processes*. New York, Harper, 1953.

Eckstein, Alexander. "Individualism and the Role of the State in Economic Growth," *Economic Development and Cultural Change,* Vol. 6 (1957/58).

Economic Planning Board (Kyongje Kihoegwŏn). *Korea Statistical Yearbook, 1961*. Seoul, 1962.

——. *1960 Population and Housing Census of Korea*, Vol. 2. Seoul, 1963.

——. *1970 Population and Housing Census Report*, Vol. 1. Seoul, 1972.

——. *Preliminary Report of 1975 Population and Housing Census*. Seoul, 1976.

——. *Major Statistics of Korean Economy, 1977*. Seoul, 1977.

——. *Report on Mining and Manufacturing Survey*, various years. Seoul.

Frank, Charles R., Jr., Kwang Suk Kim (Kwang-sŏk Kim), and Larry Westphal. *Foreign Trade Regimes and Economic Development: South Korea*, Vol. VII. New York National Bureau of Economic Research, 1975.

Geertz, Clifford. *Peddlers and Princes*. Chicago, University of Chicago Press, 1965.

Gerschenkron, Alexander. "Ideology as a System Determinant," *Comparison of Economic Systems*. Edited by Alexander Eckstein. Berkeley, University of California Press, 1971.

Ghosh, Arabind. "Role of Large Industrial Houses in Indian Industries,"

The Indian Economic Journal, April–June 1974.

Government General of Tyosen. *Annual Report on Administration of Tyosen: 1936–37*. Keizo (Keijō), Government General, December 1937.

Hagen, Everett. *The Economics of Development*. Homewood, Illinois, Richard D. Irwin, 1968.

Hahn, Bae Ho (Han, Pae-ho) and Kyu Taik Kim (Kyu-t'aek Kim). "The Political Leaders: Their Social Origins and Skills" in *Korea: A Pattern of Political Development*. Edited by C. I. Eugene Kim. Kalamazoo, Korea Research and Publications, Inc., 1964.

Han, Woo Keun (Han, U-gŭn). *The History of Korea*. Kyung-shik Lee (Kyŏng-sik Yi) trans. Grafton K. Mintz, ed. Seoul, The Eul-Yoo Publishing Company, 1970.

Han'guk Kaebal Yŏn'guwŏn (Korea Development Institute). "Kiŏp chŏng-ch'aek ŭi kibon panghyang" (The basic direction of business policy). Mimeograph. March, 1974.

Han'guk Muyŏk Hyŏphoe (Korean Traders Association). *Muyŏk yŏn'gam* (Annual trade report). Seoul, 1974.

Han'guk Saengsansŏng Ponbu (Korea Productivity Center). *Han'guk kiŏp ch'ongnam* (Directory of Korean businesses). Seoul, 1975.

Harbison, F. "Entrepreneurial Organization as a Factor in Economic Development," *Quarterly Journal of Economics*, August 1956.

Harris, John. "Industrial Entrepreneurship in Nigeria." PhD dissertation, Northwestern University, 1967.

——. "Entrepreneurship and Economic Development." Cambridge, Mass., MIT Economics Department Working Paper 69, April 1971. Reprinted in *Essays in Honor of Harold F. Williamson*. Edited by L. Cain and P. Uselding. Kent State University Press, 1973.

Heckscher, Eli F. *An Economic History of Sweden*. Cambridge, Mass., Harvard University Press, 1954.

——. "Mercantilism," *Revisions in Mercantilism*. Edited by D. G. Coleman. London, Methuen & Co., 1969.

Henderson, Gregory. *Korea: The Politics of the Vortex*. Cambridge, Harvard University Press, 1968.

——. "Japan's Chosen: Immigrants, Ruthlessness and Developmental Shock," *Korea Under Japanese Colonial Rule*. Edited by Andrew C. Nahm. Kalamazoo, Western Michigan Unviersity, 1973.

Hirschman, Albert O. *The Strategy of Economic Development*. New Haven and London, Yale University Press, 1958.

——. "Ideology: Mask or Nessus Shirt?" in *Comparison of Economic Systems*. Edited by Alexander Eckstein. Berkeley, University of California Press, 1971.

Hirschmeier, Johannes. *The Origins of Entrepreneurship in Meiji Japan.* Cambridge, Harvard University Press, 1964.

——, and Tsunehiko Yui, *The Development of Japanese Business, 1600–1978.* Cambridge, Harvard University Press, 1975.

Hong, Sŭng-jik (Hong, Sung Chick). *Chisigin ŭi kach'igwan yŏn'gu* (A study of the values of intellectuals). Seoul, Samyŏng Sa, 1972.

Hong, Wontack (Hong, Wŏn-t'aek). *Factor Supply and Factor Intensity of Trade in Korea.* Seoul, Korea Development Institute Press, 1976.

——. "Trade, Distortions and Employment Growth in Korea." Mimeographed. Seoul, Korea Development Institute, 1977.

Hoselitz, Bert. "Economic Policy and Economic Development," in *The State and Economic Growth.* Edited by Hugh J. Aitken. New York, Social Science Research Council, 1959.

Hwang, Myŏng-su. *Kiŏpka sa yŏn'gu* (A study of entrepreneurial history). Seoul, Tongguk University Press, 1976.

Hyundai Construction Company, Ltd. *Application for Prequalification.* Seoul, Hyundai Construction Co., Ltd., n.d.

Ihwa Yŏja Taehakkyo (Ewha Womans University). "Haksaeng saenghwal yŏn'gu" (A study of student life). Seoul, Ewha Womans University, 1971.

Indian Institute of Management at Bangalore. *Overview of Public Enterprise Sector in India.* Bangalore, 1976.

Johnson, Harry. "Planning and the Market in Economic Development," in *Economic Development: Readings in Theory and Practice.* Edited by Theodore Morgan and George Betz. Belmont, California, Wadsworth, 1970.

Jones, Leroy P. *Public Enterprise and Economic Development: The Korean Case.* Seoul, Korea Development Institute Press, 1976.

Juhn, Daniel Sungil. "Entrepreneurship in an Underdeveloped Economy: The Case of Korea, 1890–1940." PhD dissertation, George Washington University, 1965.

Kaplan, Eugene. *Japan: The Government-Business Relationship.* Washington, Department of Commerce, 1972.

Keynes, John Maynard. *The End of Laissez Faire.* London, Leonard and Virginia Woolf, 1927.

Kilby, Peter. "Hunting the Heffalump," in *Entrepreneurship and Economic Development.* Edited by Peter Kilby. New York, The Free Press, 1971.

Kim, Chin-hyŏn. "Pujŏng ch'ukchae ch'ŏri chŏnmalsŏ" (Report on the reversed policy toward illicit accumulation of wealth), *Sindonga,* December 1964.

Kim, Joungwon A. *Divided Korea: The Politics of Development, 1945–*

1972. Cambridge, East Asian Research Center, Harvard University, 1975.

Kim, Kwang Suk (Kim, Kwang-sŏk) and Michael Roemer. "Macroeconomic Growth and Structural Change in Korea" Seoul, Korea Development Institute Working Paper 77-05, April 1977.

Kim, Kyong-Dong (Kim, Kyŏng-dong). "Political Factors in the Formation of the Entrepreneurial Elite in South Korea," *Asian Survey*, May 1976.

Kim, Sŏng-du. *Chaebŏl kwa pin'gŏn* (Chaebŏl and poverty). Seoul, Paekkyŏng Munhwa Sa, 1964.

Kim, Yong-wan. "Kŭttae kŭ ildŭl" (Memoirs). *Dong-A Ilbo* (Dong-A daily newspaper). May 12, 1976.

Kim, Yŏn-su. "Chaegye hoego" (Memoirs) *Sŏul Kyŏngje Sinmun* (Seoul economic newspaper). January 8-July 31, 1975.

Kim, Yŏng-nok. "Han'guk kiŏpka chŏngsin ŭi pansŏng" (Reconsideration of the Korean entrepreneurial spirit). *Sasanggye*, August 1964.

Kirschen, E.S., F. Black, L. Csapo, Z. Kamecki, P. Kestens, P. Bozyk, J.M. Brabant, Z. Frank-Ossipoff, S. Gora, and L. Morrissens. *Economic Policy in Our Time*. 3 volumes. Amsterdam, North Holland, 1968.

Koh, Harold. "The Early History of U.S. Economic Assistance to the Republic of Korea, 1945-1955" Mimeographed. Cambridge, Mass., Harvard Institute for International Development, September 1975.

Koo, Hagen. "Small Entrepreneurship in a Developing Society." Mimeographed. Memphis State University, 1976.

Koopmans, Tjalling C. and John Michael Montias. "On the Description and Comparison of Economic Systems," *Comparison of Economic Systems: Theoretical and Methodological Approaches*. Edited by Alexander Eckstein. Berkeley, University of California Press, 1971.

Korea Gallup Statistical Institute. *Statistical Yearbook: 1974*. Seoul, 1975.

"Korea, Inc.,–'Volcano with the Lid On'," *Business Week*, August 1, 1977. Reprinted in *Asian Wall Street Journal*, August 4, 1977.

Kyŏngje Kihoegwŏn (Economic Planning Board). *Che samch'a yŏndo ch'ongjawŏn yesan, 1977* (Overall resources budget for 1977).

——. *Kyŏngje paekso* (Economic white paper). Various years.

Kuznets, Paul W. *Economic Growth and Structure in the Republic of Korea*. New Haven, Yale University Press, 1977.

Lee, Hahn-Been (Yi, Han-bin). *Korea: Time, Change, and Administration*. Honolulu, East-West Center Press, 1968.

Lee, Joe Won (Yi, Cho-wŏn). "Planning Efforts for Economic Development" in *Patterns of Economic Development: Korea*. Edited by Joseph S. Chung. Detroit, Cellar Book Shop for Korea Research and Publications, Inc., 1966.

Lee, Man-Gap. "Sociological Implications of Modernization in Korea". Mimeographed. Seoul, n.d.

Leibenstein, Harvey. *Economic Backwardness and Economic Growth.* New York, Wiley and Sons, 1963.

——. "Entrepreneurship and Development," *American Economic Review*, Vol. 58 (May 1968).

Lewis, W. Arthur. *Development Planning: The Essentials of Economic Policy*. London, George Allemad Union, 1966.

Lotz, Jorgen and Elliot Morss. "Measuring 'Tax Effort' in Developing Countries," *International Monetary Fund Staff Papers*, November 1967.

Maeil Kyŏngje Sinmun Sa (Daily Economic Newspaper Company). *Pak Chŏng-hŭi taet'ongnyŏng ŭi chido inyŏm kwa haengdong ch'ŏrhak* (President Park Chung Hee's philosophy of leadership and behavior). Seoul, Kwangmyŏng Ch'ulp'an Sa, 1977.

Mannari, Hiroshi. *The Japanese Business Leaders*. Tokyo, University of Tokyo Press, 1974.

Mason, Edward S. *Economic Planning in Underdeveloped Areas.* New York, Fordham University Press, 1958.

McCune, George M. *Korea Today*. Cambridge, Harvard University Press, 1950.

Meade, E. Grant. *American Military Government in Korea*. New York, Columbia University Press, 1951.

Mun, P'ar-young (Moon, Pal Yong) and Pyŏng-sŏ Yu. *Nongsanmul kagyŏk punsŏngnon* (A study of agricultural product prices). Seoul, Korea Development Institute Press, 1975.

Myrdal, Gunnar. *Asian Drama: An Inquiry Into the Poverty of Nations.* New York, Pantheon, 1968.

Nelson, R. "A Theory of the Low Level Equilibrium Trap in Underdeveloped Economies," *American Economic Review Quarterly*, December 1956.

Nevaskar, Balwant. *Capitalists Without Capitalism*. Westport, Conn., Greenwood Publishing, 1971.

No, Kyu-sik, Chŏn-bong Chang, Tong-uk Chi, and Tong-jin Hyŏn. "Palsimnyondae chaebŏl cheil ŭi kiŏp kurŭp" (The number-one enterprise group in the 1980s), *Hyŏndae kyŏngyŏng* (Modern management), Vol. 12, No. 3 (No. 125), (March 1977).

Paek, Chong-gi and Yŏng-jung Pak. *Chaebŏl samsimnyŏn sa ŭi tŭrama* (The thirty-year drama of chaebŏl). Seoul, Ch'angnam Munhwa Sa, 1976.

Pak, Pyŏng-yun. "Han'guk ŭi chaebŏl" (Korean chaebŏl). *Sindonga*, December, 1975.

Pak, Tong-sŏ (Bark, Dong Suh). "Haengjŏng kwa chŏnch'i" (Administration and politics), in *Han'guk haengjŏng ŭi yŏksajŏk punsŏk, 1948–1967* (An historical analysis of Korean administration, 1948–1967). Seoul, Han'guk Haengjŏng Munje Yŏn'guso, 1969.

Papanek, Gustav F. "The Development of Entrepreneurship," *American Economic Review Supplement*, May 1962.

——. *Pakistan's Development: Social Goals Private Incentives*. Cambridge, Mass., Harvard University Press, 1967.

Park, Chung Hee (Pak, Chŏng-hŭi). *Our Nation's Path*. Seoul, Hollym Corporation, 1970.

——. *The Country, the Revolution and I*. Seoul, Hollym Corporation, 1970.

Park, Ki Hyuk (Pak, Ki-hyŏk), et al. *A Study of Land Tenure System in Korea*. Seoul, Korea Land Economics Research Center, 1966.

Parsons, Talcott. "Some General Theories in Sociology," in *Theoretical Sociology*. Edited by John McKinney and Edward Tyriakian. New York, Appleton-Crofts, 1970.

Patrick, Hugh and Henry Rosovsky. "Japan's Economic Performance: An Overview," in *Asia's New Giant: How the Japanese Economy Works*. Edited by Hugh Patrick and Henry Rosovsky. Washington, D.C., The Brookings Institution, 1976.

Pryor, Frederic. "Public Ownership: Some Quantitative Dimensions," in *Public Enterprise*. Edited by William G. Shepherd. Lexington, Mass., D. C. Heath, 1976.

Pu, Wan-hyŏk. "Chaebŏl kwa ogaenyŏn kyehoek" (Chaebŏl and the Five-Year Plans). *Sasanggye* (August 1966).

Pyŏn, Hyŏng-yun. "Inp'ŭlle angjin kwa anjŏnghwa kiban ŭi siryŏn" (Accelerated inflation and troubled stabilization foundation). in *Han'guk kyŏngje chŏngch'aek samsimnyŏn sa* (A thirty-year history of Korean economic policy, 1975). Edited by Chŏn'guk Kyŏngjein Yŏnhaphoe (Federation of Korean Industries). Seoul, Sahoe Sasang Sa, 1975 .

Reeve, W. D. *The Republic of Korea: A Political and Economic Study*. London, Oxford University Press, 1963.

Republic of Korea. "Chŏngbu chojik kaep'yŏn e kwanhan pŏpkyu" (Law on Reforming Government Organization). July 22, 1961.

——. *The Second Five-Year Economic Development Plan, 1967–1971*. Seoul, July 1966.

——. *The Third Five-Year Economic Development Plan, 1972–1976*. Seoul, 1971.

——. (Office of National Tax Administration). *Statistical Yearbook of National Tax, 1976*.

SaKong, Il. "An Overview of Corporate Finance and the Long-term Securities Market," *Planning Model and Macroeconomic Policy Issues*. Edited by Chuk Kyo Kim (Chŏk-kyo Kim), Seoul, Korea Development Institute Press, 1977.

"Samsŏng Kujung" (Samsung Group). *Hyŏndae* 12.3 (March 1977). Kyŏngyŏng (Modern management). (No. 125), March 1977.

Samyang osimnyŏn (Fifty years of Sam Yang). Seoul, Samhwa Ch'ulp'an Sa, 1974.

Sayigh, Y. A. *Enterpreneurs of Lebanon.* Cambridge, Harvard University Press, 1962.

Schumpeter, J. A. *The Theory of Economic Development.* Cambridge, Harvard University Press, 1934.

Shin, Roy W. "The Politics of Foreign Aid: A Study of the Impact of United States Aid in Korea from 1945 to 1966," PhD dissertation, University of Minnesota, 1969.

Smith, Adam. *The Wealth of Nations.* New York, Modern Library, 1937.

Sŏng, Ch'ang-hwan. *Han'guk kyŏngjeron* (A review of the Korean economy). Seoul, Changmun'gak, 1959.

Song, In-sang. "Anjŏng kuch'uk kwa sŏngjang ŭi mosaek" (A search for stability and growth), in *Han'guk kyŏngje chŏngch'aek samsimnyŏn sa* (A thirty-year history of Korean economic policy). Edited by Chŏn'guk Kyŏngje Yŏnhaphoe (Federation of Korean Industries). Seoul, Sahoe Sasang Sa. n.d.

Suh, Sang-Chul (Sŏ, Sang-ch'ŏl). *Growth and Structural Changes in the Korean Economy, 1910–1940.* Cambridge, Council on East Asian Studies, Harvard University, 1978.

Taake, Hans-Helmut. "The Implementation of Development Plans: Organization and Policies," *The Developing Economies.* Vol. 13. March 1975.

"Taeu Kurup" (Daewoo Group). *Hyŏndae kyŏngyŏng* (Modern management). May, 1977.

Trezise, Philip and Yukio Suzuki. "Politics, Government and Economic Growth in Japan," in *Asia's New Giant: How the Japanese Economy Works.* Edited by Hugh Patrick and Henry Rosovsky. Washington, The Brookings Institution, 1976.

United Nations Command, Office of the Economic Coordinator. "Fiscal Year 1955 Congressional Presentation." Seoul, 1954.

U.S. Armed Forces in Korea–National Economic Board. *South Korea Interim Government Activities*, No. 28, November–December 1948.

Ward, Benjamin. "Organization and Comparative Economics: Some Approaches," in *Comparison of Economic Systems: Theoretical and Methodological Approaches.* Edited by Alexander Eckstein. Berkeley, University of California Press, 1971.

Waterson, Albert. "A Hard Look at Development Planning," in *Economic Development: Readings in Theory and Practice.* Edited by Theodore

Morgan and George Betz. Belmont, California, Wadsworth, 1970.

Westphal, Lawrence and Irma Adelman. "Reflections on the Political Economy of Planning: The Case of Korea," in *Basic Documents and Selected Papers of Korea's Third Five-Year Economic Development Plan (1972–1976)*. Edited by Sung Hwan Jo (Sŏng-hwan Cho) and Seong-Yawng Park (Sŭng-yong Pak). Seoul, Sogang University, 1972.

Yajima, Kinji. *Challenge of Korean Economy*. Tokyo, Japan Economic Communication, 1977.

Yamamura, Kozo. "A Reexamination of Entrepreneurship in Meiji Japan (1868–1912)," in *Entrepreneurship and Economic Development*. Edited by Peter Kilby. New York, The Free Press, 1971.

Yanaga, Chitoshi. *Big Business in Japanese Politics*. New Haven and London, Yale University Press, 1968.

Yi, Ch'ang-nyŏl. "Chaebŏl iran muŏt in'ga?" (What are chaebŏl?) *Sindon-ga*, November 1966.

Yi, Kyu-ŏk. *Sijang kujo wa tokkwajŏm kyuje* (Market structure and regulations on monopolies). Seoul, Korea Development Institute Press, 1977.

Yi, Kyŏng-nam. *Han'guk ŭi kiŏpka* (Korean entrepreneurs). Vol. 1, Seoul, Munu Sa, 1973; Vol. 2, Seoul, Munu Sa, 1976.

Yi, Kyŏng-ŭi. "Chung so kiŏp" (Small and medium enterprises). in *Han'-guk kyŏngjeron* (A review of the Korean economy). Edited by Hyŏng-yun Pyŏn and Yun-hwan Kim. Seoul, Yup'ung Ch'ulp'an Sa, 1977.

Yi, Man-gi. *Han'guk kyŏngjeron* (A review of Korean economy). Seoul, Ilsin Sa, 1973.

Yi, Pyŏng-ch'ŏl. "Chaegye hoego" (Memoirs). *Sŏul Kyŏngie Sinmun* (Seoul economic newspaper). April 7–July 26, 1976.

Yu, Hoon (Yu Hun). "Social Background of Higher Civil Servants in Korea," *Koreana Quarterly*, Spring 1968.

Yu, Hun (Yu, Hoon). *Konggiŏp imwŏn ŭi sahoejŏk paegyŏng* (The social background of public enterprise executives). Seoul, Korea Development Institute, 1974.

Zo, Ki-Zun (Cho, Ki-jun). "Types of Entrepreneur in Modernization Process of Korean Economy," in *Report of International Conference on the Problems of Modernization in Asia*. Seoul, Asiatic Research Center, 1966.

Index

Harvard East Asian Monographs

1. Liang Fang-chung, *The Single-Whip Method of Taxation in China*
2. Harold C. Hinton, *The Grain Tribute System of China, 1845–1911*
3. Ellsworth C. Carlson, *The Kaiping Mines, 1877–1912*
4. Chao Kuo-chün, *Agrarian Policies of Mainland China: A Documentary Study, 1949–1956*
5. Edgar Snow, *Random Notes on Red China, 1936–1945*
6. Edwin George Beal, Jr., *The Origin of Likin, 1835–1864*
7. Chao Kuo-chün, *Economic Planning and Organization in Mainland China: A Documentary Study, 1949–1957*
8. John K. Fairbank, *Ch'ing Documents: An Introductory Syllabus*
9. Helen Yin and Yi-chang Yin, *Economic Statistics of Mainland China, 1949–1957*
10. Wolfgang Franke, *The Reform and Abolition of the Traditional Chinese Examination System*
11. Albert Feuerwerker and S. Cheng, *Chinese Communist Studies of Modern Chinese History*
12. C. John Stanley, *Late Ch'ing Finance: Hu Kuang-yung as an Innovator*
13. S. M. Meng, *The Tsungli Yamen: Its Organization and Functions*
14. Ssu-yü Teng, *Historiography of the Taiping Rebellion*
15. Chun-Jo Liu, *Controversies in Modern Chinese Intellectual History: An Analytic Bibliography of Periodical Articles, Mainly of the May Fourth and Post-May Fourth Era*
16. Edward J. M. Rhoads, *The Chinese Red Army, 1927–1963: An Annotated Bibliography*
17. Andrew J. Nathan, *A History of the China International Famine Relief Commission*
18. Frank H. H. King (ed.) and Prescott Clarke, *A Research Guide to China-Coast Newspapers, 1822–1911*
19. Ellis Joffe, *Party and Army: Professionalism and Political Control in the Chinese Officer Corps, 1949–1964*
20. Toshio G. Tsukahira, *Feudal Control in Tokugawa Japan: The Sankin Kōtai System*

21. Kwang-Ching Liu, ed., *American Missionaries in China: Papers from Harvard Seminars*
22. George Moseley, *A Sino-Soviet Cultural Frontier: The Ili Kazakh Autonomous Chou*
23. Carl F. Nathan, *Plague Prevention and Politics in Manchuria, 1910–1931*
24. Adrian Arthur Bennett, *John Fryer: The Introduction of Western Science and Technology into Nineteenth-Century China*
25. Donald J. Friedman, *The Road from Isolation: The Campaign of the American Committee for Non-Participation in Japanese Aggression, 1938–1941*
26. Edward Le Fevour, *Western Enterprise in Late Ch'ing China: A Selective Survey of Jardine, Matheson and Company's Operations, 1842–1895*
27. Charles Neuhauser, *Third World Politics: China and the Afro-Asian People's Solidarity Organization, 1957–1967*
28. Kungtu C. Sun, assisted by Ralph W. Huenemann, *The Economic Development of Manchuria in the First Half of the Twentieth Century*
29. Shahid Javed Burki, *A Study of Chinese Communes, 1965*
30. John Carter Vincent, *The Extraterritorial System in China: Final Phase*
31. Madeleine Chi, *China Diplomacy, 1914–1918*
32. Clifton Jackson Phillips, *Protestant America and the Pagan World: The First Half Century of the American Board of Commissioners for Foreign Missions, 1810–1860*
33. James Pusey, *Wu Han: Attacking the Present through the Past*
34. Ying-wan Cheng, *Postal Communication in China and Its Modernization, 1860–1896*
35. Tuvia Blumenthal, *Saving in Postwar Japan*
36. Peter Frost, *The Bakumatsu Currency Crisis*
37. Stephen C. Lockwood, *Augustine Heard and Company, 1858–1862*
38. Robert R. Campbell, *James Duncan Campbell: A Memoir by His Son*
39. Jerome Alan Cohen, ed., *The Dynamics of China's Foreign Relations*
40. V. V. Vishnyakova-Akimova, *Two Years in Revolutionary China, 1925–1927*, tr. Steven I. Levine
41. Meron Medzini, *French Policy in Japan during the Closing Years of the Tokugawa Regime*
42. *The Cultural Revolution in the Provinces*
43. Sidney A. Forsythe, *An American Missionary Community in China, 1895–1905*
44. Benjamin I. Schwartz, ed., *Reflections on the May Fourth Movement: A Symposium*
45. Ching Young Choe, *The Rule of the Taewŏn'gun, 1864–1873: Restoration in Yi Korea*

46. W. P. J. Hall, *A Bibliographical Guide to Japanese Research on the Chinese Economy, 1958–1970*
47. Jack J. Gerson, *Horatio Nelson Lay and Sino-British Relations, 1854–1864*
48. Paul Richard Bohr, *Famine and the Missionary: Timothy Richard as Relief Administrator and Advocate of National Reform*
49. Endymion Wilkinson, *The History of Imperial China: A Research Guide*
50. Britten Dean, *China and Great Britain: The Diplomacy of Commerical Relations, 1860–1864*
51. Ellsworth C. Carlson, *The Foochow Missionaries, 1847–1880*
52. Yeh-chien Wang, *An Estimate of the Land-Tax Collection in China, 1753 and 1908*
53. Richard M. Pfeffer, *Understanding Business Contracts in China, 1949–1963*
54. Han-sheng Chuan and Richard Kraus, *Mid-Ch'ing Rice Markets and Trade, An Essay in Price History*
55. Ranbir Vohra, *Lao She and the Chinese Revolution*
56. Liang-lin Hsiao, *China's Foreign Trade Statistics, 1864–1949*
57. Lee-hsia Hsu Ting, *Government Control of the Press in Modern China, 1900–1949*
58. Edward W. Wagner, *The Literati Purges: Political Conflict in Early Yi Korea*
59. Joungwon A. Kim, *Divided Korea: The Politics of Development, 1945–1972*
60. Noriko Kamachi, John K. Fairbank, and Chūzō Ichiko, *Japanese Studies of Modern China Since 1953: A Bibliographical Guide to Historical and Social-Science Research on the Nineteenth and Twentieth Centuries, Supplementary Volume for 1953–1969*
61. Donald A. Gibbs and Yun-chen Li, *A Bibliography of Studies and Translations of Modern Chinese Literature, 1918–1942*
62. Robert H. Silin, *Leadership and Values: The Organization of Large-Scale Taiwanese Enterprises*
63. David Pong, *A Critical Guide to the Kwangtung Provincial Archives Deposited at the Public Record Office of London*
64. Fred W. Drake, *China Charts the World: Hsu Chi-yü and His Geography of 1848*
65. William A. Brown and Urgunge Onon, translators and annotators, *History of the Mongolian People's Republic*
66. Edward L. Farmer, *Early Ming Government: The Evolution of Dual Capitals*
67. Ralph C. Croizier, *Koxinga and Chinese Nationalism: History, Myth, and the Hero*
68. William J. Tyler, tr., *The Psychological World of Natsumi Sōseki*, by Doi Takeo

69. Eric Widmer, *The Russian Ecclesiastical Mission in Peking during the Eighteenth Century*
70. Charlton M. Lewis, *Prologue to the Chinese Revolution: The Transformation of Ideas and Institutions in Hunan Province, 1891–1907*
71. Preston Torbert, *The Ch'ing Imperial Household Department: A Study of its Organization and Principal Functions, 1662–1796*
72. Paul A. Cohen and John E. Schrecker, eds., *Reform in Nineteenth-Century China*
73. Jon Sigurdson, *Rural Industrialization in China*
74. Kang Chao, *The Development of Cotton Textile Production in China*
75. Valentin Rabe, *The Home Base of American China Missions, 1880–1920*
76. Sarasin Viraphol, *Tribute and Profit: Sino-Siamese Trade, 1652–1853*
77. Ch'i-ch'ing Hsiao, *The Military Establishment of the Yuan Dynasty*
78. Meishi Tsai, *Contemporary Chinese Novels and Short Stories, 1949–1974: An Annotated Bibliography*
79. Wellington K. K. Chan, *Merchants, Mandarins, and Modern Enterprise in Late Ch'ing China*
80. Endymion Wilkinson, *Landlord and Labor in Late Imperial China: Case Studies from Shandong by Jing Su and Luo Lun*
81. Barry Keenan, *The Dewey Experiment in China: Educational Reform and Political Power in the Early Republic*
82. George A. Hayden, *Crime and Punishment in Medieval Chinese Drama: Three Judge Pao Plays*
83. Sang-Chul Suh, *Growth and Structural Changes in the Korean Economy, 1910–1940*
84. J. W. Dower, *Empire and Aftermath: Yoshida Shigeru and the Japanese Experience, 1878–1954*

STUDIES IN THE MODERNIZATION OF THE REPUBLIC OF KOREA: 1945–1975

86. Kwang Suk Kim and Michael Roemer, *Growth and Structural Transformation*
87. Anne O. Krueger, *The Developmental Role of the Foreign Sector and Aid*
88. Edwin S. Mills and Byung-Nak Song, *Urbanization and Urban Problems*
89. Sung Hwan Ban, Pal Yong Moon, and Dwight H. Perkins, *Rural Development*
90. Noel F. McGinn, Donald R. Snodgrass, Yung Bong Kim, Shin-Bok Kim, and Quee-Young Kim, *Education and Development in Korea*

91. Leroy P. Jones and Il SaKong, *Government, Business, and Entrepreneurship in Economic Development: The Korean Case*

92. Edward S. Mason, Dwight H. Perkins, Kwang Suk Kim, David C. Cole, Mahn Je Kim, et al., *The Economic and Social Modernization of the Republic of Korea*